C Programming

The Peter Norton Programming Series

D0861415

Who This Book Is For

Introductory for intermediate C programmers who want to develop and extend their programming expertise and add new performance to their programs.

What's Inside

- More than 100 ready-to-run programs that show the best ways to handle the keyboard, files and disks, graphics and the screen, the mouse, and more

- Expert tips and hints for writing better programs, including how to interface with assembly language for more speed and power programming

- A learn-by-doing approach to programming that shows code in action in a direct, highly readable style

About the Peter Norton Microcomputer Libraries from Brady Publishing

All of the volumes in the Peter Norton Libraries, written in collaboration with Peter Norton Computing, provide clear, in-depth discussions of the latest developments in computer hardware, operating systems, and programming. Fully tested and rigorously reviewed by the experts at Peter Norton Computing, these libraries deserve a special place on your bookshelf. These libraries are comprised of two series:

The Peter Norton Hardware Library gives you an insider's grasp of your computer and the way it works. Included are such best-selling classics as *Inside the IBM PC, Inside the Apple Macintosh,* and *The Hard Disk Companion.*

The Peter Norton Programming Library focuses on creating programs that work right away and offers the best tips and techniques in the industry. It includes *Advanced BASIC, Advanced Assembly Language, C++ Programming, QBasic Programming, Advanced DOS,* and more.

C Programming

Steve Holzner
Peter Norton Computing

Brady Publishing

New York London Toronto Sydney Singapore Tokyo

Brady Publishing

A Divison of Simon & Schuster, Inc.
15 Columbus Circle
New York, NY 10023

Manufactured in the United States of America
10   9   8   7   6   5   4   3   2   1

Library of Congress Cataloging-in-Publication Data

Holzner, Steven.
    C Programming / Steven Holzner and Peter Norton Computing.
         p.   cm.
    Includes index.
    1. C (Computer programming language) I. Peter Norton
Computing   II.   Title.
QA76.73.C15H658   1991
005.26'2–dc20   91-12884
                                                                           CIP

ISBN 0-13-663162-2

Produced by Micro Text Productions

Contents

———

Introduction   xi

CHAPTER 1

Welcome to C   1

    A Brief History of C   2
    Our First Programs   4
    Introduction to Data in C   14
    Arithmetic Operators in C   18
    Operator Precedence in C   25
    How to Use All the C Data Types   28
    Data Type Modifiers   32
    C Type Conversions   34

CHAPTER 2

Reading from the Keyboard   39

    The scanf( ) Function for Reading Keys   40
    The if Statement   45
    Relational and Logical Operators   51

A Simple Calculator Example   54
The for Loop   59
The while Loop   69
The do-while Loop   71
Writing Our Own C Functions   74

CHAPTER 3

Organizing Your Data and Pointers 83

Keeping Data in Arrays   84
Two-Dimensional Arrays in C   87
Our Database Program   91
Character Strings in C   95
Data Structures in C   107
All about Pointers   114

CHAPTER 4

Welcome to C Graphics   123

Video Modes in C   124
Coloring a Screen Pixel   125
Drawing Lines   128
Drawing Rectangles   131
Drawing Ellipses   134
Filling Shapes with Color   136
C Screen Modes   138
Animation with Getimage( ) and Putimage( )   152
Graphics Viewports   158

CHAPTER 5

Using Files in C   163

Streams and Files in C   163
A File Writing Example   165
A File Reading Example   168
The EOF Marker   171
Binary and ASCII Files in C   172
File Records   174
File Errors — Errno and Perror( )   182

The UNIX File Functions   185
Reading Command Line Parameters   195

CHAPTER 6

The Mouse   199

Starting with the Mouse   200
Interrupts in Your Computer   200
Initializing the Mouse   205
Making the Mouse Cursor Visible   206
Hiding the Mouse Cursor   208
Reading Immediate Mouse Information   210
Moving the Mouse Cursor   215
Reading the Button Pressed Queue   218
Reading the Button Released Queue   222
Restricting the Mouse Cursor Horizontally   225
Restricting the Mouse Cursor Vertically   227
Changing the Mouse Cursor Appearance   229

CHAPTER 7

How to Use Memory in C   235

Memory Use in C   235
The Code   237
C's Data Areas   239
The Heap   248
The Stack   260

CHAPTER 8

Advanced Pointers   271

From Arrays to Pointers   271
Two-Dimensional Arrays   278
Pointers to Structures   283
Fast Sorting Techniques   285
Pointers to Functions   295
Linked Lists   300

CHAPTER 9

How to Debug C Programs   303

Using Assertions in Your Programs   303
Interactive Debugging   306
Dedicated C Debuggers   320

CHAPTER 10

Welcome to C++   349

Screen Output in C++   350
Keyboard Input in C++   353
How to Use C++ Classes   355
A Stack — An Object Example   358
Function Overloading in C++   369
C++ Inheritance   378

CHAPTER 11

Welcome to Assembly Language   389

Machine Language   389
Assembly Language   390
An Assembly Language Example   393
Our First Program   396
A Review of Memory Segmentation   399
Assembler Directives   403
Assembling PRINTZ.ASM   407
Adding Data   408
Strings in Memory   412
Accepting Keyboard Input   415
Conditional Jumps   418
DEHEXER.ASM   420
Assembly Language Procedures   437

CHAPTER 12

Connecting Assembly Language to C   443

Using In-Line Assembly Language   443
Understanding the Internal C Data Formats   448

Passing Parameters   456
Returning Values from Functions   462
Linking in External Assembly Language Files   465
Linking Assembly Language Functions to C   470
Linking C into Assembly Language   477

CHAPTER 13

Assembly Language Routines for C Programmers   481

Some Fast Math   481
High Precision Adding   482
High Precision Subtracting   482
High Precision Multiplying   483
High Precision Dividing   484
Pixel Graphics in Assembly Language   493
How to Create Assembly Language Libraries   504

APPENDIX

BIOS and DOS Reference   513

BIOS Interrupts   513
DOS Interrupts   533

Index   565

Limits of Liability and Disclaimer of Warranty

The authors and publisher of this book have used their best efforts in preparing this book and the programs contained in it. These efforts include the development, research, and testing of the theories and programs to determine their effectiveness. The authors and publisher make no warranty of any kind, expressed or implied, with regard to these programs or the documentation contained in this book. The authors and publisher shall not be liable in any event for incidental or consequential damages in connection with, or arising out of, the furnishing, performance, or use of these programs.

Trademarks

Most computer and software brand names have trademarks or registered trademarks. The individual trademarks have not been listed here.

Introduction

The Spirit of C

There are many different computer languages; the list is long. For example, there are teaching languages, highly structured languages, number crunching languages, elegant languages, and programmer's languages. C, the subject of this book, is a programmer's language. That is to say, it is not as elegant and educational as some languages nor is it as highly structured and theoretical as others.

What it is, however, is probably the most popular language for microcomputers today. And rightly so. In fact, if you want to be a programmer on the PC these days, you almost have to know C. C is the programmer's language and it has grown in popularity since it was first invented by Dennis Ritchie almost 20 years ago. There are many reasons that programmers like C, but they can all be summed up in the guiding spirit behind the language: C is the only high level language that lets the programmer be king. It is designed as a true working tool, not as a hindrance.

C lets us get almost as close to the machine — that is, as close to the language of the microprocessor itself — as we can get. The real name for the microprocessor's native language is assembly language, and assembly language is just one step up from the bits and bytes that your computer understands. Although assembly language can't be beat for speed or efficiency, it's not easy to write long programs in it. C is the language that comes the closest to assembly language while smoothing the rough edges at the same time; it's certainly much easier to program in C for most applications. And, with the most modern versions of C, our programs will come close even to assembly language in speed. Today, C is where the power is.

Our Approach

Because C is a language for programmers and because this is a book for would-be programmers, we are going to orient the book towards seeing our programs work. In other words, we want to see what the language can do for us, not the other way around. We're not going to work through long, academic arguments about abstractions — those kinds of discussions would be out of place. This is a book for programmers, not theoreticians. In other words, we intend to unleash the full power of C in its own environment, and that power is outstanding.

However, we should know from the beginning that there is a good deal we have to learn before we can really use C. There is no way around learning the difference between a modifier and an operator or between a statement and a directive. We'll have to learn about for loops, while loops, and do...while loops; about unary and binary operators; and about typecasts, structures, and unions. In other words, we're going to get serious about learning C. In fact, we're going to explore it from the inside out — and there's a lot to learn. However, we'll find that, despite the amount of material we have to cover, C is here to make our life easier. That is, it is truly the programmer's tool; as we write more and more code, it will start to come naturally.

For that reason, we'll fill this book with dozens of ready-to-run examples. There's no better way to learn than by example, and we'll see some good ones here. In addition, we'll develop the longer examples line by line, using arrows to indicate where we are as we work through a program. There'll be frequent figures, notes, and, especially, tips. The tips are included to give you something extra. A tip might be a method of making a program run twice as fast, it might be about some other part of C that is unexpectedly handy at the present moment or it might even give us some insights about what's going on behind the scenes in C. Whatever it is, the tips will show us some aspects of C from the professional programmer's point of view — giving us a little extra power, a little extra control.

In addition, there is a certain C **style**, and, as we work through this book, we'll cultivate it. The C style has much to do with good programming practice. Over the years, programmers have come to establish certain conventions for C. Even though these conventions are not neccessary to make our programs run, we'll see how they often make programming and debugging easier.

That's our approach. We'll learn C by seeing it work, starting at the beginning and building our expertise carefully. We'll go from the most basic — the very beginning — up to the most powerful in C, from the most simple to the most unexpected. Whether or not you've had a little programming experience, you'll become a master of C by the time this book is over. Let's take a moment now to see what's ahead.

What's in This Book

With our emphasis on results, we'll start by writing our first C programs and getting them to produce something visible on the screen. Next, we'll start accepting keyboard input so that we can have some data to work on. At that point, we'll be ready to start organizing and handling that data the best way. As we work through this process, elaborating and fleshing out our programs, we'll learn a lot about C — about what's available and what kind of tool it is.

After we get accustomed to the basic use of C, we'll go on to explore the extraordinarily powerful libraries that come with C. Libraries are special sub-parts of the language built to handle graphics, files, the mouse, and memory.

Then, we'll get a little more advanced, seeing the way C really uses memory and how it can work to our advantage, including some advanced pointer work (even how to write database programs that sort pointers, not records, for super speed). We'll get a grip on C's use of memory and learn dozens of professional tricks. We'll even get a peek at C++, C's object-oriented bigger brother (programmers usually start using C++ when programs exceed 50 pages). The C language itself is an astonishing tool, capable of wonderful speed and precision — and we're going to put it to work. Here's an overview of the subjects we'll gain mastery of:

- Screen output
- Keyboard input
- Organizing data
- Graphics

- Files
- The mouse
- Using memory in C
- Pointers and advanced pointers
- Debugging
- Some C++
- Assembly language
- A C–assembly language interface

You might have noticed that we'll spend some time near the end of the book investigating the C–assembly language connection. We'll do this for a very important reason: Most C programmers know a little assembly language and frequently they drop into assembly language for speed and power. In fact, among programmers, the most common programming environment today is a mix of C and assembly language. This combination is hard to beat for both speed and ease of programming — high-level languages like C make the programming easier, and assembly language makes it fast. For that reason, this book is specially designed to include a simple assembly language primer (not a complete text) for C programmers.

In those types of programs, you can accelerate your code, speed any graphics, or shorten critical sections when you need to. We'll find that assembly language is much like C in many ways. (Needless to say, if you're only interested in C, you can skip that section; but, taking a look at assembly language from the C point of view is usually very fruitful for the C programmer.)

What You'll Need

Since this book is designed to be put to work, we're going to need some software. The compiler you have must be one (or more) of the following: Microsoft C, Turbo C, Quick C, Turbo C++, Turbo C++ Pro, or Borland C++. This book is designed to be used with any of those packages — all you need is one of them and you're set. For the assembly language sections later in the book, we'll use MASM (the Microsoft Macro Assembler; we'll need version 5.1 or later) as well as TASM (the Turbo Assembler, any version). In addition, in the debugging chapter (Chapter 9), we cover the Turbo Debugger.

You'll also need an editor to type in the programs we develop. Almost any editor will do (particularly the built-in editors in Quick C or Turbo C). If the editor can print out intelligible English, the compilers and assemblers can read it. (Please note that word processors that store text in their own proprietary format may not work.) That is all the software we'll need.

Now we're ready to begin to unleash the full power of C. We're going to see it at work almost immediately because, in programming, there is no substitute for the real thing — seeing it in action. If you want to master C and become a power programmer, let's start at once with Chapter 1, where we'll see our very first C programs.

Welcome to C

Welcome to C — one of the most exciting languages now available for microcomputers and just about the most popular. In this book, we're going to learn C in the best way — by seeing it at work. We'll avoid the dry cataloging type of teaching, which piles incomprehensible layer upon layer of formal theory. Instead, we'll see the language in its own environment, giving us a working knowledge of just what it can do. In this book, the programmer is king, and we're going to work deep into the heart of the C language, learning about graphics, file handling, memory control, debugging techniques, databases, and even some advanced programming methods. In other words, we're going to unwrap the full programming power of C here — and that power is extraordinary.

That's not to say that there isn't a lot to learn; there is. We'll dissect C, seeing how its programming constructs work, how to use and manipulate data, and how to write good program code. In fact, there may be more to learn in C before becoming proficient than in any other popular language. In other languages, it's just a matter of adding more and more instructions. C is different, however; it is a language rich in new methods and powerful techniques. For example, we'll get many of the essentials down in the first couple of chapters, but then we'll meet pointers, and whole new avenues of possibility will open up. Or, again, we'll get a taste of object oriented programming when we meet C++, and things will change once more. As vista after vista opens

1

before us, we'll see just how rich C really is — and how much of an asset it will be to us as programmers.

In this chapter, we'll get our first introduction to the C language. We'll see our first C programs and learn exactly what makes them tick. First, we'll see how to write a C program and get some tangible results that we can print on the screen. We'll go on to add data to our programs, learning about the C operators that let us manipulate it, and the different ways that C can store it. By the time the chapter is over, we'll be familiar with the basics of data handling in C — and of C programming in general.

A Brief History of C

Let's start our guided tour of C with a look at its history, which will be important as we progress. The reason the language is called C is that it is the successor to (no kidding) the language called B. That language was developed by Ken Thompson in 1970 while working on a DEC PDP-7, a much less powerful machine than most modern PCs. The original UNIX operating system ran on that machine, and that's also where B got its start. (B itself was the successor to a language called BCPL, which had been written by Martin Richards.)

However, B was a little restricted. In 1972, Dennis Ritchie and Ken Thompson created the C language to augment B's power. C did not become immediately popular after its creation; in fact, it remained almost an esoteric topic for the next six years. In 1978, however (a historic year for C programmers), Brian Kernighan and Dennis Ritchie wrote a famous book — *The C Programming Language* (Prentice Hall, 1978). And that simple book changed everything.

Once the word was out, there was an explosion of interest, and C was implemented on 8-bit computers under the CP/M operating system. It wasn't until the introduction of the IBM PC in 1981, however, that C really came into its own. When the PC revolution began, C was in a perfect place to take advantage of it. As the number of PCs shot upwards, so did the number of C users. C broke away from its original UNIX background and became a popular language on microcomputers.

It's worth stressing that C became popular for a very good reason — programmers liked using it. Unlike many other languages, C gives the programmer a great deal of control over the computer. With that control comes responsibility — there are many things you can do in C that will ruin your program or crash your computer. That is, you have the power to do things in C that other languages would never allow you to do. And programmers liked that very much; they liked finding a language that was a tool, not an obstacle.

Until that time, the only true way to get complete control over your computer was to use assembly language — the native language of the 80×86 microprocessor itself (we'll use the term 80×86 to stand for any of the Intel chip series from the 8088 up to the 80486). The 80×86 interprets the bytes and words it sees in memory as instructions, and when we give English language names to those low-level instructions, it's called assembly language. This is the true language of your computer, the instructions that are built into the actual microprocessor, the 80×86.

Yet it is difficult to write long or user friendly programs in assembly language — in fact, it may take you dozens of pages of frustration to get where you want to go. C builds on that original foundation; many C instructions are quite close to their assembly language equivalents. But many more powerful instructions have been added, as well as whole libraries of prewritten programs ready for us to use. To programmers, C was much like assembly language without the drawback of having to do everything for yourself — in other words, C was the perfect combination of control and programming power.

ANSI Standardizes C

All this made for such a popular language that different companies started to bring out their own versions of C, and each one began to go in a different direction. The C revolution was in danger of splintering into many incompatible programming packages. For that reason, the American National Standards Institute (ANSI) created a special subcommittee named X3J11 to create a standard version of C. This was an extremely important development for C programmers; the language, which had been going off in all directions at the same time, became standardized and coherent once more. For that reason, ANSI C did indeed become standard C, and we'll make many references to ANSI C in this book.

On the other hand, ANSI was interested in codifying C for *all* computers, not just the PC. But there are many things that are specific to the PC which do not really apply to, say, mainframe computers. For example, one important area is the way the PC handles memory, which is quite unlike any computer which is not 80x86-based. For that reason, most implementations of C now adhere to the ANSI standard as far as it goes, and then they add their own extensions. The two versions of C that we're covering in this book, one from Borland and one from Microsoft, agree in most particulars; however, they start to differ when there is no ANSI standard to agree on. The ANSI standard says nothing about screen graphics, for example, so we'll see in Chapter 4, our graphics chapter, that there is considerable difference between Turbo and Microsoft C when it comes to drawing pictures.

That's it, then. Now that we know the history of C — as well as what ANSI C is and where it came from — we're ready to see some code. Let's get started with our first, tiny program.

Our First Programs

Some of our C programs are going to get pretty long in this book, so let's start with a look at the shortest possible C program. Here is the absolute shortest possible (legal) C program:

```
main(){}
```

That's it. That's all we need. This is a working C program. On the other hand, this tiny program produces no visible results at all. What's happening here?

Usually, when we start a program, DOS loads it and transfers control to it. In order to do that, DOS has to know where to enter a program and start executing. That's what the term **main( )** is for — DOS looks for the part of the program labeled **main( )** and starts there. In other words, **main( )** is the label that tags the beginning of the program. Later, the parentheses after the word main will enclose some information that DOS will pass to us, but for now we won't use that information so we're leaving them empty.

Following the parentheses in **main( )** is the program body, enclosed in curly braces. The program body here is remarkably small. In fact, we have given it no length at all. Although you can run this program, it does nothing. DOS loads the program and starts at **main( )**, but all that happens is that control is returned immediately to DOS and the program ends. Usually the curly braces enclose more program lines, such as in this case:

```
#include <stdio.h>

/* Prints "Hello, world." on the screen */

main()
{
    printf("Hello, world.");

    return(0);
}
```

Here, something is really going on; there is a real program body between the curly braces. (In fact, this is the traditional first program of C books.) This program indicates a few more things about writing C programs — especially about the actual format of the program. The curly braces have been split, and one is directly above the other. The program lines — `printf("Hello, world.");` and `return(0);` — are indented.

This kind of format, while not required, helps make C programs easier to use, and it is commonly used by C programmers. In particular, we'll find it helpful to align the curly braces, one on top of the other, and indent the body of the program as we've done above. This is an example of the C style, and the reason we use it will become clearer as our programs grow more complex.

Another example of the C style is the use of lowercase for most of the words in a program. Special words that are reserved for C are always written in lowercase — and C is sensitive to the case of those words (e.g., **printf** and **PrInTf** are two different words to C).

TIP When looking through C programs, you may be startled to find certain words in capital letters. That's also part of the C style; certain names may be assigned constant values — in fact, they are named **constants** — and constants are always written in uppercase. We'll see more about them soon.

Let's make this program run. First, we can type it into a file named, say, hello.c. Then we need to use a **compiler** to make an executable file. A compiler is responsible for taking the program as we've typed it in and translating it into something that the computer can understand. For example, to make this program run under the Quick C compiler, we can type qc hello.c and press Enter.

NOTE   Every time you boot, and before using the Quick C compiler, you should run the batch file named new-vars.bat by typing **new-vars** and pressing Enter. This lets Quick C know where it will find all the information it requires to compile and run your program.

In this case, the Quick C screen appears, and we see the program there. We select the Compile File option in the Make menu. Quick C takes the program hello.c and produces a new file, hello.obj. This is the **object file**, and it's the first step towards seeing our program run. This file is written in the language of the microprocessor, all byte-sized instructions and data. However, it's not a program we can execute yet. Quick C next uses its own **linker** to add the prewritten code for the C **functions** that we've used.

A function in C is a part of a program specially designed to handle a discrete programming task. For example, the **printf( )** function that we've used here is responsible for printing what we pass to it inside the parentheses; in our case, **printf( )** will send the words "Hello, world." to the screen. This function is defined in one of the C **libraries**, and these libraries are just collections of such functions, ready to be used. In fact, we can write our own functions too. For example, **main( )** is really the function that holds the body of our program, and we'll see a great deal more about that soon.

In our case, then, the Quick C linker finds the definition of the function **printf( )** in one of the C libraries and adds it to our program, creating the final file named hello.exe. Quick C then runs hello.exe, and you see this appear on the screen:

```
Hello, world.
```

The **printf( )** function has done its work — our first program has produced some output: two words on the screen. To do the same thing under Turbo C or Turbo C++, start it up like this: type tc hello.c and press Enter. If you're using Borland C++, type bc hello.c instead. The program appears on the screen; select the Make EXE File option in the Compile menu, and the compiler will produce hello.exe. Next, select the Run option in the Run menu, and the compiler will run the program, producing the same output as above.

NOTE Although the Borland products produce the same output, they switch us back to the program editor so fast that we don't see the words "Hello, world." on the screen. To switch back to the output screen (what Borland products call the user screen) and see those words, select the User Screen option from the Run menu. After that, type any key to get back to the program editor. In addition, we'll be using Turbo C++ and Borland C++ the same way as we use Turbo C in this book (with the exception of the C++ chapter), so if you have Turbo C++, use tc.exe as indicated; if you have Borland C++, use bc.exe instead.

If you have Microsoft C instead of Quick C, you can produce hello.exe with this command — type cl hello.c and press Enter. Microsoft C produces the object file and then links it (the CL command stands for Compile and Link), leaving you with hello.exe. To run it, just type hello and press Enter.

Since this is our first program, let's take the time to take it apart line by line; this dissection is going to tell us exactly what's happening here.

#include <stdio.h>

The most important line in the whole program is the line with **printf( )**:

```
#include <stdio.h>

/* Prints "Hello, world." on the screen */

main()
{
→       printf("Hello, world.");

        return(0);
}
```

This is where we tell C that we have something to display, and it is the most common way of printing on the screen. But, surprisingly, **printf( )** is not a built-in part of the C language at all. C is really divided into two major sections: the C language proper, and the C libraries. As we've mentioned, the C libraries are vast collections of functions like **printf( )**. (When we're talking about a function in this book, we'll put a pair of parentheses after its name.)

Here, we are telling the **printf( )** function that we want it to print the words "Hello, world." on the screen. A function can read what we pass to it inside the parentheses, do something, and even return some data to us. For this reason, when we use a function, C has to know how it's going to behave. What kind of data will it take? What kind of data will it return?

When we define our own functions, it will be up to us to inform C of all of these things. But because there are literally hundreds of functions already available to us in the C libraries, it would be difficult to remember what to tell C for each one of them. For that reason, C has a number of **header files** that hold the information it needs to know about the library functions.

In our case, we can provide C with everything it needs to know about **printf( )** by including the correct header file; for **printf( )**, this file is named stdio.h (depending on your version of C, there might be several dozen different header files available). The **printf( )** function has a line in that file telling C what kind of data it takes and what kind it returns, and, if C is going to use any function in a program, it needs that kind of information about it. Many functions are included in each header file, so we're including information about dozens of functions besides **printf( )**, but C ignores all the information that it doesn't need.

TIP There is an easy way of knowing what header file you have to include: When you look up a function in the C documentation, the description of each function will also mention which header file the function requires. For example, the documentation for **printf( )** also says that we have to include stdio.h.

The **#include** instruction is a special type of instruction called a **preprocessor directive**. This is an instruction to the compiler — it doesn't appear in the final program. Directives like this one simply tell the compiler to do something. In our case, **#include** tells the compiler to take the entire file stdio.h and place it in the program here:

```
→    #include <stdio.h>

     /* Prints "Hello, world." on the screen */

     main()
     {
```

```
        printf("Hello, world.");

        return(0);
    }
```

As mentioned, including this entire file adds information about many more functions than just **printf( )**, but C ignores the information about functions that it doesn't need. After this line is executed by the compiler, C knows what it needs to know about the function **printf( )**.

/* Prints "Hello, world." on the screen */

The next line in our program is a **comment**. The compiler treats comments as though they weren't there at all. In fact, comments are entirely for our benefit. We use them as notes to tell us what's going on in the program. In this case, our comment tells us what the program is for:

```
    #include <stdio.h>

→   /* Prints "Hello, world." on the screen */

    main()
    {
        printf("Hello, world.");

        return(0);
    }
```

In C, a comment starts with the characters /*, and, when it's done, ends with the matching characters */. As soon as the compiler sees /* it stops reading and interpreting; only after it sees the closing */ marker will it begin reading the program again. Comments are added to make the code more readable, so you can go back to your program some time in the future and still understand what the program does. They may be placed anywhere in the program, as long as you don't obstruct parts of the program that you want compiled. For example, our program could look like this:

```
  #include <stdio.h>    /* The required header file for printf() */

  /*    This program prints */
  /*    the words "Hello, world."    */
  /*    on the screen.        */

  main()                    /* The main function. */
```

```
{
    printf("Hello, world.");     /* Use printf() to print out\
                                   message. */

    return(0);
}
```

There is more information here, so what is actually happening is clearer. Note in particular the comment:

```
/*     This program prints */
/*     the words "Hello, world."    */
/*     on the screen.        */
```

Because the compiler stops interpreting what's between the /* and */ markers, we could have done that this way instead:

```
/* This program prints
the words "Hello, world."
on the screen.*/
```

Both work as comments, but it's more clear that the entire text in the first case is a comment; the C style is usually to place /* and */ markers on each line of a multi-line comment to avoid confusion.

We'll see comments frequently in this book, and it's good programming practice to include them since it makes the code easier to read, change, or debug; in other words, adding comments can actually help you be a more efficient programmer.

main( )

The next line has the label **main( )** in it. We already know a little about **main( )** — it represents the place where the program starts. And, as we've mentioned, it is a function.

Every single line of C that does anything must be inside some function before it can be executed. We've already seen another example of a function, **printf( )**. Functions are used in C to compartmentalize a large programming task into smaller tasks that are easier to work with. The work done in one function is separate from the work done in another, making our code

modular, which is another way of saying that it's broken up into manageable pieces. Later, when we write our own functions, we'll see how that works.

The **main( )** function is the one that we always need even if we don't have any others because it's the one where our program starts. The **statements** that make up the body of a function follow the name of that function and are enclosed by curly braces — in our case, the only statements are `printf("Hello, world.");` and `return(0);` like this:

```
#include <stdio.h>

/* Prints "Hello, world." on the screen */

main()
{
→       printf("Hello, world.");

        return(0);
}
```

In C, whatever is between curly braces is referred to as a **block**. In particular, the body of a function like this one is always enclosed in curly braces, so it is an example of a block. We will also use blocks as a way of tying statements together to make a group of statements. Keep in mind that the indentation and physical arrangement of statements in a block is up to us. We could equally as well have done this:

```
#include <stdio.h>

/* Prints "Hello, world." on the screen */

main(){printf("Hello, world.");
return(0);}
```

However, as our programs become longer, we'll find it much more useful to indent the program body so that it's more readable.

NOTE   Together, the curly braces make up what is called a **delimiter pair** in C. Other delimiter pairs (i.e., if you find one, the other must be coming up) are { }, [ ], ( ), <I>, /**/, " ", and ' '.

---

printf( ) and the C Library

Now we reach the meat of the program, the part where we use the **printf( )** function. Here's how it looks:

```
#include <stdio.h>

/* Prints "Hello, world." on the screen */

main()
{
    printf("Hello, world.");

    return(0);
}
```

This line is a good example of a statement in C. Statements like this end with a semicolon (;), referred to as the **statement terminator**. Each action in C is a statement, and each one must be ended by a semicolon. In practice, this means that just about every line of a C program is ended with a semicolon (there are exceptions, as we'll see). This terminator tells the compiler that the present statement is complete.

TIP Probably the most common error among beginning C programmers is to leave out semicolons. However, the compiler catches this type of error and asks us to correct it before compiling the program.

This is the typical way to use a function — by placing the data we want it to use between the parentheses. The data that is passed to a function makes up the function's **arguments**. In this case, the **printf( )** function only receives one argument, and that is the **character string** "Hello, world." We'll see soon that there are many different forms of data that we can manipulate in a C program, and one of them is called a character string — a sequence of characters. For example, "Hello, world." is a character string thirteen characters long, and it makes up the argument we are sending to **printf( )**.

Because **printf( )** is the normal way of printing on the screen in C, it's pretty powerful. We are not limited to just printing words; we also have control over the way we print those words on the screen. For example, we can place the characters \t and \n in the character string like this:

```
#include <stdio.h>

/* Prints "Hello, world." on the screen */

main()
{
→       printf("Hello\t world.\n");

        return(0);
}
```

Now the program prints out "Hello," followed by a tab, followed by " world." and then a carriage return, which takes us to the next line on the screen. The \t sequence causes **printf( )** to print a tab on the screen, and the \n sequence, called the newline sequence, makes **printf( )** skip to the beginning of the next line. There are a number of these codes, called **backslash codes**, that we can use to manipulate the appearance of **printf( )**'s output, and they appear in Table 1-1. Whenever you use one of these codes (such as \t) at a particular place, it is converted to what it stands for (a tab in the case of \t) at that same place in the output.

Code	Meaning
\a	alert (ring bell)
\n	newline (<cr><lf> pair on screen)
\b	backspace
\r	carriage return
\f	formfeed
\t	tab
\v	vertical tab
\\	backslash (two needed)
\'	single quote mark
\"	double quote mark
\0	null

Table 1-1. printf( ) Backslash Codes.

return(0);

The last line of our first program is `return(0);`:

```
#include <stdio.h>

/* Prints "Hello, world." on the screen */

main()
{
    printf("Hello, world.");

    return(0);
}
```

$\rightarrow$

We include this statement because **main( )** itself is a function, and C expects functions to return some value unless we explicitly indicate that they will not. In particular, we have not indicated a return value for **main( )**, so C assumes that it will return an integer value (which is the default for functions). To make sure we comply with this expectation, we return a value of 0 at the end of our program (the Borland compilers insist that **main( )** return a value, the Microsoft ones do not). This will be the usual last statement in our programs — we'll return a value of 0 from **main( )** if everything went well, and a value of 1 if not. We'll see a great deal about returning values from functions later.

That's it for our first program, then; the return(0) statement completes it. We've been pretty successful so far, and we've been able to use **printf( )** to print on the screen. However, **printf( )** is far more powerful than what we've used it for; it will also let us print out all kinds of data on the screen. In fact, now that we have the essentials down, data handling is our next topic.

Introduction to Data in C

Our first program, HELLO.C, is alright as far as it goes, but that's not very far. It's limited to one not very bright action — printing out "Hello, world." There's more to computing than that, however, so we'll see how to store and handle some data in the remainder of this chapter (after all, that's what computers were designed for, processing our data).

For example, let's say that we wanted to keep track of the current chapter number of this book in a program. When the program was run, it could print out the chapter number like this: "This is Chapter 1." Our program would also be free to work on that data, and, in the following chapter, the chapter number could be updated to 2.

In C, we store data by setting aside space for it in memory and by giving it a name. The space we set aside for the data depends on what kind of data we have, and there are several predefined types of data that we can select from in C. One very popular type of data object is the **integer**, which takes up two bytes of memory storage. Those two bytes (which make up 16 bits of memory) can hold integer numbers ranging from -32,768 to 32,767 (omit the commas in numbers like this in your programs). That's large enough to hold chapter numbers, so let's set up an integer in memory named **chapter_number**. We can do that and set it equal to 1 at the same time like this:

```
#include <stdio.h>

/* Print "This is Chapter 1." */

main()
{
    int chapter_number = 1;

    printf("This is Chapter %d.\n", chapter_number);
    return(0);
}
```

Let's interpret this statement. Because we want C to set aside space for our data, we have to let it know how much space to set aside. This is true of every data item that we want to use; when we set aside space for our data and give it a name, we are creating a *variable*, such as **chapter_number**, and we have to declare each of our variables.

In our case, the **data type** of **chapter_number** is **integer**, which is abbreviated as **int** in C. As we set aside space for it, we also direct C to store the value 1 in it like this: int chapter_number = 1;. This is called **initializing** the variable. (Note that there is a semicolon at the end of this C statement as well.)

So far, then, we have set up a variable, an integer named **chapter_number** which holds the value 1. There are rules in C about the naming of **identifiers**: the names that we can give to functions, variables, or labels. Here they are:

- The first character of the identifier must be a letter or an underscore (_). The first character cannot be a number (because C might think the whole thing is a number).

- The rest of the characters must be numbers, letters, or an underscore.
- Only the first 32 letters count; that's all C actually reads (some compilers read even less).
- C is case sensitive: upper- and lowercase letters in identifiers are different.

Now let's continue with the program. To check the value of **chapter_number**, we print it out like this:

```
#include <stdio.h>

/* Print "This is Chapter 1." */

main()
{
    int chapter_number = 1;

    printf("This is Chapter %d.\n", chapter_number);

    return(0);
}
```

Here we're passing two arguments to **printf( )**; the first is a character string, and the second is the name of our variable, **chapter_number**. The string we pass to **printf( )** is actually called the **format string**. In our previous example, the format string contained no formatting characters — it was only the string "Hello, world." Now, however, we are printing out data, and we have to format what we print.

If you study the format string, "This is Chapter %d.\n", you'll see the **format specification** %d (in addition to the **newline** backslash code). This informs **printf( )** that we wish to print out an integer in decimal format — the **d** in %d stands for decimal — and that it should come at exactly this position in the string. In other words, the result of this program is to print the following line on the screen:

```
This is Chapter 1.
```

Notice that the value of **chapter_number**, 1, was substituted exactly where the %d used to be in the format string:

```
              ↓
This is Chapter %d.\n
```

College Marketing Group
50 Cross Street
Winchester, MA 01890

ATT: **Cheryl Read**

If we had another variable to hold the number of the next chapter, we might name it next and include it in the format string like this:

```
#include <stdio.h>

/* Print "This is Chapter 1, next is 2." */

main()
{
    int chapter_number = 1;
    int next = 2;

    printf("This is Chapter %d, next is %d.\n",\
    chapter_number, next);

    return(0);
}
```

In this case, the value of the first variable, **chapter_number**, is substituted for the first **%d**, and the value of the variable named **next** is substituted for the second **%d**. This program prints out:

```
This is Chapter 1, next is 2.
```

There are many different variable types in C, and, as you might expect, there are different **printf( )** codes like %d for each one of them, as we'll see soon.

NOTE You might notice that we've been defining our variables in the beginning of the function **main( )**. Declaring variables inside a function like that is only one of three possible places to declare them, and we'll see the others when we start working with other functions.

There are other ways of reaching the value inside a variable besides initializing it. For example, we can do this:

```
#include <stdio.h>

/* Print "This is Chapter 1." */

main()
{
    int chapter_number;

    chapter_number = 1;
```

```
        printf("This is Chapter %d.\n", chapter_number);

        return(0);
}
```

In this case, we didn't initialize **chapter_number**. Instead, we assigned a value to it like this:

```
chapter_number = 1;
```

> **TIP**   A variable that was not initialized cannot be counted on to hold 0 when the program starts. In fact, it may hold whatever value was in memory when the program first started. In other words, don't make the mistake of assuming that uninitialized variables are set to 0; setting variables to zero is compiler dependent.

Assignments like this always take the value on the right-hand side, 1 in this case, and assign it to the variable on the left. The expression on the right doesn't have to be a constant like 1 — it can be another variable, or, as we'll see, even a function. (In fact, it can be anything at all as long as C is able to evaluate it and give that value to the variable on the left side.)

The = sign is called the **assignment operator**, and we can use it to put values into variables. In fact, C has three different types of operators: arithmetic operators; relational and logical operators; and bitwise operators. We're ready to take a look at arithmetic operators, so let's do that next, saving the others for when they'll be useful to us.

We'll work through arithmetic operators with the variable type we already know: integers. And, after we become familiar with those operators, we'll be able to move on to explore the other data types C has to offer us besides integers.

Arithmetic Operators in C

Arithmetic operators are the ones that do math for us. This is where we find the familiar operations of addition, subtraction, and so on. Let's see an example. If you had three oranges and four apples, and you wanted to add them, you could do it this way:

```
#include <stdio.h>

/* This program adds apples and oranges. */

main()
{
    int apples, oranges, sum;

    oranges = 3;
    apples = 4;
→   sum = apples + oranges;
    printf("Total fruit inventory is %d apples and\
    oranges.\n", sum);

    return(0);
}
```

There are two new things here. First, note that we can set up a number of integer variables on the same line, like this:

```
#include <stdio.h>

/* This program adds apples and oranges. */

main()
{
→   int apples, oranges, sum;

    oranges = 3;
    apples = 4;
    sum = apples + oranges;
    printf("Total fruit inventory is %d apples and\
    oranges.\n", sum);

    return(0);
}
```

If we had wanted to, we could even have initialized their values right there, like this:

```
int apples = 4, oranges = 3, sum;
```

Instead, we used the assignment operator to make **apples** equal to 4 and **oranges** equal to 3:

```
#include <stdio.h>

/* This program adds apples and oranges. */

main()
{
    int apples, oranges, sum;

    oranges = 3;
    apples = 4;
    sum = apples + oranges;
    printf("Total fruit inventory is %d apples and\
    oranges.\n", sum);

    return(0);
}
```

With our variables set, we can add apples and oranges like this:

```
#include <stdio.h>

/* This program adds apples and oranges. */

main()
{
    int apples, oranges, sum;

    oranges = 3;
    apples = 4;
    sum = apples + oranges;
    printf("Total fruit inventory is %d apples and\
    oranges.\n", sum);

    return(0);
}
```

In this case, the value in **apples** is added to the value in **oranges**, and the result is placed in the variable sum (neither the value in **apples** nor the value in **oranges** is affected). Then the program prints out the total fruit inventory, 7 apples and oranges.

TIP   The assignment operator has a time-saving feature that you should be aware of. Let's say you wanted to assign the value of **apples** + **oranges** to two variables, both **sum** and **total**. You could do it like this in C: `sum = total = apples + oranges;` — all on one line. Although this saves the need for assignments on different lines, it can be confusing to do it this way, and for that reason, we'll avoid that usage in this book.

Besides addition, we also have subtraction. Let's say that we started with four apples and then ate one. This program would let us know how many we had left:

```
#include <stdio.h>

/* This program adjusts apples. */

main()
{
    int apples;

    apples = 4;
    apples = apples - 1;
    printf("You now have %d apples left.\n", apples);

    return(0);
}
```

You might notice something interesting here; **apples** appears on both sides of the equals sign:

```
    apples = apples - 1;
```

What happens here is that the original value of **apples**, 4, has 1 subtracted from it, and then is assigned back to **apples** again. (We are intentionally changing the value of **apples** in this case, and assigning it a new number.) Then the program prints out the new value, 3.

Besides addition and subtraction, there are also multiplication, division, modulus, and other arithmetic operators, as shown in Table 1-2. The **modulus operator** %, which returns the modulus of one number with respect to another, might be unfamiliar. This operator simply returns the remainder of an integer division (for example, 16 / 3 is 5 with a remainder of 1, and 16 % 3 equals 1). We'll see most of these operators in many places throughout the book.

Combining Arithmetic and Assignment Operators

Because changing the value of a variable by adding or subtracting another value is so common, C has a shortcut method that comes in handy (and which works for all the arithmetic operators). All we have to do is to combine the symbols we want to use like this: + and = becomes +=, - and + becomes -=, and so on. In other words, these lines are equivalent:

Operator	Function
-	Subtraction
+ -	Addition
*	Multiplication
/	Division
%	Modulus
- -	Decrementing
++	Incrementing

Table 1-2.   C's Arithmetic Operators.

```
apples = apples - 1;
apples -= 1;
```

So are these:

```
double_me = double_me * 2;
double_me *= 2;
```

And these:

```
halve_me = halve_me / 2;
halve_me /= 2;
```

This kind of shortcut is typical of C. Much of its attraction to programmers comes from the shortcuts that make writing programs a little easier and more compact. In fact, we're about to see another example of that right now.

The Increment and Decrement Operators

The last two arithmetic operators are the **increment** and **decrement** operators, ++ and - -. These operators also provide us with shortcuts.

> **NOTE**   This is another case when C is close to assembly language, and, in particular, to the 80×86 increment and decrement instructions, INC and DEC.

A few pages ago, we had a program that displayed the new number of apples after we had eaten one; we could have done that this way:

```
main()
{
    int apples;

    apples = 4;
→   apples = --apples;
    printf("You now have %d apples left.\n", apples);

    return(0);
}
```

Here, we're subtracting 1 (i.e., decrementing) the number of apples with the line `apples = --apples;`. The decrement operator, - -, automatically subtracts one from the values of **apples**. In fact, C allows us this further shortcut:

```
main()
{
    int apples;

    apples = 4;
→   --apples;
    printf("You now have %d apples left.\n", apples);

    return(0);
}
```

All we had to do was to include the statement `--apples` in order to decrement the value in apples by one. The ++ and - - operators are favorites among C programmers, and we'll see them continually in this book. (You are probably already familiar with the ++ operator from the name C++, an inside pun meaning incremented or augmented C.)

TIP   Probably the most common place to use ++ or - - is in a loop statement, as we'll see in the next chapter.

We should note, however, that ++ and - - can be either **postfix** or **prefix** operators. For example, we could have used either `--apples` or `apples--`. Both statements decrement the value of **apples**, but what is important is when they do it. For example, we can use ++ (or - -) as a prefix operator, as in this case:

```
fruits = --apples;
```

Here, the value of **apples** is first decremented, and then it is assigned to the variable **fruits**. If apples held 4, then after this statement is executed, **apples** and **fruits** will both hold 3. On the other hand, look at this statement:

```
fruits = apples--;
```

Using ++ (or --) as a postfix operator like this means that it will be applied only after the rest of the statement has been executed. If **apples** held 4, then 4 would be assigned to **fruits**. After the statement had been executed, the -- operator would be applied to **apples**, decrementing it to 3. When we move on to the next line, **fruits** would be left holding 4, and **apples** would be left holding 3.

This can lead to unexpected results. For example, you might think that the following program would print out "You now have 3 fruits left.", but it actually prints out "You now have 4 fruits left." because -- is a postfix operator here, applied only after the original value in **apples** is assigned to **fruits**:

```
main()
{
    int apples, fruits;

    apples = 4;
→   fruits = apples--;
    printf("You now have %d fruits left.\n", fruits);

    return(0);
}
```

Because of the possible confusion here, it is usually best to break such lines up into two statements (i.e., `apples--;` and `fruits = apples;`).

Now we've seen the arithmetic operators at work — but what about the case when we start working with multiple operators in the same statement? For example, what is the result of this statement:

```
my_int = 9 + 6 / 3;
```

Is **my_int** given a value of 5 or 11? The answer to that question makes up an important operator topic, and it's coming up next.

Operator Precedence in C

Every now and then, operator expressions can become complicated, and we need to know how operators combine. In our example — `my_int = 9 + 6 / 3;` — the division operator / has **precedence** over the addition operator +, so the result is 9 + 2, or 11. In fact, both the multiplication and division operators have precedence over addition and subtraction. Here are some examples:

$$3 + 4 * 5 \quad \rightarrow \quad 23$$
$$8 / 2 + 1 \quad \rightarrow \quad 5$$
$$9 * 2 - 1 \quad \rightarrow \quad 17$$

In each case, the operator with higher precedence is used first. Table 1-3 shows the operator precedence for all the C operators (the operators with the highest precedence are the highest in the table — don't memorize them; we'll meet most of these operators later) and you can refer to it whenever there's a question.

For example, this expression evaluates to 15 - 2 + 1, or 14:

$$3 * 5 - 4 / 2 + 1$$

Operator	Description	Associativity
( )	function call	left to right
[ ]	array element	left to right
.	structure member	left to right
->	pointer to a structure member	left to right
!	logical NOT	right to left
~	one's complement	right to left
-	minus (the neg operator)	right to left
++	increment	right to left
--	decrement	right to left
&	address of	right to left
*	contents of	right to left
(vble type)	typecast operator	right to left
sizeof	returns in bytes	right to left

Table 1-3. Operator Precedence in C.

*	multiply	left to right
/	divide	left to right
%	modulous	left to right
+	add	left to right
-	subtract	left to right
<<	left shift	left to right
>>	right shift	left to right
<	less than	left to right
<=	less than or equal to	left to right
>	greater than	left to right
>=	greater than or equal to	left to right
==	equality	left to right
!=	not equal	left to right
&	bit-by-bit AND	left to right
^	bit-by-bit XOR	left to right
¦	bit-by-bit OR	left to right
&&	logical AND	left to right
¦ ¦	logical OR	left to right
?:	conditional	right to left
=	assignment	right to left
*= /= %= +=	compound assignment	right to left
-= <<= >>=	compound assignment	right to left
&= ^= ¦=	compound assignment	right to left
,	comma operator	left to right

Table 1-3.   (continued)

There's one sure way of clearing up any confusion; we can use parentheses in our statements to indicate which operands we want to go with which operators. For example, this expression evaluates to $3 * 2 / 2 + 1$, or 4:

$3 * (5 - 3) / 2 + 1$

And this one is $3 * 1 / 3$, or 1:

$3 * (5 - 4) / (2 + 1)$

Parentheses can come in very handy, and we'll use them frequently to make our code clearer. Wherever there's a problem about operator precedence — that is, which operations C will perform first — parentheses can solve it.

The Resulting Data Type

The last point we might notice about arithmetic operators is that when we operate on two variables with the same data type — say, integer — that the result is also of that type. For example, if we add two integers, the result will be an integer. This is worth noticing when you divide two integers; the result is an integer, which cannot contain fractions. For example, look at this program:

```
#include <stdio.h>

/* This program calculates employee share. */

main()
{
    int profits, employees, share;

    profits = 3;
    employees = 2;
→   share = profits/employees;
    printf("Each employee gets %d.", share);

    return(0);
}
```

In this case, we are trying to divide a profit of three over two employees. We might think that 3 divided by 2 should yield 1.5, but when we assign 1.5 to the integer variable (named **share**), the fractional part is truncated and the program actually prints out:

```
Each employee gets 1.
```

In this case, we should not have used integer variables. Instead, we should have used a type that was capable of handling floating point numbers, such as C's **float** type. And, now that we're finished with arithmetic operators, we should look at data types like **float** next so that we can handle the cases that integers can't. In fact, the rest of this chapter will be about the rest of the C data types, taking us far beyond integers.

How to Use All the C Data Types

We've gotten a good introduction to the arithmetic operators in C, but, so far, we've worked only with one type of variable: integers. However, the world is a place filled with quantities that won't fit into the integer range of -32,768 to 32,767. Some quantities are a great deal larger, some are a great deal smaller (i.e., less than one). Other quantities have fractional parts associated with them. A calculator can handle these numbers; surely our computer should also. In C, there are five basic data types: **char** (1 byte long), **int** (2 bytes), **float** (4 bytes), **double** (8 bytes), and **void** (0 bytes). Table 1-4 shows what kinds of values they can hold.

You may not have been expecting this last data type: a void quantity has no value. Void is used as a keyword to indicate to C that a function takes (or returns) no data, and we won't worry about it until we start working with functions in earnest. The other data types are more interesting, however. Let's examine them now.

Data Type char

The char data type is one byte (eight bits) long, and its name is an abbreviation for character; the numbers we can store in a char range from 0 to 255. The reason a byte is called a **char** is that each of the PC's characters, all the letters, numbers, and text symbols that it can display, are given code numbers and stored that way. For example, the letter 'A' is stored as 65, the letter 'B' as 66. A space is stored as 32. Here are some more examples:

'A' = 65	'a' = 97	'0' = 48
'B' = 66	'b' = 98	'1' = 49
'C' = 67	'c' = 99	'2' = 50
:	:	:
'Z' = 90	'z' = 122	'9' = 57

These codes are called *ASCII codes*, and there are 256 of them, which means that the PC can display a total of 256 symbols (there is a complete list of ASCII codes in your C documentation). If you set aside one byte of memory, you can store the ASCII code for exactly one character in the PC's character set. That's why this type is referred to as a **char**. It is just the right size to store the ASCII code for one character.

Data Type	Signed?	Bytes	Range
char	signed	1	-128 to 127
int	signed	2	-32,768 to 32,768
float	signed	4	3.4E+-38 [7 digits accuracy]
double	signed	8	1.7E+-308 [15 digits accuracy]
void	neither	0	without value

Table 1-4. C Data Types.

For instance, we could modify our example that prints out the chapter number as an integer to print out the character '1' instead. The ASCII code of '1' is 49, so we can print "This is Chapter 1." like this:

```
#include <stdio.h>

/* Print "This is Chapter 1." */

main()
{
    char chapter_number;

    chapter_number = 49;
    printf("This is Chapter %c.\n", chapter_number);
    return(0);
}
```

Note that in this case, we have declared **chapter_number** as a char, not as an int. Then we assign the ASCII code 49 to it, which stands for the character '1'; in addition, the **printf( )** format code for printing chapter_number has changed from **%d** (which prints out decimal integers) to **%c**, which tells **printf( )** that we want to print out this value as an ASCII character. That means that **printf( )** interprets the value passed to it, 49, as an ASCII code. In fact, there is a shortcut for this process; if we enclose the character in single quotation marks, like this: '1', then that automatically stands for the corresponding ASCII code (49 here) in any C program:

```
#include <stdio.h>

/* Print "This is Chapter 1." */

main()
```

```
         {
              char chapter_number;

  →          chapter_number = '1';
              printf("This is Chapter %c.\n", chapter_number);

              return(0);
         }
```

We should also note that single and double quotation marks mean something quite different in C. Double quotation marks indicate that we're talking about a **string** of characters, such as "Hello, World.", and we'll see more about strings soon.

Data Type int

The **int** type we have already seen. It can hold numbers from -32,768 to 32,767. This range seems unsymetrical; there seem to be more negative numbers than positive ones. In fact, the way that the computer stores positive and negative numbers makes it treat 0 as part of the positive range (and we'll see why when we investigate the internal representation of C data in Chapter 12).

Data Types float and double

Next are the two floating point types, **float** and **double**. The float type takes up four bytes, the double type eight bytes. With the float type, you can store floating point numbers numbers ranging from 3.4E-38 to 3.4E+38 (where the E means Exponent) with seven digit accuracy. With double, you can store floating point numbers from 1.7E-308 to 1.7E+308 with 15 digits of accuracy. This is quite a range. Let's use the float type in our chapter example:

```
         #include <stdio.h>

         /* Print "This is Chapter 1.000000" */

         main()
         {
  →           float chapter_number;

              chapter_number = 1.0;
              printf("This is Chapter %f.\n", chapter_number);

              return(0);
         }
```

This example prints out "This is Chapter 1.000000.". Note that we're using a new format specification, **%f.**, to print out a floating point number here. In fact, **%f.** prints out the chapter number to far greater precision than we need, and we can change that by adding a **precision specifier**. That works like this: **%.#f.** tells printf( ) that we want to print out # digits past the decimal point; **%.2f.** in our example would print out "This is Chapter 1.00." That means we can print "This is Chapter 1." with **%.0f.** like this:

```
#include <stdio.h>

/* Print "This is Chapter 1." */

main()
{
    float chapter_number;

    chapter_number = 1.0;
→   printf("This is Chapter %.0f.\n", chapter_number);

    return(0);
}
```

So far, we've seen the **%d** format specifiers for decimal integers, **%c** for ASCII characters, and now **%f** for floating point There are even more options available, however. Table 1-5 shows all the **printf( )** format specifications, from characters to hexadecimal values.

Hexadecimal is, of course, just base 16, and it's very popular in computers. The numbers run from 0 to 9, exhausting all the decimal digits, and then continue with the letters a–f. We can indicate to C that a number is in hexadecimal format by prefixing it with the characters **0x**, as in **0x1a** or **0x15ff**. For example, the hexadecimal digit **0xa** is equal to 10 decimal; the next digit, **0xb**, is equal to 11, and so on. We'll see a great deal more about hexadecimal numbers later.

We've covered the five basic data types and how to print them out; however, that's only part of the data type story, because C also allows us to add special keywords called **data type modifiers** to our variable declarations as well. For example, two of the modifiers are short and long, which means that we can use not only ints, but also short ints and long ints. Let's take a look at this topic next as we continue our discussion of data storage in C.

Specifier	Meaning
%c	Character
%d	Decimal Integer
%i	Integer (same as %d)
%e	Scientific notation (e.g., 3.4e-3)
%E	Scientific notation (e.g., 3.4E-3)
%f	Floating Point
%g	Scientific notation or floating point, whichever is shorter (lowercase e used)
%G	Scientific notation or floating point, whichever is shorter (uppercase E used)
%n	Argument is an integer pointer; number of characters printed so far is placed in that integer
%o	Octal
%p	Prints a pointer
%s	Character String
%u	Unsigned Integer
%x	Hexadecimal, lowercase letters (e.g., 1a4c)
%X	Hexadecimal, uppercase letters (e.g., 1A4C)
%%	Percent sign

Table 1-5.   printf( ) Format Specifications.

Data Type Modifiers

So far, we've covered the basic variable types; however, to extend our data-handling power further, C adds four modifiers that may be used with some of those basic data types. The modifiers are **signed**, **unsigned**, **long**, and **short**.

These data type modifiers may only be applied to the char and int types, although long may also be applied to double. In Table 1-6, you'll find a list of the possible combinations of the basic data types and the modifiers (note the tremendous range of the long double type).

TIP   The long double type is 10 bytes long, and it corresponds exactly to the internal format of floating point numbers as they're stored in the 80×87. When we discuss assembly language later, you'll be able to slip these numbers to and from the 80×87 without modification.

Declaration	Signed?	Bytes	Range
char	signed	1	-128 to 127
int	signed	2	-32,768 to 32,768
short	signed	2	-32,768 to 32,768
short int	signed	2	-32,768 to 32,768
long	signed	4	-2,147,483,648 to 2147483647
long	intsigned	4	-2,147,483,648 to 2147483647
unsigned char	unsigned	1	0 to 255
unsigned	unsigned	2	0 to 65,535
unsigned int	unsigned	2	0 to 65,535
unsigned short	unsigned	2	0 to 65,535
unsigned long	unsigned	4	0 to 4,294,967,295
signed char	signed	1	-128 to 127
signed int	signed	2	-32,768 to 32,768
signed	signed	2	-32,768 to 32,768
signed long	signed	4	-2,147,483,648 to 2147483647
enum	unsigned	2	0 to 65,535
float	signed	4	3.4E+-38 (7 digits accuracy)
double	signed	8	1.7E+-308 (15 digits accuracy)
long double	signed	10	3.4E-4932 to 1.1E+4932

Note that some of these are duplicates of each other. For example, int, short, and short int are all names for the same thing.

Table 1-6.   C Variable Types with Modifiers.

We can declare our variables to be any of the types listed in that table. The unsigned types can only handle numbers starting at 0 and working upwards; the signed types can handle both positive and negative numbers. You can see the trade-off here when you note that an unsigned int can hold numbers from 0 to 65,535, while a signed int can hold numbers from -32,768 to 32,767. In other words, if you're sure that your values will be positive, using unsigned variables will effectively double your range. Note also that, by default, char and int are signed; if you declare a variable as int, for example, the compiler assumes you mean signed int (with a range of -32,768 to 32,767).

Now we've seen what variable types we can use in our programs, what the data type modifiers do, and even how to print our variables out. But there is one other topic that we should cover before we are through setting up our variables; we have to see what happens when we start to mix variables of different types in the same statement.

C Type Conversions

When our programs get long and more complex, we'll have plenty of variables in them. Sooner or later, we might find that we want to add the value in, say, a char named **my_char** to an integer named **my_integer**. Will C handle this correctly?

In general, it will. If C is expected to combine two operands in some way, like **my_char** and **my_int**, it will elevate both of them to the same level before performing the operation. In this case, C will temporarily make **my_char** into an int before adding it to **my_int**, and the result will be an int. The rule is that no accuracy should be lost; when a char and an int are addded, the char is converted temporarily into an int; when an int and a float are added, the int is converted temporarily into a float. The result of the operation will have the largest type.

In general, this is the way it goes (apply these rules in order): if one operand is a long double, C converts the other one to a long double as well. Next, if either of the operands is a double, the other is converted to a double too. Next, if one is a long, the other is converted to long also. Finally, if one is unsigned, the other is converted to unsigned also. Let's look at some examples:

```
my_answer = my_char + my_int;
```

In this case, **my_char** is temporarily converted to an int and then added to **my_int**. However, the next case is a little different:

```
my_answer = my_int + my_float;
```

Here, we are mixing a floating point number and an integer. In this case, to preserve accuracy, **my_int** is temporarily made into a float and added to **my_float**. Now look at this one:

```
my_answer = my_char + my_int + my_float + my_double;
```

In this case, all operands are made into doubles before being added, since double is the largest type present. The answer, **my_answer**, is also of type double.

C is very agile at converting your variables to different types to preserve accuracy, so you usually don't have to worry about the result of such an operation. In fact, it even lets you temporarily convert your variables to a different type yourself.

Type Casts in C

Let's take a look at a program that we developed earlier in this chapter, when we tried to divide profits between two employees. That program looked something like this:

```
#include <stdio.h>

/* This program calculates employee share. */

main()
{
    int profits, employees;

    profits = 3;
    employees = 2;
    printf("Each employee gets %d.", profits/employees);

    return(0);
}
```

We know that the fractional part of a value gets cut off when C is working with integers, so the result is "Each employee gets 1." Now, however, we're in a position to change that with a temporary override of type. We can convert the variable profits from an int to a float temporarily and do the calculation like this:

```
#include <stdio.h>

/* This program calculates employee share. */

main()
{
    int profits, employees;
```

```
          profits = 3;
          employees = 2;
  →       printf("Each employee gets %f.", (float)\
          profits/employees);

          return(0);
      }
```

When we preface **profits** with (float), its type becomes a float temporarily. Since we are dealing with a float, the variable employees is also made into a float, the division is performed, and then the program prints out "Each employee gets 1.500000." (Notice that we also changed the **%d** format specification in the format string to **%f** to print out a float.) In fact, we shouldn't rely on C to upgrade employees by itself; instead, it would be better and clearer to do this:

```
      #include <stdio.h>

      /* This program calculates employee share. */

      main()
      {
          int profits, employees;

          profits = 3;
          employees = 2;
  →       printf("Each employee gets %f.", (float)\
          profits/ (float) employees);

          return(0);
      }
```

You can temporarily override any variable's type this way, with what is called a **cast**. All you need to do is to preface the variable with the new type in parentheses, and C will treat it as though it had that new type. For example, here are some casts: (double) **my_float**, (int) **my_char**, or (float) **my_int**. Note that the variable and the variable's type are not really altered; the change is only in effect when a variable is prefaced with the cast.

That's it, then, for data storage and handling. We've seen the arithmetic operators; what the basic data types are in C; how to print them out; how to extend them with data type modifiers; even how to mix them. In just one short chapter, we've become pretty proficient with setting up C programs and with handling data in those programs. Our tour of C is on track.

On the other hand, now we're going to need some actual data to handle in those programs. Let's move on to Chapter 2, *Reading from the Keyboard*, so that we will be able to read real data from the keyboard, which will give us something to work on.

Reading from the Keyboard

In this chapter, we'll start reading data from the keyboard to work on in our programs. So far, our programs have been very good at printing on the screen and storing data in a variety of ways, but now it's time to go further. In this chapter, we'll learn how to read what we type at the keyboard and — just as importantly — we'll learn more about manipulating that data.

We'll see how program control works in this chapter as well, introducing the **if statement** and others that let us check on the value of our data and take the appropriate action. We'll be able to compare what we read to make sure it's in specific limits, and handle the cases where it's not. We'll also be introduced to the idea of **loops**, which lets a program repeat a certain procedure over and over, often breaking a single large task into many small, repetitive ones. Toward the end of the chapter, our programs will get a little longer, so we'll see that it makes sense sometimes to break them up into smaller pieces. In doing that, we'll see how to write our own functions. In other words, this chapter will introduce us to a great deal of C power, so let's get started by reading keys from the keyboard.

The scanf( ) Function for Reading Keys

Take a look at the program in Listing 2-1; this program reads a key that you type at the keyboard by using the library function **scanf( )**. This program asks you to type a key and, when you do, it types it out again.

Listing 2-1. Example Using scanf( ).

```
#include <stdio.h>

/* Read keys from the keyboard with scanf() */

main()
{
    char my_char;

    printf("Please type a character: ");
    scanf("%c", &my_char);

    printf("Thank you. That character was %c\n.", my_char);

    return(0);
}
```

We start off by including the header file stdio.h so that C knows how to handle scanf( ) and printf( ):

```
#include <stdio.h>

/* Read keys from the keyboard with scanf() */
    :
    :
```

Next, we set up main( ) and type out a prompt, indicating that we are waiting for a key to be typed at the keyboard:

```
        #include <stdio.h>

        /* Read keys from the keyboard with scanf() */

        main()
        {

→           printf("Please type a character: ");
            :
            :
```

Now we're ready to read the key that was typed, and to do that, we use **scanf( )**. This function is the major keyboard-input function of C, and the way you use it is a little like the way you use **printf( )**. You have to set up a format string, but in this case, the format string lets C know what kind of **input** to expect from the keyboard. In our case, we're just expecting a single character (which has the format specification **%c**). We can store that character as **my_char**, so we use **scanf( )** like this:

```
#include <stdio.h>

/* Read keys from the keyboard with scanf() */

main()
{
→       char my_char;

        printf("Please type a character: ");
→       scanf("%c", &my_char);
           :
           :
```

Note that we also declared the variable **my_char** to hold our keyboard data. In this case, the format string is extraordinarily simple, and just consists of "**%c**". However, our format strings will get more complex in this chapter; we'll have to tell C what to expect as input, and we have to plan it first in the format string. If our input characters are separated by spaces, for example, our format string might look like this: "**%c %c %c**", matching what C receives from the keyboard.

You might also notice something here that differs a little from our use of **printf( )**. The variable we pass to **scanf( )**, **my_char**, is preceded by an &, which wouldn't happen in **printf( )** because the corresponding **printf( )** statement would be `printf("%c", my_char);`:

```
#include <stdio.h>

/* Read keys from the keyboard with scanf() */

main()
{
        char my_char;

        printf("Please type a character: ");
→       scanf("%c", &my_char);
           :
           :
```

The use of **&** here takes a little bit of explaining, which we'll do at the end of this chapter as our lead-in to pointers. But for now we can think of it as a character that lets C functions modify the values of the parameters that we pass to them. In other words, without the **&**, **scanf( )** would not be able to change the value stored in **my_char**, which means that it could not store the value of the key that we typed. That is, the **&** gives the function access to **my_char** which it would otherwise not have, and we'll have to precede each variable that we want to fill with **&** when we use **scanf( )**.

After **scanf( )** is executed, the character that we typed (actually, its ASCII code) is stored in the variable **my_char**, and we can print it out with **printf( )**, like this:

```
#include <stdio.h>

/* Read keys from the keyboard with scanf() */

main()
{
    char my_char;

    printf("Please type a character: ");
    scanf("%c", &my_char);

    printf("Thank you. That character was %c.\n", my_char);

    return(0);
}
```

Using this little program, **char.c**, looks something like this on the screen:

```
H:\>char
Please type a character:
```

We can type a character — say we type 'a', followed by Enter:

```
H:\>char
Please type a character: a[Enter]
Thank you. That character was a.
```

The program politely tells us what we've typed, and finishes up. That's all there is to it; we've read a key from the keyboard, stored it, and managed to print it back out.

On the other hand, this program isn't that exciting. We already know what key we've typed without the program printing it out for us. Let's do a little more data manipulation here by, say, capitalizing the letter before printing it out. We can do that easily enough; there is a function in C named **toupper( )** which does this; i.e., capitalizes lowercase letters. We can change the prompt of our program to ask for a lowercase letter:

```
#include <stdio.h>
#include <ctype.h>

/* Capitalize keys read from the keyboard */

main()
{
    char my_char;

    printf("Please type a lowercase letter: ");
        :
        :
```

> **TIP**
>
> There's another way of capitalizing lowercase letters that programmers often use. Characters in C are just stored as their ASCII codes; the letters a–z have ASCII codes 97–122, and A–Z have codes 65–90. To capitalize my_char, all you have to do is to subtract 'a' - 'A' = 32 from it like this:
> `my_char = my_char - ('a' - 'A');.]`

Functions in C can *return* a value, and the value that **toupper( )** returns is the uppercase letter (i.e., of type char). Since this return value is a value like any other, we can assign it to **my_char** like this:

```
#include <stdio.h>
#include <ctype.h>

/* Capitalize keys read from the keyboard */

main()
{
    char my_char;

    printf("Please type a lowercase letter: ");
    scanf("%c", &my_char);
    my_char = toupper(my_char);
```

```
        printf("Thank you. The uppercase version is %c\n.",\
        my_char);

        return(0);
}
```

Here, we're passing the ASCII value in **my_char** to **toupper( )**, which capital-izes it and sends it back. The return value from **toupper( )** is then assigned to **my_char**, and all that remains is to print it out.

In fact, we could have saved a little time here. All we wanted to see on the screen was the uppercase version of **my_char**, and we could do that like this:

```
#include <stdio.h>
#include <ctype.h>

/* Capitalize keys read from the keyboard */

main()
{
    char my_char;

    printf("Please type a lowercase letter: ");
    scanf("%c", &my_char);

→       printf("Thank you. The uppercase version is\
        %c\n.",toupper(my_char));

    return(0);
}
```

In this case, **printf( )** prints out the format string until it comes to the **%c** format specifier. Then it checks the variables following the format string (what's called the **parameter list**) for the character to print out, and it en-counters **toupper(my_char)**. This expression evaluates to a character (the up-percase version of **my_char**) and **printf( )** prints that result out.

Now our program does something a little more interesting, but, since we're accepting unrestricted input, we have to plan for something that we haven't seen before: the possibility of errors. In particular, our program is meant only to capitalize lowercase letters. What if someone types 3 or @ or Z? These cannot be capitalized, so we should let the user know by checking what they type and letting them know if there is an error.

The if Statement

Checking our input for invalid responses is an important part of programming, and it will introduce us to the idea of making choices in our programs. In this case, we are faced with two choices: we can either accept the input or reject it. That kind of decision is made with the **if** statement.

Here, we want to check the character that's been typed. If it's not a lowercase letter, we want to inform the user that we cannot capitalize it. We know that C stores characters as ASCII codes. For example, if we type 'A', ASCII code 65, the value 65 is stored in **my_char**. As we saw in the last chapter, the letters 'a'–'z' use ASCII codes 97–122, and the letters 'A'–'Z' use ASCII codes 65–90. This means that we can check whether the key we got from the keyboard is a lowercase letter by checking its **numerical value**. If **my_char** is less than 'a' or greater than 'z', it's not a lowercase letter, and we should report an error.

We can check that value easily by breaking it up into two steps. First, we make sure that **my_char** is not less than 'a'; then we check that it is not greater than 'z'. We can compare it to 'a' like this, with an **if** statement:

```c
#include <stdio.h>
#include <ctype.h>

/* Capitalize keys read from the keyboard */

main()
{
    char my_char;

    printf("Please type a lowercase letter: ");
    scanf("%c", &my_char);

    if (my_char >= 'a') printf("In uppercase: %c\n.",\
    toupper(my_char));

    return(0);
}
```

Here, we check that the value in **my_char** is greater than or equal to 'a', and, if it is, we print out the uppercase version. Note the form of this statement; we start out with if, followed by a **condition**, which is enclosed in parentheses. That condition is my_char >= 'a', and it is true if **my_char** is greater than or equal to 'a'.

Conditions in C can be either true or false. Properly read, the **if** statement reads: if **my_char** is greater than or equal to 'a' then execute the following **printf( )** statement. The general form of an **if** statement is like this:

```
if( condition ) statement;
```

Here are a few examples:

```
if(my_int > 5) printf("Your variable is greater than 5.\n");

if(at_least_1 < 1) at_least_1 = 1;

if(x > y) bigger_val = x;
```

In addition, we should note the **>=** relational operator. The last chapter only dealt with arithmetic operators; here, we'll start using relational operators. These operators compare the relation between two values, and they're used in C conditions. For that reason, the value that these operators return is either true or false. The relational operator here is **>=**, and it means greater than or equal to. We'll meet other relational operators shortly.

As far as the program we've been developing goes, we check **my_char** against 'a', and, if it's greater, we print out the capitalized version. Otherwise, we do nothing. There are two obvious problems here: First, we're not checking if **my_char** is greater than 'z'; and second, we're not printing out any error message if the character is less than 'a'. We can rectify the second problem with the second part of the if statement — **else**. Take a look at the program in Listing 2-2.

Listing 2-2. if...else Example.

```
#include <stdio.h>
#include <ctype.h>

/* Capitalize keys read from the keyboard */

main()
{
    char my_char;

    printf("Please type a lowercase letter: ");
```

Listing 2-2. *(continued)*

```
    scanf("%c", &my_char);

    if (my_char < 'a') printf("Sorry, I cannot capitalize\
    that.\n");
    else printf("Thank you. In uppercase: %c.",\
    toupper(my_char));

    return(0);
}
```

We've improved our program by using the relational operator <, which stands for "is less than"; if **my_char** is less than 'a', we print out an error message. Take a look at these two lines:

```
if (my_char < 'a') printf("Sorry, I cannot capitalize
that.\n"); else printf("Thank you. In uppercase %c.",
toupper(my_char));
```

If **my_char** is less than 'a' (i.e., if the condition is true), we print out the error message "Sorry, I cannot capitalize that."; otherwise, (if the condition is false), the statement following the **else** is executed, and we print out the capitalized letter. Here's how it looks in general (the **else** is always optional, but if you use it, it must follow an **if** statement):

```
if (condition) statement;
else statement;
```

And here are some examples:

```
if (my_int > 0) printf("%d", my_int);
else printf ("Caution, your number is negative.\n");

if (x > y) bigger_val = x;
else bigger_val = y;
```

You use **if** together with **else** when you have a choice that can go in either of two ways, and you want to perform a different action in each of those cases.

if-else-if Ladders

In fact, our problem here is that we don't have just two possible outcomes. We have three:

- my_char < 'a'

- my_char > 'z'

- my_char is legal — print out toupper(my_char)

So far, we've only handled the first and last of these conditions, but C allows us to handle all three. In particular, it allows us to chain **if...elses** together into what is called an **if-else-if ladder**, and we can see how that works in Listing 2-3.

Listing 2-3. if-else-if ladder Example.

```
#include <stdio.h>
#include <ctype.h>

/* Capitalize keys read from the keyboard */

main()
{
    char my_char;

    printf("Please type a lowercase letter: ");
    scanf("%c", &my_char);

    if (my_char < 'a')
        printf("Sorry, I cannot capitalize that.\n");
    else if (my_char > 'z')
        printf("Sorry, I cannot capitalize that.\n");
    else
        printf("Thank you. In uppercase: %c\n.",\
        toupper(my_char));

    return(0);
}
```

Here's the important part of that program:

```
if (my_char < 'a')
    printf("Sorry, I cannot capitalize that.\n");
else if (my_char > 'z')
    printf("Sorry, I cannot capitalize that.\n");
```

```
else
    printf("Thank you. In uppercase: %c\n.", toupper(my_char));
```

This is an **if-else-if** ladder. In it, we first test to see if **my_char** is less than 'a'; if it is, we print out the error message. Next, we go one step down the ladder and check to see if **my_char** is greater than 'z'; if it is, we print out the error message. Otherwise, if we passed both tests, we print out the uppercase version of the character, and we're done.

Managing Blocks of Code

Our example was a pretty easy one. In particular, we only had one line of code to execute for each case in the **if-else-if** ladder. However, it turns out that it's just as easy in C to handle many statements as one in cases like these: we can group statements together into a **code block** using curly braces like the example shown in Listing 2-4.

Listing 2-4. Blocks of Code Example.

```
#include <stdio.h>
#include <ctype.h>

/* Capitalize keys read from the keyboard */

main()
{
  char my_char;

  printf("Please type a lowercase letter: ");
  scanf("%c", &my_char);

  if (my_char < 'a'){
      printf("Sorry, ");
      printf("I cannot ");
      printf("capitalize that.\n");
  }
  else if (my_char > 'z'){
      printf("Sorry, ");
      printf("I cannot ");
      printf("capitalize that.\n");
  }
  else
      printf("Thank you. In uppercase: %c.", toupper(my_char));

    return(0);
    }
```

Let's take a closer look at the body of that program:

```
if (my_char < 'a'){
    printf("Sorry, ");
    printf("I cannot ");
    printf("capitalize that.\n");
}
else if (my_char > 'z'){
    printf("Sorry, ");
    printf("I cannot ");
    printf("capitalize that.\n");
}
else
    printf("Thank you. In uppercase: %c.", toupper(my_char));
```

Here we have grouped several statements into blocks of code. C treats blocks of code themselves as a single statement; any time you can use a C statement, you can also use a block of statements enclosed by curly braces. To C they are the same. This allows us to perform multiple actions in the body of **if** statements, as above, or as in this example:

```
if (time == new_years_eve){
    printf("Happy New Year!!\n");
    ++current_year;
}
```

There are two things to notice here. The first is the indentation. You might notice that we placed the first curly brace after the parentheses surrounding the **if** condition, while the second curly brace is aligned with the **if** above it. If we had aligned the curly braces as we have been doing when we define the **main( )** function, however, they would have looked like this:

```
        if (time == new_years_eve)
→       {
            printf("Happy New Year!!\n");
            ++current_year;
        }
```

Both methods are valid, and both will of course compile. However, the C style has gradually become to move the first curly brace up after the parentheses. This saves vertical space in long programs, and we will do it that way as well in this book.

NOTE The alignment of the curly braces defining the body of the **main( )** function is usually as we have been doing it, one above the other, and we'll keep doing it that way.

The second thing to notice is the new relational operator = =, which means "is equal to", and that brings us to our next topic, an overview of all the relational and logical operators.

Relational and Logical Operators

We can find a list of C's relational and logical operators in Tables 2-1 and 2-2, respectively. We've already seen a number of these operators, including >=, >, <, and, now, = =. The = = operator (two equal signs are used to differentiate it from the = assignment operator) stands for "is equal to," and it's one of the most common operators in if statements. Its counterpart is **!=**, which means "is not equal to."

The relational and logical operators differ from the arithmetic operators that we've seen so far in one primary way: their operands, and their results, are not numbers but logical values, true or false. For example, C evaluates an expression like (5 = = 3) as false.

Numerically, **false** is represented as 0 in C, and any nonzero value, if it appears as a logical or relational operand, is regarded as **true**. That means that if **my_int** was 3, (`my_int == 3`) is true, and has a nonzero value. In fact, even the expression (`my_int = 3`) has a nonzero value. C evaluates an assign-

Operator	Meaning
>	Is greater than
>=	Is greater than or equal to
<	Is less than
<=	Is less than or equal to
= =	Is equal to
!=	Is not equal to

Table 2-1. Relational Operators.

Operator	Meaning
&&	AND
¦ ¦	OR
!	NOT

Table 2-2. Logical Operators.

ment expression like this from right to left, so not only is **my_int** given the value 3, but the value of the whole expression itself is 3 and is therefore true.

TIP   You actually can use = instead of = = in the conditional part of an if state-ment. For example, if(my_int = her_int) printf("Ok."); does two things: It assigns the value of **her_int** to **my_int**, and it tests that value; e.g., if it's nonzero, "Ok." is printed. Many programmers use this property of C as a shortcut, and we'll do it occasionally, too. However, please note that we'll only use it rarely, because it can be confusing (i.e., when reading quickly, the = may be taken as a = =).

The logical operators are of particular value when you want to tie certain conditions together to form one. For example, you might recall that in our earlier capitalizing program, there were two possible ways of disqualifying an incoming character. The character was invalid if either of these conditions were true:

my_char < 'a'
my_char > 'z'

Using the logical operator ¦ ¦, which stands for "or," we can make both of these into one condition like this: (my_char < 'a') ¦ ¦ (my_char > 'z'), which you can read as (my_char < 'a') OR (my_char > 'z'). In other words, if either of the two conditions are true, the whole condition to be true. That means that we can collapse our **if-else-if** ladder this way:

```
#include <stdio.h>
#include <ctype.h>

/* Capitalize keys read from the keyboard */
```

```
main()
{
    char my_char;

    printf("Please type a lowercase letter: ");
    scanf("%c", &my_char);

→           if (my_char < 'a' || my_char > 'z')
            printf("Sorry, I cannot capitalize that.\n");
    else
        printf("Thank you. In uppercase: %c.",\
        toupper(my_char));

    return(0);
}
```

In this way, we have shortened the **if-else-if** ladder into a single if...else statement. The **AND** logical operator, **&&**, is different — for it to be true, *both* operands must be true (nonzero). Here's an example:

```
if((month == 12) && (day == 25)) printf("Merry Christmas!!\n");
```

Here we are testing to see whether it's Christmas; for that to be true, the variable **month** must equal 12 AND the **day** must equal 25. If both conditionals are satisified, then the Merry Christmas message is typed out.

Since true and false can be represented by nonzero and zero values, respectively, we can put them together into a table, as below (nonzero, that is, true values are represented by 1):

OR	0	1		AND	0	1
0	0	1		0	0	0
1	1	1		1	0	1

The **Not** logical operator, !, has the unique ability to reverse the logical value of an expression. With it, true becomes false, and false becomes true. For example, `!(5==3)` is true. This operator is good when the expression you want to test is (inconveniently) the logical reverse of what you would like it to be. We'll see it throughout the book as well. Since the **Not** operator only needs one operand, it is called a unary operator. Since || and && need two, they are called **binary** operators.

Now that we have some of the rudiments of data manipulation down, let's see if we can't progress beyond reading and capitalization, and introduce an example of more interest.

A Simple Calculator Example

The **scanf( )** function can do more than read single characters, of course. Let's say that we wanted to design a calculator program that would accept floating point expressions, calculate the result, and print that result out.

For example, we might type "5.3 + 4.6", and we'd expect it to print out an answer of 9.9. In this case, the characters received by the program make up a floating point number, a space, an operator (say +, -, *, or /), another space, and a second floating point number. We could easily handle that in **scanf( )** with a format string like this: "**%f %c %f**". We can start out the program by reading the correct values, operator and operands, like this:

```
#include <stdio.h>

/* A calculator example. */

main()
{
    char the_operator;
    float operand_1, operand_2, result;

    printf("Please type the expression to be\
    calculated: ");
→   scanf("%f %c %f", &operand_1, &the_operator,\
    &operand_2);
       :
       :
```

Now that the operands are loaded into **operand_1** and **operand_2**, we have to test the character in **the_operator** to learn what we should do with them. That can be done with an **if-else-if** ladder like this:

```
#include <stdio.h>

/* A calculator example. */

main()
{
    char the_operator;
```

```
        float operand_1, operand_2, result;

        printf("Please type the expression to be calculated: ");
        scanf("%f %c %f", &operand_1, &the_operator, &operand_2);

        if (the_operator == '+')
            result = operand_1 + operand_2;
        else if (the_operator == '-')
            result = operand_1 - operand_2;
        else if (the_operator == '*')
            result = operand_1 - operand_2;
        else if (the_operator == '/')
            result = operand_1 / operand_2;
        else{
            printf("Sorry, I cannot understand %c.\n",\
            the_operator);
            return(0);
        }
        printf("Thank you. The result is %f\n.", result);

        return(0);
    }
```

This will do the job. We can type in our expressions (4.8 + 12.0, 9.17 / 43.99, -2.1 + 6.9 — anything we wish), and the calculator program will print out the answer for us.

Note in particular the `return(0);` statement.

```
        :
        else{
            printf("Sorry, I cannot understand %c.\n",\
            the_operator);
→           return(0);
        }
        printf("Thank you. The result is %f.", result);
        :
```

We use this statement if we cannot understand what has been typed (i.e., the_operator is not '+', '-', '*', or '/'), and we wish to quit without proceeding to the next stage (where we print out the result). The return statement causes us to exit a function and return a value — in this case, we leave the **main( )** function, so the program as a whole terminates. We'll see much more about return later. At this point, however, it provides us with a clear way of ending the program so that we do not type out a misleading result.

As you can see, our **if-else-if** ladder is getting longer, which means it's also getting a little harder to read. It's not so easy to take in what's going on here at a glance. In fact, there is a better and more clear way to do this in C, and we can use it when **if-else-if** ladders grow to be too long.

The Switch Statement

C has a built-in way of handling situations that seem to call for long if-else-if ladders, and it is called the **switch** statement. In its general form, it looks like this:

```
switch(variable){
    case constant_1:
        statement(s);
        break;
    case constant_2:
        statement(s);
        break;
    case constant_3:
        statement(s);
        break;
        :

        :
    default:
        statement(s);
}
```

To use **switch**, we must choose some variable whose value determines what action we should take; in our case, that variable is **the_operator**. The **switch** statement should compare the value in **the_operator** to each of the possible choices: '+', '-', '*', and '/'. When it finds a match, it should execute the statements associated with that operator. We can do that as shown in Listing 2-5.

Listing 2-5. Calculator Example with Switch.

```
#include <stdio.h>

/* A calculator example with switch. */

main()
{
    char the_operator;
    float operand_1, operand_2, result;
```

Listing 2-5. *(continued)*

```
printf("Please type the expression to be calculated: ");
scanf("%f %c %f", &operand_1, &the_operator, &operand_2);

switch (the_operator){
    case '+':
        result = operand_1 + operand_2;
        break;
    case '-':
        result = operand_1 - operand_2;
        break;
    case '*':
        result = operand_1 * operand_2;
        break;
    case '/':
        result = operand_1 / operand_2;
        break;
    default:
        printf("Sorry, I cannot understand %c.\n", the_operator);
        return(0);
}
printf("Thank you. The result is %f.", result);

return(0);
}
```

The **switch** statement there looks like this:

```
switch (the_operator){
    case '+':
        result = operand_1 + operand_2;
        break;
    case '-':
        result = operand_1 - operand_2;
        break;
    case '*':
        result = operand_1 * operand_2;
        break;
    case '/':
        result = operand_1 / operand_2;
        break;
    default:
        printf("Sorry, I cannot understand %c.\n",\
        the_operator);
        return(0);
}
```

Here, we compare the value in **the_operator** to each of the **cases** '+', '-', '*', and '/'; if we find a match, we execute the lines following it. For example, if **the_operator** held '+', we'd execute these lines:

```
    switch (the_operator){
        case '+':
→            result = operand_1 + operand_2;
→            break;
```

Note that the statements for each case include a **break** statement. This is an exceptionally useful statement, and in C it gets us out of the current **switch** or loop construction. When we encounter a break here, we leave the **switch** statement entirely and proceed with the rest of the program.

We should also know that if we left a **break** statement out of a particular case, then we would not leave the **switch** statement at all but would continue on to the statements in the next case and execute them. For example, if we had typed 3 + 2 to the calculator program, but had left out the **break** in the '+' case, it would look like this:

```
    switch (the_operator){
        case '+':
            result = operand_1 + operand_2;
→       /* break; used to be here */
        case '-':
            result = operand_1 - operand_2;
            break;
            :
```

Then we would execute the '+' code (result = operand_1 + operand_2;), immediately followed by the code for the '-' case (result = operand_1 - operand_2;), and would have been startled to learn that 3 + 2 = 1. Leaving out a **break** statement this way and inadvertantly continuing on through the next case is probably the most common programming error when working with **switch**.

TIP   You can omit the **break** statement on purpose, creating an intentional waterfall effect in your code. For example, if your program was printing out the lines of the song "The Twelve Days of Christmas," you could leave all the **breaks** out of the 12 descending cases; case 12 would then print out all the lines of the song, down to the partridge in the pear tree.

We should also note that although **switch** is extremely useful, especially when dealing with menu selection choices, it doesn't completely replace **if-else-if** ladders. This is because **switch** relies on equality (i.e., the variable being tested must exactly equal one of the case constants), while the **if-else-if** ladder can include the usual relational operators like > or <. On the other hand, note that the **switch** statement can end with a catch-all default case that does not demand equality:

```
switch (the_operator){
    case '+':
        result = operand_1 + operand_2;
        break;
          :
          :
    default:
        printf("Sorry, I cannot understand %c.\n",\
        the_operator);
        return(0);
}
```

This last, optional, case (it must be last because it matches any value of the variable we've been checking, eclipsing whatever cases come after it) scoops up everything that does not match one of the cases. If no cases match, and you leave the default case out, control continues to the next part of the program, as it would with an **if-else-if** ladder.

This is all fine as far as our calculator goes, but it's an odd calculator that can only be used to solve one problem and then it quits. A program like that should keep repeating, leaving the choice of whether or not to quit up to you. There are special constructions in programming that are included precisely for this kind of repetition, and they are called *loops*. And, in our case, we're going to start with the one that's probably the most popular — the **for** loop.

The for Loop

This is a big one; one of a computer's most important attributes is the ability to perform repeatedly certain actions quickly, and loops are at the very heart of that. The **for** loop lets us keep performing an action over and over on our data until a condition (which we specify) becomes true. The general form of the **for** loop looks like this:

```
for(initialization; condition; increment) statement;
```

Here, `initialization` is a statement that is executed when the loop begins, often setting a *loop counter* to 0, `condition` is the end condition, checked every time the body of the loop is about to execute, and `increment` is a statement that is executed at the end of the loop, just before the condition is tested to see if we should loop again.

When the condition becomes false (keep in mind that you can connect a number of conditions together here with relational operators), the **for** loop stops and the program continues with the lines of code following it. The body of the loop is made up of `statement` above, and, as is always true in C, that statement can be made up of a block of code that is enclosed in curly braces.

This kind of material is always easier to see in an example, so let's take a look at one immediately:

```
main()
{
    int loop_index;

    for(loop_index = 0; loop_index < 10; loop_index++){
        printf("Hello, world.\n");
    }

    return(0);
}
```

Let's dissect this code; at the beginning of the **for** loop, the loop counter or index, which we've called **loop_index**, is set to 0 (this is the initialization statement in our case):

```
              ↓
for(loop_index = 0; loop_index < 10; loop_index++){
    printf("Hello, world.\n");
  }
```

Then the termination condition is tested:

```
                          ↓
for(loop_index = 0; loop_index < 10; loop_index++){
    printf("Hello, world.\n");
  }
```

If it is false, the loop is done and we go on with the program. Note that the condition is tested *before* the loop executes at all — if the condition here had been `loop_index > 0`, for example, the loop wouldn't even execute once. However, the condition is `loop_index < 10`; since **loop_index** is now 0, the body of the loop is executed, printing "Hello, world.\n" on the screen. At the end of the body of the loop, the increment statement is executed, and **loop_index** is incremented to 1:

```
                                        ↓
for(loop_index = 0; loop_index < 10; loop_index++){
    printf("Hello, world.\n");
}
```

Next, the termination condition is checked (is **loop_index** < 10?), and, since **loop_index** is 1, the body of the loop is executed again. This keeps going until "Hello, world.\n" has been printed out exactly 10 times.

That means that we can add a measure of repetition to our calculator program this way, making it loop 10 times before quitting:

```
#include <stdio.h>

/* Calculator example with a for loop */

main()
{
    int loop_index;
    char the_operator;
    float operand_1, operand_2, result;

    for (loop_index = 0; loop_index < 10; loop_index++){
        printf("Please type the expression to be\
        calculated: ");
        scanf("%f %c %f", &operand_1, &the_operator,\
        &operand_2);

        switch (the_operator){
            case '+':
                result = operand_1 + operand_2;
                break;
            case '-':
                result = operand_1 - operand_2;
                break;
```

```
                   case '*':
                       result = operand_1 * operand_2;
                       break;
                   case '/':
                       result = operand_1 / operand_2;
                       break;
                   default:
                       printf("Sorry, I cannot understand %c.\n",\
                       the_operator);
                       continue;
           }        /* end of switch */
           printf("Thank you. The result is %f.\n", result);
       } /* end of for loop */

       return(0);
   }
```

The continue Statement

One important thing in our new version of the calculator program is what we've done to the **return 0** statement. You may recall that if some operator other than '+', '-', '*', or '/' was typed, we printed out the error message ("I cannot understand...") and exited the program with **return 0**. Now that we've added a loop, that's not such a good option — we should let the user try again, so we can no longer use **return 0** to exit the entire program.

What we do instead is to use the C **continue** statement. Like **break**, **continue** affects the operation of a loop. Unlike **break**, however, **continue** is not designed to exit the loop, but to cause the loop to continue with the next iteration; that is, the next time through.

When you execute **continue** in a loop, the body of the loop stops executing, the increment statement is executed, and the next iteration of the loop starts (if there is to be one; it depends on the loop's termination condition). That's just right for us here — if we can't read the operator, we want to go on to the next iteration of the loop, reading in a new expression to evaluate:

```
   for (loop_index = 0; loop_index < 10; loop_index++){

       switch (the_operator){
           case '+':
               result = operand_1 + operand_2;
```

```
              break;
              :
              :
          default:
              printf("Sorry, I cannot understand %c.\n",\
              the_operator);
→             continue;        /* get a new expression */
      }        /* end of switch */
      printf("Thank you. The result is %f.\n", result);
  }        /* end of for loop */
```

With **continue**, we've taken care of that problem neatly. However, the loop itself is not ideal — why should we loop exactly 10 times? It turns out that the **for** loop is a great deal more flexible than this in C, so let's take a look.

It might surprise you to learn, for example, that all the parts of a **for** loop — initialization, condition, increment, and statement — are optional. You can omit any one you wish; in fact, you can omit them all like this:

```
for(;;);
```

This loop is legal, but not very exciting; all it does is keep executing forever (i.e., the termination condition is never met). This called an infinite loop, and while unintentional infinite loops are something you should certainly avoid, intentional ones are a different story. That is, while the loop itself may look like an infinite loop, there are other ways of getting out of it — notably with the break statement.

TIP   Sometimes, loops without bodies are executed as timing loops, like this: for (i=0; i<99999; i++);. In this case, the loop will take some time to execute, delaying the program.

Using break in Loops

The **break** statement is by no means confined to use in a **switch** statement; it can be a very valuable part of a loop. Just as **continue** forces the next iteration of a loop, **break** forces the end of the loop altogether.

> **NOTE**   It is legal in C to have loops inside loops; however, **break** will only end the
> current loop.

Here's an example of a loop that looks infinite at first but is not:

```
for(loop_index = 0;;){
    loop_index++;
    if (loop_index == 1000) break;
}
```

This loop will keep going until **loop_index** becomes equal to 1,000. Programmers often use **break** to save time. Something may occur in a loop that means that the loop is over, and, for time reasons, they don't want to wait for the rest of the loop execute and the termination condition to be checked. Instead, they want to exit now.

Using **break** is valid for such a reason, and it's also valid to use when your loop is controlled by some unexpected outside event (such as a key being struck, the computer's clock reaching a certain value, or a disk event completing). However, using break can make your program less structured; your program can become harder to read and the flow of control less well defined. For that reason, you should not use **break** in a loop unless you need it.

Writing unstructured code is really valid for only one reason: speed. That's why the **break** statement is popular in loops: It can get you out of a loop quickly. However, you might be inside a loop which is itself inside a loop — this is called **nested** loops — and **break** will only get you out of the current loop to the next level up. C has an additional statement that comes in handy in this case, and that's the **goto** statement.

The goto Statement

In general, the **goto** statement looks like this:

```
goto label;
```

We can label any statement in our program by preceding it with the label name and a colon. For instance, let's modify our break example to use **goto**, like this:

```
#include <stdio.h>

/* A goto Example */

main()
{
    int loop_index;

    for(loop_index = 0;;){
        loop_index++;
→       if (loop_index == 1000) goto finish_up;
    }
finish_up: printf("Goodbye\n");

    return(0);
}
```

We keep going in the loop until **loop_index** reaches 1,000, at which time we go to the label **finish_up**. That label is in front of the statement `printf("Goodbye\n");`, so the program prints "Goodbye\n" and quits. The goto statement, while fast, is about as unstructured as you can get (i.e., program control can jump all over the program). That means that unless it's really a question of speed, C programmers usually avoid **goto**.

TIP   goto statements are regarded as legitimate when you need to get out of heavily nested loops in a hurry, and that's a job goto does well.

Going Wild with for Loops

We can get much more advanced with loops; the C language is so flexible that the termination condition in a **for** loop may be any valid C expression. For example, we can modify our calculator program so that it asks us if we want to continue after each calculation with the prompt "Type c to continue, q to quit:" and still use a **for** loop. That might look like the program in Listing 2-6.

Listing 2-6. Calculator Example with Continuation Prompt.

```
#include <stdio.h>

/* Calculator Example With Continuation Prompt */

main()
```

(continued)

Listing 2-6. *(continued)*

```c
{
    char cntrl, the_operator;
    float operand_1, operand_2, result;

    for (cntrl=' '; toupper(cntrl) != 'Q'; cntrl = getche()){

        printf("\nPlease type the expression to be\
        calculated: ");
        scanf("%f %c %f", &operand_1, &the_operator,\
        &operand_2);

        switch (the_operator){
            case '+':
                result = operand_1 + operand_2;
                break;
            case '-':
                result = operand_1 - operand_2;
                break;
            case '*':
                result = operand_1 * operand_2;
                break;
            case '/':
                result = operand_1 / operand_2;
                break;
            default:
                printf("Sorry, I cannot understand %c.\n",\
                the_operator);
                continue;
        }        /* end of switch */
        printf("Thank you. The result is %f.\n", result);
        printf("Type c to continue, q to quit: ");
    }            /* end of for loop */

    return(0);
}
```

At first, this example seems very confusing. Take a look at the new for statement:

```c
for (cntrl=' '; toupper(cntrl) != 'Q'; cntrl = getche()){
```

When we begin the loop, we initialize a character we've named **cntrl** to a space, ' '. Then the body of the loop executes once, and we perform one calculation. At the end of the loop, we've added this prompt:

```
printf("Type c to continue, q to quit: ");
```

This appears on the screen, and the loop finishes. C then executes the increment section of the **for** loop, which looks like this:

```
cntrl = getche()
```

This introduces the **getche( )** function, get character with screen echo. This function reads a single character from the keyboard and returns it; in our case, we assign that character to the char **cntrl**.

TIP If you just want to check whether a key has been hit on the keyboard, you should use a function named kbhit( ). This function does not wait for a key; instead, it returns a 1 if there is a key waiting to be read, and a 0 otherwise.

You might wonder why we don't use **scanf( )** here. It turns out that there is a peculiarity in **scanf( )** that we should be aware of when reading characters. When we use **scanf( )**, we terminate input by pressing <Enter>, which sends a carriage-return line-feed pair — two characters, ASCII 13 and 10 — to the program. That's the way the <Enter> key works: The carriage return sends the cursor back to the beginning of the line, and the line feed moves it down to the next line. In C, however, the end of a line is only marked by a carriage return, ASCII 13, and this is an important fact.

This means that **scanf( )** stops reading input when it reads the carriage return, leaving the line feed in the keyboard buffer. The next time we use **scanf( )**, the leftover line feed character is still waiting. To get rid of it, we would have to read two characters with **scanf( )**; the first time to get rid of the unwanted line feed, and the second time to read the actual control character ('c' or 'q') that the user typed in response to our prompt. That might look like this:

```
for (cntrl=' '; toupper(cntrl) != 'Q'; scanf("%c%c", &cntrl,\
    &cntrl)){
```

Clearing the keyboard buffer like this is called "teaching" **scanf( )** about carriage returns line feeds. However, most programmers find it easier to not worry about the leftover line feed, and they use **getche( )** when reading single characters.

TIP	You should also know that if we had been waiting for anything but a character, like a float or an int, this problem would not have occurred — the **scanf( )** function skips over "whitespace" characters like line feeds in search of numbers. It was only because we were trying to read a character (which the leftover line feed qualifies as) that we would have had problems.

After the increment part of the **for** loop is done, C checks the termination condition to see if it's true:

```
for (cntrl=' '; toupper(cntrl) != 'Q'; cntrl = getche()){
```

In our case, that termination condition was this:

```
toupper(cntrl) != 'Q'
```

We can check whether the just read-in character, now in **cntrl**, was either 'q' or 'Q' this way. If one of these characters was typed, the condition becomes false, and we quit the **for** loop. Note that any other response ('c' or any other character) would have sent us back for another interation of the loop. And that's it. This example works as we'd expect it to.

One last topic deserves our attention here before finishing with the **for** loop, and that is using multiple expressions in a **for** loop with the **comma** operator. Using the comma operator, we can string a number of operations together. They are evaluated left to right, and the value of the rightmost expression becomes the final value of the whole expression. For example, this line first assigns a value of 30 to minutes, and then a value of 30×60 to seconds:

```
seconds = (minutes = 30, minutes * 60);
```

This can give us a great deal of power in a **for** loop. For example, we can work with multiple indices, like this:

```
        #include <stdio.h>

        /* Demonstrate the comma operator */

        main()
        {
            int index1, index2;

→           for (index1 = 0, index2 = 0; index1 < 100;\
```

```
        index1++, index2++)
            printf("index 1, index 2 are: %d %d", index1,\
            index2);

        return(0);
    }
```

The comma operator is legal programming, and when you want to do a number of things in the same place in a C program, it can come in handy. However, lines like

```
    seconds = (minutes = 30, minutes * 60);
```

can be quite confusing in code, so we'll usually avoid them as much as possible.

Now that we've seen many of the possibilities of the **for** loop, it's time to turn to the other two kinds of loops in C: the **while** loop and the **do-while** loop.

The while Loop

The **while** loop acts a little like a **for** loop but — unlike a **for** loop — it doesn't usually have a loop index associated with it. In its general form, it looks like this:

```
    while(condition) statement;
```

The **while** loop continues to execute as long as the condition — which can be any expression — remains true (numerically, that means nonzero). The statement, of course, can be any block of code as long as you enclose it in curly braces. Note that, like the **for** loop, the **while** loop evaluates its condition at the top, so if the condition is false to begin with, the body of the loop will never be executed at all.

Here's a simple **while** loop example; this program keeps asking you to guess a number until you hit it:

```
    #include <stdio.h>

    /* A while loop example */

    main()
```

```
{
    int my_number = 10, user_guess = 0;

    while(user_guess != my_number){
        printf("Guess my number: ");
        scanf(" %i", &user_guess);
    }
    printf("Good work!!\n");

    return(0);
}
```

It keeps looping until the read-in value, user_guess, equals my_number, which is set to 10 here:

```
→    while(user_guess != my_number){
        printf("Guess my number: ");
        scanf(" %i", &user_guess);
    }
```

In the same way, we can modify our calculator example to use a while loop as shown in Listing 2-7.

Listing 2-7. Calculator Example Using a while Loop.

```
#include <stdio.h>

/* Calculator Example Using a While Loop */

main()
{
    char cntrl, the_operator;
    float operand_1, operand_2, result;
    cntrl = ' ';
    while(toupper(cntrl) != 'Q'){

        printf("\nPlease type the expression to be\
        calculated: ");
        scanf("%f %c %f", &operand_1, &the_operator,\
        &operand_2);

        switch (the_operator){
            case '+':
                result = operand_1 + operand_2;
                break;
            case '-':
```

Listing 2-7. *(continued)*

```
                        result = operand_1 - operand_2;
                        break;
                case '*':
                        result = operand_1 * operand_2;
                        break;
                case '/':
                        result = operand_1 / operand_2;
                        break;
                default:
                        printf("Sorry, I cannot understand %c.\n",\
                        the_operator);
                        continue;
        }       /* end of switch */
        printf("Thank you. The result is %f.\n", result);
        printf("Type c to continue, q to quit: ");
        cntrl = getche();
    }           /* end of while loop */

    return(0);
}
```

We use a **while** loop with this condition:

```
        cntrl = ' ';
→       while(toupper(cntrl) != 'Q'){
                :
                :
            printf("Type c to continue, q to quit: ");
            cntrl = getche();
        } /* end of while loop */
```

Although this works, we still have to set the character **cntrl** to a space before beginning, as we did with the **for** loop. However, with the next and last loop construction, we won't have to do that.

The do-while Loop

The **do-while** loop is different from the other two types of loops; here, the body of the loop is always executed at least once because the condition isn't checked until the end of the loop. The general form looks like this:

```
do{
    statement;
} while(condition);
```

This loop keeps executing while the condition is true. There are times that you'll want the body of the loop to execute at least once, such as when you're allowing choices to be made from a menu (to quit, you'd have to select the quit choice). We can convert our earlier **while** loop example into a **do-while** loop example like this:

```
#include <stdio.h>

/* A do-while loop example */

main()
{
    int my_number = 10, user_guess;

    do{
        printf("Guess my number: ");
        scanf(" %i", &user_guess);
    } while(user_guess != my_number);

    printf("Good work!!\n");

    return(0);
}
```

Note that we did not need to initialize **user_guess** because it is not checked at the top of the loop, only at the bottom:

```
      do{
          printf("Guess my number: ");
          scanf(" %i", &user_guess);
  →   } while(user_guess != my_number);
```

In addition, we can convert our calculator example to a **do-while** loop as well, as in Listing 2-8.

Listing 2-8. Calculator Example Using a do-while Loop.

```
#include <stdio.h>

/* Calculator Example Using a Do-while Loop */
/* Demonstrates that cntrl is never used. */
```

Listing 2-8. *(continued)*

```
main()
{
    char cntrl, the_operator;
    float operand_1, operand_2, result;
    do{

        printf("\nPlease type the expression to be\
        calculated: ");
        scanf("%f %c %f", &operand_1, &the_operator,\
        &operand_2);

        switch (the_operator){
            case '+':
                result = operand_1 + operand_2;
                break;
            case '-':
                result = operand_1 - operand_2;
                break;
            case '*':
                result = operand_1 * operand_2;
                break;
            case '/':
                result = operand_1 / operand_2;
                break;
            default:
                printf("Sorry, I cannot understand %c.\n",\
                the_operator);
                continue;
        }       /* end of switch */
        printf("Thank you. The result is %f.\n", result);
        printf("Type c to continue, q to quit: ");
    } while(cntrl = toupper(getche()) != 'Q');

    return(0);
}
```

Let's take a quick look at the **do...while** loop in that listing:

```
do{
    :
    :
} while(cntrl = toupper(getche()) != 'Q');
```

We did not need to initialize the control character, **cntrl**, with an artificial space character before beginning our loop. In fact, since **cntrl** now appears —

and is tested — in only one place, we can get rid of it completely, like this (in fact, the Borland compilers give us a warning that cntrl is never used):

```
do{
   :
   :
} while(toupper(getche()) != 'Q');
```

Even so, our calculator program is getting pretty long now. In fact, it's usually a good idea to break larger programs up into smaller, manageable, pieces, which brings us to the last major topic that we should cover before finishing this chapter — how to write our own C functions.

Writing Our Own C Functions

The C libraries are filled with functions, and we've already seen four of them — **scanf( )**, **printf( )**, **getche( )**, and **toupper( )**. As it turns out, we can write our own functions in C, and it's remarkably easy to do. We'll see a great deal more about this process throughout this book, but we can introduce ourselves to it now. The general form for a function looks like this:

```
return_type function_name (parameter list)
{
    statement(s);
}
```

That's all there is to it. A function can take a number of arguments, as we've seen with **printf( )** and **scanf( )**, and even return a value (but there may be only one return value) as we've seen with **toupper( )**, which returns a capitalized letter.

Let's put together our own simple function named **get_char( )**; all it will do when called is to read a character from the keyboard and return it like this:

```
#include <stdio.h>

/* Read keys from the keyboard with scanf() */

char get_char(void);

main()
{
    printf("Please type a character: ");
    printf("Thank you. That character was %c.", get_char());
```

```
        return(0);
    }

→   char get_char(void)
    {
        char my_char;

        scanf("%c", &my_char);
        return my_char;
    }
```

There are a number of points that we should notice here. First, at the start of the whole program, we tell C about the function **get_char( )** — in particular, that it takes no arguments and that it returns a value of type char — with a **function protoype**:

```
    #include <stdio.h>

    /* Read keys from the keyboard with scanf() */

→   char get_char(void);
    :
```

The keyword **void** tells C that **get_char** receives no parameters, and the keyword **char** indicates that its return value is of type **char**. If there was no return value (which is perfectly legal), we could have used the protoype `void get_char(void)`.

Later in the program, when C comes across our use of **get_char( )**, it will know what to expect — it already knows that this is a function that takes no parameters and returns a parameter of type **char**. The prototype is very important; in fact, the header files that we've been including all along hold the function prototypes for the C library functions.

A prototype for a function that takes two integer parameters and returns a float value might look like this:

```
float my_func(int a, int b);
```

In the pre-ANSI C days, you could use a partial prototype, without specifying the parameters, like this:

```
float my_func();
```

Although you can still omit the types of the parameters this way, it's not a good idea — leaving them in lets C check to make sure that the types of the variables being passed are correct. Next in our program, we can use **get_char( )** like this:

```
#include <stdio.h>

/* Read keys from the keyboard with scanf() */

char get_char(void);

main()
{
    printf("Please type a character: ");
    printf("Thank you. That character was %c.",\
    get_char());

    return(0);
}
    :
    :
```

Since the return value of **get_char( )** is the character that was typed, we can just put it into the **printf( )** statement directly; when it's evaluated, its value will be the value it returns. Finally, we can define the function **get_char( )** itself:

```
#include <stdio.h>

/* Read keys from the keyboard with scanf() */

char get_char(void);

main()
{
    printf("Please type a character: ");
    printf("Thank you. That character was %c.",\
    get_char());

    return(0);
}

    char get_char(void)
{
    char my_char;

    scanf("%c", &my_char);
    return my_char;
}
```

Note that the definition begins with a line much like the function's prototype, except that it is not followed by a semicolon. The body of the function itself is defined after this first line.

We should also note the variable **my_char**, which is defined inside **get_char( )**. Because it is internal to **get_char( )**, it is not available in the rest of the program. It is a **local** variable, available to **get_char( )** only, which means that you cannot use it in the **main( )** function. If, on the other hand, we had defined **my_char** outside *any* function, like this:

```
#include <stdio.h>

/* Read keys from the keyboard with scanf() */

char get_char(void);

main()
{
    printf("Please type a character: ");
    printf("Thank you. That character was %c.",\
    get_char());

    return(0);
}

        char my_char;

char get_char(void)
{
    scanf("%c", &my_char);
    return my_char;
}
```

→

Then it is a **global** variable, and you can use it at any place inside the program. We'll see more about local and global variables in Chapter 7. In the meantime, we should note that the variables defined inside a function are purely local to that function. This is one of the ways that functions help compartmentalize our programs and make them more modular.

TIP   Modular, compartmentalized programs, where all tasks are broken up into functions, are a good idea for two reasons: 1) they help contain the spread of possible bugs; and 2) they divide the whole programming task into discrete chunks that are more easily managed.

The return Statement

Note that we use the **return** statement to return a value from **get_char( )**, like this:

```
char get_char(void)
{
    char my_char;

    scanf("%c", &my_char);
→   return my_char;
}
```

We've already seen **return**, and it's how we return values from functions — with the **return** statement (the parentheses around the return values are optional). In this case, we are returning the value of **my_char**. That's it for **get_char( )**.

That was a pretty easy example; let's take a look now at a more involved case. We might have a function named **addem( )** that takes two integer parameters, adds them, and returns the sum as another integer. That program might look like this:

```
#include <stdio.h>

/* A function example with parameters. */

int addem(int a, int b);

main()
{
    int i_1 = 1, i_2 = 2;

    printf("Adding the two numbers gives %d.", addem(i_1, i_2));

    return(0);
}

int addem(int a, int b)
{
    return a + b;
}
```

Here the prototype looks like this:

```
int addem(int a, int b);
```

And the function itself looks like this:

```
int addem(int a, int b)
{
    return a + b;
}
```

Note that we declared the two variables used in **addem( )** (i.e., the local names we give to the two integer arguments passed to the function) in the first line:

```
→   int addem(int a, int b)
    {
        return a + b;
    }
```

This is the third place that you're allowed to declare variables in C (the other two are inside and outside functions). We could have done it this way:

```
    int addem(a, b)
    {
→       int a, b;

        return a + b;
    }
```

However, this way we run the risk of confusing the variables passed as parameters with the variables internal to the function. The modern C style is the first way, declaring the variables in the first line. Of course, if the function itself had internal variables in addition to parameters, we could declare them like this:

```
    int addem(int a, int b)
    {
→       int c, d;

        c = a;
        d = b;
        return c + d;
    }
```

In this way, we keep the parameters and the internal variables from getting confused. While we're on the subject of parameters, there's one more topic we should cover before finishing up with functions, and that's *how* parameters get passed to functions in C.

How C Passes Parameters to Functions

There are two different ways of passing parameters to a function, by value and by reference. When you pass a parameter by value, you pass the value of the parameter; when you pass by reference, you pass the parameter's **address**. C passes by value. For example, let's take a look at our **addem( )** example again:

```
#include <stdio.h>

/* A function example with parameters. */

int addem(int a, int b);

main()
{
    int integer1 = 1, integer2 = 2;

    printf("Adding the two gives %d.", addem(integer1,\
    integer2));

    return(0);
}

int addem(int a, int b)
{
    return a + b;
}
```

When we pass **integer1** and **integer2** to **addem( )**, we are actually passing their values, 1 and 2. That's fine since that's all **addem( )** needs to add them: 1 + 2 = 3. Then it can return that value. On the other hand, there's no way that **addem( )** can actually affect the values stored in the variables **integer1** and **integer2** directly because all it has is a copy of those values.

There's no problem here, but if we want to use a function like **scanf( )** to read characters for us, it has to be able to place the values of the characters it reads into the correct variables, which means that we have to pass more than a copy of the current value of the variable to **scanf( )**. Let's take a look at this example from the beginning of the chapter:

```
#include <stdio.h>

/* Read keys from the keyboard with scanf() */
```

```
main()
{
    char my_char;

    printf("Please type a character: ");
    scanf("%c", &my_char);

    printf("Thank you. That character was %c.", my_char);

    return(0);
}
```

Here, **scanf( )** needs to be able to access **my_char** directly to place the ASCII code that it reads into it. This is when passing by reference (which is the default in a language like FORTRAN) comes in handy. If we pass **my_char's** address to **scanf( )**, **scanf( )** can place the ASCII code it read directly into the variable **my_char**. And that's what we're doing here. The & operator returns a variable's address. That means that we are passing **my_char's** address to **scanf( )** when we do this:

```
scanf("%c", &my_char);
```

The address of a variable is also called a **pointer**, and in fact that's what we are passing to **scanf( )**; a pointer to **my_char**. With that address — that pointer — **scanf( )** knows where **my_char** is in memory, so it can change its value. That kind of operation is very important in C, and it's one of the major topics of the next chapter where we start to take a closer look at data organization, and at pointers.

Organizing Your Data and Pointers

In this chapter, we're going to learn more about organizing our data. We already know the basics of storing data in C; we can store values in variables. We've seen that the five basic data types (along with the four data type modifiers) provide a good way of holding the information we need to manipulate in our programs. But now it's time to take the next step. For example, what if we needed to handle a whole set of data, not just a single value?

What if we were responsible, say, for the grades of an entire class of students? In that case, it would be awkward indeed to have to assign a different variable for each student. C provides us with ways of handling problems like this, and we'll see them in this chapter. In particular, we'll see how to use arrays of data — special constructs that are designed to hold data sets — as well as character strings, and data strutures.

In addition to those, C provides us with another powerful technique of organizing our data and storing it with ready access, and that method is the use of **pointers**. We'll get an introduction to pointers in this chapter, and — in our later chapter on advanced pointers — we'll see how they can replace arrays altogether.

Also in this chapter, we'll develop a simple database program as the backbone of our data-organizing efforts. It won't be a particularly dazzling program as far as databases go, but it will illustrate the major points in this chapter. With all that in mind, then, let's dig in and see how data organization in C really works.

Keeping Data in Arrays

Let's say that you were tutoring a student named George in the use of C, and that you wanted to record his score on a test (he got a 92, not bad). You could do that like this in a program:

```
#include <stdio.h>

/* Record George's test score. */

main()
{
    int Georges_score;

    Georges_score = 92;
    printf(" The test score is: %d", Georges_score);

    return(0);
}
```

If you were teaching an entire class in C, however, it would be a different story. Imagine a program that started like this:

```
#include <stdio.h>

/* Record test grades. */

main()
{
    int Georges_score;
    int Bettys_score;
    int Toms_score;
    int Tanyas_score;
    int Bruces_score;
            :
```

The problem here is that we have a different variable for each student even though it holds the same class of data; i.e., a test score. What we have is a **data set**, and it doesn't make sense to have an independent variable for each member of such a set. C has a special construction for use with data sets called

arrays. Arrays are at the root of many powerful programming techniques because they allow parallel operations to take place on all the variables in a data set.

In particular, we could set up an array to hold our student's scores like this:

```
#include <stdio.h>

/* Record test scores. */

main()
{
→       int scores[5];
        :
        :
}
```

This statement informs C that we wish to set up an array named **scores[]** that will hold five integers; we say that this an **array of type integer**. Now we can place the student's scores into that array like this:

```
#include <stdio.h>

/* Record test scores. */

main()
{
    int scores[5];

→       scores[0] = 92;
        scores[1] = 73;
        scores[2] = 57;
        scores[3] = 98;
        scores[4] = 89;
        :
        :
}
```

In other words, we are treating the array **scores[]** as though it were simply a variable with an index. That index can range from 0 to 4, which covers all the five integers that we wish to store in the array. That's how we handle a data set, by giving the set one name (**scores**) and an index, which can range over the individual members of the set.

This is especially convenient because now we can refer to each member of the set with one index whose value we can readily change. As mentioned, this allows us to perform a parallel operation on all members of the set. For example, we could print out all the scores with a **for** loop like this:

```
#include <stdio.h>

/* Record test scores. */

main()
{
    int loop_index, scores[5];

    scores[0] = 92;
    scores[1] = 73;
    scores[2] = 57;
    scores[3] = 98;
    scores[4] = 89;

    for (loop_index = 0; loop_index < 5; loop_index++)
        printf("Student's score: %d\n",\
        scores[loop_index]);

    return(0);
}
```

Being able to reach each member of the set with a numeric index like this makes arrays an extraordinarily powerful construction because the program itself can manipulate that index. We just have to set up the operation we want performed on one member of the set and then let the index vary over all members. For example, what if we wanted to find the average grade of all the students? We'd want to add all the scores into a running total, and we could do that like this:

```
#include <stdio.h>

/* Find average of test scores. */

main()
{
    int i, sum, scores[5];

    scores[0] = 92;
    scores[1] = 73;
    scores[2] = 57;
```

```
        scores[3] = 98;
        scores[4] = 89;

→       for (i = 0, sum = 0; i < 5; i++)
            sum = sum + scores[i];

        printf("Average test score: %f\n", (float) sum / 5);

        return(0);
    }
```

Here we just loop over all the test scores, adding them up, and then we print out that total after dividing by 5 (after using a (**float**) cast so that the result will be a floating point number).

TIP   Note that we took advantage of the comma operator here to set not only the loop's index to 0 in the initialization part of the **for** loop but also the running **sum**. Adding that statement to the loop initialization is not only convenient; it also indicates that we're zeroing that variable specifically for use in the following loop.

This is pretty good as far as it goes, but it would be a lucky bunch of students that only had one test a term. Let's say that you gave them three tests over the duration of the course, and you'd like to keep track of all those scores. You can do that in C with a **two-dimensional array**.

Two-Dimensional Arrays in C

So far, we've filled up our array scores like this:

```
scores[0] = 92;
scores[1] = 73;
scores[2] = 57;
scores[3] = 98;
scores[4] = 89;
```

That gives us a data set like this:

	Student Number	→		
0	1	2	3	4
92	73	57	98	89

← Test Scores

But if there were three tests a term, we might want our data set to look like this:

Test Number ↓	Student Number →					
	0	1	2	3	4	
0	92	73	57	98	89	← Row 0: Test 0 Scores
1	88	76	23	95	72	← Row 1: Test 1 Scores
2	94	82	63	99	94	← Row 2: Test 2 Scores

This is a two-dimensional array. In programming, an array like this is broken up into **rows** and **columns**. The rows make up the test scores for a particular test, and the columns make up the test scores for an individual student.

C allows us to set up a data set like this by giving our array two indices. The first index (**rows**) will run over test number, the second index (**columns**) will run over students:

```
#include <stdio.h>

/* Record three tests. */

main()
{
    int scores[3][5];
        :
```

NOTE   C is different from other computer languages that you might be familiar with in that it gives separate array indices separate pairs of braces, like this: `scores[3][5]`. This notation, in fact, mirrors the same use in assembly language.

Now it's easy: We can use the first index to select the test number, 0-2, and the second to select the student, 0-4; the first index is always the row index, and the second is the column index. We can load the values shown above into our array like this:

```
#include <stdio.h>

/* Record three tests. */

main()
{
    int i, sum, scores[5];

    scores[0][0] = 92;   /* Test 0 scores */
    scores[0][1] = 73;
    scores[0][2] = 57;
    scores[0][3] = 98;
    scores[0][4] = 89;

    scores[1][0] = 88;   /* Test 1 scores */
    scores[1][1] = 76;
    scores[1][2] = 23;
    scores[1][3] = 95;
    scores[1][4] = 72;

    scores[2][0] = 94;   /* Test 2 scores */
    scores[2][1] = 82;
    scores[2][2] = 63;
    scores[2][3] = 99;
    scores[2][4] = 94;
        :
        :
```

This looks a little tedious, however, and in fact there is a better way that makes more sense. Just as we can initialize simple variables when we declare them, we can also do the same with arrays. For a two-dimensional array, the initialization just spells out the array row by column like this:

```
#include <stdio.h>

/* Record three tests. */

main()
{
    int i, sum, scores[3][5] = {
        { 92 , 73 , 57 , 98 , 89 },
        { 88 , 76 , 23 , 95 , 72 },
        { 94 , 82 , 63 , 99 , 94 }
    };


        :
        :
```

TIP   C actually allows you a shortcut here: When you're initializing a multi-dimensional array, you can always omit the first index (C can figure out what it is because of the number of elements in the initialization list). That means that the declaration line could have read: `int i, sum, scores[][5] = {.`

NOTE   Initializing a single-dimensional array is even easier; we could have done that like this: `int scores[5] = {92 , 73 , 57 , 98 , 89};.`

Now, if we like, we can print out the average test score for each test:

```c
#include <stdio.h>

/* Record three tests. */

main()
{
    int i, j, sum, scores[3][5] = {
        { 92 , 73 , 57 , 98 , 89 },
        { 88 , 76 , 23 , 95 , 72 },
        { 94 , 82 , 63 , 99 , 94 }
    };

    for (i = 0; i < 3; i++){   /* loop over tests. */
        for (j = 0, sum = 0; j < 5; j++)\
        sum = sum + scores[i][j];
        printf("Average for test %d is %f.\n", i,\
        (float) sum / 5);
    }

    return(0);
}
```

And that's it. We can also add even more dimensions to an array in C; such arrays as `int big_array[3][4][5]` are certainly possible, depending on how many indices your data set has. But keep in mind that your program has to supply memory for each entry in the array. To find out how much that is, multiply the indices together to find the total number of elements, 3×4×5 = 60, and then multiply by the number of bytes in each element. An integer is 2 bytes long, so the total number of bytes for this array are 60×2 or 120.

Our Database Program

With all this in mind, we can start our database program, which will provide us with a practical example of how to organize our data. Let's say that we were keeping track of nine products. We might have different quantities of those nine products:

```
tomatoes: 5
cucumbers: 7
oranges: 3
apples: 17
cabbages: 8
bananas: 12
mushrooms: 19
potatoes: 6
broccoli: 3
```

Our database's job is to store and maintain this data. In other words, it should be able to both accept and display data about each product. For example, we might have it come up with this prompt when it starts:

```
Do you want to (r)ead, (w)rite or (q)uit?
```

If we wanted to check on the number of cucumbers, product 1, we'd ask to read data by typing 'r'. The program should then ask us what product we wish to read about, and we could type 1, for cucumbers:

```
Do you want to (r)ead, (w)rite or (q)uit? r   ←we type this
Please select a product number: 1             ←we type this
```

It should then check its internal data, print out the number of cucumbers, and get ready to work with another product like this:

```
Do you want to (r)ead, (w)rite or (q)uit? r
Please select a product number: 1
No. of product 1: 7                            ←program types this

Do you want to (r)ead, (w)rite or (q)uit?
```

Let's begin writing the program. We start with storage space for the number of each product:

```
#include <stdio.h>

/* Database to keep track of products. */

main()
{
        int prod[9];
              :

}
```

Now we have to set up a loop that lets us accept commands. The commands we want include (r)eading a record, (w)riting a record, and (q)uitting; we print those choices in our prompt. Then we can accept a one-character response, **the_command**, with **getche( )**:

```
#include <conio.h>
#include <stdio.h>
#include <ctype.h>

/* Database to keep track of products. */

main()
{
    char the_command;
    int prod[9];

    do{
        printf("Do you want to (r)ead, (w)rite or (q)uit? ");
        the_command = getche();
                 :

                 :
    } while(toupper(the_command) != 'Q');

    return(0);
}
```

NOTE   Since the prototype for **getche( )** appears in **conio.h**, we had to include that header file as well.

Now, as usual with a menu, we use a switch statement to handle the different cases, (r)ead, (w)rite, or (q)uit:

```
#include <conio.h>
#include <stdio.h>
#include <ctype.h>
```

```
/* Database to keep track of products. */

main()
{
    char the_command;
    int prod[9];

    do{
        printf("\nDo you want to (r)ead, (w)rite or (q)uit? ");
        the_command = getche();
        switch (toupper(the_command)){
          case ('R'):
                  :
            break;
          case ('W'):
                  :
            break;
          case ('Q'):
            break;
          default:
            printf("I'm sorry, I cannot undertand that.\n");
        }
    } while(toupper(the_command) != 'Q');

    return(0);
}
```

Whether we put a new value into our array **prod[ ]** or read what's there, we'll
have to ask for a product number, which we can store as **prod_num**. After we
do that, it's easy to work on the quantity of that product, which is just stored in
prod[prod_num]. The whole program appears in Listing 3-1.

Listing 3-1. Database Program, Version 1.0.

```
#include <conio.h>
#include <stdio.h>
#include <ctype.h>

/* Database to keep track of products. */

main()
{
    char the_command;
    int prod_num, prod[9];

    do{
        printf("\nDo you want to (r)ead, (w)rite or (q)uit? ");
```

(continued)

Listing 3-1. *(continued)*

```
        the_command = getche();
        switch (toupper(the_command)){
          case ('R'):
            printf("\nPlease select a product number: ");
            scanf("%d", &prod_num);
            printf("No. of product %d: %d\n", prod_num,\
            prod[prod_num]);
            break;
          case ('W'):
            printf("\nPlease select a product number: ");
            scanf("%d", &prod_num);
            printf("New quantity of product %d: ", prod_num);
            scanf("%d", &prod[prod_num]);
            break;
          case ('Q'):
            break;
          default:
            printf("I'm sorry, I cannot undertand that.\n");
        }
      } while(toupper(the_command) != 'Q');

      return(0);
    }
```

Let's make sure this works. We can start the program and we'll get this prompt:

```
Do you want to (r)ead, (w)rite or (q)uit?
```

We might be interested in oranges, product 2. In that case, we'll want to put some data into that record because there's nothing there now. We select 'w' for write, and the program responds like this (note that we should make sure to write data into this program before trying to read it):

```
Do you want to (r)ead, (w)rite or (q)uit? w ← Please select a
product number:
```

It is asking us for a product number. Oranges are product number 2, so we can give that response. The program then asks for a new quantity of oranges:

```
Do you want to (r)ead, (w)rite or (q)uit? w
Please select a product number: 2 ←
New quantity of product 2:          ←
```

The program is waiting for us to enter our data on oranges. Let's say we have 3 oranges. We can enter that like this:

```
Do you want to (r)ead, (w)rite or (q)uit? w
Please select a product number: 2
New quantity of product 2: 3        ←

Do you want to (r)ead, (w)rite or (q)uit?
```

The program accepts the number and then asks us whether we want to (r)ead, (w)rite, or (q)uit. Let's take a look at oranges again to make sure our data got into the program. We type ′r′, followed by 2 to read read about product 2, and we get this:

```
Do you want to (r)ead, (w)rite or (q)uit? w
Please select a product number: 2
New quantity of product 2: 3

Do you want to (r)ead, (w)rite or (q)uit? r ←

Please select a product number: 2 ←

No. of product 2: 3

Do you want to (r)ead, (w)rite or (q)uit?
```

Our database program tells us that the quantity of product 2 is 3, so it worked. That's fine, but as you can see, it's a little hard to remember just what all the products are by number. It would be much easier if the program could tell us that we were looking at the data for oranges. And it can, as we'll see in the next topic, character strings.

Character Strings in C

Take a look at this array, of type char:

```
char product_1[8] = {'c','u','c','u','m','b','e','r'};
```

This produces an array named product_1[], filled like this:

'c'	'u'	'c'	'u'	'm'	'b'	'e'	'r'

If we wanted to, that means that we could type the word cucumber out with a loop:

```
#include <stdio.h>

/* Print out "cucumber". */

main()
{
    char product_1[8] = {'c','u','c','u','m','b','e','r'};
    int i;

    for (i = 0; i < 8; i++) printf("%c", product_1[i]);

    return(0);
}
```

This program types the word cucumber (note that we should always place values in an array before trying to read from it). In this way, we're able to put individual characters together into a **string**. String handling in C once again points out the division between the C library functions and the built-in C statements; there is no **string** type in C (as there are **ints** or **floats**). Instead, strings are supported only by the library functions. For example, one library function that supports the use of strings is **printf( )**, which has a format specifier especially for strings — **%s**. Here are some other ones and what they do:

gets( )	Get a string from the keyboard
strcpy( )	Copy a string
strcat( )	Concatenate two strings
strlen( )	Return the length of a string
strcmp( )	Compare the dictionary order of two strings

The functions that begin with **str** have their protoypes in **string.h** (**gets( )** is in **stdio.h**), so we'll have to include that when we use these functions. To use strings, we have to end them with a zero, or null character. In C, that character is expressed with a backslash code; e.g., '\0'. We can make **product_1[ ]** into a true C string and use **printf( )** to print it out like this:

TIP   The null character '\0' really is a zero byte. When you're poking around the data of a C program, you will see a single byte of value 0 marking the end of strings.

```
#include <stdio.h>

/* Print out "cucumber". */

main()
{
→      char product_1[] = {'c','u','c','u','m','b','e','r', '\0'};
       int i;

       printf("%s", product_1);

       return(0);
}
```

In C, we use double quotes to indicate a string; that is, an array of type **char** ending with a null character (which is all what a string is, nothing more). In fact, we can initialize our string **product_1** like this:

```
#include <stdio.h>

/* Print out "cucumber". */

main()
{
→      char product_1[] = "cucumber";
       int i;

       printf("%s", product_1);

       return(0);
}
```

Note that we did not have to indicate the number of characters in the **product_1** string (which is now 9 counting the terminating null) because the compiler could count them itself when we initialize that string.

Because the C language itself doesn't really have built-in string features, we can't just assign strings using the assignment operator this way (remember that as far as C is concerned, a string is an array):

```
product_1 = "cucumber";       /* NOT LEGAL */
```

On the other hand, most of the normal C capabilities have been duplicated with library functions. To assign one string to another, we can use the string copying function, **strcpy( )**:

```
strcpy(product_1, "cucumber");
```

Let's see an example of this. The following program reads a string with **gets( )** (although we could also use **scanf( )** with a **%s** format specifier), assigns it to the string named **copy_of_string**, and then prints out the copy:

```
#include <string.h>
#include <stdio.h>

/* Read in a string, assign it, and print it out. */

main()
{
    char read_in_string[80], copy_of_string[80];

    gets(read_in_string);
    strcpy(copy_of_string, read_in_string);
    printf("%s", copy_of_string);

    return(0);
}
```

We can also **concatenate** — that is, join — the two strings with **strcat( )** and type the resulting string out. Because that string may be longer than the screen is wide (80 characters), however, we should test its length with **strlen( )** first:

```
      #include <string.h>
      #include <stdio.h>

      /* Read in a string, assign it, concatentate the two,\
      print it out. */

      main()
      {
          char read_in_string[80], copy_of_string[160];

          gets(read_in_string);
→         strcpy(copy_of_string, read_in_string);
→         strcat(copy_of_string, read_in_string);
          if (strlen(copy_of_string) > 80)
               printf("Final string is too long.");
          else
               printf("%s", copy_of_string);

          return(0);
      }
```

Condition	Return Value
string1 < string2	< 0
string1 = = string2	0
string1 > string2	> 0

Table 3-1. strcmp( ) Return Values.

For example, if we type "tes" to this program, it would type back "testt-est". Let's see one more string example before updating our database program to include strings. The **strcmp( ) function takes the place of the relational operators > and < for strings.** If compares the dictionary order of two strings as in strcmp(string1, string2). If string1 comes before string2 alphabetically, then we say that string1 < string2. The possible returns from **strcmp( )** appear in Table 3-1.

Here's a short program that reads two strings and then types them out in alphabetic order:

```
#include <string.h>
#include <stdio.h>

/* Read two strings and print them out in dictionary\
order. */

main()
{
    char string1[80], string2[80];

    gets(string1);
    gets(string2);
    if (strcmp(string1, string2) < 0){
        printf("%s\n", string1);
        printf("%s\n", string2);
    }
    else{
        printf("%s\n", string2);
        printf("%s\n", string1);
    }

    return(0);
}
```

Of course, we can always construct our strings character by character, treating them as arrays if we wish. For example, take a look at this program, which converts a positive decimal integer into a hex value and prints it out. Because we strip off the hex digits in reverse order, it's convenient to be able to treat the resulting string like an array and fill it using an index we can increment or decrement:

```c
#include <stdio.h>

main()
{
    unsigned int i = 0, index = 0;
    char out_string[10];

    printf("Type a positive integer please ");
    scanf("%d", &i);

    do{
    out_string[index++] = (i%16 > 9 ? i%16 - 10 + 'a' :\
    i%16 + '0');
    }while(i /= 16);

    printf("That number in hexadecimal is ");
    while(index) printf("%c", out_string[--index]);

    return(0);
}
```

Notice in particular the line that converts a hex digit into ASCII:

```c
out_string[index++] = (i%16 > 9 ? i%16 - 10 + 'a' : i%16 + '0');
```

If the current hex digit is in the range 0–9, we just want to add the ASCII value '0' to turn it into something we can print out. Otherwise, the digit is in the range 0xa–0xf (where the 0x prefix indicates a hex number), and we have to subtract 10 and add 'a' to it. We can do all of that with a **conditional operator**.

The Conditional Operator

The general form of the conditional operator is this:

```c
condition ? expression 1 : expression 2;
```

If the condition is true, the value of the statement is the value of expression 1. Otherwise, it is the value of expression 2. Conditional operators like this provide a quick way of deciding between two choices, and they can make code very compact. In our case, this is our conditional operator:

```
out_string[index++] = (i%16 > 9 ? i%16 - 10 + 'a' :\
i%16 + '0');
```

Here, we compare the value of **i%16** (the current hex digit we're stripping off the input number we read, i) against 9. If it's greater than 9 (that is, in the range of 0xa to 0xf), we assign **out_string[index++]** the value **i%16 - 10 + 'a'**. Otherwise, we set it equal to **i%16 + '0'**. This loads the character string **out_string** in reverse order; at the end of the program, we print out the digits backwards to correct that:

```
printf("That number in hexadecimal is ");
while(index) printf("%c", out_string[--index]);
```

Now we've gained a good working feel for character strings; we know enough now to modify our database program so that it can store the names as well as the numbers of the products. The products and the numbers we've assigned to them were these:

0	tomatoes
1	cucumbers
2	oranges
3	apples
4	cabbages
5	bananas
6	mushrooms
7	potatoes
8	broccoli

Let's augment our program to type out this list — that is, which product corresponds to which number — with the new (l)ist command:

```
Do you want to (l)ist, (r)ead, (w)rite or (q)uit? l ←
0  tomatoes
1  cucumbers
2  oranges
3  apples
4  cabbages
5  bananas
```

```
6   mushrooms
7   potatoes
8   broccoli

Do you want to (l)ist, (r)ead, (w)rite or (q)uit?
```

There are a number of strings here, so we will use an **array of strings** (which is actually the same as a two-dimensional array of type char). We can set that up like this:

```
#include <conio.h>
#include <stdio.h>
#include <ctype.h>

/* Database to keep track of products. */

main()
{
    char the_command, name[9][20] = {
        "tomatoes",
        "cucumbers",
        "oranges",
        "apples",
        "cabbages",
        "bananas",
        "mushrooms",
        "potatoes",
        "broccoli"};
    int i, prod_num, prod[9] = {5, 7, 3, 17, 8, 12, 19, 6, 3};
        :
        :
```

The first index stands for the number of the string we want. For example, to print out tomatoes, we would use `printf("%s", name[0])`. Note that, as we did for single strings, we omit the last index number here. We are just passing the name of the array to **printf( )** (we'll see more about this later). To type out this list, we add a new case to the switch statement in our program:

```
      switch (toupper(the_command)){
→       case ('L'):
          for(i = 0; i < 9; i++) printf("\n%d %s", i, name[i]);
          break;
        case ('R'):
            :
```

In addition, now that we're handling strings, the program should type out not only the quantity of that product, but also the name. And when we write that record, we should be able to change the name of the product as well. That's easy enough with **printf( )** and **scanf( )**:

```
switch (toupper(the_command)){
    case ('L'):              /* list products */
        for(i = 0; i < 9; i++) printf("\n%d %s", i, name[i]);
        break;
    case ('R'):              /* Read product data */
        printf("\nPlease select a product number: ");
        scanf("%d", &prod_num);
→       printf("Product name: %s\n", name[prod_num]);
        printf("Quantity of product: %d\n", prod[prod_num]);
        break;
    case ('W'):              /* Write product data */
        printf("\nPlease select a product number: ");
        scanf("%d", &prod_num);
        printf("New name of product %d: ", prod_num);
→       scanf("%s", name[prod_num]);
        printf("New quantity of product %d: ", prod_num);
        scanf("%d", &prod[prod_num]);
        break;
```

The new version of the database program appears in Listing 3-2. When we run the program, we see this new prompt:

```
Do you want to (l)ist, (r)ead, (w)rite or (q)uit?
```

Listing 3-2. Database Program, Version 2.0.

```
#include <conio.h>
#include <stdio.h>
#include <ctype.h>

/* Database to keep track of products. Version 2.0 */

main()
{
    char the_command, name[9][20] = {
        "tomatoes",
        "cucumbers",
        "oranges",
        "apples",
        "cabbages",
```

(continued)

Listing 3-2. *(continued)*

```
                "bananas",
                "mushrooms",
                "potatoes",
                "broccoli"};
        int i, prod_num, prod[9] = {5, 7, 3, 17, 8, 12, 19, 6, 3};

        do{
            printf("\nDo you want to (l)ist, (r)ead, (w)rite or\
            (q)uit? ");
            the_command = getche();
            switch (toupper(the_command)){
              case ('L'):
                for(i = 0; i < 9; i++) printf("\n%d %s", i,\
                name[i]);
                break;
              case ('R'):
                printf("\nPlease select a product number: ");
                scanf("%d", &prod_num);
                printf("Product name: %s\n", name[prod_num]);
                printf("Quantity of product: %d\n",\
                prod[prod_num]);
                break;
              case ('W'):
                printf("\nPlease select a product number: ");
                scanf("%d", &prod_num);
                printf("New name of product %d: ", prod_num);
                scanf("%s", name[prod_num]);
                printf("New quantity of product %d: ", prod_num);
                scanf("%d", &prod[prod_num]);
                break;
              case ('Q'):
                break;
              default:
                printf("I'm sorry, I cannot undertand that.\n");
            }
        } while(toupper(the_command) != 'Q');

        return(0);
    }
```

Let's say that we want to replace cabbages with corn, but that we forget what product number cabbages corresponds to. We can list all the names of the records with the l command:

```
Do you want to (l)ist, (r)ead, (w)rite or (q)uit? l ←
0    tomatoes
1    cucumbers
```

```
2  oranges
3  apples
4  cabbages  ←
5  bananas
6  mushrooms
7  potatoes
8  broccoli

Do you want to (l)ist, (r)ead, (w)rite or (q)uit?
```

We see that cabbages is product number 4. We can modify that record with the (w)rite command:

```
Do you want to (l)ist, (r)ead, (w)rite or (q)uit? l
0  tomatoes
1  cucumbers
2  oranges
3  apples
4  cabbages
5  bananas
6  mushrooms
7  potatoes
8  broccoli

Do you want to (l)ist, (r)ead, (w)rite or (q)uit? w  ←
Please select a product number: 4  ←
New name of product 4:
```

Now the program is waiting for the name of the new product, and we type corn:

```
Do you want to (l)ist, (r)ead, (w)rite or (q)uit? l
0  tomatoes
1  cucumbers
2  oranges
3  apples
4  cabbages
5  bananas
6  mushrooms
7  potatoes
8  broccoli

Do you want to (l)ist, (r)ead, (w)rite or (q)uit? w
Please select a product number: 4
New name of product 4: corn  ←
New quantity of product 4:
```

Next we have to fill in an amount for corn, so let's say 10 and then read the record back to see whether it worked:

```
Do you want to (l)ist, (r)ead, (w)rite or (q)uit? l
0   tomatoes
1   cucumbers
2   oranges
3   apples
4   cabbages
5   bananas
6   mushrooms
7   potatoes
8   broccoli

Do you want to (l)ist, (r)ead, (w)rite or (q)uit? w
Please select a product number: 4
New name of product 4: corn
New quantity of product 4: 10 ←

Do you want to (l)ist, (r)ead, (w)rite or (q)uit? r ←
Please select a product number: 4 ←
Product name: corn
Quantity of product: 10

Do you want to (l)ist, (r)ead, (w)rite or (q)uit?
```

The program types back the name, **corn**, and the quantity, 10. If we listed the products, we'd find that corn has replaced cabbages. It looks as though our database program is functioning quite well, keeping track of our data.

On the other hand, from a programming point of view, we've made things a little more complex, because now we have two types of arrays to keep track of, **name[ ][ ]** (the product's names) and **prod[ ]** (the product's quantities):

```
char name[9][20] = {
    "tomatoes",
    "cucumbers",
    "oranges",
    "apples",
    "cabbages",
    "bananas",
    "mushrooms",
    "potatoes",
    "broccoli"};
int prod[9] = {5, 7, 3, 17, 8, 12, 19, 6, 3};
```

If we had dozens of quantities to keep track of for each product, this would be difficult to manage. In fact, however, C allows us to combine even different types of arrays like this into a super data type, which we call **structures**, and they're the next step up in organizing our data.

Data Structures in C

As we can see in our database example, it would occasionally be helpful to associate different types of data together under one name. In our databse example, we'd like to keep track of both the name of the product and its quantity. C provides **data structures** for just this purpose, and data structures let us wrap different data types together under the same name so they can be accessed easily.

TIP   We'll see later that this kind of conglomeration of data can be extended into a conglomeration of data and functions, which is the basis of forming objects in C++.

When we define a data structure, we're setting up a new data type of our own (i.e., to add to the predefined types of char, **int**, **float**, **double**, and **void**). For example, let's say that we wanted to keep track of the height and weight of some friends. We can set up a structure that looks like this:

```
struct my_record {
    int height;
    int weight;
};
```

After we've defined this structure named **my_record**, it becomes a new data type. In other words, we've created an entirely new type and we can use it in a program to declare variables like this:

```
#include <stdio.h>

/* Struct example */

main()
{
    struct my_record {
```

```
            int height;
            int weight;
         };
```

→   `struct my_record george, frank;`
                :

Now we have two variables of type **my_record** named **george** and **frank**. Each has associated with it two integers, **height** and **weight**, stored in the order shown above. To reach, say, George's height, we can use the **dot operator** (formally called the **member operator**) like this: `george.height = 72;`. This places a value of 72 (inches) into George's height. We can load and use the variables associated with our structures as easily as that, as shown in this example:

```
#include <stdio.h>

/* Struct example */

main()
{
   struct my_record {
       int height;
       int weight;
   };
   struct my_record george, frank;

   george.height = 72;   /* inches */
   george.weight = 180;  /* pounds */

   printf("George is %d inches, %d lbs.", george.height,\
   george.weight);

   return(0);
}
```

In general, defining a structure looks like this:

```
struct name_of_struct_type {
    type first_member_name;
    type second_member_name;
             :

             :
    type last_member_name;
} variables_of_this_type;
```

Note that we can declare a number of **variables** of this type in the structure declaration by placing them after the curly braces. For example, we could have declared **george** and **frank** like this:

```
#include <stdio.h>

/* Struct example */

main()
{
    struct my_record {
        int height;
        int weight;
    } george, frank;

    george.height = 72;    /* inches */
    george.weight = 180;   /* pounds */

    printf("George is %d inches, %d lbs.", george.height,\
    george.weight);

    return(0);
}
```

We are not limited to using only simple data types as the members of structures. We can use whole arrays inside our structures. One common example is the use of strings; if we wanted to store our friend's names as well as their heights and weights, we could do that by adding a string like this:

```
struct my_record {
    char name[20];
    int height;
    int weight;
} george, frank;
```

TIP   Enclosing an array inside a structure is also part of a programmer's trick. In C, when you pass arguments to a function, they are passed by value, except for arrays. When you pass an array to a function, it is passed by reference; that is, its address is passed. However, you can pass the whole thing by enclosing it in a structure because, when you pass a structure, the entire structure is passed. We'll talk more about argument passing later in this book.

In fact, we can even use arrays of structures. This is actually a common thing to do when you're formatting records that you want to write to a file. In our case, we can set up an array named **friends[ ]** made up of 10 of these structures this way:

```
struct my_record {
    char name[20];
    int height;
    int weight;
} friends[10];            ←
```

We've included space for the person's name, so we can record the data we have on George this way (keep in mind that we have to use **strcpy( )** to assign one string to another):

```
#include <string.h>
#include <stdio.h>

/* Array of structures example */

main()
{

    struct my_record {
        char name[20];
        int height;
        int weight;
    } friends[10];

→       strcpy(friends[0].name, "George");
→       friends[0].height = 72;    /* inches */
→       friends[0].weight = 180;   /* pounds */

    printf("%s is %d inches tall, weighs %d lbs.\n",\
    friends[0].name, \
        friends[0].height, friends[0].weight);

    return(0);
}
```

| TIP | Notice that the **printf( )** line in this example was very long, and that we broke it up into two lines, which you can do in C if you use a backslash, \, at the end of the first line. This tells the compiler that the current statement continues on the next line. You actually don't need a \ if you're breaking the line after a comma (unless the comma is inside quotation marks), but we put it in here to make the code more clear. |

This is very convenient because now the program can let the array index vary over all the records we have. For example, if we had recorded five friends, we could print their data out like this with a **for** loop:

```
for (i=0; i < 5; i++)
    printf("%s is %d inches tall, weighs %d lbs.\n",
friends[i].name, \
        friends[i].height, friends[i].weight);
```

In this way, we have collected different types of data under the same name:

```
friends[i].name
friends[i].height
friends[i].weight
```

In fact, we've done even more than that; we've made an array of these collections, which lets us refer to them by index. Structures are a natural for database programs, and we can modify ours to use them. In our case, we want to keep track of both the name and number of various products, so we start off by setting up a structure like this:

```
#include <conio.h>
#include <stdio.h>
#include <ctype.h>

/* Database to keep track of products. Version 3.0 */

main()
{
        struct my_record {
            char name[20];
            int num;
        } recs[9];
```

We've defined an array of structures, which we name **recs[ ]**. Now we have to fill up our array with the values we want:

```
#include <conio.h>
#include <stdio.h>
#include <ctype.h>

/* Database to keep track of products. Version 3.0 */

main()
{
    struct my_record {
```

```
        char name[20];
        int num;
} recs[9];
char the_command;
int i, prod_num;

strcpy(recs[0].name, "tomatoes");
strcpy(recs[1].name, "cucumbers");
strcpy(recs[2].name, "oranges");
strcpy(recs[3].name, "apples");
strcpy(recs[4].name, "cabbages");
strcpy(recs[5].name, "bananas");
strcpy(recs[6].name, "mushrooms");
strcpy(recs[7].name, "potatoes");
strcpy(recs[8].name, "broccoli");

recs[0].num = 5;
recs[1].num = 7;
recs[2].num = 8;
recs[3].num = 17;
recs[4].num = 8;
recs[5].num = 12;
recs[6].num = 19;
recs[7].num = 6;
recs[8].num = 3;
        :
        :
```

And then we just replace the old references to variables in our program with the new array references as in this case, where we're printing out the name of each product:

```
switch (toupper(the_command)){
  case ('L'):
    for(i = 0; i < 9; i++) printf("\n%d %s", i,\
    recs[i].name);
    break;
```

The new, more advanced database program may be found in Listing 3-3. Of course, it's not a very professional database. That kind of database has to be able to search through records, as well as sort them. And in professional databases, that's usually done with **pointers**, which is the topic we'll cover next.

Listing 3-3. Database Program, Version 3.0

```c
#include <conio.h>
#include <stdio.h>
#include <ctype.h>

/* Database to keep track of products. Version 3.0 */

main()
{
    struct my_record {
        char name[20];
        int num;
    } recs[9];
    char the_command;
    int i, prod_num;

    strcpy(recs[0].name, "tomatoes");
    strcpy(recs[1].name, "cucumbers");
    strcpy(recs[2].name, "oranges");
    strcpy(recs[3].name, "apples");
    strcpy(recs[4].name, "cabbages");
    strcpy(recs[5].name, "bananas");
    strcpy(recs[6].name, "mushrooms");
    strcpy(recs[7].name, "potatoes");
    strcpy(recs[8].name, "broccoli");

    recs[0].num = 5;
    recs[1].num = 7;
    recs[2].num = 8;
    recs[3].num = 17;
    recs[4].num = 8;
    recs[5].num = 12;
    recs[6].num = 19;
    recs[7].num = 6;
    recs[8].num = 3;

    do{
        printf("\nDo you want to (l)ist, (r)ead, (w)rite or\
        (q)uit? ");
        the_command = getche();
        switch (toupper(the_command)){
          case ('L'):
            for(i = 0; i < 9; i++) printf("\n%d %s", i,\
            recs[i].name);
            break;
          case ('R'):
```

(continued)

Listing 3-3. *(continued)*

```
                printf("\nPlease select a product number: ");
                scanf("%d", &prod_num);
                printf("Product name: %s\n", recs[prod_num].name);
                printf("Quantity of product: %d\n",\
                recs[prod_num].num);
                break;
            case ('W'):
                printf("\nPlease select a product number: ");
                scanf("%d", &prod_num);
                printf("New name of product %d: ", prod_num);
                scanf("%s", recs[prod_num].name);
                printf("New quantity of product %d: ", prod_num);
                scanf("%d", &recs[prod_num].num);
                break;
            case ('Q'):
                break;
            default:
                printf("I'm sorry, I cannot undertand that.\n");
        }
    } while(toupper(the_command) != 'Q');

    return(0);
}
```

All about Pointers

Pointers are one of the most central topics in C and learning how to use them is exceptionally important, especially if you want your programs to execute faster, manipulate memory, and let functions change the arguments they were called with. So, what is a pointer?

Pointers Are Just Addresses

The answer to that question is very simple: pointers are just addresses. Every item of data that we store in a program is stored at a particular address in memory. For example, in a program like the following one, **my_int** is the label given to a location in memory at which the program stores an integer:

```
#include <stdio.h>

/* Example of integer storage. */
```

```
      main()
      {
→         int my_int;

          my_int = 1;

          printf("The value of my_int is: %d", my_int);

          return(0);
      }
```

That integer is two bytes long, so if the address it is stored at in memory is 3985, both bytes 3985 and 3986 are set aside to hold **my_int** (we'll see more about the details of addressing memory directly later). On the other hand, if we were storing a floating point variable, **my_float**, we would need four bytes.

NOTE   The popularity of pointers in C in fact follows their popularity in assembly language. This is another case in which the two are very similar, and we'll see how to use pointers in assembly language starting in Chapter 11.

Declaring a pointer is the same as declaring any other variable, except that we use the pointer operator * (also called the **indirection operator**). For instance, if we wanted to declare a pointer named **my_pointer** in our program, we could do it like this:

```
      #include <stdio.h>

      /* Example of integer storage. */

      main()
      {
→         int my_int, *my_pointer;

          my_int = 1;

          printf("The value of my_int is: %d", my_int);

          return(0);
      }
```

In this case, **my_pointer** is a pointer to a variable of type **int**. In C, we say that **int** is the pointer's **base type**. This base type is very important. For example, you can't mix a pointer to an **int** with a pointer to a **float**. In general, we declare a pointer like this:

```
type *pointer_name;
```

You read a declaration like this backwards. For example, you can read the following line as "**my_pointer** is a pointer to type **int**":

```
int *my_pointer;
```

TIP   The reason the * is associated with the pointer name and not the declaration type is to allow you to declare both variables and pointers to variables of that type in the same line, making a statement like this possible: int my_int, *my_pointer;.

As it stands, **my_pointer** doesn't point to anything yet. We have to load it with another operator named the **address operator**, **&**. When you see & in a program, it helps to read it as "the address of." We can use it like this here:

```
#include <stdio.h>

/* Example of integer storage. */

main()
{
    int my_int, *my_pointer;

    my_int = 1;
    my_pointer = &my_int;

    printf("The value of my_int is: %d", my_int);

    return(0);
}
```

The statement my_pointer = &my_int; may be read as "**my_pointer** gets the address of **my_int**." Now **my_pointer** points to **my_int**. Using **my_pointer**, we can reach **my_int** with the * operator, the **indirection operator**. When you find * in a program, it helps to read it as "the value at address." Here's how we might print out the value in **my_int**, using its address as stored in **my_pointer**:

```
#include <stdio.h>

/* Example of pointer usage. */

main()
{
    int my_int, *my_pointer;

    my_int = 1;
    my_pointer = &my_int;

→   printf("The value of my_int is: %d", *my_pointer);

    return(0);
}
```

If you keep in mind that * can be read as "the value at address," then *my_pointer simply means "the value at address **my_pointer**." We're asking **printf( )** to print out the value at address **my_pointer**, which is **my_int**. This program produces the same results as the previous one:

```
The value of my_int is: 1
```

It is helpful to think of pointers simply as variables, and that these variables are used to hold addresses. For example, we can assign pointers to each other, as we can with variables:

```
#include <stdio.h>

/* Example of pointer usage. */

main()
{
    int my_int, *my_pointer, *my_other_pointer;

    my_int = 1;
    my_pointer = &my_int;
→   my_other_pointer = my_pointer;

    printf("The value of my_int is: %d", *my_other_pointer);

    return(0);
}
```

We can even perform addition and subtraction on pointers, as you might expect on variables that hold addresses. (Note, however, that multiplying or dividing, or any other such math operation on such a variable is meaningless.)

Using Addition and Subtraction with Pointers

Let's say that we had an array of five integers named **my_int_array[ ]**, and that it held the values 1, 2, 3, 4, and 5. In this case, the integers would be stored in ascending order in memory:

5	my_int_array[4]
4	my_int_array[3]
3	my_int_array[2]
2	my_int_array[1]
1	my_int_array[0]

← 2 bytes →

We can set up a pointer, **my_pointer**, to point at the first of these elements:

	5	my_int_array[4]
	4	my_int_array[3]
	3	my_int_array[2]
	2	my_int_array[1]
my_pointer →	1	my_int_array[0]

← 2 bytes →

In a program, that might look like this:

```
#include <stdio.h>

/* Example of pointer usage. */

main()
```

```
{
     int i, *my_pointer, my_int_array[] = {1, 2, 3, 4, 5};

→    my_pointer = &my_int_array[0];
     :
```

Now, there is a special quality to pointer addition and subtraction, and it comes from the same reason that the base type of a pointer is so important. When we add 1 to **my_pointer**, we'd expect to point to the next element up in memory, like this:

5	my_int_array[4]
4	my_int_array[3]
3	my_int_array[2]
2	my_int_array[1]
1	my_int_array[0]

my_pointer → (points to my_int_array[1] row, value 2)

← 2 bytes →

In fact, we should notice that each element of the array is an integer, which means that it's two bytes long. Because memory addresses go byte by byte, if we just add 1 to the value of an address, we would be left pointing at the next byte along. Here, however, we have to point to the location two bytes up.

C takes care of this automatically because it knows the base type of the pointer. If we were to add 1 to **my_pointer**, C would realize that **my_pointer** is a pointer to an **int**, and integers are two bytes long, so it really adds 2 to **my_pointer**. In the same way, if **my_pointer** pointed to **floats**, four bytes long, an operation like my_pointer = my_pointer + 1 would actually add 4 to **my_pointer** so that we end up pointing to the next float in memory.

If you're ever in doubt about the size of a data item (structures included), you can use the C operator **sizeof( )**. For example, sizeof(my_int) would return a value of 2. On a floating point number, **sizeof( )** would return 4.

NOTE   In spite of looking very much like a C library function, **sizeof( )** is actually a built-in C operator.

We can even use expressions like `my_pointer++`. Let's print out the contents of the array **my_int_array[ ]** that way:

```
#include <stdio.h>

/* Example of pointer usage. */

main()
{
    int i, *my_pointer, my_int_array[] = {1, 2, 3, 4, 5};

    my_pointer = &my_int_array[0];

    for (i = 0; i < 5; i++){
        printf("Element %d is: %d\n", i, *my_pointer);
        my_pointer++;
    }

    return(0);
}
```

We start off by pointing to the first element in **my_int_array[ ]**, which is **my_int_array[0]**, and we print that out by referencing it as ***my_pointer** ("the value at address **my_pointer**"). Next, we increment **my_pointer** so that it points to the next element, using **my_pointer++**, and we print that out. This is one of the places that pointers can come in handy; if data items are stored sequentially, one after the other, we can start at the beginning and just work our way up by incrementing an address.

In fact, here's something that may surprise you: the name of the array we set up, **my_int_array[ ]**, is actually a pointer itself. That is, array names (including the names of character strings) are actually pointers. For example, if we treat the name **my_int_array** as a pointer, then it points to the beginning of the array, like this:

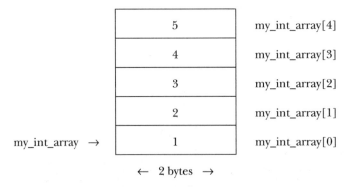

Note that when we refer to it as a pointer, we omit the [] after the name. If this is the case, then my_int_array + 1 must point to the next element in the array, and in fact it does:

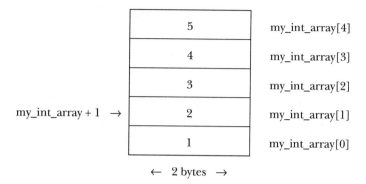

How would we reach the element stored at my_int_array[1] using pointer notation? We'd just call it *(my_int_array + 1). In other words, these two expressions are interchangeable:

$$*(my\_int\_array + n) \longleftrightarrow my\_int\_array[n]$$

Let's see what that means in our program. We can take out **my_pointer** altogether, and just add the printing loop index directly to **my_int_array** like this:

```
#include <stdio.h>

/* Example of pointer usage. */

main()
{
    int i, my_int_array[] = {1, 2, 3, 4, 5};

    for (i = 0; i < 5; i++){
        printf("Element %d is: %d\n", i,\
        *(my_int_array + i));
    }

    return(0);
}
```

As you can see, there's more to pointers than you might think at first. Let's finish up with something to think about. If a one-dimensional array name is just a pointer, what is a two-dimensional array name? It turns out that you can think of a two-dimensional array as an array of one-dimensional arrays. That is, each two-dimensional array is actually a one-dimensional array of rows. And that makes each two-dimensional array name — a pointer to a pointer.

TIP   In fact, we'll see how to get substitute pointers for arrays entirely in certain cases later, and doing so will make our programs faster and more efficient in memory usage.

We'll go into depth like this in Chapter 8, our advanced pointer chapter, where we'll have the time to work through these kinds of ideas. In the meantime, let's take a break. We've looked at the language itself for three straight chapters now; let's look at some library functions next — and nowhere are the library functions more fun than when it comes to graphics.

Welcome to C Graphics

So far, we've gotten a pretty good picture of many of the basics in C. But now it's time to put them to work and investigate some of the available library functions that make C so rich. For example, there are a tremendous number of graphics routines in C for the PC and PS/2; this is one place that C gets to shine. In this chapter, we will develop a paintlike program that draws on the screen. As we develop it, we will explore many of the graphics options available in both the Microsoft C and Turbo C libraries. Before we're done, we'll be drawing lines, ellipses, and rectangles — even animating figures on the screen.

It is very important to note, however, that graphics is one area of C that is not specified by the ANSI standard. As a result, Microsoft C (including Quick C) and Turbo C (including Turbo C++) diverge here, and we will have to keep track of both of them. On the other hand, all that we're going to do in this chapter can be done with either compiler. Let's begin immediately. Before doing anything else in graphics, we have to set the screen the way we want it, and we'll do that first.

Video Modes in C

There are many different monitors out there for the PC, including the CGA, the EGA, and the VGA. For the purposes of our demonstration program, and because there are so many different types of monitors, we'll pick a graphics mode that just about any PC with graphics can support — the CGA medium-resolution mode (320 × 200 pixels, four colors). We'll investigate other modes later.

Setting the video mode is done differently in the Microsoft and Turbo compilers — already the two compilers diverge. In Microsoft C, you use the function **_setvideomode( )** and pass it constants predefined in the graph.h header file. In Turbo C, you use the function **setgraphmode( )**, constants from the **graphics.h** header file, and you have to specify a graphics driver file. We will investigate the details of setting all video modes under both compilers later. To get our demonstration program going and to set the video mode to low-resolution CGA mode, let's concentrate on Microsoft C. Later, we'll see the whole program written in Turbo C.

We'll start by including the **graph.h** header file because it has the prototypes and constant definitions that we'll need (Turbo: graphics.h):

```
→      #include <stdio.h>
→      #include <graph.h>

     main()
     {
     }
```

In order to set up our graphics mode, we call **_setvideomode( )**. (Turbo: **setgraphmode( )**). There are a number of different constants already defined in **graph.h** that we can use with **setvideomode( )**. We will see all of them later, but now we will only use one of them, **_MRES4COLOR**, to set up the CGA four-color mode in our program (Turbo: **mode CGAC3** — you can see that, without a standard to adhere to, just about no two C compilers would be alike):

```
     #include <stdio.h>
     #include <graph.h>

   main()
```

```
        {

→               _setvideomode(_MRES4COLOR);
                 :
                 :
        }
```

Coloring a Screen Pixel

After the video mode is set, we're ready to draw on the screen. Since our paint program is only intended as a graphics demonstration, we'll make it keyboard driven (if you like, you can add a mouse interface after reading Chapter 6). When the program begins, we might start at the top left of the screen:

One of the capabilities of our paint program should be to simply draw on the screen; that is, to turn individual pixels on (the dots on the screen). To set the pixel at our current location, for example, we might type 'p'. If we wish, we can move around using the cursor keys, typing 'p' at each place and leaving a trail of lit pixels:

When a 'q' is typed, we can exit the program. The cursor keys are a little tricky, however. None of the standard character-reading C routines acknowledges the cursor keys as typed keys, but, nonetheless, it's important to learn how to use them. The **getche( )** function that we've already seen has a counterpart that is called **getch( )**. The **getche( )** function reads a single key, and echoes it on the screen. The **getch( )** function does the same thing, except that it doesn't echo on the screen (the second **e** in **getche( )** stands for **echo**). This way, our graphics screen won't become crowded with unwanted characters as we move our position around the screen.

If we press a cursor key, **getch( )** returns 0. If we see that value, we will use **getch( )** again, and this time, we will get the **scan code** for the key (this works the same for **getche( )**). For each of the 83 or 101 keys on the keyboard, there is a unique code called the scan code. These codes were used because the ASCII codes do not cover all possible key strokes from the keyboard. They do not cover F5, for example, or shift-F5, or any of the function and cursor keys. However, there is a unique scan code for each key or key combination, and you can find tables of scan codes in your C documentation.

TIP   To find scan codes quickly, you can write a small C program using **getche( )** or **getch( )** to print them out. This can save you the time needed to find the correct table.

After looking up the scan codes, we can use the cursor keys easily. The scan code for the up arrow is 208, 200 for the down arrow, 205 for right, and 203 for left. We'll just check to see if they've been typed, and we'll be home free.

We'll also need to keep track of our present screen position, and we can use two variables for that: **x_location** and **y_location**. In other words, (x_location, y_location) will always represent our current location on the screen. In the graphics mode we have chosen, the screen is 200 pixels vertically (the y direction) and 320 pixels horizontally (the x direction). Furthermore, the origin (0, 0) is in the upper left-hand corner of the screen. The lower, right-hand corner is (199, 319):

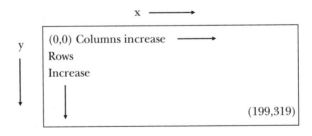

Now let's continue with our program, which we can call **painter.c**. When 'p' is typed, we'll set the pixel at the current location (x_location, y_location) with the graphics function named _setpixel(x_location, y_location) (Turbo: putpixel(x_location, y_location, 1), where 1 is the pixel color).

We've already set the video mode in our program. Now we have to start reading keys from the keyboard which we can interpret as commands. For example, the 'q' command means quit:

```
#include <stdio.h>
#include <graph.h>

/* painter.c -- a paint program */

main()
{
    int in_key;
    int x_location = 0, y_location = 0;

    _setvideomode(_MRES4COLOR);

→   while((in_key = getch()) != 'q'){
        :

        :
    }
```

If **in_key** turns out to be 0, a control key — such as a cursor key — was used; we have to use **getch( )** a second time and add 128 to get the scan code. Next, we can use a switch statement to either update the current screen location (assuming a cursor key was typed) or to set a pixel (assuming 'p' was typed) like this:

```
#include <stdio.h>
#include <graph.h>

/* painter.c -- a paint program */

main()
{
    int in_key;
    int x_location = 0, y_location = 0;

    _setvideomode(_MRES4COLOR);

    while((in_key = getch()) != 'q'){
→       if (!in_key) in_key = getch() + 128;
    :       switch (in_key){
    :           case 208:                   /* up arrow */
                    y_location++;
                    break;
                case 203:                   / left arrow */
                    x_location--;
```

```
                          break;
                case 205:              /* right arrow */
                     x_location++;
                     break;
                case 200:              /* down arrow */
                     y_location--;
                     break;
                case 'p':              /* set the screen pixel */
                     _setpixel(x_location, y_location);
                     break;
                default:
                     ;
          }
     }

     return(0);
}
```

NOTE   Recall that the **Not operator** ! changes the logical value of its operand, so if **in_key** is 0, which is interpreted as false, then ! in_key is true.

We can use **painter.c** already. It will set pixels anywhere on the screen. Just move around with the cursor keys and when you type 'p', the program will turn the pixel at the current location on.

Drawing Lines

Turning dots on the screen on is interesting, but it falls short of exciting. Let's add a few more features to **painter.c**. First, let's add color. We'll get a more comprehensive discussion of color after we discuss screen modes, but, for now, if we include the line in our program, the pixels you turn on the screen will be cyan, not white (Turbo: setcolor(1)):

```
#include <stdio.h>
#include <graph.h>

/* painter.c -- a paint program */

main()
{
     int in_key;
     int x_location = 0, y_location = 0;

     _setvideomode(_MRES4COLOR);
```

→   `_setcolor(1);`
                :
                :
      `}`

In other words, **_setcolor( )** sets the drawing color to use. Let's take advantage of more C library functions now to draw a cyan line on the screen.

To draw a line on the screen, we start at a particular position:

To anchor this point as one end of our line, we make it into what C calls the current **graphic output position**. In other words, if the current graphic output position was at position x as shown above, then we could use the **_lineto( )** function (Turbo: **lineto( )**) to draw a line from x to a point we indicate. If we passed the coordinates of, say, y, to **_lineto( )**, then the screen would look like this:

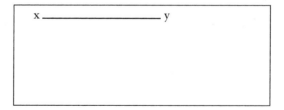

To set the current graphics output position, and therefore anchor one end of the line, we use the function named **_moveto( )** (Turbo: **moveto( )**). Next, we pass the coordinates of y to **_lineto( )** to draw the line. That means that we'll set x with **_moveto( )**, move around using the cursor keys, and then draw the line when we're at the new location, y.

Let's put this in our program. We have to specify two points, x and y. We can use the program's pixel-setting ability to mark one end of the line, x, by typing 'p':

(type 'p')

Then we move around using the cursor keys and type, say, 'l' to draw a line from the pixel we just set to the place where we are now, y:

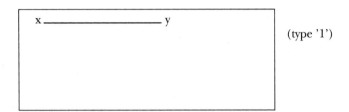

(type 'l')

We can do this by augmenting the 'p' command not only to set a pixel, but also to set the current graphic output location, *x*, at the same place. Then we can move around the screen using the cursor keys. When we type 'l', a (cyan) line will be drawn from the pixel we set, *x*, to the position we moved to, *y*. Here's how it looks with **_moveto( )** and **_lineto( )**:

```
#include <stdio.h>
#include <graph.h>

/* painter.c -- a paint program */

main()
{
    int in_key;
    int x_location = 0, y_location = 0;

    _setvideomode(_MRES4COLOR);

    _setcolor(1);
    while((in_key = getch()) != 'q'){
        if (!in_key) in_key = getch() + 128;
        switch (in_key){
            case 208:      /* up arrow */
                y_location++;
                break;
```

```
                case 203:       /* left arrow */
                    x_location--;
                    break;
                case 205:       /* right arrow */
                    x_location++;
                    break;
                case 200:       /* down arrow */
                    y_location--;
                    break;
                case 'p':
                    _setpixel(x_location, y_location);
→                   _moveto(x_location, y_location);
                    break;
→             case 'l':
→                   _lineto(x_location, y_location);
→                   break;
                default:
                    ;
            }
        }

        return(0);
    }
```

That's all there is to it. To draw a line, we move around, press 'p' to tack down one end of the line, move again, and type 'l' to draw the line. However, the C library offers us more than lines. For example, we can draw rectangles almost as easily.

Drawing Rectangles

There is a **_rectangle( )** function in the Microsoft C library (Turbo: **rectangle( )**). This function differs from **_lineto( )** in that it requires two sets of coordinates, the upper, left-hand and lower, right-hand coordinates of the rectangle:

The call to the function **_rectangle( )** is made this way:

```
_rectangle(control, x_top, y_top, x_bot, y_bot);
```

(**Turbo**: `rectangle(x_top, y_top, x_bot, y_bot)`). Microsoft C gives you the option of filling the rectangle in: the parameter named control in the above call is given the value of one of two constants: **_GFILLINTERIOR** or **_GBORDER** (both defined in **graph.h**). If you select **_GFILLINTERIOR**, the rectangle that is drawn is filled with the current drawing color (in our case, cyan). If you choose **_GBORDER**, as we will here, only the border will be drawn.

To draw rectangles, we have to establish two pairs of coordinates on the screen, (**x_top**, **y_top**) and (**x_bot**, **y_bot**). An easy way to do this is to set the first pair when we use the pixel command, 'p', and to add another command, 'r', to draw the rectangle after we've moved to the correct position.

In other words, we'll move to the upper, left-hand corner of the rectangle we want to draw and press 'p'. A pixel appears, marking that location and setting (**x_top**, **y_top**):

(type 'p')

Next, we move to the lower, right-hand corner and press 'r'. When we do, our present position on the screen is taken as (**x_bot**, **y_bot**), and the rectangle is drawn:

(type 'r')

We can add these lines to case 'p' to set (**x_top, y_top**):

```
case 'p':
    _setpixel(x_location, y_location);
    _moveto(x_location, y_location);
    x_top = x_location;        ←
    y_top = y_location;        ←
    break;
case 'l':
```

NOTE Note that the 'p' command now sets both (**x_top, y_top**) for drawing rectangles and the current graphics output position for drawing lines.

Then we add the following lines to the program for the new case, case 'r', to draw rectangles:

```
#include <stdio.h>
#include <graph.h>

/* painter.c -- a paint program */

main()
{
    int in_key;
    int x_location = 0, y_location = 0, x_top = 0,\
    y_top = 0;

    _setvideomode(_MRES4COLOR);

    _setcolor(1);

    while((in_key = getch()) != 'q'){
        if (!in_key) in_key = getch() + 128;
        switch (in_key){
            case 208:      /* up arrow */
                y_location++;
                break;
            case 203:      /* left arrow */
                x_location--;
                break;
            case 205:      /* right arrow */
                x_location++;
                break;
```

```
                         case 200:      /* down arrow */
                             y_location--;
                             break;
                         case 'p':
                             _setpixel(x_location, y_location);
                             _moveto(x_location, y_location);
                             x_top = x_location;
                             y_top = y_location;
                             break;
                         case 'l':
                             _lineto(x_location, y_location);
                             break;
→                         case 'r':
→                             _rectangle(_GBORDER, x_top, y_top, \
                                 x_location,  y_location);
→                             break;
→                         default:
                                 ;
                 }
         }

         return(0);
 }
```

When you press 'r', a rectangle will be drawn from the last pixel you turned on to the current location. Since the method for drawing ellipses is very similar, we can add that immediately to our program.

Drawing Ellipses

It's as easy to draw an ellipse as it is to draw a rectangle. All we have to do is to supply the function **_ellipse( )** (Turbo: **ellipse( )**) with the same coordinates as we might supply to **_rectangle( )**. The pair of coordinates you pass to **_ellipse( )** define a box, and the ellipse is drawn so that it touches this box at four points. Again, you can use the two constants **_GFILLINTERIOR** or **_GBORDER** in Microsoft C. Here's the new addition:

```
#include <stdio.h>
#include <graph.h>

/* painter.c -- a paint program */

main()
{
    int in_key;
```

```
int x_location = 0, y_location = 0, x_top = 0,\
y_top = 0;

_setvideomode(_MRES4COLOR);

_setcolor(1);
while((in_key = getch()) != 'q'){
    if (!in_key) in_key = getch() + 128;
    switch (in_key){
        case 208:       /* up arrow */
            y_location++;
            break;
        case 203:       /* left arrow */
            x_location--;
            break;
        case 205:       /* right arrow */
            x_location++;
            break;
        case 200:       /* down arrow */
            y_location--;
            break;
        case 'p':
            _setpixel(x_location, y_location);
            _moveto(x_location, y_location);
            x_top = x_location;
            y_top = y_location;
            break;
        case 'l':
            _lineto(x_location, y_location);
            break;
        case 'r':
            _rectangle(_GBORDER, x_top, y_top, \
                x_location,  y_location);
            break;
        case 'e':
            _ellipse(_GBORDER, x_top, y_top, \
                x_location,  y_location);
            break;
        default:
            ;
    }
}

return(0);
}
```

In Turbo C, however, this process is significantly different. The call to **el-lipse( )** takes these parameters: **ellipse(x, y, 0, 360, xradius, yradius)**, where (**x,y**) is the location of the exact center of the ellipse, the beginning and ending angles 0 and 360 indicate that we want a closed figure to be drawn, **xradius** is the radius of the ellipse in the x direction, and **yradius** is the radius in the y direction. When we rewrite our painting program in Turbo C, we'll make our call to **ellipse( )** this way: `ellipse((x_top + x_bot)/2,` `(y_top + y_bot)/2, 0, 360, abs(x_bot - x_top)/2, abs(y_bot` `- y_top)/2)`.

Filling Shapes with Color

So far, our paint program just draws the outline of shapes; we can, however, modify it to fill shapes in. Microsoft C provides the **_floodfill( )** function to do exactly that (Turbo: **floodfill( )**). All you have to do is specify the point on the screen and the color of the border of the area you want filled. The **_floodfill( )** function then fills in the area with the current color, which is cyan for us (set with **_setcolor( )**).

For example, if you had drawn a rectangle on the screen in our default color, cyan, the **_floodfill( )** function could fill it in by coloring until it reaches that boundary color. All you have to do is specify a location on the screen to start filling with color.

To fill an area with color, let's modify our program again to accept the 'f' command. Use the cursor keys to move into a shape that you have already drawn and press 'f'. The area will be colored in solidly. To use **_floodfill( )**, we have to pass it the position on the screen, (**x_location**, **y_location**) and the boundary color. Since we are only drawing shapes in cyan (color = 1), this is what our call to **_floodfill( )** looks like:

```
#include <stdio.h>
#include <graph.h>

/* painter.c -- a paint program */

main()
{
    int in_key;
    int x_location = 0, y_location = 0, x_top = 0,\
    y_top = 0;

    _setvideomode(_MRES4COLOR);

    _setcolor(1);
```

```
        while((in_key = getch()) != 'q'){
            if (!in_key) in_key = getch() + 128;
            switch (in_key){
                case 208:       /* up arrow */
                    y_location++;
                    break;
                case 203:       /* left arrow */
                    x_location--;
                    break;
                case 205:       /* right arrow */
                    x_location++;
                    break;
                case 200:       /* down arrow */
                    y_location--;
                    break;
                case 'p':
                    _setpixel(x_location, y_location);
                    _moveto(x_location, y_location);
                    x_top = x_location;
                    y_top = y_location;
                    break;
                case 'l':
                    _lineto(x_location, y_location);
                    break;
                case 'r':
                    _rectangle(_GBORDER, x_top, y_top, \
                        x_location, y_location);
                    break;
                case 'e':
                    _ellipse(_GBORDER, x_top, y_top, \
                        x_location, y_location);
                    break;
                case 'f':
                    _floodfill(x_location, y_location, 1);
                    break;
                default:
                    ;
            }
        }

    return(0);
}
```

The call is just this: _floodfill(x_location, y_location, 1) (Turbo: floodfill(x_location, y_location, 1).) The area on the screen bordered by the specified color — cyan — will be filled in solidly with the current drawing color (set with **_setcolor( )** or **setcolor( )**). You can experiment with filling in different colors by passing new values to **_setcolor( )** before choosing the 'f' option; in our current four-color CGA mode, **_setcolor( )** can take values from 0 to 3 (we will get a full description of what these values correspond to later).

Now our program can fill in shapes on the screen. The only thing we can't do in the **painter.c** program is to change colors easily. When we draw, it's in cyan, and this is a distinct drawback if you had wanted to use, say, magenta. Let's add the ability to choose different colors to **painter.c**.

There are many colors available on the PC (in the case of the VGA, an enormous number), but, to learn to work with them, we have to understand how the different PC screen modes work. Some colors that are available under one screen mode, for example, will not be available under others. For that reason, we'll undertake a tour of the possible screen modes next.

C Screen Modes

Displays on the PC machines have gotten steadily better over time, and it's been a popular improvement. The original Color Graphics Adapter (CGA) could only display four colors at a time, with a poor resolution of 320×200 (320 vertical colums, 200 horizontal rows). And it flickered badly.

The other option at that time, the Monochrome Display Adapter (MDA) didn't flicker, had good resolution, but it also didn't do graphics: all it could use were alphanumeric characters. With the introduction of other, competing, computers, it became clear that graphics was an up and coming issue in hardware, and IBM eventually followed the lead.

In 1984, IBM introduced the Enhanced Graphics Adapter (EGA). The EGA can select 16 colors to display at once from a selection of 64; it doesn't flicker; and it has pretty good resolution: 640×350 (almost as good as the monochrome display, which has a resolution of 720×350).

In addition, the EGA could display anything that the CGA or MDA could; it even used the same character set as the monochrome screen. The improvement can be readily seen in the difference in memory size allocated to the CGA, which is 16K, versus the EGA with an allocation of up to 256K.

Then, in April 1987, along with the introduction of the PS/2, the Video Graphics Adapter (VGA) was born. The Video Graphics Adapter can do everything the EGA can do and more. Specifically, of course, there was a tremendous expansion in the numbers of colors that could be displayed. In one (low-resolution) mode, the VGA can display 256 colors at once, chosen from a selection of 256K possibilities. This immense number is slightly qualified by the poor resolution of this mode: only 320 × 200 pixels. Other VGA graphics modes allow higher resolution display (such as 640 × 480), but with a correspondingly fewer number of available colors.

Finally, in late 1990, IBM announced the XGA, with a resolution of 1,024 × 768. Clearly, high-resolution displays had arrived at last. (Note, however, that neither Borland nor Microsoft C compliers support the XGA yet, so we won't work with it.)

Let's put all this together; a list of all the available graphics modes, their resolutions and number of colors appears in Table 4-1.

Mode	Display Lines	Number of Colors	Adapters
0	40×25	B&W text	CGA, EGA, VGA
1	40×25	Color text	CGA, EGA, VGA
2	80×25	B&W text	CGA, EGA, VGA
3	80×25	Color text	CGA, EGA, VGA
4	320×200	4	CGA, EGA, VGA
5	320×200	B&W	CGA, EGA, VGA
6	640×200	2 (on or off)	CGA, EGA, VGA
7	80×25	Monochrome	MDA, EGA, VGA
8	160×200	16	PCjr
9	320×200	16	PCjr
0xa	640×200	1	PCjr
0xb	Reserved for future use.		
0xc	Reserved for future use.		
0xd	320×200	16	EGA, VGA
0xe	640×200	16	EGA, VGA
0xf	640×350	monochrome	EGA, VGA
0x10	640×350	16	EGA, VGA
0x11	640×480	2	VGA
0x12	640×480	16	VGA
0x13	320×200	256	VGA

Table 4-1. All the Screen Modes.

Some of these modes are alphanumeric; that is, they are text modes that don't support graphics (i.e., modes 0–3, and 7). You can still use text as usual in graphics modes, however.

In graphics modes, the cursor will not appear on the screen.

We can see how the modes are partitioned by adapter; Modes 0–6 are used on the CGA (and EGA and VGA, since they're compatible); mode 7 is for the MDA (and EGA and VGA again since they can mimic the MDA); modes 8–0xa were for the PCjr; modes 0xd–0x10 are for the EGA and VGA (here the VGA is emulating the EGA for compatibility). Modes 0x11–0x13 are just for the VGA (mode 0x13 is the 256-color mode):

Mode	Display Adapter		
0	CGA	EGA	VGA
1			
2			
3			
4			
5			
6			
7	MDA		
0xd			
0xe			
0xf			
0x10			
0x11			

Setting Video Modes in Microsoft C

When we use graphics, the first step is often checking what the current video mode is. We can do that with Microsoft C by calling the function **_getvideoconfig( )**. This fills a structure of type **videoconfig** (defined in **graph.h**). We can declare one of these structures simply like this:

```
struct videoconfig myvid;
```

Then we pass the name of our structure to **_getvideoconfig( )** like this:

```
_getvideoconfig(&myvid);
```

All these fields are filled in the structure **myvid** (and they are all ints):

myvid.numxpixels	=	number of pixels on X axis
myvid.numypixels	=	number of pixels on Y axis
myvid.numtextcols	=	number of text columns available
myvid.numtextrows	=	number of text rows available
myvid.numcolors	=	number of actual colors
myvid.bitsperpixel	=	number of bits per pixel
myvid.numvideopages	=	number of available video pages
myvid.mode	=	current video mode
myvid.adapter	=	active display adapter
myvid.monitor	=	active display monitor
myvid.memory	=	adapter video memory in K bytes

TIP

To see what kind of adapter card is in place, check the adapter field of the **videoconfig** structure, **myvid.adapter**, against these constants (the constants are defined in **graph.h**, and you can use them if you include that file):

_MDPA	Monochrome Display Adapter
_CGA	Color Graphics Adapter
_EGA	Enhanced Graphics Adapter
_VGA	Video Graphics Array
_MCGA	MultiColor Graphics Array
_HGC	Hercules Graphics Card

To check what kind of monitor is installed, check the monitor field, myvid.monitor, against these constants:

_MONO	Monochrome
_COLOR	Color (or Enhanced emulating color)
_ENHCOLOR	Enhanced Color
_ANALOGMONO	Analog Monochrome only
_ANALOGCOLOR	Analog Color only
_ANALOG	Analog Monochrome and Color modes

Mode	Description
_DEFAULTMODE	Restore screen to original mode
_TEXTBW40	40-column text, 16-tone gray
_TEXTC40	40-column text, 16/8 color
_TEXTBW80	80-column text, 16-tone gray
_TEXTC80	80-column text, 16/8 color
_MRES4COLOR	320×200, 4 color
_MRESNOCOLOR	320×200, 4 gray
_HRESBW	640×200, BW
_TEXTMONO	80-column text, BW
_HERCMONO	20×348, BW for HGC
_MRES16COLOR	320×200, 16 color
_HRES16COLOR	640×200, 16 color
_ERESNOCOLOR	640×350, BW
_ERESCOLOR	640×350, 4 or 16 color
_VRES2COLOR	640×480, BW
_VRES16COLOR	640×480, 16 color
_MRES256COLOR	320×200, 256 color

Table 4-2. Names of Screen Modes in Microsoft C.

Now let's see if we can't learn how to set the video mode ourselves. The choices of possible video modes that you can use in Microsoft C (and therefore also Quick C) appears in Table 4-2.

To select one of these modes, pass one of these constants to **_setvideomode( )**. For example, in painter.c we set four-color medium CGA resolution with _setvideomode(_MRES4COLOR):

```
#include <stdio.h>
#include <graph.h>

/* painter.c -- a paint program */

main()
{
    int in_key;
    int x_location = 0, y_location = 0, x_top = 0,\
    y_top = 0;
```

```
→          _setvideomode(_MRES4COLOR);

           _setcolor(1);
           while((in_key = getch()) != 'q'){
               :
```

That's all there is to it; just select the video mode you want from Table 4-2, use **_setvideomode( )**, and you're in business. Now that we've set the video mode, we have a range of colors to select from (as indicated in the same table), so the question now becomes: How do we select one of those colors for drawing?

Selecting Colors in Microsoft C

It turns out that selecting a color is as easy as passing a parameter to **_setcolor( )**. These 16 colors are already set up by default in Microsoft C:

_BLACK	_BROWN	_LIGHTRED	_RED
_MAGENTA	_LIGHTCYAN	_CYAN	_LIGHTBLUE
_LIGHTGREEN	_GREEN	_GRAY	_LIGHTYELLOW
_BLUE	_WHITE	_LIGHTMAGENTA	_BRIGHTWHITE

When you include graph.h, these constants are already defined. If you have selected an EGA or VGA mode capable of supporting 16 colors, you can select a color as easily as using **_setcolor( )**, as we've already seen in painter.c:

```
   _setcolor(_RED);
```

This selects the **drawing color**. From now on, all the drawing operations will use this color until we change it.

NOTE You can use these predefined constants even if you are using 256-color VGA mode.

TIP Color mixing is another story: If you want to change the default colors, the EGA is capable of displaying 16 colors at once out of a selection of 64, and the VGA is capable of displaying up to 256 colors out of a selection of 256K. You can set which 16 or 256 colors are available from those ranges by dipping into assembly language and using BIOS interrupt 0x10. For more information, see the appendix in the back of this book.

Palette Number	Color Value 1	Color Value 2	Color Value 3
0	Green	Red	Brown
1	Cyan	Magenta	Light grey
2	Light green	Light red	Yellow
3	Light cyan	Light magenta	White

Table 4-3.   CGA Palettes.

Not all screen modes support 16 colors, however. When you're using an EGA or VGA, there is no problem. But a CGA is a little more complex. In CGA four-color mode, you must select a background color and three foreground colors. Although you can select the background color from the above range of 16 possible choices, you are not free to choose any three foreground colors. You must choose between a choice of four **palettes**. That's the way the CGA works (EGA and VGA modes do not have this drawback).

After you select a palette, the palette colors make up color values 1, 2, and 3 (the background color will make up color value 0). These color values are the values you pass to _setcolor( ) to select the drawing color. Table 4-3 shows the CGA palettes under Microsoft C.

For example, let's say we want to choose CGA palette 1. Reading across, that means that color value 1 would become cyan; color value 2, magenta; and color value 3, light gray. We can select this palette with a call to **_selectpalette( )** like this:

```
_selectpalette(1);
```

Now we can choose drawing colors by passing a color value to **_setcolor( )**. Since we have selected the cyan/magenta/light gray palette, color 1 will be cyan; color 2 will be magenta; and color 3 will be light gray. To draw in magenta, make this call:

```
_setcolor(2);
```

Color values 1–3 are the palette colors, and color value 0 is the background color, which you set with **_setbkcolor( )**. We can choose the background color out of 16 choices above. For example, to make the background color blue, we would use this call:

```
_setbkcolor(_BLUE);
```

TIP It is important to realize that when you select the background color that the whole background changes to that color. In this case, the background will now be blue, no longer black.

Selecting the background color sets color value 0. When you want to draw in the background color (which would be the same as erasing in our paint program), pass a value of 0 to **_setcolor( )**. Now that we have a grasp of how to select a video mode and drawing color in Microsoft C, let's see how that process works in Turbo C.

Setting Video Modes in Turbo C

If we want to set the video mode in Turbo C, we must first make sure that the appropriate **graphics driver** is loaded. (This is a step we didn't need to make in Microsoft C.) To load a graphics driver, we use the **initgraph( )** function. This function is called like this: `initgraph(&grdiver, &grmode, grpath)`. Here, **grdriver** stands for a graphics driver, and there is a different one for each video card, as defined in Table 4-4 (all of these constants may be used as soon as you include the file **graphics.h**). The constant **grmode** defines the actual video mode, as defined in Table 4-5 (these constants may also be used as soon as you include **graphics.h**).

The **grpath** variable is a string indicating where the driver software (which comes with Turbo C since these files have the extension **.BGI**) for the particular monitor is to be found. If the driver software is in the current subdirec-

Graphics Drivers
CGA
MCGA
EGA
EGA64
EGAMONO
IBM8514
HERCMONO
ATT400
VGA
PC3270

Table 4-4. Turbo C Graphics Drivers.

Graphics Modes	Means
CGAC0	320×200 palette 0
CGAC1	320×200 palette 1
CGAC2	320×200 palette 2
CGAC3	320×200 palette 3
CGAHI	640×200
MCGAC0	320×200 palette 0
MCGAC1	320×200 palette 1
MCGAC2	320×200 palette 2
MCGAC3	320×200 palette 3
MCGAMED	640×200
MCGAHI	640×480
EGALO	640×200 16 color
EGAHI	640×350 16 color
EGA64LO	640×200 16 color
EGA64HI	640×350 4 color
EGAMONOHI	640×350
HERCMONOHI	720×348
VGALO	640×200 16 color
VGAMED	640×350 16 color
VGAHI	640×480 16 color

Table 4-5.   Turbo C Graphics Modes.

tory, just set **grpath** to a null string, " ". For example, to load the CGA driver, we might use this code:

```
int g_driver, g_mode;

g_driver = CGA;
g_mode = CGAC3;

initgraph(&g_driver, &g_mode, "");
```

TIP   In Turbo C, you can detect what graphics equipment and mode is currently installed with **detectgraph( )**. The way you call it is like this:

```
detectgraph(&grdriver, &grmode);
```

Both **grdriver** and **grmode** are int variables that you declare yourself. Check the returned value of **grdriver** against the list in Table 4-4, and the value of **grmode** against the value in Table 4-5.

After you've installed the driver software, you do not need to install it again to switch modes. Instead, you can call **setgraphmode( )** to set a new mode (as long as the video monitor supports the requested mode):

```
int g_driver, g_mode;

g_driver = CGA;
g_mode = CGAC3;

initgraph(&g_driver, &g_mode, "");

→    setgraphmode(CGAC3);
```

That's how to select a video mode in Turbo C; now let's see how to select a drawing color.

Selecting Colors in Turbo C

Just as in Microsoft C, there are 16 predefined constants in Turbo C (in graphics.h) for the 16 default colors:

BLACK	RED	DARKGRAY	LIGHTRED
BLUE	MAGENTA	LIGHTBLUE	LIGHTMAGENTA
GREEN	BROWN	LIGHTGREEN	YELLOW
CYAN	LIGHTGRAY	LIGHTCYAN	WHITE

In 16-color modes, you select the current drawing color using **setcolor( )**. For example, if we wanted to draw in brown, we would make this call:

```
setcolor(BROWN);
```

From then on, the drawing color remains brown until we change it. In the four-color CGA mode, we can select the background color (only) from the full choice of 16. For example, to make the background magenta, we would make this call:

```
setbkcolor(MAGENTA);
```

We can select the CGA palette when we set the mode (since the mode constants are defined for each CGA mode). The four palettes used in Turbo C are shown in Table 4-6.

Palette Number	Color Value 1	Color Value 2	Color Value 3
0	Light green	Light red	Yellow
1	Light cyan	Light magenta	White
2	Green	Red	Brown
3	Cyan	Magenta	Light gray

Table 4-6.   CGA Palettes.

For example, to select palette 0, we would set the mode to **CGAC0** like this:

```
setgraphmode(CGAC0);
```

Once we've selected a palette, we've selected colors 1–3. If we wanted to draw in light green (color 1 of palette 0) after making this call, we would simply make this next call to **setcolor**:

```
setcolor(1)
```

That's it; we've seen how to select video modes and drawing colors in both Microsoft and Turbo C. As you can see, it takes a little effort (which is why we didn't discuss it immediately at the beginning of the chapter). But now that we know how to do it, we can let **painter.c** select among the four available CGA colors.

Adding Color to painter.c

Let's use the command 'c' to set colors in **painter.c**. Every time we type 'c', we can increase the current drawing color's color value, 1–3 (0 corresponds to the background color), until we get to 3, after which we can reset it to 1. This way we'll cycle through the available colors.

In addition, note that when we draw in the background color, it's like erasing. This means we can delete images if we add a delete command, 'd'. All 'd' will do is set the color used to 0 (the background color). And that's it; the final program (for Quick C and Microsoft C) appears in Listing 4-1.

Listing 4-1. Microsoft C Version of painter.c.

```c
#include <stdio.h>
#include <graph.h>

/* painter.c -- a paint program */

main()
{
    int in_key, index = 1;
    int x_location = 0, y_location = 0, x_top = 0,\
    y_top = 0;

    _setvideomode(_MRES4COLOR);

    _setcolor(1);

    while((in_key = getch()) != 'q'){
        if (!in_key) in_key = getch() + 128;
        switch (in_key){
            case 208:     /* up arrow */
                y_location++;
                break;
            case 203:     /* left arrow */
                x_location--;
                break;
            case 205:     /* right arrow */
                x_location++;
                break;
            case 200:     /* down arrow */
                y_location--;
                break;
            case 'p':     /* put pixel */
                _setpixel(x_location, y_location);
                _moveto(x_location, y_location);
                x_top = x_location;
                y_top = y_location;
                break;
            case 'l':     /* draw line */
                _lineto(x_location, y_location);
                break;
            case 'r':     /* draw rectangle */
                _rectangle(_GBORDER, x_top, y_top, \
                    x_location,  y_location);
                break;
            case 'e':     /* draw ellipse */
                _ellipse(_GBORDER, x_top, y_top, \
```

(continued)

Listing 4-1. *(continued)*

```
                            x_location,  y_location);
                        break;
                  case 'f':      /* fill */
                      _floodfill(x_location,  y_location, 1);
                      break;
→               case 'c':      /* change color */
→                   (index >= 3 ? index = 1 : index++);
→                   _setcolor(index);
→                   break;
→               case 'd':      /* delete */
→                   _setcolor(0);
→                   break;
                  default:
                      ;
            }
        }

        return(0);
    }
```

For almost every subject in this book, Microsoft C and Turbo C will overlap
well enough not to be considered as separate. However, graphics is an exception. As we've seen, we have to load a graphics driver, select modes, and make
different calls in Turbo C. For that reason, we can write **painter.c** in Turbo C,
and that program appears in Listing 4-2.

Listing 4-2. Turbo C Version of painter.c.

```
#include <stdio.h>
#include <graphics.h>

main()
{
    int in_key, index = 1;
    int x_location = 0, y_location = 0, x_top = 0, y_top = 0;
    int g_driver, g_mode;

    g_driver = CGA;
    g_mode = CGAC3;

    initgraph(&g_driver, &g_mode, "");

    setgraphmode(CGAC3);
```

Listing 4-2. *(continued)*

```
setcolor(1);

while((in_key = getch()) != 'q'){
    if (!in_key) in_key = getch() + 128;
    switch (in_key){
        case 208:      /* up arrow */
            y_location++;
            break;
        case 203:      /* left arrow */
            x_location--;
            break;
        case 205:      /* right arrow */
            x_location++;
            break;
        case 200:      /* down arrow */
            y_location--;
            break;
        case 'p':      /* put pixel */
            putpixel(x_location, y_location,1);
            moveto(x_location, y_location);
            x_top = x_location;
            y_top = y_location;
            break;
        case 'l':      /* draw line */
            lineto(x_location, y_location);
            break;
        case 'r':      /* draw a rectangle */
            rectangle(x_top, y_top, x_location,\
            y_location);
            break;
        case 'e':      /* draw ellipse */
            ellipse((x_top + x_location)/2,      \
                (y_top + y_location)/2, 0, 360, \
                abs(x_location - x_top)/2,       \
                abs(y_location - y_top)/2);
            break;
        case 'f':      /* fill */
            floodfill(x_location,  y_location, 1);
            break;
        case 'c':      /* change color */
            (index >= 3 ? index = 1 : index++);
            setcolor(index);
            break;
        case 'd':      /* delete */
```

(continued)

Listing 4-2. *(continued)*

```
                    setcolor(0);
                    break;
                default:
                    ;
        }
    }

    return(0);
}
```

And that's it for **painter.c**. We've seen how to start up the graphics system, set pixels on the screen, draw lines, rectangles, and ellipses, as well as select the drawing color and even erase mistakes. We've come very far in graphics, in just one short chapter. Now, however, let's go even farther with another very popular topic, screen animation.

Animation with Getimage( ) and Putimage( )

There are many things you can do with graphics images, and surely one of the most attractive is animation. We can do that in Microsoft C with **_getimage( )** and **_putimage( )** (Turbo: **getimage( )** and **putimage( )**). If we store images and then restore them, we can animate action on the screen.

In order to store an image, all you have to do is pass **_getimage( )** the upper, left-hand coordinates, the lower, right-hand coordinates, and the address of the area in memory to store it. Once it's in memory we can pop it back on the screen when required with **_putimage( )**.

We'll need to set aside memory space to store images. How much space is required for a graphics image? It turns out that we can just use the **_imagesize( )** (Turbo: **imagesize( )**) function. Just pass the coordinates of the image on the screen (i.e., four integers), and **_imagesize( )** will return the number of bytes needed to store the image. Next, we'll have to set up some space in memory to store our images in.

To store that image, we could set up, say, a large array that would handle any size image in our program. However, such a method is wasteful of memory: If we planned for any size image and the image turned out to be tiny, much of the memory space would be unused. If we use **_imagesize( )**, we won't really know how much memory we need until the program runs.

C has a number of special functions, however, that are specifically designed to let us manage memory as our program runs. One of them is named **malloc( )**, for memory allocation. In this way, C allows us to allocate memory **dynamically** — on the fly, matching the needs of our program. This is an enormously popular function, and we'll study it in detail when we cover memory use in Chapter 7. However, we can get an introduction to it right now. In C, the usual method is to refer to allocated memory spaces with a pointer. For example, we could set up a pointer to a byte like this:

```
char *images;
```

This is a pointer to a byte, as yet uninitialized. Now we can use **malloc( )**. When we ask it for a specific number of bytes of memory — let's say 100 — it returns a pointer to the newly allocated memory. We can assign that pointer to the pointer images like this:

```
        char *images;

  →     images = malloc(100);
```

Now we have a pointer to (that is, the address of) the block of memory allocated to us:

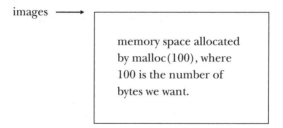

That address is exactly what we have to pass to the **_getimage( )** function to store an image in memory, so let's get started. In particular, let's say that our image on the screen goes from location (0, 0) to (150, 150). We can use **_imagesize( )** to get the number of bytes we'll need and simultaneously assign that memory to our pointer like this, using **malloc( )**:

```
        char *images;

  →     images = malloc(_imagesize(0, 0, 150, 150));
```

Now we know how to set up the memory space we'll need; let's put animation into action by writing a program that draws a succession of multicolored rectangles on the screen, stores each image in memory, and then replays them. We can call it animate.c.

We have to start **animate.c** by setting the graphics mode. Since we are drawing in different colors this time, let's use a 16- color, 640×350 mode, like **_ERES-COLOR** (in Turbo, this would be EGAHI):

```
#include <stdio.h>
#include <graph.h>

main()
{

→    _setvideomode(_ERESCOLOR);
                   :
                   :
}
```

Next, we have to set aside memory space for our images. Let's generate rectangles inside the region $(0, 0)$ to $(50, 50)$. In fact, we can use all available EGA colors, creating 16 rectangles of steadily expanding sizes, and then flash them one by one on the screen as our animation example. We can get the size requirements for 16 rectangles from **_imagesize( )** and use **malloc( )** all at once:

```
#define MAXX 50
#define MAXY 50
#include <stdio.h>
#include <graph.h>
#include <malloc.h> /* Borland products:\
                       include alloc.h instead. */

main()
{
→            char *images;

      _setvideomode(_ERESCOLOR);

→            images = malloc(16 * _imagesize\
             (0, 0, MAXX, MAXY));
                :
                :
}
```

The #define Directive

Note that we've used the **#define** compiler directive to define two constants here, **MAXX** and **MAXY**. That's what **#define** does: It allows us to define constants. From now on, when the compiler sees **MAXX** or **MAXY**, it will replace them with 50. We did it this way so that it would make it easy for us to change the size of our rectangle if we wanted to. We'd only have to change **MAXX** and **MAXY** in one place: at the beginning of the program.

TIP The C style is to capitalize the names of constants like **MAXX** and **MAXY**. If you see what appear to be variable names capitalized in a C program, look around for a **#define** statement. If you see one, the names are probably constants.

Now we have to include a variable to hold the color value (0–15) and enter our drawing loop. We'll use a **for** loop, and, each time through, we can increase the size of our rectangle like this:

```
#define MAXX 50
#define MAXY 50
#include <stdio.h>
#include <graph.h>
#include <malloc.h> /* Borland products:\
                    include alloc.h instead. */

main()
{
    char *images;
→        int colorval, x = MAXX/16, y = MAXY/16;

    _setvideomode(_ERESCOLOR);

    images = malloc(16 * _imagesize(0, 0, MAXX, MAXY));

→        for(colorval = 0; colorval < 16;\
         colorval++, x+= MAXX/16, y+= MAXY/16){
→            _setcolor(colorval);
→            _rectangle(_GBORDER, 0, 0, x, y);
    }

    return(0);
}
```

We also want to save our images, so we use **_getimage( )**. To do that, we have to pass it the screen coordinates of the image, as well as the memory address at which to save that image. Memory addresses in C are just pointers, so we can pass the pointer we've already named **images**. Note that to avoid writing over an image, we'll have to point to successively later places in memory, which means that we can update **images** like this each time through the loop:

```
#define MAXX 50
#define MAXY 50
#include <stdio.h>
#include <graph.h>

main()
{
    char *images;
    int colorval, x = MAXX/16, y = MAXY/16;

    _setvideomode(_ERESCOLOR);

    images = malloc(16 * _imagesize(0, 0, MAXX, MAXY));

    for(colorval = 0; colorval < 16; colorval++,\
    x+= MAXX/16, y+= MAXY/16){
        _setcolor(colorval);
        _rectangle(_GBORDER, 0, 0, x, y);
        _getimage(0, 0, MAXX, MAXY, images);
→       images += _imagesize(0, 0, MAXX, MAXY);
    }

    return(0);
}
```

Now that the images are stored, we blank the screen with _clearscreen(_GCLEARSCREEN) (Turbo: cleardevice( ) with no parameters) and then put them back, one by one. We can add a pointer named start to get the images back (i.e., we've already incremented the pointer-named images to the end of the allocated memory space when we stored the images). This new pointer will point to the current image; every time through the retrieval loop, we can get an image and then increment the pointer by the size of that image to point to the next one:

```
#define MAXX 50
#define MAXY 50
#include <stdio.h>
#include <graph.h>
#include <malloc.h>

main()
{
    char *images, *start;
    int colorval, x = MAXX/16, y = MAXY/16;
    int size;

    _setvideomode(_ERESCOLOR);

    images = malloc(16 * _imagesize(0, 0, MAXX, MAXY));
    start = images;

    for(colorval = 0; colorval < 16; colorval++,\
    x+= MAXX/16, y+= MAXY/16){
        _setcolor(colorval);
        _rectangle(_GBORDER, 0, 0, x, y);
        _getimage(0, 0, MAXX, MAXY, images);
        images += _imagesize(0, 0, MAXX, MAXY);
    }

    _clearscreen(_GCLEARSCREEN);

    for(colorval = 0; colorval < 16; colorval++){
        _putimage(0, 0, start, 0);
        start += _imagesize(0, 0, MAXX, MAXY);
    }

    return(0);
}
```

That's it. When you run the program, the rectangles appear, each one larger than the last. After the last colored rectangle appears, the screen is cleared, and the sequence repeats. The second time, however, we are retrieving the images from memory and playing them back.

Of course, there are other images that we could animate besides rectangles. Let's take a look at one last graphics program before leaving the subject.

Graphics Viewports

Let's say we wanted to draw a stick figure on the screen:

```
(0,0)xxxx
      x    x
       xxxx  (6,6)
        x
       xx(4,8)
      x x x
     x   x   x
(0,14)x   x    x(8,14)
       x x
      x   x
     x       x
(0,25)x        x(8,25)
```

We could draw this figure easily with the **_moveto( )** and **_lineto( )** functions, using these statements:

```c
#include <stdio.h>
#include <graph.h>

main()
{
    _setvideomode(_MRES4COLOR);
    _ellipse(_GFILLINTERIOR, 0, 0, 6, 6);
    _moveto(4,8);
    _lineto(0,14);
    _moveto(4,8);
    _lineto(8,14);
    _moveto(4,8);
    _lineto(4,14);
    _lineto(0,25);
    _moveto(4,8);
    _lineto(8,25);

    return(0);
}
```

If we wanted to animate the figure, we could then add the next image:

```
    (0,0)xxxx
        x    x
        xxxx (6,6)
         x
        xx(4,8)
        x x  x
        x x   x
(2,14) x x     x(10,14)
        x  x
        x   x
        x    x
  (4,25) x       x(12,25)
```

In code, that would look like this:

```c
#include <stdio.h>
#include <graph.h>

main()
{
    _setvideomode(_MRES4COLOR);
    _ellipse(_GFILLINTERIOR, 0, 0, 6, 6);
    _moveto(4,8);
    _lineto(0,14);
    _moveto(4,8);
    _lineto(8,14);
    _moveto(4,8);
    _lineto(4,14);
    _lineto(0,25);
    _moveto(4,8);
    _lineto(8,25);

    _moveto(4,8);
    _lineto(2,14);
    _moveto(4,8);
    _lineto(10,14);
    _moveto(4,8);
    _lineto(4,14);
    _lineto(4,25);
    _moveto(4,8);
    _lineto(12,25);

    return(0);
}
```

Now that we have our code for drawing two images of the figure, we could store both images and alternate them across the screen (passing different coordinates to **_putimage( )**) and create the illusion that the figure is walking.

However, there is another way to do the same thing; we can use **viewports**. In Microsoft and Turbo C, we can define a viewport on the screen, which is an area like this:

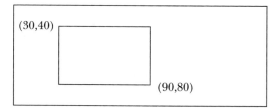

If we pass these coordinates to **_setviewport( )** (Turbo: **setviewport( )**), then this area becomes the only active area on the screen. Attempting to draw outside it does nothing. The top, left-hand corner of the viewport becomes the new (0,0):

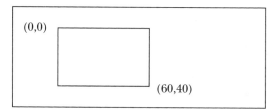

NOTE   Keep in mind that once you set a viewport, you will not be able to draw outside it.

Since the origin is set every time we set the viewport, we can move our figure across the screen simply by using **_setviewport( )**, like this:

```
#include <stdio.h>
#include <graph.h>

main()
```

```
{
    int i;

    _setvideomode(_MRES4COLOR);

    for (i = 0; i < 100; i++){
        _setviewport(100-i , 0, 125 - i, 25);      ←
        _ellipse(_GFILLINTERIOR, 0, 0, 6, 6);
        _moveto(4,8);
        _lineto(0,14);
        _moveto(4,8);
        _lineto(8,14);
        _moveto(4,8);
        _lineto(4,14);
        _lineto(0,25);
        _moveto(4,8);
        _lineto(8,25);

        _clearscreen(_GCLEARSCREEN);

        _moveto(4,8);
        _lineto(2,14);
        _moveto(4,8);
        _lineto(10,14);
        _moveto(4,8);
        _lineto(4,14);
        _lineto(4,25);
        _moveto(4,8);
        _lineto(12,25);

        _clearscreen(_GCLEARSCREEN);
    }

    return(0);
}
```

That's all there is to it. If you run this program, a one-inch high figure appears to run across the screen from right to left. What is happening is that as we continue to draw the figure on the screen, we are also shifting the screen coordinates with _setviewport( ). The origin of the screen moves across the screen, and our figure — defined with respect to that origin — moves along with it.

That's it for graphics. There are topics we didn't cover. Graphics itself could make up a book. For example, you can use various graphic fonts under either

Microsoft or Turbo C (but they are a little complex to use, and their use varies significantly between compilers). Nonetheless, we've gotten a good introduction to the subject.

In fact, now that we know something about some of the C library functions, let's take a look at more of them in Chapter 5.

Using Files in C

We've come far already. We've written many good programs. But we have yet to produce anything permanent in the computer, something that will last after we turn the machine off. Certainly, unless computers allowed us to store data in some such permanent fashion, we'd be in trouble. Of course, we can store data on computer disks in the form of **files**, and that's what this chapter is about. Working with files is integral to programming, and the file-handling capabilities in C are good. In fact, the selection of library functions is almost too good: Sometimes it's hard to wade through all the choices available, as we'll see. Let's start by seeing how C approaches the whole idea of files.

Streams and Files in C

C places a large emphasis on **portability**, on code that can be transferred between different types of computers without many changes. This is one of C's selling points over assembly language. C is portable between different computers to a large extent, and assembly language is definitely not (since it is the native language of the central processor itself).

However, the actual details of different computers can differ enormously — how to work with monitors, keyboards, disk files, printers, or even tape drives — and that makes it difficult for a language that seeks to be completely

Stream	Is Connected To
stdout	The screen
stdin	The keyboard
stprn	The printer
stdaux	The screen
stderr	The screen

Table 5-1.   Standard Streams and Their Physical Connections.

portable. For that reason, C's input/output (I/O) system disconnects us from many of the details of the actual devices.

Theoretically, C's I/O functions work on **streams** of data. Streams may then be connected to actual devices, which C calls **files** (in this sense, a C file really stands for a physical device). A stream is a sequence of data, and there are two kinds of streams: text streams, which are streams of ASCII characters, and binary streams, which are streams of raw bytes. Most of the C I/O functions are intended to operate on streams, and the streams are flexible because they can be assigned to different actual devices. In fact, some of these connections are already made for us; when we start our program, five standard streams are set up and connected to various physical devices already, and we will find them in Table 5-1.

Again theoretically, C's I/O funtions are designed to work on streams such as these. For example, **printf( )** is actually the short form of **fprintf( )**; **fprintf( )** is designed to work with any stream; and **printf( )** is dedicated to working with the **stdout** — that is, screen — stream (because printing on the screen is so common). As an example, the following program uses **fprintf( )** in the same way we'd use **printf( )**: to print on the screen. To use **fprintf( )**, we specify the **stdout** stream, which is already connected to the screen:

```
        #include <stdio.h>

        main()
        {
→           fprintf(stdout, "Hello, world.\n");

            return(0);
        }
```

When we work with a disk file in this chapter, we'll associate a stream with it by *opening* that file. Then we'll be able to print to that file with **fprintf( )**, which allows us to choose what stream we want to print to (as opposed to **printf( )**, which does not). Now let's see how all this works in practice.

A File Writing Example

In a practical sense, we've already learned much that we need to know about the C I/O system. The only difference here is that we're going to use the I/O functions that can be associated with a particular stream instead of those that use streams already connected to physical devices.

In many cases, the C functions that let us specify a stream are just the versions we're familiar with, prefixed with an 'f': **scanf( )** becomes **fscanf( )**; **getc( )** (get character) becomes **fgetc( )**; and **printf( )** becomes **fprintf( )**. Let's try a small program immediately. This program writes our "Hello, world.\n" string to a disk file named **hello.txt**:

```c
#include <stdio.h>

main()
{
    FILE *file_pointer;

    if((file_pointer = fopen("hello.txt", "w")) != NULL){
        fprintf(file_pointer, "Hello, world.\n");
        fclose(file_pointer);
    }
    else printf("Error writing hello.txt\n");

    return(0);
}
```

When you run the program, you'll find a 15-byte file named **hello.txt** on the disk, and typing it reveals our message. Here's the way it works. First we include the I/O function header **stdio.h**. Next, we associate a stream with a physical file by opening that file for writing with the function **fopen( )**:

```c
#include <stdio.h>

main()
{
    FILE *file_pointer;
```

File-opening Option	Means
"r"	Open (existing) file for reading
"w"	Open (create if necessary) file for writing
"a"	Open (create if necessary) file for appending
"r+"	Open (existing) file for reading and writing
"w+"	Create and open file for reading and writing
"a+"	Open (create if necessary) file for reading and appending
"rb"	Open a binary file for reading
"wb"	Open a binary file for writing
"ab"	Open a binary file for appending
"rt"	Open a text file for reading
"wt"	Create a text file for writing
"at"	Open a text file for appending
"r+b"	Open a binary file for reading and writing
"w+b"	Create a binary file for writing
"a+b"	Open a binary file for appending
"r+t"	Open a text file for reading and writing
"w+t"	Create a text file for reading and writing
"a+t"	Open a text file for reading and writing

Table 5-2. File Opening Options.

```
→       if((file_pointer = fopen("hello.txt", "w")) != NULL){
            fprintf(file_pointer,"Hello, world.\n");
            fclose(file_pointer);
        }
        else printf("Error writing hello.txt\n");

        return(0);
    }
```

The **fopen( )** function does the work of associating a stream with the actual disk file **hello.txt**. Here we specify both the name of the file ("**hello.txt**") and the fact that we intend to write to it (by including the character string "**w**"). There are many file-opening options with the **fopen( )** function, and you will find them in Table 5-2.

The **fopen( )** function returns a pointer to a structure of type FILE, which we name **file_pointer**. In other words, the name of our stream is **file_pointer**, and it is connected to the the disk file **hello.txt** (much as stdout is connected to the screen):

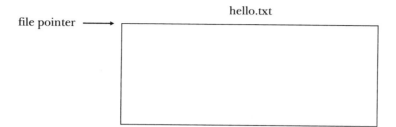

Since the internal makeup of the FILE structure is handled by the file functions themselves, we won't concern ourselves with it here. All we need is the file pointer.

If the file could not be opened, a **NULL pointer** is returned. **NULL** is a predefined constant in C (its value is 0), and we can check for it. In that case, the program should terminate and print an error message. Let's also note the typical economy of C here. We can both assign the file pointer to . **file_pointer** and check its value in the same statement (this is the usual way of opening files in C):

```
if((file_pointer = fopen("hello.txt", "w")) != NULL){
```

If you had wanted to specify a pathname for the file, for example, `c:\hello.txt`, note that we should make the string in the **fopen( )** call `"c:\\hello.txt"`, since a single backslash would be interpreted as part of an escape sequence otherwise.

On the other hand, if the file was opened successfully, we want to write the data string to it. Since we are familiar with **printf( )**, let's use its analog, **fprintf( )**. We have to include a format string, as usual, as well as the stream to write to. This means that we have to pass **fprintf( )** the file pointer for the file we want to use. In this case, that's **file_pointer**:

```
#include <stdio.h>

main()
{
    FILE *file_pointer;

    if((file_pointer = fopen("hello.txt", "w")) != NULL){
```

→
```
            fprintf(file_pointer, "Hello, world.\n");
            fclose(file_pointer);
    }
    else printf("Error writing hello.txt\n");

    return(0);
}
```

The **fprintf( )** function does the work for us:

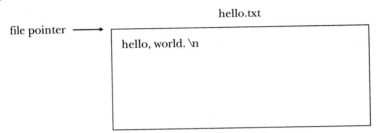

hello.txt

file pointer ⟶

hello, world. \n

Following it, we close the file (so that DOS may update the file's directory information). To close a file, all you need to do is to pass the file pointer to the **fclose( )** function, and that function disconnects the stream we've opened from the actual disk file. That's all there is to it. We've written our first disk file.

A File Reading Example

In a similar way, now that we have the file **hello.txt** on the disk, we can read it in and print it out. The easiest way to read a string from the file is to use **fgets( )**, the counterpart of **gets( )** — get string. We also have to provide storage space for the string in memory, and we can use a string called **temp[ ]** for that purpose. Here, then, is our reading program:

```
#include <stdio.h>

main()
{
    FILE *file_pointer;
    char temp[80];

    if((file_pointer = fopen("hello.txt", "r")) != NULL){
        if(fgets(temp, sizeof(temp), file_pointer) != NULL){
            printf("%s", temp);                    /* print string */
            fclose(file_pointer);
        }
```

```
            else printf("Error reading hello.txt\n"); /* error */
      }
      else printf("Error opening hello.txt\n");        /* error */

      return(0);
}
```

First, we define **temp[ ]**, the buffer for the file's data, and open the file:

```
      #include <stdio.h>

      main()
      {
          FILE *file_pointer;
→         char temp[80];

→         if((file_pointer = fopen("hello.txt", "r")) != NULL){
                  ... get string and print it ...
          }
→         else printf("Error opening hello.txt\n");

          return(0);
      }
```

If we cannot open the file, we print an error message. If we can open the file, our next step is to read the data in. Since our data is simply a character string, we can use **fgets( )**, file get string, which is tailor-made for us. The **fgets( )** function requires three arguments: a pointer to a string buffer; the length of the string buffer in memory; and a file pointer.

The name of an array is really a pointer. This means that the pointer to the buffer in memory is really just the name **temp**. As far as the length of the buffer in memory goes, we know that C treats a character string like **temp[80]** as an array, so we can easily find the size of an array (if we did not already know it was 80) with the **sizeof( )** operator. Finally, the file pointer here is simply **file_pointer**. Here, then, is how we get the string from the file and put it into **temp[ ]**:

```
      #include <stdio.h>

      main()
      {
          FILE *file_pointer;
          char temp[80];

          if ((file_pointer = fopen("hello.txt", "r")) != NULL){
```

```
→                        if((fgets(temp, sizeof(temp), file_pointer))\
                         != NULL){
                                  ... print string and close file ...
                         }
→                        else printf("Error reading hello.txt\n");
                  }
                  else printf("Error opening hello.txt\n");

                  return(0);
           }
```

Note that if **fgets( )** fails, it returns a **NULL** pointer, and in our program we print out an error message. All that remains is to print the string now in **temp[ ]** and to close the file. We can do that easily, and our program is done:

```
           #include <stdio.h>

           main()
           {
               FILE *file_pointer;
               char temp[80];

               if((file_pointer = fopen("hello.txt", "r")) != NULL){
                   if((fgets(temp, sizeof(temp), file_pointer))\
                   != NULL){
→                      printf("%s", temp);            /* print string */
→                      fclose(file_pointer);
                   }
                   else printf("Error reading hello.txt\n");\
                   /* error */
               }
               else printf("Error opening hello.txt\n");\
               /* error */

               return(0);
           }
```

Give it a try. The program will open **hello.txt** and print the contents of the file out on the screen. Now we've been able to read in a file that we also created. However, we may not always know the size of the file we're reading, or we may not know that it contains exactly one character string, as we knew here. Let's move from these specific examples to the more general case, where we'll read in from a file until we reach the end of file. After that, we'll go to an even lower level, where the functions we use simply return the number of bytes they've read, and we won't search for the end of the file at all.

The EOF Marker

When you read a file in byte by byte, you will eventually reach the end of the file. When that happens, the next thing you read is the end-of-file marker (in C, this is an integer with the value 0xffff). This mark is not actually at the end of files; it's just returned by the C file-reading functions to inform you that there is nothing more to read from the file.

Here's a program that demonstrates the use of the EOF mark:

```c
#include <stdio.h>

main()
{
    int buff1;
    FILE *file_pointer;

    if(file_pointer = fopen("hello.txt", "r")){
        while((buff1 = fgetc(file_pointer)) != EOF)
            printf("%c", buff1);
        printf("\n");
        fclose(file_pointer);
    }
    else printf("Couldn't open hello.txt\n");

    return(0);
}
```

This program is like our earlier reading program. It too reads in the file **hello.txt** and prints it out on the screen, but this program does it byte by byte, not relying on the fact that there is only one character string in the file. We've already seen the functions **getch( )** and **getche( )**, which read individual bytes. However, they are tied to the stream already connected to the keyboard (**stdin**). The version that lets us specify the stream ourselves is **fgetc( )**. Using **fgetc( )**, we just keep going with a while loop until the read-in character is the end-of-file, or EOF, marker:

```c
#include <stdio.h>

main()
{
    int buff1;
    FILE *file_pointer;

    if(file_pointer = fopen("hello.txt", "r")){
```

```
→        while((buff1 = fgetc(file_pointer)) != EOF)
→            printf("%c", buff1);
→        printf("\n");
→        fclose(file_pointer);
    }
    else printf("Couldn't open hello.txt\n");

    return(0);
}
```

TIP   Notice that the variable we fill when we read in from the file, **buff1**, is declared as an integer, and not a char variable. This is important. Using an integer-sized variable lets us accept and test values that can include the EOF mark, even if we only read in one byte at a time. The reason for this is that the EOF mark is one word long, not one byte long. In order to test **buff1** against EOF, **buff1** must be an int.

So far, we've learned that we can write files, and we can read them. When we read them, C will tell us when there is no more data to be read by passing us the EOF mark. However, we still don't have a good feel for the internal structure of a file. Some programs format the files they write under all circumstances. Does C? Can we store, say, a data structure in a file and retrieve it? Can we section a file up into records? Let's examine the answers to those questions next.

Binary and ASCII Files in C

The C language treats files in two different ways: as either ASCII files or as binary files. If you specify that a file is to be treated as a binary file, C does not interpret the file's contents when it reads or writes data to or from it. In this case, the data in the file is just data, nothing more. (Soon we are going to write a program that copies one file over into another, and we'll treat the files as binary so C doesn't do anything fancy.)

ASCII files are not radically different. In fact, there are only two differences. First, if C finds a ^Z (ASCII 26) in the file when it's reading, it treats the ^Z as an end-of-file character and assumes the end of the file has been reached. (Although C does not write these characters at the end of ASCII files, you can explicitly put them in.) The second difference is that on the disk, the newline character '\n' is stored as an ASCII 13 10 (ASCII <carriage return> and <line feed>), and in memory it is stored only in C's internal format for an end-of-line character, 10 alone (ASCII <lf>).

The fact that C stores newline characters internally as only ASCII 10 and on the disk (in ASCII format) as 13 10 has some interesting consequences. When we wrote our original string "Hello, world.\n" out to disk, the file was 15 bytes long:

$$H \quad e \quad l \quad l \quad o \quad , \quad \quad w \quad o \quad r \quad l \quad d \quad . \quad 13\ 10$$
$$\longleftarrow \text{———— 15 bytes ————} \longrightarrow \qquad \text{(ASCII Mode)}$$

That's because the default file mode is ASCII. If we wrote the string out to match what's in memory (in other words, in binary mode), we'd get a file that's only 14 bytes long, since the ASCII 13 is missing:

$$H \quad e \quad l \quad l \quad o \quad , \quad \quad w \quad o \quad r \quad l \quad d \quad . \quad 10$$
$$\longleftarrow \text{———— 14 bytes ————} \longrightarrow \qquad \text{(Binary Mode)}$$

To read and write in binary format, it's only necessary to add "b" to the option string passed to **fopen( )**. For example, here's our first file-writing program converted to write a binary (i.e., uninterpreted) version of the string in memory (note the `"wb"` instead of the `"w"`):

```
#include <stdio.h>

main()
{
    FILE *file_pointer;

    if((file_pointer = fopen("hello.txt", "wb")) != NULL){
        fprintf(file_pointer, "Hello, world.\n");
        fclose(file_pointer);
    }
    else printf("Error writing hello.txt\n");

    return(0);
}
```

When we run *this* program, **hello.txt** ends up being 14 bytes long on the disk.

NOTE The reason "**\n**" is stored internally as only **10** is because Unix — the operating system that fostered C — does it that way. The **13** is added in disk files so that when you type a file out at DOS level, it will print correctly on the screen.

When do you use ASCII format and when do you use binary format? If you are dealing with only strings, as we have been doing until now, it is best to use only ASCII format (once you pick one format, stick with it throughout the entire program). On the other hand, if you want a literal copy of a disk file (e.g., to copy it), use binary format. Now that we've got a handle on of files, let's press on to see how we can structure them inside.

File Records

Most languages let you write files in what are called **records**. Data files, for example, are commonly made up of records. Let's say you had an account book that you wanted to keep track of on your computer. One "record" might look like this:

```
Name: "Bob Crachit"
Owes: $312.59
```

There is both an ASCII string and a floating point number in such a record. In C, we might put together a data structure for this record like this:

```
struct entry
{
    char[20] name;
    float owes;
}
```

Writing File Records

In order to store such structures, we can build a file of them, one after the next; that's how records are used in data files:

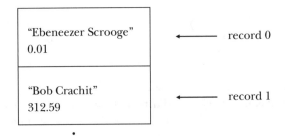

Let's give it a try by writing a short program called **writer.c** to write these records to a file. We can start by setting up an array of **array** of **struct entry**:

```
#include <stdio.h>
#define INDEX 15

struct entry{
    char name[20];
    float owes;
}

main()
{
    FILE *file_pointer;
→   struct entry my_data[INDEX];
        :
```

Next, let's put data into our array:

```
#include <stdio.h>
#define INDEX 15

struct entry{
    char name[20];
    float owes;
}

main()
{
    FILE *file_pointer;
    struct entry my_data[INDEX];

→      strcpy(my_data[0].name,"Ebeneezer Scrooge");
→      my_data[0].owes = 0.01;
→      strcpy(my_data[1].name,"Bob Crachit");
→      my_data[1].owes = 312.59;
            :
```

Now we can write these records to a file. Instead of **fprintf( )** (which demands a format string), let's use the two file functions **fwrite( )** and **fread( )**. These two functions are really the basis of writing data to, or reading data from files in C. That is, the most common file functions programmers use are **fopen( )**, **fread( )**, **fwrite( )**, and **fclose( )**, all of which adhere to the ANSI standard. In our case, we can write our data out to a file named **writer.dat** like this:

```
#include <stdio.h>
#define INDEX 15

struct entry{
    char name[20];
    float owes;
}

main()
{
    FILE *file_pointer;
    struct entry my_data[INDEX];

    strcpy(my_data[0].name,"Ebeneezer Scrooge");
    my_data[0].owes = 0.01;
    strcpy(my_data[1].name,"Bob Crachit");
    my_data[1].owes = 312.59;

    if((file_pointer = fopen("writer.dat", "w")) != NULL)
        fwrite(my_data, sizeof(struct entry), INDEX,\
        file_pointer);
    else printf("Error writing writer.dat\n");
                    :
}
```

Finally, we close the file:

```
#include <stdio.h>
#define INDEX 15

struct entry{
    char name[20];
    float owes;
}

main()
{
    FILE *file_pointer;
    struct entry my_data[INDEX];

    strcpy(my_data[0].name,"Ebeneezer Scrooge");
    my_data[0].owes = 0.01;
    strcpy(my_data[1].name,"Bob Crachit");
    my_data[1].owes = 312.59;

    if((file_pointer = fopen("writer.dat", "w")) != NULL)
        fwrite(my_data, sizeof(struct entry), INDEX,\
        file_pointer);
```

```
       else printf("Error writing writer.dat\n");

→       fclose(file_pointer);

       return(0);
}
```

Now we've written our data to the file **writer.dat** on disk. It's about 360 bytes long, and contains 15 records. We've written our data file. Now it's time to read it.

Reading File Records

We can read **writer.dat** in and print out the first two records. All we need to do is to develop a program that uses **fread( )** instead of **fwrite( )**, and open the file for reading, not writing. Here is the new program, which we might call **reader.c**:

```
       #include <stdio.h>
       #define INDEX 15

       struct entry{
           char name[20];
           float owes;
       }

       main()
       {
           FILE *file_pointer;
           struct entry my_data[INDEX];

→          if((file_pointer = fopen("writer.dat", "r")) != NULL)
→              fread(my_data, sizeof(struct entry), INDEX,\
                   file_pointer);
               else printf("Error reading writer.dat\n");

→          printf("%s owes $%.2f\n", my_data[0].name,\
               my_data[0].owes);
→          printf("%s owes $%.2f\n", my_data[1].name,\
               my_data[1].owes);

           fclose(file_pointer);

           return(0);
       }
```

When you run this new program, it does just the reverse of the earlier one. It opens **writer.dat** and reads it in and then prints out the first two (formatted) records.

Of course, if you had 3,000 such entries, it would be more difficult to read them all in at once and to provide memory space for each one. The C language uses something called a **position pointer** inside a file to solve this problem. With it, we can position ourselves inside the file and read whatever record we want. In that case, since we're only reading one record at a time, we only need to provide memory storage for that record.

The File Position Pointer

Let's say we had a file filled with data like this:

data data data data data data data data data data	Record 0
data data data data data data data data data data	Record 1
data data data data data data data data data data	Record 2
data data data data data data data data data data	Record 3

In this case, we can use the position pointer in the file to position ourselves wherever we want:

position pointer ⟶

data data data data data data data data data data	Record 0
data data data data data data data data data data	Record 1
data data data data data data data data data data	Record 2
data data data data data data data data data data	Record 3

Originally, it's at the beginning of the file, but you can place it anywhere you want with a function called **fseek( )**, like this:

TIP You can also return the position pointer to the beginning of the file with a function called **rewind( )**, passing it the file pointer.

The position pointer is the new location from which, or to which, data is read or written. Let's put this information to work. We could rewrite our program **writer.c** to fill only record number 9, like this:

```c
#include <stdio.h>
#define INDEX 15

struct entry{
    char name[20];
    float owes;
}

main()
{
    FILE *file_pointer;
    struct entry my_data[INDEX];

→   strcpy(my_data[9].name,"Ebeneezer Scrooge");
→   my_data[9].owes = 0.01;

    if((file_pointer = fopen("writer.dat", "w")) != NULL)
        fwrite(my_data, sizeof(struct entry), INDEX,\
        file_pointer);
    else printf("Error writing writer.dat\n");
```

```
        fclose(file_pointer);

        return(0);
    }
```

Our new version of **writer.dat** contains all uninitialized records, except for record 9. Now we want to read that record from the file. This is a common problem in database programs: How would you read, say, record 37281 in a file of 93,829 records?

Using **fseek( )** to position ourselves in **writer.dat**, the solution is easy. We can modify **reader.c** — the program that reads data from **writer.dat** — so it only has memory space for one record, uses **fseek( )** to set the position pointer in the file, and reads in only one record at a time. We can ask the user which record to read, and store that value in **rec_num**. The we just use **fseek( )** like this:

```
        #include <stdio.h>
        #include <io.h>
        #define INDEX 15

        struct entry{
            char name[20];
            float owes;
        }

        main()
        {
            FILE *file_pointer;
→           struct entry buffer;
            int rec_num;

            if((file_pointer = fopen("writer.dat", "r")) != NULL){
                printf("Type the record number to recover: ");
                scanf("%d",&rec_num);
→               fseek(file_pointer, (long)\
                (rec_num*sizeof(struct entry)), 0);
                fread(&buffer, sizeof(struct entry),\
                1, file_pointer);
            }
            else printf("Error reading writer.dat\n");

            printf("%s owes $%.2f\n",buffer.name,buffer.owes);

            fclose(file_pointer);

            return(0);
        }
```

Let's take a closer look at the use of **fseek( )**:

```
fseek(file_pointer, (long) (rec_num*sizeof(struct entry)), 0);
```

We have already stored the record number we want **rec_num**. To position the file pointer correctly in the file, we have to move rec_num * sizeof(struct entry) bytes into the file. In other words, if rec_num was 2, that would look like this:

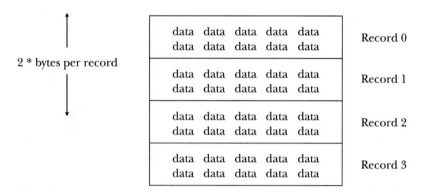

Note also that we use a type cast of (long) before passing this product to **fseek( )**. This is because **fseek( )** expects a long integer value here, allowing us to move through files larger than 64K.

The final parameter in our call to **fseek( )** is the **origin** value. This is the initial position in the file; the position pointer is set with respect to this origin. Since we know the number of bytes we want to position ourselves from the beginning of the file (i.e., rec_num * sizeof(struct entry)), we use an origin of zero in this case. In other cases, you can use the present position in the file as the origin and set the position pointer with respect to it.

Although we didn't check it, **fseek( )** returns a value of 0 if the seek was unsuccessful. If we were going to develop our program, we should check the return value as a matter of course (what if someone requested record 2,432 from our 15-record file?)

When we run the new program, it asks for the record to read, uses **fseek( )** to position us correctly in the file, and then it prints out the record it reads at that position. On the screen, we see this:

```
Type the record number to recover: 9   ←
Ebeneezer Scrooge owes $0.01
```

That's how we use records in files. Making up a record's structure is up to us. In C you can use structures as templates for records. Then, you can use **fopen( )** to open files, **fread( )** to read them, **fwrite( )** to write them, **fseek( )** to look around inside them, and **fclose( )** to close them. All of these functions are ANSI standard functions.

Random versus Sequential Access

Using files in this way — picking out records at random locations in the file — is called **random access**. The other method of file access is **sequential access**. If you are reading a file sequentially, you have to read all the records in order before coming to the one you want. That's the way you read files normally. With the file position pointer, you can use random access. In other words, you can just specify a record number and reach in to pick it out. If we didn't have the position pointer, we'd have to use sequential access. The difference is like finding a song on a tape (sequential access) or finding an article in a magazine (random access).

Now we've seen the basics about file handling, from creating and filling them to working inside them, and we can proceed to slightly more advanced topics. In particular, our error-checking hasn't been very good. All we've done is print out rudimentary error messages. However, since so many things can go wrong when you use files, C provides some error functions that can be helpful. Let's take a brief excursion into error-checking right now.

File Errors — Errno and Perror( )

There are two functions, **errno( )** and **perror( )**, which are designed to let us know what's going on if there is an error during file handling. If there is an error in a file operation, C places the error number in a variable called **errno** (declared in **errno.h**). We can print that number out, but since the number itself often isn't that much help, there is another option: We can ask C to print out the error in English with **perror( )**.

For example, we could modify our terse error message in the above record-reading program, **reader.c**, to this:

```
#include <stdio.h>
#include <io.h>
#define INDEX 15
```

```
extern int errno;

struct entry
{
    char name[20];
    float owes;
}

main()
{
    FILE *file_pointer;
    struct entry buffer;
    int rec_num;

    if((file_pointer = fopen("writer.dat", "r")) != NULL){
        printf("Type the record number to recover:");
        scanf("%d",&rec_num);
        fseek(file_pointer, (long)\
        (rec_num*sizeof(struct entry)), 0);
        fread(&buffer, sizeof(struct entry), 1,\
        file_pointer);
    }
    else{
        printf("Error number:%d returned.\n",errno);
        perror("Error reading writer.dat.\n");
    }
    printf("%s owes $%.2f\n",buffer.name,buffer.owes);

    fclose(file_pointer);

    return(0);
}
```

Here we can use **errno** and **perror( )**. Note that since **errno** is not defined in this program, we had to declare it **external** like this: `extern int errno;`. This way, the compiler knows that **errno** is not set or defined in the present file, but that we want to use it, and that it will be available when the program runs.

An external variable usually means that the variable is actually defined in another file, and that that file will be linked in before we run the whole program. We'll see much more about declaring objects external this way when we start working with assembly language, but this gives us a small introduction to the subject. As soon as we declare **errno** external, then, we're set.

If we ran this modified program, it will look for **writer.dat**; if the file does not exist, there will be an error. Let's see what happens:

```
D:\>del writer.dat

D:\>reader
Error number:2 returned.
Error reading writer.dat.
: No such file or directory

D:\>
```

A number of error messages were returned. The first one indicates that **errno** was set to 2. The second one was the standard error message that we had put into the program ourselves. The third one, however, is **perror( )**'s explanation of what is going on — ": No such file or directory". This kind of information can be very useful when working with files, and complete error handling is an asset to any program.

That's how to work with files in C, then. Open a file with **fopen( )**; use one of the writing functions like **fwrite( )** to write to it; and close it with **fclose( )**. To read from it, use **fseek( )** to position yourself in the file, and use one of the reading functions like **fread( )** to get data. We now know enough to work with files efficiently.

On the other hand, there is a another set of file functions in C that most programmers know about and sometimes use. The functions we've covered so far are ANSI standard functions; they are detailed by the ANSI standard, so they're safe to use.

However, C grew up under the UNIX operating system, which means that it also supports the UNIX style file functions — **open( )**, **close( )**, **read( )**, and **write( )**. (Note that the ANSI style file functions begin with 'f' and the UNIX style ones do not.) Even though the UNIX functions are nonstandard, programmers still use them because they can be slightly faster than the ANSI functions; the UNIX functions are not internally **buffered**. When you write data, it goes directly to the file. The ANSI versions, **fread( )** and **fwrite( )**, are buffered, which means that data has to be written to an internal buffer before it goes to the disk. Because **read( )** and **write( )** are so popular, we should take a look at them here, and that will be our last major file topic.

The UNIX File Functions

Neither **read( )** nor **write( )** — nor the associated UNIX functions (**lseek( )**, **open( )**, **close( )**) — are part of the ANSI C standard C library. Yet you can find them in all popular C compilers for the PC and PS/2 (including Microsoft and Turbo C).

For that reason, we should take a look at these UNIX file functions. As a demonstration, we can write a program that copies files for us. All it will do is to make a copy of a file: We'll tell it the name of the file to copy and the new filename, and it will produce the copy. Let's call this program **copier.c**.

Copying Files — copier.c

Before doing anything in **copier.c**, we have to include all these header files:

```
#include <stdio.h>
#include <fcntl.h>
#include <sys\types.h>
#include <sys\stat.h>
#include <io.h>

main()
   :
```

In addition, we also have to set up a buffer in memory for our data. In **copier.c**, we should use a large-sized buffer to make reading and writing faster (otherwise, we'd have to read and write many times). Let's use a buffer size of, say, 32K bytes. But we can't just declare a large data area like an array of 32K without special preparation. If we just put it into our program:

```
→    #define BUFFSIZE 32*1024
     #include <stdio.h>
     #include <fcntl.h>
     #include <sys\types.h>
     #include <sys\stat.h>
     #include <io.h>

     main()
     {
→    char buffer[BUFFSIZE];
       :
```

Then space would have to be allocated for it on the stack when the program runs. The stack is an internal section of memory used by the computer, and that's where the space for variables is often allocated, as we'll see when we cover memory use in C. It can be any size; however, the default Quick C stack is only about 2K long, 4K in Turbo C. The first thing that would happen in our program is that we would get a **stack overflow**, which means that there's not enough room on the stack. Instead, we can use **malloc( )** to allocate the memory ourselves.

In our case, we need 32K bytes in an array of type char, which we can name **buffer[ ]**. The **malloc( )** function returns a pointer of type **void**, and we can assign it to a pointer of type **char** without a type **cast**. In other words, we can use **malloc( )** to set up our data buffer like this (for Borland products, include **alloc.h**, not **malloc.h**):

```
#define BUFFSIZE 32*1024
#include <stdio.h>
#include <fcntl.h>
#include <sys\types.h>
#include <sys\stat.h>
#include <io.h>
#include <malloc.h>           /* Borland products:\
                                 #include <alloc.h> */

main()
{
→       char *buffer;

→       if((buffer = malloc(BUFFSIZE)) == NULL){
            printf("Malloc could not allocate.")
            return(1);
        }
        :
```

If **malloc( )** returns a NULL pointer, it did not allocate memory, so we terminate the program with return(1). If the program runs correctly, **malloc( )** will allocate 32K bytes for our use, and supply us with a pointer to it (which we name buffer).

Now that we have the space in memory for the data we are going to read in, we have to know what file to read. We can read that from the keyboard when the program is running; let's get the information using **scanf( )** and a prompt like this:

```
#define BUFFSIZE 32*1024
#include <stdio.h>
#include <fcntl.h>
#include <sys\types.h>
#include <sys\stat.h>
#include <io.h>
#include <malloc.h>            /* Borland products:\
                                  #include <alloc.h> */

main()
{
    char *buffer;
    char source_file_name[50];
    char target_file_name[50];

    if((buffer = malloc(BUFFSIZE)) == NULL){
        printf("Malloc could not allocate.");
        return(1);
    }

→   printf("Source file:");
→   scanf("%s",source_file_name);
        :
```

After we use **scanf( )**, the character string named **source_file_name** will hold the name of the file that is to be copied. We also need the name of the destination or target file, the file that will be created when the copy is made. We can read that into a string named **target_file_name** like this:

```
#define BUFFSIZE 32*1024
#include <stdio.h>
#include <fcntl.h>
#include <sys\types.h>
#include <sys\stat.h>
#include <io.h>
#include <malloc.h>            /* Borland products:\
                                  #include <alloc.h> */

main()
{
    char *buffer;
    char source_file_name[50];
    char target_file_name[50];

    if((buffer = malloc(BUFFSIZE)) == NULL){
        printf("Malloc could not allocate.");
        return(1);
    }
```

```
        printf("Source file:");
        scanf("%s", source_file_name);
→       printf("Target file:");
→       scanf("%s", target_file_name);
        :
```

After we have both names, we can open both files. Under the UNIX file functions, we will use **open( )** to do this. Here are the lines that open the source and target files:

```
#define BUFFSIZE 32*1024
#include <stdio.h>
#include <fcntl.h>
#include <sys\types.h>
#include <sys\stat.h>
#include <io.h>
#include <malloc.h>              /* Borland products:\
                                   #include <alloc.h> */

main()
{
    char *buffer;
    char source_file_name[50];
    char target_file_name[50];
    int source_handle;
    int target_handle;

    if((buffer = malloc(BUFFSIZE)) == NULL){
        printf("Malloc could not allocate.");
        return(1);
    }

    printf("Source file:");
    scanf("%s", source_file_name);
    printf("Target file:");
    scanf("%s", target_file_name);

→   if((source_handle = open(source_file_name,\
    O_RDONLY | O_BINARY)) == -1){
→       printf("Couldn't open source file.\n");
→       return(1);
→   }

→   if((target_handle = open(target_file_name, O_CREAT\
        | O_WRONLY \
→       | O_BINARY, S_IWRITE )) == -1){
→       printf("Couldn't open target file.\n");
→       return(1);
→   }
```

Flag	Means
O_RDONLY	Open for reading only
O_WRONLY	Open for writing only
O_RDWR	Open for reading and writing
O_APPEND	Open to append
O_CREAT	Creates file
O_TRUNC	If file exists
O_BINARY	Make this a binary file
O_TEXT	Make this a text file

Table 5-3. The open( ) Function Flags.

The **open( )** function takes many constants as parameters, and we can find them in Table 5-3. There are many possibilities: we can create files, open them as read-only or write-only, open them for appending, or open them as ASCII or binary files. If we open files for appending, anything we write to them will be placed at the end of the current file on disk; if we open a file with the **O_TRUNC** flag, the file is truncated to zero length (that is, zeroed) and then opened.

Note that we can use as many of these options as are consistent with each other. To use more than one option, they may be **OR'ed** together, as we have done in our program:

```
→        if((source_handle = open(source_file_name, O_RDONLY\
             ¦ O_BINARY)) == -1){
         printf("Couldn't open source file.\n");
         return(1);
     }
```

Bitwise Operators

The OR operation is a member of a new class of C operators, **bitwise operators**. We've already covered the other types of operators: arithmetic operators like +, - and *, as well as relational and logical operators like ¦¦ and &&. In fact, bitwise operators are very close to logical operators, except that they operate on the individual bits of variables and constants.

For example, we've already seen the **AND (&&)** logical operator. We use it when we want to connect two conditions together:

```
if((month == 12) && (day == 25)) printf("Merry Christmas!!\n");
```

For this joint condition to be true, the month has to be 12 AND the day has to be 25. We can work on individual bits in the same way, with the bitwise **AND** operator, **&**. For example, if we had two bytes which looked like this in binary (8 bits make up a byte):

01010101
11101110

then we could **AND** them together bit by bit (i.e., bitwise). **AND**ing two bits only yields 1 if *both* original bits were 1; otherwise, it yields 0. In other words, our example would look like this:

```
     01010101
&    11101110
     ────────
     01000100
```

In this way, **&** works on each bit of its two operands to produce each bit of the result. When we use bitwise **OR**, its symbol is ¦ and *either* bit can be 1 (or both can be 1) to yield a 1 in the result, like this:

```
     01010101
¦    11101110
     ────────
     11111111
```

In addition, there is also the bitwise **NOT** operator, which flips the bits of its operand (0s become 1s and 1s become 0s), and the exclusive **OR** operator, **XOR**, which is like **OR** except that `1 XOR 1 = 0`. The symbol for bitwise **NOT** is ~, and the symbol for bitwise **XOR** is ^. The action of these operators is detailed below:

OR	0	1		AND	0	1		XOR	0	1
0	0	1		0	0	0		0	0	1
1	1	1		1	0	1		1	1	0

The open options of the UNIX **open( )** statement are designed to be OR'ed together like this: **O_RDONLY | O_BINARY**. This combines the bits of the two options in a way that indicates we want to open the file as a read-only file, as well as a binary file. All we needed to pass were the file's name and the options we wanted, like this:

```
if(source_handle = open(source_file_name, O_RDONLY\
   | O_BINARY) == -1){
   printf("Couldn't open source file.\n");
   return(1);
}
```

Next, we have to open the target file to hold the copy. This file doesn't exist yet, but we can create it with **open( )**. When we create a file with **open( )** (as opposed to opening an existing one), we need to do two things: 1) We must include the **O_CREAT** option in our call; and 2) we must add a third parameter to **open( )**, as we have done here:

```
       if(source_handle = open(source_file_name, O_RDONLY\
          | O_BINARY) == -1){
          printf("Couldn't open source file.\n");
          return(1);
       }

→      if((target_handle = open(target_file_name, O_CREAT\
          | O_WRONLY \
→         | O_BINARY, S_IWRITE )) == -1){
          printf("Couldn't open target file.\n");
          return(1);
       }
```

Here we've asked for shared permission to write to the file by setting the third parameter (used only when we want to create a file) equal to **S_IWRITE**. The other two possibilities for this third parameter are the flags **S_IREAD** and **S_IWRITE | S_IREAD**, which would open the newly created file for reading, or for reading and writing, respectively.

The reason for all these options is that, under UNIX, other programs can access the same files we're using at the same time, and the situation can get complicated. For that reason, the UNIX functions allow us to specify how access to this new file may be shared between programs; however, the third parameter is only used under UNIX. We could as well have set it to 0 under DOS (and many programs do).

The **open( )** function does not return a pointer to a file structure. Instead, (and like assembly language functions) it returns a **file handle**. This handle is an integer, and we can use it with all the UNIX file-handling routines instead of a file pointer. We can set aside two integers, **source_handle** and **target_handle**, to store those handles in. Those are the values we'll pass to the functions that actually do the reading and writing, **read( )** and **write( )**.

Let's do that now. The two files are open, one with data in it, and one with none:

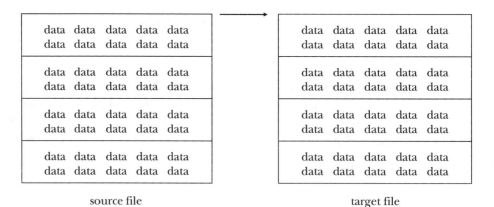

And now we have to keep copying the data in 32K chunks until we're all done:

This means that we're ready for the real meat of the program, the two lines that actually do all the copying:

```
#define BUFFSIZE 32*1024
#include <stdio.h>
#include <fcntl.h>
#include <sys\types.h>
#include <sys\stat.h>
#include <io.h>
#include <malloc.h>              /* Borland products:\
                                   #include <alloc.h> */

main()
{
    char *buffer;
    char source_file_name[50];
    char target_file_name[50];
    int source_handle;
    int target_handle;
    int number_read;

    if((buffer = malloc(BUFFSIZE)) == NULL){
        printf("Malloc could not allocate.");
        return(1);
    }
    printf("Source file:");
    scanf("%s", source_file_name);
    printf("Target file:");
    scanf("%s", target_file_name);

    if((source_handle = open(source_file_name, O_RDONLY\
        | O_BINARY)) == -1){
        printf("Couldn't open source file.\n);
        return(1);
    }

    if((target_handle = open(target_file_name, O_CREAT\
        | O_WRONLY
        | O_BINARY, S_IWRITE )) == -1){
        printf("Couldn't open target file.\n);
        return(1);
    }

    while (number_read = read(source_handle, buffer,\
    BUFFSIZE))
        write(target_handle, buffer, number_read);
            :
            :
```

In the **while( )** statement, we keep reading bytes from the file. The **read( )** function returns the number of bytes actually read, and as long as it wasn't zero, we write them out again. When these two lines are completed, we have copied the whole source file into the target file. Except for cleanup, the program is done.

After the files have been copied, we close them both. The source file has now been duplicated in the target file, and you can find the whole program in Listing 5-1. After all the preliminary setup, the actual work of the program was accomplished in just two lines. That's it; this program, **copier.c**, is able to copy files in large, 32K chunks. Give it a try.

Listing 5-1. copier.c — Copies Files.

```c
#define BUFFSIZE 32*1024
#include <stdio.h>
#include <fcntl.h>
#include <sys\types.h>
#include <sys\stat.h>
#include <io.h>
#include <malloc.h>              /* Borland products:\
                                   #include <alloc.h> */

main()
{
    char *buffer;
    char source_file_name[50];
    char target_file_name[50];
    int source_handle;
    int target_handle;
    int number_read;

    if((buffer = malloc(BUFFSIZE)) == NULL){
        printf("Malloc could not allocate.");
        return.(1);
    }
    printf("Source file:");
    scanf("%s", source_file_name);
    printf("Target file:");
    scanf("%s", target_file_name);

    if((source_handle = open(source_file_name, O_RDONLY\
        | O_BINARY)) == -1){
        printf("Couldn't open source file.\n");
        return(1);
    }
```

Listing 5-1. *(continued)*

```
    if((target_handle = open(target_file_name, O_CREAT \
       | O_WRONLY
       | O_BINARY, S_IWRITE )) == -1){
       printf("Couldn't open target file.\n);
       return(1);
    }

    while (number_read = read(source_handle, buffer,\
    BUFFSIZE))
        write(target_handle, buffer, number_read);

    close(source_handle);
    close(target_handle);

    return(0);
}
```

Reading Command Line Parameters

The **copier.c** program is good, but we can make it still better. As it stands, it relies on prompts like this:

```
G:\>copier
Source file: my_file.dat
Target file: her_file.dat
```

That's not very professional. It would be better if we could simply pass the names of the source and target files to copier directly:

```
G:\>copier my_file.dat her_file.dat
```

In fact, we can do this; C lets us pass command line parameters like these as parameters to the **main( )** function. All we need to do is to declare the parameters that C actually passes to **main( )** like this:

```
#define BUFFSIZE 32*1024
#include <stdio.h>
#include <fcntl.h>
#include <sys\types.h>
#include <sys\stat.h>
```

```
#include <io.h>
#include <malloc.h>              /* Borland products:\
                                    #include <alloc.h> */


→    main(int argc, char *argv[])
     {
       :
```

In other words, **main( )** can take two parameters, an integer named **argc** and an array named **argv[ ]**. The **argc** parameter holds the number of command line arguments (which will be three for us since C counts the name of the program itself, **copier**, as a command line argument), and **argv[ ]** is an array of strings (which means it's really a two-dimensional array of type **char**). C fills these values for us. **argv[1]** will hold the name of the source file and **argv[2]** the name of the target file. We can use them like this:

```
#define BUFFSIZE 32*1024
#include <stdio.h>
#include <fcntl.h>
#include <sys\types.h>
#include <sys\stat.h>
#include <io.h>
#include <malloc.h>              /* Borland products:\
                                    #include <alloc.h> */

main(int argc, char *argv[])
{
    char *buffer;
    char source_file_name[50];
    char target_file_name[50];
    int source_handle;
    int target_handle;
    int number_read;

    if((buffer = malloc(BUFFSIZE)) == NULL){
        printf("Malloc could not allocate.");
        return(1);
    }

→    strcpy(source_file_name, argv[1]);
→    strcpy(target_file_name, argv[2]);
       :
```

And that's all there is to it. Now we can pass the names of the source and target files directly to **copier**, giving our program a very professional feel. The modified program appears in Listing 5-2.

Listing 5-2. copier.c Using Command Line Arguments.

```c
#define BUFFSIZE 32*1024
#include <stdio.h>
#include <fcntl.h>
#include <sys\types.h>
#include <sys\stat.h>
#include <io.h>
#include <malloc.h>           /* Borland products:\
                                #include <alloc.h> */

main(int argc, char *argv[])
{
    char *buffer;
    char source_file_name[50];
    char target_file_name[50];
    int source_handle;
    int target_handle;
    int number_read;

    if((buffer = malloc(BUFFSIZE)) == NULL){
        printf("Malloc could not allocate.");
        return(1);
    }

    strcpy(source_file_name, argv[1]);
    strcpy(target_file_name, argv[2]);

    if((source_handle = open(source_file_name, O_RDONLY\
        | O_BINARY)) == -1){
        printf("Couldn't open source file.\n);
        return(1);
    }

    if((target_handle = open(target_file_name, O_CREAT\
        | O_WRONLY
        | O_BINARY, S_IWRITE )) == -1){
        printf("Couldn't open target file.\n);
        return(1);
    }

    while (number_read = read(source_handle, buffer,\
    BUFFSIZE))
        write(target_handle, buffer, number_read);

    close(source_handle);
    close(target_handle);

    return(0);
}
```

That's it for files. We've seen how to write them as either ASCII or binary files, and how to read them as well. We've also examined the idea of using file records and the position pointer to give us control over our data. Sometimes, sequential access is appropriate (if we are, for example, writing text files), and sometimes random access using the position pointer is more appropriate (as in databases). We've even seen the UNIX file functions; there are many options available in C, represented by a rich assortment of library functions.

Now, however, it's time to turn to another part of the computer entirely, as we augment what we can do by adding the mouse to our programs. This will also introduce us to the next step up in C programming, accessing the operating system directly.

CHAPTER 6

The Mouse

In this chapter, we're going to add support for the mouse to our programs. Actually, neither Microsoft C (including Quick C) nor Turbo C support the mouse, but that is not a problem. We can do it ourselves. When we want to use the mouse, we load the mouse's driver software, and that's what provides the necessary support. That driver enables DOS interrupt 0x33 (51 decimal), the mouse interrupt, and we'll learn how to use it directly in this chapter.

As we work through this chapter, we'll see how to initialize the mouse, read position and button information from it, and work with the mouse cursor. We'll also see plenty of examples, showing how to make use of mouse information. Using the mouse is becoming more and more common on the PC (especially in graphics programs or with pull-down menus), and if we're going consider ourselves proficient programmers, we'll have to be able to provide mouse support. In addition, this chapter will teach us how to interface directly to the operating system, DOS, and that information will be very valuable later.

Starting with the Mouse

It turns out that there are two separate things we need to do before we start using the mouse. First, you must load the mouse driver software for your mouse, and you can do that by running the .COM file that comes with the mouse (e.g., MOUSE.COM for an IBM, Microsoft, or Logitech mouse, or MOUSESYS.COM for a Mouse Systems mouse). It's important to realize that you must run this driver program *before* any program can use your mouse. The driver initializes interrupt 0x33, which is the basis of this chapter. For more information, consult your mouse's documentation.

Second, we have to initialize the mouse before using it. We'll start this chapter by developing a function named **mouse_initialize( )** to do exactly that. Before we can use the mouse, we'll call **mouse_initialize( )**. After that, we can use any other mouse function in whatever order we want, as demonstrated by the examples coming up. Let's get started, then, by seeing how to interface our C code to the mouse interrupt, DOS interrupt 0x33.

TIP   In many programs, use of a mouse is optional and depends on whether or not a mouse and mouse driver are installed. You should know that, even if a mouse is optional, you can call and use the mouse functions here without problem. If there is no mouse, you'll simply see no mouse "events" like cursor movements or button presses. (And you should make sure you don't loop forever, waiting for such events.) In other words, using the mouse functions developed here will cause no errors if there is no mouse.

Interrupts in Your Computer

One of the strongest ways of augmenting the power of C is to use the resources available to us in the computer's operating system. Each interrupt is a prewritten program already in memory, ready for us to use. The commands you use at DOS level (e.g., COPY, TIME, VER, XCOPY, or FORMAT) all make use of the built-in interrupts — and now we, as C programmers, can too. It's like adding a whole new language to our programming capabilities.

The way we pass and receive data to and from interrupt routines is by using the C **int86( )** function, and the 80×86's **registers**. The microprocessor handles data in 16-bit registers, and you can think of them as the computer's built-in variables. The ones we'll see most are named **ax**, **bx**, **cx**, and **dx**, and they store data in the computer's Central Processing Unit, the CPU:

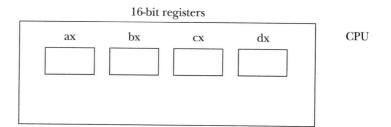

16-bit registers

Each interrupt examines the way we've loaded some or all of these registers, and takes action accordingly. For a complete listing of each interrupt service and how to load the registers, look at the appendix of this book. It shows you what must be in each register before calling **int86( )** or **int86x( )**, and what kinds of output you can expect to find.

NOTE **int86( )** and **int86x( )** are the same, except that **int86x( )** allows you to use a few more registers.

Since each register is 16 bits long, it is exactly like a C int, and we can load integer values into them like 53, 3,251, or -219:

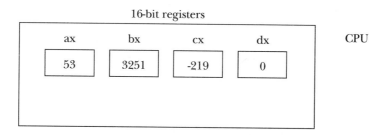

16-bit registers

To the computer, however, each register can also be thought of as two bytes, so you can also break up these registers into a high eight-bit register and a low eight-bit register. For example, the high eight-bit part of **ax** (**bx**, **cx**...) is called **ah** (**bh**, **ch**...), and the low eight-bit part of **ax** (**bx**, **cx**...) is called **al** (**bl**, **cl**...):

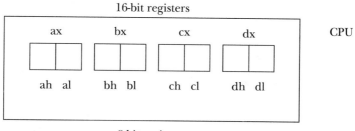

16-bit registers

8-bit registers

Frequently, we'll have to load one of these eight-bit registers, such as **ah**, with a particular value to use an interrupt, and we work with registers, we'll use hexadecimal values. Hexadecimal is useful because a 16-bit binary number — the size of each full register — makes up four hexadecimal digits. That means that the values we can place in the 80×86's registers go from 0 to 0xffff (65,535):

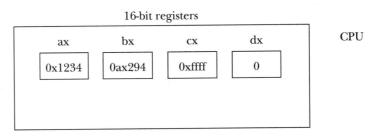

In addition, eight bits (a byte) make up exactly two hex digits like this: 0x12 or 0x34, so a byte can hold values from 0 to 0xff (255). Because we can divide registers like **ax** into **ah** and **al**, the top byte in a 16-bit word (i.e., a word is two bytes) like **ax** is simply the first two hex digits, and the bottom byte is the bottom two. For example, if **ax** held 0x1234, then **ah** contains 0x12 and **al** contains 0x34:

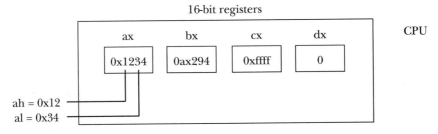

To reach the 80×86's registers from C, we first have to set up two data structures, which we'll call **in_regs** and **out_regs**, as type **REGS** (this type is defined in **dos.h**). Because the registers can be accessed as either bytes or as words, **REGS** is made up from two structures named **WORDREGS** and **BYTEREGS**:

```
struct WORDREGS {
     unsigned int ax;
     unsigned int bx;
     unsigned int cx;
     unsigned int dx;
     unsigned int si;
```

```
    unsigned int di;
    unsigned int cflag;
};

struct BYTEREGS {
    unsigned char al, ah;
    unsigned char bl, bh;
    unsigned char cl, ch;
    unsigned char dl, dh;
};
```

The union Data Type

These two are then merged in a clever way using the C **union** data type. A union is much like a **struct**, except that it uses the same memory space for its variables; in other words, it overlays them, allowing us to refer to the same memory locations by different names. For example, if we stored an int named **a** and a char named **b** in a structure, it might look like this:

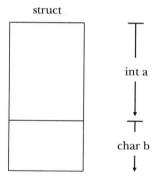

In a union, however, the first byte of space would be shared, and could be reached through either **a** or **b**:

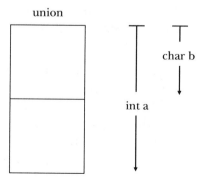

Unions are typically used to get around C's relatively strong data typing regulations.

In our case, this is how the union **REGS** is set up to handle both word-sized and byte-sized registers:

```
union REGS {
    struct WORDREGS x;
    struct BYTEREGS h;
}in_regs;
```

This allows us to refer to the **ax** register as **in_regs.x.ax** and the **ah** register (the top byte of **ax**) as **in_regs.h.ah**; note that we indicate which scheme of addressing we want (i.e., words or bytes) by using a dot operator followed by **x** or **h** as defined in **REGS** above. This is exactly what unions are for: letting us address a memory location by different names or data types.

We might also note that some new registers were defined in the **WORDREGS** and **BYTEREGS** structures. These match what is available in the microprocessor:

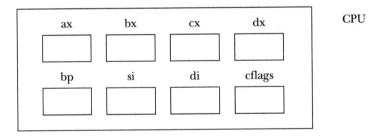

The high and low bytes of these new registers cannot be addressed separately; for example, **si** does not split into **sh** and **sl**.

We won't see these new registers until we start to deal with assembly language. For example, the **bp** register is normally used in manipulating stack data, and we'll use it in Chapter 13. The **si** and **di** registers are used by the 80×86 to manipulate strings, and the **cflags** register holds the result of certain operations we'll also learn more about later.

That's it. Now we're ready for the mouse. To use the mouse interrupt, 0x33, we can simply use the **int86( )** function like this:

```
#include <dos.h>

main()
{
    union REGS in_regs, out_regs;

    in_regs.x.ax = 0;
→   int86(0x33, &in_regs, &out_regs);

    return(0);
}
```

We just set up two unions named **in_regs** and **out_regs**, both of type **REGS**, and then we can reach interrupt 0x33 like this: int86(0x33, &in_regs, &out_regs);. Note that we included **dos.h** for the prototype of **int86( )** (as well as the definition of **REGS**), and that we passed the address of each union to **int86( )** so it can place values in them. In this case, we passed a value of 0 in the ax register to interrupt 0x33, which initializes the mouse. Now that we've worked out the interface, the remainder of the chapter will simply be an exploration of the services offered by interrupt 0x33; in fact, let's start that exploration immediately.

Initializing the Mouse

Initializing the mouse is a necessary first step towards using it. We can do that with interrupt 0x33, service 0. If this service returns a nonzero value, the mouse is initialized; otherwise, the mouse cannot be used (because it's not installed in the computer or the mouse driver is missing). In that case, and if your program depends on the use of a mouse, you should print out an error message and quit.

Once the mouse is initialized, we're all set until the computer is turned off. We don't have to initialize it again (although doing so does no harm). Note that initializing the mouse does not display the mouse cursor. To display the cursor, use the function we'll develop next, **mouse_show_cursor( )**.

mouse_initialize( )

This function just uses interrupt 0x33 service 0 (i.e., **ah** = 0) to initialize the mouse system. As mentioned, this is the necessary first step to using any other mouse function. Here's all we do: Load **ah** with 0 and send it to interrupt 0x33, and then set **mouse_initialize** to the value returned in **ax**:

```
#include <dos.h>
#include <stdio.h>

int mouse_initialize(void);

main()
{

    if (!mouse_initialize()){
        printf("Mouse could not be initialized.\n");
        exit(1);
    }
    printf("Mouse initialized.\n");

    return(0);
}

int mouse_initialize(void)
{
    union REGS in_regs, out_regs;

    in_regs.x.ax = 0;
    int86(0x33, &in_regs, &out_regs);
    return out_regs.x.ax;
}
```

In the program, we check the value returned by **mouse_initialize( )**. If it's zero, we print out an error message ("Mouse could not be initial-ized.\n") and quit. Otherwise, we print "Mouse initialized\n." and then quit. Now that we've set up the mouse system for use, let's get things rolling by displaying the mouse cursor itself.

Making the Mouse Cursor Visible

The next step in using the mouse is to show the mouse cursor on the screen. In text mode, this cursor appears as a solid block (although you can change that with **mouse_set_cursor( )**, developed later in this chapter), and in graphics mode as an arrow. Let's write a small subprogram named **mouse_show_cursor( )** to do the work for us.

mouse_show_cursor( )

Like all of the mouse functions and subprograms we'll write, we just use another interrupt 0x33 service here; in this case, we use service 1, which displays the mouse cursor:

```
void mouse_show_cursor(void)
{
    union REGS in_regs, out_regs;

→   in_regs.x.ax = 1;
→   int86(0x33, &in_regs, &out_regs);
}
```

When you use **mouse_show_cursor( )**, the cursor appears on the screen. Here's how our program looks now:

```
#include <dos.h>
#include <stdio.h>

int mouse_initialize(void);
void mouse_show_cursor(void);

main()
{

    if (!mouse_initialize()){
        printf("Mouse could not be initialized.\n");
        exit(1);
    }
    printf("Mouse initialized.\n");

→   mouse_show_cursor();

    return(0);
}

int mouse_initialize(void)
{
    union REGS in_regs, out_regs;

    in_regs.x.ax = 0;
    int86(0x33, &in_regs, &out_regs);
```

```
        return out_regs.x.ax;
}

void mouse_show_cursor(void)
{
    union REGS in_regs, out_regs;

    in_regs.x.ax = 1;
    int86(0x33, &in_regs, &out_regs);
}
```

Notice that we first initialize the mouse with the function **mouse_initialize( )**, and, if that worked, then we display the cursor with **mouse_show_cursor( )**.

If the mouse system is not initialized for some reason, calls to interrupt 0x33 have no effect. That is, we could have called **mouse_show_cursor( )** whether or not we were able to initialize the mouse system.

Now that we've displayed the mouse cursor on the screen, our next step will be to hide it.

Hiding the Mouse Cursor

There are times when the mouse cursor can be a distraction on the screen, and we'll fix that problem here. Let's write the function to hide the mouse cursor, **mouse_hide_cursor( )**.

If the mouse cursor is already off, it stays off when we hide it.

There is one more little-known — but very important — reason for hiding the mouse cursor. As the mouse cursor moves over the screen, the mouse driver software reads the character at the present screen position before displaying the mouse cursor. Then, when the mouse cursor moves on, that character is restored. However, if you've changed the screen display behind the mouse cursor, it will still restore the original (and wrong) character. To avoid this problem, you should always turn the mouse cursor off when displaying a window or overwriting the mouse cursor in any way (using the function we're about to write, **mouse_hide_cursor( )**), and turn it on again immediately afterwards (using **mouse_show_cursor( )**). This solves the problem completely.

mouse_hide_cursor( )

Here we just make use of interrupt 0x33 service 2, which hides the mouse cursor:

```
void mouse_hide_cursor(void)
{
    union REGS in_regs, out_regs;

    in_regs.x.ax = 2;
    int86(0x33, &in_regs, &out_regs);
}
```

And here's what the mouse program that we've been developing looks like, ready to roll:

```
        #include <dos.h>
        #include <stdio.h>

        int mouse_initialize(void);
        void mouse_show_cursor(void);
        void mouse_hide_cursor(void);

        main()
        {

            if (!mouse_initialize()){
                printf("Mouse could not be initialized.\n");
                exit(1);
            }
            printf("Mouse initialized.\n");

            mouse_show_cursor();

→           printf("Press any key to hide the mouse cursor.\n");
→           getch();
→           mouse_hide_cursor();

            return(0);
        }

        int mouse_initialize(void)
        {
            union REGS in_regs, out_regs;

            in_regs.x.ax = 0;
            int86(0x33, &in_regs, &out_regs);
```

```
        return out_regs.x.ax;
}

void mouse_show_cursor(void)
{
    union REGS in_regs, out_regs;

    in_regs.x.ax = 1;
    int86(0x33, &in_regs, &out_regs);
}

void mouse_hide_cursor(void)
{
    union REGS in_regs, out_regs;

    in_regs.x.ax = 2;
    int86(0x33, &in_regs, &out_regs);
}
```

Again, we initialize the mouse system, and, if successful, show the mouse cursor and print out the prompt: `"Press any key to hide the mouse cursor\n."` When a key is pressed, we hide the mouse cursor with **mouse_hide_cursor( )**.

At this point, we've been able to set the mouse system up, show the cursor and hide it at will. Those are good beginning steps, but now it's time to start reading information from the mouse. For example, we may want to check the status of the mouse at some given time: Is there a button being pressed? And where is the mouse cursor? We'll work out the answer to these questions next.

Reading Immediate Mouse Information

There is one way of getting information from the mouse. Interrupt 0x33 service 3 returns the immediate status of the left and right buttons, as well as the row and column number of the mouse cursor's position. When we call it, it returns this information encoded in the **bx**, **cx**, and **dx** registers, providing us with a snapshot of what the mouse is doing now. Here's how the registers are set on return:

bx = 0 → No button down
1 → Right button down
2 → Left button down
3 → Both buttons down

> **cx** = screen column of mouse cursor (using pixel ranges)
>
> **dx** = screen row of mouse cursor (using pixel ranges)

Let's write a function to report these things to us.

mouse_information( )

Since we want to learn about four things (the status of the right and left buttons and the present row and column location of the mouse cursor), it would be ideal to have a function we could use this way:

```
void mouse_information(&right, &left, &row, &col);
```

Note that since we want to change the values in the variables **right**, **left**, **row**, and **col** that we had to pass pointers to them. This is the first time that a function that we develop will change its calling parameters. We're getting pointers passed to us, so we declare **mouse_information( )** this way:

```
void mouse_information(int *right, int *left, int *row,\
int *col);
```

Now, inside **mouse_information( )**, we're free to change the value of, say, right by referring to it as ***right** (keep in mind that * means "the value at address"). The variables we pass could be set this way on return:

right	0	→	Right mouse button is up
	1	→	Right mouse button is down

left	0	→	Left mouse button is up
	1	→	Left mouse button is down

row	Current text-mode screen row of mouse cursor (Range 1–25)
col	Current text-mode screen column of mouse cursor (Range 1–80)

This function is designed to return a snapshot of the mouse's present state. As we saw, interrupt 0x33 service 3 returns button information in **out_regs.bx**. If this value is 1, the left button only is down. If it's 2, the right button only is down. If 3, both are down. (And if 0, neither are down). Here's how we can decode that information into the parameters right and left:

```
void mouse_information(int *right, int *left, int *row, int *col)
{
    union REGS in_regs, out_regs;
```

```
        in_regs.x.ax = 3;
        int86(0x33, &in_regs, &out_regs);
        *right = *left = 0;
        switch( out_regs.x.bx){
            case 1:
                *left = 1;
                break;
            case 2:
                *right = 1;
                break;
            case 3:
                *left = 1;
                *right = 1;
        }
        :
        :
    }
```

Next, **out_regs.dx** now holds the present screen row in **pixels**, and **out_regs.cx** holds the present screen column also in pixels; this is the usual way that the mouse services return location information, in screen pixels (i.e., in ranges like 0–199 and 0–639). The mouse and menu work we're going to do will usually be in text mode, however, so let's report screen row and column numbers (i.e., 1–25 and 1–80, not pixel ranges like 0–199 and 0–639). We can convert from pixel ranges to the normal screen row and column ranges like this (assuming the standard 8×8 pixel size for each screen character):

```
void mouse_information(int *right, int *left, int *row,\
int *col)
{
    union REGS in_regs, out_regs;

    in_regs.x.ax = 3;
    int86(0x33, &in_regs, &out_regs);
    *right = *left = 0;
    switch( out_regs.x.bx){
        case 1:
            *left = 1;
            break;
        case 2:
            *right = 1;
            break;
        case 3:
            *left = 1;
            *right = 1;
    }
```

```
→          *row = out_regs.x.dx / 8 + 1;
→          *col = out_regs.x.cx / 8 + 1;
     }
```

And we're set. Here's the whole mouse program as it stands so far:

```
#include <dos.h>
#include <stdio.h>

int mouse_initialize(void);
void mouse_show_cursor(void);
void mouse_hide_cursor(void);
void mouse_information(int *right, int *left, int *row, int
*col);

main()
{
    int right, left, row, col;

    if (!mouse_initialize()){
        printf("Mouse could not be initialized.\n");
        exit(1);
    }
    printf("Mouse initialized.\n");
    mouse_show_cursor();

    printf("Press any key to hide the mouse cursor.\n");
    getch();
    mouse_hide_cursor();

    printf("Press any key to show the mouse cursor.\n");
    getch();
    mouse_show_cursor();

    mouse_information(&right, &left, &row, &col);
    if (right) printf("Right mouse button is down.\n");
    if (left) printf("Left mouse button is down.\n");
    printf("Cursor row: %d, cursor column: %d.\n", row, col);

    return(0);
}

int mouse_initialize(void)
{
    union REGS in_regs, out_regs;

    in_regs.x.ax = 0;
```

```
        int86(0x33, &in_regs, &out_regs);
        return out_regs.x.ax;
}

void mouse_show_cursor(void)
{
    union REGS in_regs, out_regs;

    in_regs.x.ax = 1;
    int86(0x33, &in_regs, &out_regs);
}

void mouse_hide_cursor(void)
{
    union REGS in_regs, out_regs;

    in_regs.x.ax = 2;
    int86(0x33, &in_regs, &out_regs);
}

void mouse_information(int *right, int *left, int *row,\
int *col)
{
    union REGS in_regs, out_regs;

    in_regs.x.ax = 3;
    int86(0x33, &in_regs, &out_regs);
    *right = *left = 0;
    switch( out_regs.x.bx){
        case 1:
            *left = 1;
            break;
        case 2:
            *right = 1;
            break;
        case 3:
            *left = 1;
            *right = 1;
    }

    *row = out_regs.x.dx / 8 + 1;
    *col = out_regs.x.cx / 8 + 1;
}
```

Here we used **mouse_information( )** and then simply decoded the returned values **right**, **left**, **row**, and **col**. To use this program, make sure you've loaded the mouse driver as outlined in the beginning of this chapter. When you press any key on the keyboard, this program will report the present mouse state.

The most severe limitation here is that **mouse_information( )** only provides an instant snapshot of what's going on with the mouse. If you want to use it for mouse input, you have to keep **polling** it; that is, looping over it until something happens.

A better option will be to use the functions we develop later that use other, specialized interrupt 0x33 services. In them, button action is stored in a **queue**, and it waits until we call for it. This way, we won't have to catch a button being pressed at the time that it is being pressed. We can find out about it when we're ready to deal with it (much like reading keys from the keyboard buffer rather than catching them in the act of being pressed).

TIP   Also, you might prefer to have the row and column numbers returned in pixel format rather than text format (i.e., in ranges like 0–199 and 0–639 rather than 1–25 and 1–80). If so, just set **row** and **col** equal to **out_regs.x.dx** and **out_regs.x.cx**, respectively, at the end of **mouse_information( )**:

```
*row = out_regs.x.dx;
*col = out_regs.x.cx;
```

You should note that in text mode, the mouse cursor jumps from character position to character position anyway. The pixel value that is returned corresponds to the top left corner of the character position.

Let's continue our exploration of the mouse now with service 4, which lets us move the mouse cursor at will from inside our program.

Moving the Mouse Cursor

With service 4, we'll gain control over the mouse cursor. Up to this point, the only way to make the mouse cursor move was to move the mouse (as soon as you show the mouse cursor, it responds to mouse movements). However, we can develop a function named **mouse_move_cursor( )** to position the mouse cursor as we want it.

mouse_move_cursor( )

It would be simplest if we could position the mouse by just passing the desired screen row and column numbers like this:

```
mouse_move_cursor (row, col);
```

To write **mouse_move_cursor( )**, we'll just make use of interrupt 0x33 service 4. We have to pass the mouse cursor's new location in **dx** (rows) and **cx** (columns). Because we are using text-mode rows and columns, we first convert that location into pixel ranges like this (again, assuming the standard 8 × 8 pixel size for screen characters):

```
        void mouse_move_cursor(int row, int col)
        {
            union REGS in_regs, out_regs;

→           in_regs.x.dx = 8 * (row - 1);
→           in_regs.x.cx = 8 * (col - 1);
            in_regs.x.ax = 4;
            int86(0x33, &in_regs, &out_regs);
        }
```

Even if you request a position far off the screen, this service does not return an error (which is why **mouse_move_cursor( )** does not produce any output); it simply places the cursor at the edge of the screen. Here's a program to put it to use:

```
        #include <dos.h>
        #include <stdio.h>

        int mouse_initialize(void);
        void mouse_show_cursor(void);
        void mouse_move_cursor(int row, int col);

        main()
        {
            int right, left, row, col;

            if (!mouse_initialize()){
                printf("Mouse could not be initialized.\n");
                exit(1);
            }
            printf("Mouse initialized.\n");

            mouse_show_cursor();

            printf("Press any key to move the mouse cursor to\
            (1, 1).\n");
            getch();
→            mouse_move_cursor(1, 1);
```

```
        return(0);
    }

    int mouse_initialize(void)
    {
        union REGS in_regs, out_regs;

        in_regs.x.ax = 0;
        int86(0x33, &in_regs, &out_regs);
        return out_regs.x.ax;
    }

    void mouse_show_cursor(void)
    {
        union REGS in_regs, out_regs;

        in_regs.x.ax = 1;
        int86(0x33, &in_regs, &out_regs);
    }

    void mouse_move_cursor(int row, int col)
    {
        union REGS in_regs, out_regs;

        in_regs.x.dx = 8 * (row - 1);
        in_regs.x.cx = 8 * (col - 1);
        in_regs.x.ax = 4;
        int86(0x33, &in_regs, &out_regs);
    }
```

You can see that it's easy to use **mouse_move_cursor( )**, just pass the desired row and column number. Of course, getting no error back from this service is both a blessing and a curse. On one hand, you're not troubled by error messages; on the other, if you made a genuine error in placing the mouse cursor, you should know about it.

TIP One reasonable change to **mouse_move_cursor( )** is to check the row and column number requested. If they're out of range, you should still move the cursor, but you can pass back an error code.

The next interrupt 0x33 service is among the most useful. Service 5 tells us how many times a specific button was pressed since the last time we inquired, and using this service means that we won't have to catch button presses as they happen.

Reading the Button Pressed Queue

It would be useful to develop the mouse equivalent of **scanf( )**. We already have **mouse_information( )**, but you must catch mouse events as they happen to use it. Instead, it would be much better if they could be stored and we could read them as we require them (like reading keys from the keyboard buffer).

We can do that with service 5. This service lets us read the number of times a specific button has been pressed since we last checked. It also gives us the row and column screen position of mouse cursor the *last* time the button was pressed. Pressing a mouse button is usually more significant than just moving the mouse cursor around the screen. For that reason, we can treat this service as the primary mouse input service.

Let's write a function called, say, **mouse_times_pressed( )**, to connect service 5 to C. We should call **mouse_times_pressed( )** when we start accepting input to clear the mouse queue, then loop over and call it periodically to see if anything else has happened, much like we'd use **scanf( )**.

mouse_times_pressed( )

We need to query service 5 about the number of times a specific button — right or left — was pressed. We can indicate which button we're interested in by passing a value in a variable named **mouse_button**. Let's use the same values for **mouse_button** as the interrupt 0x33 services themselves use, a value of 0 for the left button, and 1 for the right button.

$$\downarrow$$

```
mouse_times_pressed(mouse_button, ...);
```

The return values we expect are the number of times the button has been pressed, and the mouse cursor's position the last time the button was pressed. In other words, we can set up **mouse_times_pressed( )** like this:

```
mouse_times_pressed(mouse_button, &number_times, &row, &col);
```

We'll be able to read the return variables like this:

number_times   The number of times the specified button was pushed since
                          the last time **mouse_times_pressed( )** was called.

row   The screen row (1–25) of the mouse cursor the last time that button was pressed.

col   The screen column (1–80) of the mouse cursor the last time that button was pressed.

Using interrupt 0x33 service 5 makes this function pretty easy. We just place the button number (0 for the left button, 1 for the right) into **in_regs.bx** and invoke service 5:

```
       void mouse_times_pressed(int mouse_button,\
       int *number_times, int *row, int *col)
       {
           union REGS in_regs, out_regs;

           in_regs.x.bx = mouse_button;
           in_regs.x.ax = 5;
→          int86(0x33, &in_regs, &out_regs);
               :
               :
       }
```

The results come back in **bx**, **cx**, and **dx**. The **bx** register holds the number of times the specified button, left or right, was pressed since the last time service 5 was used. The **dx** register holds the screen (pixel) row where the button was last pushed, and **cx** holds the corresponding (pixel) column. We can convert these to text-mode row and column ranges (1–25 and 1–80) and return:

```
       void mouse_times_pressed(int mouse_button,\
       int *number_times, int *row, int *col)
       {
           union REGS in_regs, out_regs;

           in_regs.x.bx = mouse_button;
           in_regs.x.ax = 5;
           int86(0x33, &in_regs, &out_regs);

→          *number_times = out_regs.x.bx;
           *row = out_regs.x.dx / 8 + 1;
           *col = out_regs.x.cx / 8 + 1;
       }
```

This example program shows **mouse_times_pressed( )** at work. All it does is to ask you to press the right mouse button a number of times and then press any

key on the keyboard. When you do, this program reports the number of times
you've clicked the button, and the last position at which you did so:

```
#include <dos.h>
#include <stdio.h>

int mouse_initialize(void);
void mouse_show_cursor(void);
void mouse_move_cursor(int row, int col);
void mouse_times_pressed(int mouse_button,\
int *number_times, int *row, int *col);

main()
{
    int mouse_button, number_times, row, col;

    if (!mouse_initialize()){
        printf("Mouse could not be initialized.\n");
        exit(1);
    }
    printf("Mouse initialized.\n");

    mouse_show_cursor();

    mouse_times_pressed(0, &number_times, &row, &col);\
    /* clear queue */
    printf("Press the left mouse button some times,\
    then any key.\n");
    getch();

    mouse_times_pressed(0, &number_times, &row, &col);
    printf("You pressed it %d times.\n", number_times);
    printf("Last time at (%d, %d).\n", row, col);

    return(0);
}

int mouse_initialize(void)
{
    union REGS in_regs, out_regs;

    in_regs.x.ax = 0;
    int86(0x33, &in_regs, &out_regs);
    return out_regs.x.ax;
}

void mouse_show_cursor(void)
```

```
    {
        union REGS in_regs, out_regs;

        in_regs.x.ax = 1;
        int86(0x33, &in_regs, &out_regs);
    }

void mouse_times_pressed(int mouse_button,\
int *number_times, \
    int *row, int *col)
    {
        union REGS in_regs, out_regs;

        in_regs.x.bx = mouse_button;
        in_regs.x.ax = 5;
        int86(0x33, &in_regs, &out_regs);

        *number_times = out_regs.x.bx;
        *row = out_regs.x.dx / 8 + 1;
        *col = out_regs.x.cx / 8 + 1;
    }
```

Let's go through the steps: We initialize the mouse with **mouse_initialize( )**; display the cursor with **mouse_show_cursor( )**; and then use **mouse_times_pressed( )** *before* printing out the prompt which asks the user to press the mouse button. This is to clear the mouse queue and discard any information that was waiting there (note that we're only clearing the left mouse button's queue, since we set **mouse_button** to 0). Next, we print out the prompt, wait for a key, and then use **mouse_times_pressed( )** to read what happened.

One limitation here is that **mouse_times_pressed( )** only returns the cursor location the *last* time a specific button was pressed. If you're interested in the location of every mouse button press, you should check **mouse_times_pressed( )** frequently enough to make sure that mouse events don't get a chance to stack up in the queue.

Another limitation is that we're often more interested in when the mouse button was *released*, not pressed. For example, releasing the mouse button is important when you're dragging an object across the screen or making a menu selection. The next interrupt 0x33 service, service 6, lets us handle that.

Reading the Button Released Queue

We can use service 6 to write a function that will give us button-release information; let's call this function **mouse_times_released( )**. It should give us information about the number of times a particular button was released since we called it, and the screen position of the mouse cursor when it was last released.

mouse_times_released( )

Here's how we might use **mouse_times_released( )**:

```
mouse_times_released(mouse_button, &number_times, &row, &col);
```

Again, we set **mouse_button** to 0 if we want right button information, and to 1 for the left button. And, following **mouse_times_pressed( )**, this is how we can interpret the return values:

number_times	The number of times the specified button was released since the last time **mouse_times_released( )** was called.
row	The screen row (1–25) of the mouse cursor the last time that button was released.
col	The screen column (1–80) of the mouse cursor the last time that button was released.

This function is very like **mouse_times_pressed( )**, except that we use interrupt 0x33 service 6, not 5:

```
      void mouse_times_released(int mouse_button, \
          int *number_times, int *row, int *col)
      {
          union REGS in_regs, out_regs;

          in_regs.x.bx = mouse_button;
→         in_regs.x.ax = 6;
          int86(0x33, &in_regs, &out_regs);
                  :
                  :
      }
```

After invoking **int86( )**, we decode the information exactly the same way as we did for **mouse_times_pressed( )**:

```
        void mouse_times_released(int mouse_button,\
        int *number_times, \
            int *row, int *col)
        {
            union REGS in_regs, out_regs;

            in_regs.x.bx = mouse_button;
            in_regs.x.ax = 6;
            int86(0x33, &in_regs, &out_regs);

→           *number_times = out_regs.x.bx;
→           *row = out_regs.x.dx / 8 + 1;
→           *col = out_regs.x.cx / 8 + 1;
        }
```

And that's it; now let's put it to work. This example program is just like the one
for **mouse_times_pressed( )**, except that it indicates the number of times the
button was released, not pressed:

```
        #include <dos.h>
        #include <stdio.h>

        int mouse_initialize(void);
        void mouse_show_cursor(void);
        void mouse_move_cursor(int row, int col);
        void mouse_times_released(int mouse_button,\
        int *number_times, \
            int *row, int *col);

        main()
        {
            int mouse_button, number_times, row, col;

            if (!mouse_initialize()){
                printf("Mouse could not be initialized.\n");
                exit(1);
            }
            printf("Mouse initialized.\n");

            mouse_show_cursor();

→           mouse_times_released(0, &number_times, &row, &col);
            printf("Press the left mouse button some times,\
            then any key.\n");
            getch();

→           mouse_times_released(0, &number_times, &row, &col);
```

```
        printf("You released it %d times.\n", number_times);
        printf("Last time at (%d, %d).\n", row, col);

        return(0);
}

int mouse_initialize(void)
{
    union REGS in_regs, out_regs;

    in_regs.x.ax = 0;
    int86(0x33, &in_regs, &out_regs);
    return out_regs.x.ax;
}

void mouse_show_cursor(void)
{
    union REGS in_regs, out_regs;

    in_regs.x.ax = 1;
    int86(0x33, &in_regs, &out_regs);
}

void mouse_times_released(int mouse_button,\
int *number_times, \
    int *row, int *col)
{
   union REGS in_regs, out_regs;

   in_regs.x.bx = mouse_button;
   in_regs.x.ax = 6;
   int86(0x33, &in_regs, &out_regs);

   *number_times = out_regs.x.bx;
   *row = out_regs.x.dx / 8 + 1;
   *col = out_regs.x.cx / 8 + 1;
}
```

In this example, we initialize the mouse, show the mouse cursor and, after a key is pressed, read mouse information from **mouse_times_released( )**. That's all we have to do. Let's continue our exploration of the interrupt 0x33 services now with the next service, service 7, which will allow us to restrict the mouse cursor to a specific range of columns on the screen.

TIP　Using this service, together with service 8 (which restricts the row range), you can restrict the mouse cursor to a specific window on the screen, giving a very professional effect.

Restricting the Mouse Cursor Horizontally

Service 7 restricts the mouse cursor, and therefore mouse events, to a specified range of columns. We can put together a function to interface with this service like this:

```
mouse_horizontal_range(right, left);
```

Where we fill the variables like this:

right	Right column of allowed mouse cursor range (range: 1–80)
left	Left column of allowed mouse cursor range (range: 1–80)

Now all that remains is to write the code.

mouse_horizontal_range( )

This service lets us restrict the mouse cursor's horizontal range by specifying the right column of that range in **cx** and the left column in **dx**. We simply convert to pixel ranges and use interrupt 0x33 to make this function work:

```
void mouse_horizontal_range(int right, int left)
{
    union REGS in_regs, out_regs;

    in_regs.x.cx = 8 * (right - 1);
    in_regs.x.dx = 8 * (left - 1);
    in_regs.x.ax = 7;
    int86(0x33, &in_regs, &out_regs);
}
```

And that's all there is to it (service 7 does not return any values). Now let's see it in action. In this example program, we restrict the mouse cursor to the left half of the screen by passing a left hand column of 1 and a right-hand column of 40. Service 7 sorts out the two values (as you can imagine, the left-hand column has to be less than or equal to the right-hand column), so it actually does not matter if we specify mouse_horizontal_range(40, 1) or mouse_horizontal_range(1, 40):

```
#include <dos.h>
#include <stdio.h>

int mouse_initialize(void);
void mouse_show_cursor(void);
```

```
        void mouse_move_cursor(int row, int col);
        void mouse_horizontal_range(int right, int left);

        main()
        {
            int mouse_button, number_times, row, col;

            if (!mouse_initialize()){
                printf("Mouse could not be initialized.\n");
                exit(1);
            }
            printf("Mouse initialized.\n");
            mouse_show_cursor();

            printf("Press a key to restrict the cursor to\
            the left screen.\n");
            getch();

→           mouse_horizontal_range(1, 40);

            return(0);
        }

        int mouse_initialize(void)
        {
            union REGS in_regs, out_regs;

            in_regs.x.ax = 0;
            int86(0x33, &in_regs, &out_regs);
            return out_regs.x.ax;
        }

        void mouse_show_cursor(void)
        {
            union REGS in_regs, out_regs;

            in_regs.x.ax = 1;
            int86(0x33, &in_regs, &out_regs);
        }

        void mouse_horizontal_range(int right, int left)
        {
            union REGS in_regs, out_regs;

            in_regs.x.cx = 8 * (right - 1);
            in_regs.x.dx = 8 * (left - 1);
            in_regs.x.ax = 7;
            int86(0x33, &in_regs, &out_regs);
        }
```

If you'd like to use graphics mode, you can change **mouse_horizontal_range( )** to use pixel ranges rather than column ranges. That's it. The next service, service 8, does the same thing, except that it restricts vertical, not horizontal motion. Let's look into it.

Restricting the Mouse Cursor Vertically

After **mouse_horizontal_range( )**, **mouse_vertical_range( )** is the logical next function. We can design it to retrict the mouse cursor to a specified vertical range of screen rows (1–25). Here's the way we might use it:

```
mouse_vertical_range (top, bottom);
```

Where these are the inputs:

top	Top row of allowed mouse cursor movement (range: 1–25)
bottom	Bottom row of allowed mouse cursor movement (range: 1–25)

Developing this function will be easy.

mouse_vertical_range( )

We just have to use interrupt 0x33 service 8 in much the way we used service 7. Now, however, we are restricting the mouse cursor not to a specific set of columns, but to a specific set of rows:

```
void mouse_vertical_range(int top, int bottom)
{
    union REGS in_regs, out_regs;

    in_regs.x.cx = 8 * (top - 1);
    in_regs.x.dx = 8 * (bottom - 1);
    in_regs.x.ax = 8;
    int86(0x33, &in_regs, &out_regs);
}
```

That's all there is to it. Let's see an example. In this program, we restrict the mouse cursor to the top half of the screen by calling `mouse_verti-cal_range(12, 1)`, and the left half of the screen as well with `mouse_horizontal_range(1, 40)`. Like service 7, service 8 sorts out the two values (the top row has to be less than or equal to the bottom row), so it

does not matter if we specify mouse_vertical_range(12, 1) or
mouse_vertical_range(1, 12):

```
#include <dos.h>
#include <stdio.h>

int mouse_initialize(void);
void mouse_show_cursor(void);
void mouse_move_cursor(int row, int col);
void mouse_horizontal_range(int right, int left);
void mouse_vertical_range(int top, int bottom);

main()
{
    int mouse_button, number_times, row, col;

    if (!mouse_initialize()){
        printf("Mouse could not be initialized.\n");
        exit(1);
    }
    printf("Mouse initialized.\n");

    mouse_show_cursor();

    printf("Press a key to restrict cursor to the\
    top left screen.\n");
    getch();

    mouse_horizontal_range(1, 40);
    mouse_vertical_range(1, 12);

    return(0);
}

int mouse_initialize(void)
{
    union REGS in_regs, out_regs;

    in_regs.x.ax = 0;
    int86(0x33, &in_regs, &out_regs);
    return out_regs.x.ax;
}

void mouse_show_cursor(void)
{
    union REGS in_regs, out_regs;
```

```c
        in_regs.x.ax = 1;
        int86(0x33, &in_regs, &out_regs);
    }

    void mouse_horizontal_range(int right, int left)
    {
        union REGS in_regs, out_regs;

        in_regs.x.cx = 8 * (right - 1);
        in_regs.x.dx = 8 * (left - 1);
        in_regs.x.ax = 7;
        int86(0x33, &in_regs, &out_regs);
    }

    void mouse_vertical_range(int top, int bottom)
    {
        union REGS in_regs, out_regs;

        in_regs.x.cx = 8 * (top - 1);
        in_regs.x.dx = 8 * (bottom - 1);
        in_regs.x.ax = 8;
        int86(0x33, &in_regs, &out_regs);
    }
```

There is one more interrupt 0x33 service that is of interest to us. Service 0xa lets us set the style of the mouse cursor itself. This will be our last mouse topic.

Changing the Mouse Cursor Appearance

Service 0xa lets us set the text-mode (only) mouse cursor to whatever ASCII character we want. To use it, we have to define two "masks": a **screen mask** and the **cursor mask**. Each mask consists of both a character and attribute byte, and understanding how to use them takes some time and experimentation. Let's start by understanding how characters are displayed on the screen using attributes bytes.

Screen Attributes

The attribute is a one-byte long value that determines how characters appear on the screen. Each place on the screen has two bytes in the screen buffer, a character byte and an attribute byte. The character byte simply holds an ASCII value, and the attribute byte holds display information. By selecting an attribute byte in our program, we will determine how our mouse cursor will look. For example, we can select a green character on a blue background, or a yellow character on a red background. Note: Set bit to 1 to turn on that particular color. An attribute byte is diagrammed here:

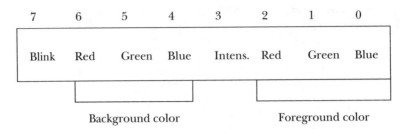

By setting the attribute, we can select the mix of red, green, and blue for both the foreground color (the color of the character) and the background color (the color of the rest of the screen). Also, we can set bit 3 for high-intensity display, and bit 7 to make the character blink. A red foreground on a green background would have an attribute byte of 00100100B, or 24H, as shown here:

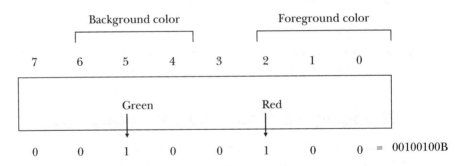

| **TIP** | You can mix the colors in a screen attribute byte by adding the respective bit values together. Here are the bit values to add in forming your attribute byte: |

Bit Value	*Color Generated*
1	Blue Foreground
2	Green Foreground
4	Red Foreground
8	High Intensity
16	Blue Background
32	Green Background
64	Red Background
128	Blinking

For example, to get a normal setting of white on black, you would turn all the foreground colors (the letter itself) on this way: 1 + 2 + 4 = 7. If you wanted to make that high intensity, you would add 8 to give 15. If you wanted blinking reverse video in white, set all the background colors on, and add 128 to make it blink: 16 + 32 + 64 + 128 = 240.

For the mouse cursor, the screen mask determines how much of a character's ASCII code to keep when the mouse cursor lands at its screen position. This mask is **AND**ed with that character's ASCII code and with the character's attribute. To keep the character at that screen position intact, use a **screen mask character** of 0xff and a **screen mask attribute** of 0xff. To overwrite it entirely, use a screen mask character and attribute of 0.

The cursor mask then determines what the cursor will look like. The **cursor mask character** and **cursor mask attribute** are **XOR**ed with the result of **AND**ing the present character and attribute with the screen mask to produce the mouse cursor (you might recall that **XOR** is the same as **OR** except that 1 **XOR** 1 = 0). Let's see how this works in practice. We might call this function **mouse_set_cursor( )**, and use it like this:

```
mouse_set_cursor (sc_mask_char, sc_mask_attr, cu_mask_char,\
cu_mask_attr);
```

Here are the inputs:

sc_mask_char	Screen mask ASCII character.
sc_mask_attr	Screen mask attribute; the screen mask character and attribute are **AND**ed with the character and attribute already on the screen. For example, to overwrite the character on the screen, set **sc_mask_char** = **sc_mask_attr** = 0. To preserve it, **sc_mask_char** = **sc_mask_attr** = 0xff.
cu_mask_char	Cursor mask ASCII character.
cu_mask_attr	Cursor mask attribute; the cursor mask character and attribute are **XOR**ed with the result of **AND**ing the character at the present position with the screen mask. That is, the cursor mask determines the shape of the mouse cursor.

For example, to use a particular ASCII character as the mouse cursor, over-write the existing screen character entirely by setting **sc_mask_char** and **sc_mask_attr** to 0. Then load the ASCII code of the character you want as the mouse cursor (such as an up-arrow, ASCII 24) into **cu_mask_char**, and the desired mouse cursor attribute (such as 7 for white on black) into **cu_mask_attr**.

TIP You can have your mouse cursor **color invert** characters on the screen by setting **sc_mask_char** to 0xff, which preserves the ASCII code of the character on the screen, and **sc_mask_attr** to 0xff to preserve its attribute byte. Then set **cu_mask_char** to 0, which will **XOR** the character with 0 and thus preserve it, and **cu_mask_attr** to 0x77 to invert its attribute with **XOR** (use 0x77, not 0xff, to avoid turning the blinking and intensity bits on). If you just want to invert the character and not the background behind it, set **cu_mask_attr** to 7.

In this function, we're simply going to use interrupt 0x33, service 0xa. To set the mouse cursor, we have to load 0 into **bx**, the full screen mask (attribute and character bytes) into **cx**, and the cursor mask (attribute and character bytes) into **dx**. In other words, we'll put **sc_mask_attr** into **ch**, **sc_mask_char** into **cl**, **cu_mask_attr** into **dh**, and **cu_mask_char** into **dl**. We can do all that this way:

```
void mouse_set_cursor (char sc_mask_char,, char\
sc_mask_attr, \
    char cu_mask_char, char cu_mask_attr)
{
    union REGS in_regs, out_regs;

    in_regs.h.ch = sc_mask_attr;
    in_regs.h.dh = cu_mask_attr;
    in_regs.h.cl = sc_mask_char;
    in_regs.h.dl = cu_mask_char;
    in_regs.x.ax = 0xa;
    in_regs.x.bx = 0;
    int86(0x33, &in_regs, &out_regs);
}
```

And now we can use it to set the mouse cursor in text mode. For example, this program sets the mouse cursor to ASCII 250, a single dot:

```
#include <dos.h>
#include <stdio.h>

int mouse_initialize(void);
void mouse_show_cursor(void);
```

```
void mouse_move_cursor(int row, int col);
void mouse_set_cursor (char sc_mask_char,\
char sc_mask_attr, \
    char cu_mask_char, char cu_mask_attr);

main()
{
    int mouse_button, number_times, row, col;

    if (!mouse_initialize()){
        printf("Mouse could not be initialized.\n");
        exit(1);
    }
    printf("Mouse initialized.\n");

    mouse_show_cursor();

    mouse_set_cursor(0, 0, 250, 7);

    return(0);
}

int mouse_initialize(void)
{
    union REGS in_regs, out_regs;

    in_regs.x.ax = 0;
    int86(0x33, &in_regs, &out_regs);
    return out_regs.x.ax;
}

void mouse_show_cursor(void)
{
    union REGS in_regs, out_regs;

    in_regs.x.ax = 1;
    int86(0x33, &in_regs, &out_regs);
}

void mouse_set_cursor (char sc_mask_char,\
char sc_mask_attr, \
    char cu_mask_char, char cu_mask_attr)
{
    union REGS in_regs, out_regs;      /

    in_regs.h.ch = sc_mask_attr;
    in_regs.h.dh = cu_mask_attr;
    in_regs.h.cl = sc_mask_char;
```

```
in_regs.h.dl = cu_mask_char;
in_regs.x.ax = 0xa;
in_regs.x.bx = 0;
int86(0x33, &in_regs, &out_regs);
}
```

Our example just changes the mouse cursor to a single dot in the middle of the character position, with a normal screen attribute (i.e., white on black) of 7. You might want to use one of the ASCII characters that look like an arrow instead (see Table 6-1).

Keep in mind that you can only use **mouse_set_cursor( )** in text mode, and you are restricted to using one of the ASCII characters. (For a complete set of the ASCII characters, see your C documentation.)

That's it. That completes our mouse support. We've set the mouse system up, displayed the mouse cursor, hidden it, read button information, and even changed the mouse cursor. Now it's time to plunge back into the C library as we see how to manipulate memory.

ASCII Number	*Character*
24	Up arrow
25	Down arrow
26	Right arrow
27	Left arrow

Table 6-1.   ASCII Arrow Characters.

How to Use Memory in C

We've come far in our study of C, but there is still much to cover. In particular, C offers us a good deal of control over our resources, and memory is a critical resource. In fact, the C programming language is more memory-conscious than most. C divides memory into four separate sections, the code area, the data area, the heap and the stack. This chapter is going to be a tour of each of these four areas, one by one, because many of the details are very important for our programs.

We'll see how to allocate and use large amounts of memory; how global and local variables work, as well as C's four **storage classes** for data in memory; how C uses the stack to pass parameters to function; what memory models are; and how to understand the duration and scope of our variables. In fact, at the end of the chapter, we'll have a good handle on how to manage memory in our C programs.

Memory Use in C

It's important to understand what is going on with memory in a C program. Few other high-level languages pay so much attention as C does to memory maintenance and allocation; for that reason, it's crucial for us as C programmers to know what's happening to our variables, how they're allocated (because when they're reallocated by a C program, the original data is lost), and how to allocate large sections of memory for ourselves.

Memory is divided into several different sections in C. There is the **code area**, where the program instructions reside. This area is not changed when a program runs. The next area is the **data area**, and this area is further divided into two sections, one for initialized data, and one for uninitialized data.

In addition, an area is set up at the top of available memory, and this region grows toward lower memory as it is filled. This is called the **stack**, and C allocates space for the majority of variables on it. The last memory area is located in low memory, above the code and data areas. This area is called the **heap**, and it can grow in size just like the stack, except that it grows toward higher memory, rather than downward toward lower memory. In fact, C itself usually maintains the stack for us, but allocating and using memory on the heap is our responsibility. There are a number of library routines that are designed to allocate memory space for us on the heap; in fact, one we've already seen, **malloc( )**, does exactly that.

This chapter is going to be a survey of what's going on in each of these memory areas, so let's take a look at how these areas might appear in a C program that's running:

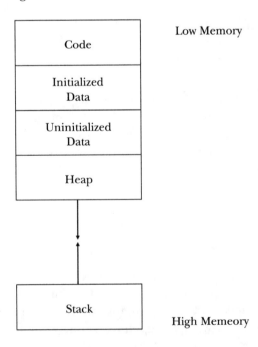

This is how a C program looks when it's working. The code and data areas are fixed in size, but the stack and the heap can change size freely. Usually, C maintains variables on the stack, but we can dynamically allocate space ourselves in the heap. The code and data areas are fixed in size when we produce our .EXE file. Now that we've got a picture of how a C program looks in memory, we can begin our survey with the first section of a C program in memory, the code area.

The Code

The code area of a C program holds, not surprisingly, the instructions that make up the code itself. For example, let's say that we had this (not very exciting) program:

```c
int my_int, his_int = 3;

main()

{
    my_int = 5;
    my_int++;
    his_int -= 10;

    return(0);
}
```

From a programmer's point of view, not much is happening here. The compiler simply translates these instructions so that the microprocessor, the 80×86, can understand what it's supposed to do. In particular, the job of the compiler here is to translate from C to **machine language**, the bits and bytes that the microprocessor reads. That is, the 80×86 has a number of built-in instructions, and the compiler has to take the C program and rewrite it using those instructions. Usually, each C statement is translated into many machine language instructions, but, in this case, each of the above simple statements can be translated into a single machine language instruction like this:

```
MOV     my_int, 5
INC     my_int
SUB     his_int, 10
```

NOTE This is actually assembly language, the English language equivalent of machine language. Machine language is just raw binary numbers.

These instructions would appear in the code area like this:

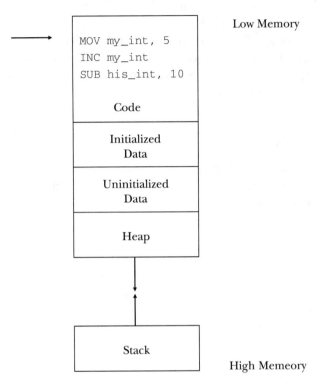

It turns out that one of C's four storage classes actually doesn't have to do with the data areas, the stack or the heap at all, but with the code area. Let's take a look at it now.

The register Storage Class

The **register** storage class concerns itself with storing data in the registers of the microprocessor, not in memory. We've already seen some of the 80×86's registers — **ax**, **bx**, **cx**, and **dx**. To load one of them, the 80×86 has to fetch data from memory, and that can take time, especially if we do it repeatedly. If we're performing an identical operation with a certain value over and over, we may want to ask the compiler to store that value in one of the 80×86's registers. That way, the value doesn't have to be loaded freshly from memory every time. It's important to realize that this is a request to the compiler, not a directive. The compiler may not be able to do it. Since the registers are only 16 bits long, we can only use the register storage class for ints and chars, like this:

```
register int my_int;
register char input_character;
```

That's all we have to do. The register storage class makes up the first of four storage classes we'll see in this chapter. Of course, data is usually stored in memory, and not kept permanently in a register. For example, let's take another look at our program:

```
int my_int, his_int = 3;

main()
{
    my_int = 5;
    my_int++;
    his_int -= 10;

    return(0);
}
```

The two integers, **my_int** and **his_int** would be stored in the data area of the C program, but in different places. Let's examine how that works next.

C's Data Areas

There are two data areas, one for initialized data, and one for uninitialized data:

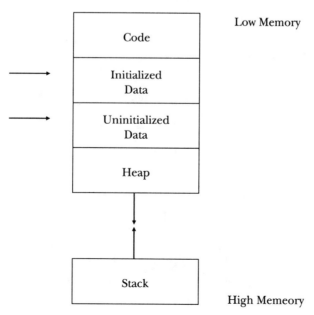

For example, in our program, **my_int** is uninitialized, and **his_int** is initialized:

```
int my_int, his_int = 3;

main()
{
    my_int = 5;
    my_int++;
    his_int -= 10;

    return(0);
}
```

That means that they would be stored in the two different areas like this:

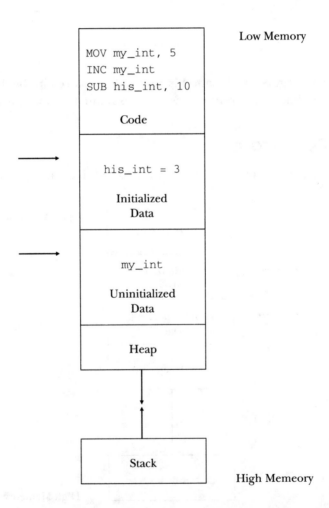

> **NOTE** The uninitialized data area is also called the **BSS** area, which stands for Block Started Segment. The reason uninitialized data is stored together is so that it can be set to zero all at once (although this is compiler dependent).

However, not all data, initialized or uninitialized, is stored in the data area. In fact, there are usually (it depends on your compiler) only three types of variables that are stored in the data area:

- global variables
- static variables
- initialized arrays and structures

We know about initialized arrays and structures, but not about the other two terms, global and static. In C, a variable can be either global or local, as well as static or automatic, so let's examine next what these terms mean.

Global versus Local Variables

A **global** variable is one that is available anywhere in the program, and we declare them outside of any code block as we've done with **my_int** and **his_int**:

```
        void my_func(void);

→       int my_int, his_int = 3;

        main()
        {
            my_int = 5;
            my_int++;
            his_int -= 10;

            return(0);
        }

        void my_func(void)
        {
            int her_int;

            her_int = 5;
            my_int = 24;
        }
```

The reason these variables are called global is because they may be referenced anywhere in the program. For example, you might notice that we've added a function to our program named **my_func( )**. That function has no difficulty in reaching and using the variable **my_int**, which is a global variable because it was declared outside of all code blocks:

```
        void my_func(void);

→    int my_int, his_int = 3;

        main()
        {
            my_int = 5;
            my_int++;
            his_int -= 10;

            return(0);
        }

        void my_func(void)
        {
            int her_int;

            her_int = 5;
→    my_int = 24;
        }
```

On the other hand, the variable **her_int** is defined inside the code block of the function **my_func( )**:

```
        void my_func(void);

        int my_int, his_int = 3;

        main()
        {
            my_int = 5;
            my_int++;
            his_int -= 10;

            return(0);
        }

        void my_func(void)
        {
→        int her_int;
```

```
→          her_int = 5;
           my_int = 24;
      }
```

This means that **her_int** is a **local variable**, local to the function **my_func( )**, and it cannot be referenced anywhere else in the program (including inside **main( )**). The regions where a variable may be referenced is called its **scope**. In particular, local variables have a restricted scope, which has advantages and disadvantages. These variables are kept private so that the rest of the program need not be concerned with the internal workings of, say, some function. A restricted scope also means that other parts of the program can't interfere (perhaps unintentionally) with a variable's value. However, you may sometimes find that you would like to reference a local variable in other places, but can't, which means you might consider expanding its scope (for example, by including it in a more inclusive code block).

You can declare a local variable inside any code block, which means that variable is local to that specific code block (and any code blocks that it in turn contains):

```
void my_func(void);

int my_int, his_int = 3;

main()
{
    my_int = 5;
    my_int++;
    his_int -= 10;

    return(0);
}

void my_func(void)
{
    int her_int;

    her_int = 5;
    my_int = 24;
    if(his_int == 3){
→       int their_int;
→       their_int = 4;
    }
}
```

This may look funny, but the declaration of **their_int** is legal. In fact, it is entirely local to the **if** code block (and we can't access its value anywhere else).

Now we know the difference between local and global variables. As we've seen, global variables are stored in C's data areas, local variables are not. In addition, one other type of variable is stored in the data areas, **static** variables.

Static versus Automatic Variables

The term **static** usually refers to a variable's **duration**, not its scope (local and global refer to scope). When we enter a code block in which variables are defined, C allocates space for those variables on the stack. It's important to realize that the space which is allocated for those variables is also deallocated when we leave the code block. This means that, for example, you cannot count on a variable in a function retaining its value between calls.

In the following program, there are two calls to **my_func( )**. The variable **her_int** is initialized to 5, incremented to 6, and then printed out. The second time around, you might expect it to be incremented to 7, but, in fact, it has been newly allocated, and after we increment it, it is 6 again:

```c
void my_func(void);

main()
{
    my_func();
    my_func();

    return(0);
}

void my_func(void)
{
    int her_int = 5;

    her_int++;
    printf("The value of her_int is: %d.\n", her_int);
}
```

This program prints out:

```
The value of her_int is: 6.
The value of her_int is: 6.
```

Variables like this (including the ones that appear inside the code block of the function **main( )**) are called **automatic** variables, and C allocates space for them on the stack; we'll see them later, when we discuss stack use. This pair makes up the next two data storage classes for C, **static** and **automatic**. Static variables are stored in the data areas and are not dynamically allocated when we enter a code block, so they may be counted on not to change their value. (Note that global variables, which are also stored in the data areas, don't change their values either.) Automatic variables are reallocated each time we enter their code block.

It is possible to override the automatic nature of variables in code blocks by using the **static keyword**, indicating that we want to use the **static** storage class for a particular variable, like this:

```
        void my_func(void);

        main()
        {
            my_func();
            my_func();

            return(0);
        }

        void my_func(void)
        {
→           static int her_int = 5;

            her_int++;
            printf("The value of her_int is: %d.\n", her_int);
        }
```

This program prints out:

```
  The value of her_int is: 6.
  The value of her_int is: 7.
```

It is also possible to have **static global** variables, and they are important. In this case, static refers not to memory allocation, but to the variable's **scope**. A static global variable like this one (below) is **private** to the current file:

```
→    static int i = 34;

     main()
     {
     ...program...
     }
```

That is, any other global variable can be referenced by code in any other file. To reach a variable in another file, we simply have to include the keyword **extern** before a variable's declaration. For example, we might want to use the variable **apples** in our file, even if it's defined in another file. We could do that like this:

```
     #include <stdio.h>
→    extern apples;

     main()
     {

→        printf("The number of apples is %d.\n", apples);

         return(0);
     }
```

Here could be what the other file looks like (notice that **apples** is a global variable):

```
→    int apples = 5;
     int oranges = 3;

     int my_func()
     {
         apples = apples + oranges;
     }
```

External variables like this make up the fourth data storage class in C. Altogether, there are **register variables**, **automatic** and **static variables**, and **external variables**. On the other hand, if we made **apples** a static global variable, then it is *not* available to the other file:

```
→    static int apples = 5;
     int oranges = 3;

     int my_func()
     {
         apples = apples + oranges;
     }
```

TIP To link **file1.c** and **file2.c** together, you can compile them separately and then use the **linker**. With Quick C, that might look like this (the **-c** option specifies that we only want **qcl.exe** to compile the files, not link them):

```
H:\>qcl file1.c -c

H:\>qcl file2.c -c

H:\>link file1+file2;
```

This produces an executable file named **file1.exe**. We'll see more about linking files together later.

Now we know about static and automatic variables, as well as local and global variables. Let's add the location of variable storage to our earlier memory chart:

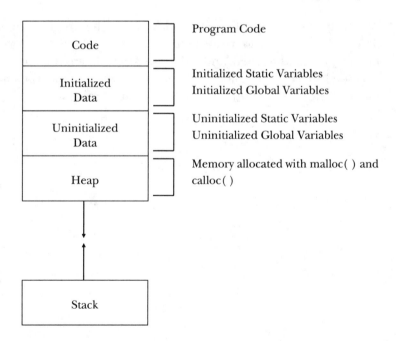

As we can see, initialized static and global data is stored in the initialized data area; uninitialized static and global data is stored in the uninitialized data area. Here's a data demonstration program indicating what goes where:

```
int i;                    [Global →  Uninitialized Data Area]
int j = 5;                [Global →  Initialized Data Area]
static int l = 5;         [Static Global → Initialized Data Area]
static int m = 5;         [Static Global → Uninitialized Data Area]

main()
{
    static int p;         [Static →  Uninitialized Data Area]
    static int q = 5;     [Static →  Initialized Data Area]
    :
    :
}
```

That completes our survey of what's stored in the two sections of the data area in C programs. Let's move on now to the next part of a C program, the heap.

The Heap

The **heap** is where we allocate memory when the program runs (i.e., at **run time**). For example, we've seen the function **malloc( )** at work: It allocates memory for us as needed, and it does so on the heap. If we took our program and used **malloc( )** to allocate memory for an array of type **char**, which we might name **my_data[10]**, this is what it would look like:

```
#include <malloc.h>

int my_int, his_int = 3;

main()
{
    char *my_data;

    my_int = 5;
    my_int++;
    his_int -= 10;
→   my_data = malloc(10);

    return(0);
}
```

The space for that array would then be set up in the heap, like this:

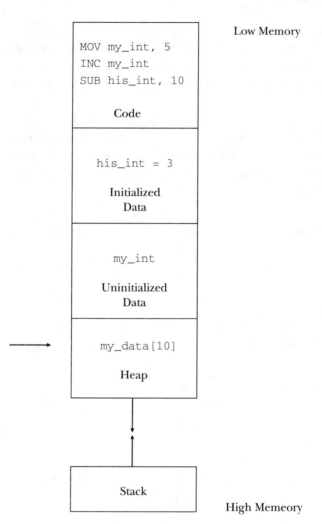

Low Memory

```
MOV my_int, 5
INC my_int
SUB his_int, 10
```

Code

his_int = 3

Initialized
Data

my_int

Uninitialized
Data

my_data[10]

Heap

Stack

High Memeory

In other words, C puts automatic variables on the stack and stores static variables in the data areas, but the heap is the part of memory that we ourselves can allocate; it's under our direct control with functions like **malloc( )**. However, to be able to do that effectively, we need to know how memory itself works in the computer.

Memory Models

Memory management in computers with 80×86s is a little complex. The 80×86 series (up to the 80386) uses 16-bit registers to keep track of data, and 16 bits can express numbers from 0 to 65,535. This means that the largest number of memory locations that we can specify with one 16-bit address is 65,536 (0 points to the first memory address), or 64K. The days of 64K computers are long gone, however; the 80×86s have to do better than that. Instead, they use two 16-bit words to specify a memory address like this, B800:0000.

The first part of this address, 0xB800, is referred to as the **segment** address. The second part, 0x0000 here, is called the **offset** address. To find the actual address that B800:0000 represents in memory, multiply the segment address by 16 (0x10) and add it to the offset address. Here, 0xb800 × 0x10 + 0x0000 = 0xB8000:

$$
\begin{aligned}
0xB800 \times 0x10 \;\; = \;\; & 0xB8000 \\
+ \;\; & 0x0000 \\
\hline
& 0xB8000
\end{aligned}
$$

The address 0040:001E (which is actually the location the keyboard buffer in memory) really stands for a linear address of 0x0041E:

$$
\begin{aligned}
0x0040 \times 0x10 \;\; = \;\; & 0x00400 \\
+ \;\; & 0x001E \\
\hline
& 0x0041E
\end{aligned}
$$

This type of address is the real address the 80×86s use, 20 bits long, which gives the 80×86 an address space of 2^{20} = 1M.

NOTE   In protected mode, the 80286 and 80386 (when it operates as an 80286) uses segment **selectors**, which represent 24 address bits and provide an address space of up to 16M.

Since real addresses use 20 bits, we need two words to specify them. This kind of addressing has consequences for compilers. If you have to call or reference some location with a different segment address, you need both the segment and offset address of the destination. If you are calling or referencing some destination within the 64K space defined by the segment address, you only need one address word, the offset address.

Model	Means
Tiny	Code and Data fit into 64K. The program can be made into a .COM file. This model is also called **Small Impure**.
Small	All data fits in one 64K segment, all code fits in one 64K segment. Maximum program size is 128K.
Medium	All data fits in one 64K segment, but code may be greater than 64K.
Compact	Data may be greater than 64K (but no single array may be), code must be less than 64K. (Turbo: static data must be less than 64K.)
Large	Both data and code may be greater than 64K, but no single array may be. (Turbo: static data must be less than 64K.)
Huge	Data, Code, and data arrays may be greater than 64K. This model is not available in Quick C.

Table 7-1. Memory Model Definitions.

In other words, all objects in memory can be thought of as having a one-word address (if you limit yourself to 64K space total) or a two-word address (if you want to reference any point in memory). That means that library functions that take pointers as parameters have to be written differently in the two cases, in one case, the pointer that is passed to them will be a two-word pointer and, in the other, a one-word pointer.

Since many functions had to be rewritten, C placed them in different libraries, where they can be linked in after you compile your program. The libraries are divided according to **memory model**. These models set the allowable sizes of the code and data areas; the calls or data references of the functions under the various memory models will have to use one- or two-word addresses depending on the model used. The memory model definitions are in Table 7-1 (and they'll be as important to us in assembly language as they are in C).

Table 7-2 shows a summary of Table 7-1.

When we compile and link, we can specify the model we want to use, small, medium, or whatever is appropriate. For example, using the command line compilers, we can indicate our choice with a switch such as **-AH**, which indicates to Microsoft C that we want to use the huge model. In Turbo C we would use the switch **-mh**.

Model	DATA versus 64K	CODE versus 64K	Arrays versus 64K
Tiny	<	<	<
Small	<	<	<
Medium	<	>	<
Compact	>	<	<
Large	>	>	<
Huge	>	>	> *

*Except in Quick C

Table 7-2. Summary of Table 7-1.

TIP   You don't have to indicate a memory model at all: If you don't specify which memory model you want to use, the default is small, limiting both code and data to 64K each.

Using memory models, we set the size limits of the code and data areas for our program. C programs always use different segments for data and for code (except for the tiny model), so, even under the small model, our program can be up to 128K long. If you have more than 64K of data, and therefore need multiple segments for data — but not for code — use the compact model. If you have more code than 64K, and so need multiple segments for code — but not for data — use the medium model. If both parts of your program are greater than 64K, use the large memory model.

There is one more option: the **huge** memory model. The difference between large and huge is only in pointer arithmetic. As you move through an array with a pointer, only the offset part of the pointer is normally incremented. For example, under the large model, when you increment the pointer 5000:FFFF, you don't get 6000:0000 as you should. Instead, you get 5000:0000. Only the offset part of the pointer has been incremented, and it is wrapped around to the bottom of the segment.

When you increment past the end of one segment while using the huge memory model, however, the pointer is handled correctly (that is, the segment address is updated to point to the next segment). Since the biggest thing we can create in C is a huge array of more than 64K, let's dig into this a little more.

A Huge Array

Here's a huge model program to make sure that the segment boundary is handled properly, and it includes an array of 75,000 bytes:

```
#include <malloc.h>
#include <stdio.h>

main()
{
    long i;
    int j = 0;
    char *array;

    array = (char *) halloc(75000, sizeof(char));
    for(i= 65535 - 10; i < 65535 + 10; i++){
        array[i] = j++;
        printf("array[%ld]: %d\n", i, array[i]);
    }

    return(0);
}
```

Note that we did not just declare the array as char **array[75000]**. That would have made it an automatic variable and undoubtedly would have given us an immediate stack overflow when the program ran. Instead, we allocate space for the array after the program has started, using a function named **halloc( )**, the function for allocating huge arrays. In Turbo C, this function is named **farmalloc( )**, and you have to use **alloc.h**, not **malloc.h**. In addition, you only include one parameter for **farmalloc( )**, the number of bytes requested. Finally, note that we had to make the array index, i, a long int.

This program will fill part of the array elements as we pass the segment boundary. We fill up the array elements across the segment boundary with the numbers 0 – 19:

```
#include <malloc.h>
#include <stdio.h>

main()
```

```
        {
            long i;
            int j = 0;
            char *array;

            array = (char *) halloc(75000, sizeof(char));
            for(i= 65535 - 10; i < 65535 + 10; i++){
→               array[i] = j++;
                printf("array[%ld]: %d\n", i, array[i]);
            }

            return(0);
        }
```

When we run the program, it produces this output:

```
D:\>huge ←
array[65525]: 0
array[65526]: 1
array[65527]: 2
array[65528]: 3
array[65529]: 4
array[65530]: 5
array[65531]: 6
array[65532]: 7
array[65533]: 8
array[65534]: 9
array[65535]: 10
array[65536]: 11
array[65537]: 12
array[65538]: 13
array[65539]: 14
array[65540]: 15
array[65541]: 16
array[65542]: 17
array[65543]: 18
array[65544]: 19
```

Mixed-Model Programs

We should also note that when we link the program, using the huge model libraries, *all* pointers in the program become two- word pointers automatically. The fact that all memory addresses may change size at once has advantages and disadvantages. If all our pointers suddenly become two words long, it can slow down our program. It takes longer to get two words out of memory than one. Also, when our functions can handle more than 64K of code, longer addresses have to be used and maintained in function calls.

There is a way of getting around all this. If we are just using, say, a few objects with two-word addresses in our program, we should consider using the **near**, **far**, or **huge** keywords, called **segment override type modifiers**. For example, let's say that we are using the default **small** model. However, we want specifically to override the type of the character pointer named **farray**, making it into a huge pointer. We can do that like this:

```
      main()
      {
→         char huge *farray;
              :
              :
      }
```

This does not mean that we can use normal library functions with **farray**, however. We will be linking to the small library functions, and they haven't changed. If they expected a one-word pointer before, they will have problems with **farray** (the other variables in the program will still be fine, of course).

NOTE   When we link, the types of the memory objects we pass as parameters are automatically converted to the type the library function requires, and that may create an error.

If we wanted to use **farray**, we could use it without library functions, like this:

```
      main()
      {
          char huge *farray;

          for(i = 0; i < 83000; i++)
→             farray[i] = i % 255;
                  :
                  :
      }
```

Here, **farray[ ]** is only used internally. We do not call any library functions with it. In other words, we could not use **farray[ ]** unless we used the **huge** keyword, but that does not mean that we had to use the **huge** model.

Keyword	Data	Code	Pointer Arithmetic
near	16-bit addresses	16-bit addresses	16-bit
far	32-bit addresses	32-bit addresses	16-bit
huge	32-bit addresses	keyword not for code	32-bit

Table 7-3. Segment Override Type Modifiers.

TIP   It turns out that, because we can use keywords and create mixed-model programs, the compact model is rarely used in practice. The compact model allows up to 64K of code and more than 64K of data. However, it is normal only to have one or two very large data structures, and large or huge keywords are usually used for those.

Table 7-3 shows a summary of the segment override type modifiers.

Now that we know what memory models are all about, let's take a new look at the heap, and how it functions in the light of memory models.

Allocating Memory in Microsoft C

Microsoft C and Quick C both use **malloc( )**, and we're familiar with its use. Under the small and medium memory models, a near pointer will be returned. Under the compact, large, or huge memory models, a far pointer will be returned (note that **malloc( )** returns a far, not huge, pointer under the huge model). When you are using **malloc( )**, include the header file **malloc.h**.

Don't use **malloc( )** when allocating huge arrays. Use **halloc( )** instead, since **malloc( )** cannot return huge pointers and **halloc( )** can. Using any other function besides **halloc( )** would return only a near or far pointer.

Allocating Memory in Turbo C

In Turbo C, the situation is different. If you want to allocate memory on the near (i.e., same segment) heap, use **malloc( )**; if you want to allocate memory on the far heap and get a two-word pointer back, use the **farmalloc( )** function. Under the compact, large, or huge memory models, just replace **mal-loc( )** with **farmalloc( )**. To use these functions, include the header file **alloc.h**.

In the large data models — compact, large, and huge — you can use **farmalloc( )** to allocate more than 64K of memory, and a two-word pointer will be returned. If you want to use the default data segment, use **malloc( )** instead, and a one-word pointer will be returned. Either of these functions can be used in any model. The length of the returned pointer depends on the memory model used (i.e., what library we link to). For example, if you use **farmalloc( )** with the small model, the returned far pointer will be made into a near pointer. In the huge model, the returned pointer will be huge.

The realloc( ) Function

There may be times when we want to readjust our memory allocation. For example, if we are working on a document with a word processor and we delete a large fraction of it, we no longer need as much memory as we did before. For cases like this, we can use the **realloc( )** function; we just need to pass it the pointer we got from **malloc( )** and the new size of the object, like this:

```
array = (char *) realloc(array,newsize);
```

The **realloc( )** function will pass back the new address. Note that the newly returned pointer may not be the same as the old pointer; both the Turbo and Microsoft compilers use some form of heap management, so the memory chunks might be moved around when they are resized.

Freeing Memory in C

To return a chunk of allocated memory to the unallocated memory pool, use **free( )**. When you release memory on the Turbo C far heap, use **farfree( )**. Just pass the pointer to the section of memory that you want to release. Microsoft C also provides the means of releasing huge arrays. This can be done with **hfree( )**, although the same thing can be done with **free( )**. If you use **hfree( )**, pass the name of the huge array; the whole array is deallocated at one time.

To sum up, then, heap management is just a process of deciding how much memory we want (if it is available), and asking for it. If the amount we want is over 64K, we have to consider which memory model we want. Let's put this information to work.

Updating the copier.c Program

We developed a small copier program in Chapter 5. That program read files in 32K chunks and wrote them out again, making a copy of the original file. Why did we use only 32K? One reason was that we were restricted to only one segment of data under the (default) small model. Since C puts some information of its own in the data segment, we didn't have the whole 64K open to us, and 32K was a good round number.

On the other hand, there is no reason why we have to restrict ourselves to just one data segment now. We can compile and link using the huge memory model, using a 64K data buffer.

You might even think that we could set up a larger memory buffer, say 128K. Unfortunately, the **read( )** function, which **copier.c** uses to read data, can only take numbers up to 64K - 2 in any memory model. It returns an int value — the number of bytes read — which already puts a limit of 65,535 on the size of the return value. However, it also returns a value of -1 if there was an error, and 65,535 (or 0xffff) is actually the way C stores a value of -1, as we'll see in Chapter 12. In other words, to C, 0xffff is equal to -1, so we couldn't tell if there had been an error or if we had actually read that many bytes. That means we can make the buffer size, **BUFFSIZE**, equal to a maximum of 64K - 2.

Even so, that's almost twice as good as before. Let's adapt **copier.c** into **copier2.c**. The change is very easy to make, since we defined **BUFFSIZE** right in the beginning of the program. All we have to do is make these changes, and then compile and link under the huge memory model (using Microsoft C here):

```
#define BUFFSIZE (64 * 1024) - 2  ←
#include <stdio.h>
#include <fcntl.h>
#include <sys\types.h>
#include <sys\stat.h>
#include <io.h>
#include <malloc.h>

main()
{
    char *buffer;
    char source_file_name[50];
    char target_file_name[50];
    int source_handle;
```

```
              int target_handle;
→     unsigned int number_read;

→     if((buffer = halloc((long) BUFFSIZE, 1)) == NULL){
              printf("Halloc could not allocate.");
              exit(1);
       }
       printf("Source file:");
       scanf("%s", source_file_name);
       printf("Target file:");
       scanf("%s", target_file_name);

       if((source_handle = open(source_file_name, O_RDONLY
           | O_BINARY)) == -1){
           printf("Couldn't open source file.");
           exit(1);
       }

   if((target_handle = open(target_file_name, O_CREAT\
           | O_WRONLY
           | O_BINARY, S_IWRITE )) == -1){
           printf("Couldn't open target file.");
           exit(1);
       }

       while (number_read = read(source_handle, buffer,\
       BUFFSIZE))
           write(target_handle, buffer, number_read);

       close(source_handle);
       close(target_handle);

       return(0);
   }
```

We didn't even have to change the declaration of **buffer**; because we are using the huge memory model, **buffer** automatically became a huge pointer.

TIP It's worth noting that we could also have used the large memory model here, not the huge one. However, we chose not to because in Microsoft C, **malloc( )** can't even allocate 64K - 2 bytes; it needs to put 20 bytes of header information in an allocated segment, and we would have had to set **BUFF-SIZE** to a maximum of 64K - 20. There is no such restriction in Turbo C. You can allocate memory space up to 65,535 bytes with **malloc( )]** (after which you must go to **farmalloc( )**).

Note that in our call to **halloc( )**, we used a type cast of long for the buffer size (**BUFFSIZE**), since **halloc( )** expects a long value. We also changed the variable that holds the number of bytes read (**number_read**) from **int** to **unsigned int**. The reason for this is that signed ints can only hold numbers up to 32,767, while unsigned ints can go up to 65,535. That completes the work we'll do here on the heap and allocating memory. Let's continue now with the stack.

The Stack

The stack is the section of memory set up and maintained by the C program for three purposes:

- Storing automatic variables
- Passing parameters to functions
- Storing return addresses

We'll cover these topics in the following pages. Let's start immediately with automatic variables.

Automatic Variables

By default, all variables in a C program that are inside a code block are **automatic**. As we've seen, that means that C allocates memory space for them when it enters their code block. All variables are automatic except for global variables (which are defined outside any code block); static variables (expressly declared with the keyword static so that they are stored in the data areas, not the stack); initialized arrays and structures (usually stored in the data areas, although that is compiler dependent); and register variables (which are stored in a microprocessor register if possible). We've already seen an example of how automatic variables work:

```
void my_func(void);

main()
{
    my_func();
    my_func();

    return(0);
}
```

```
        void my_func(void)
        {
→           int her_int = 5;

            her_int++;
            printf("The value of her_int is: %d.\n", her_int);
        }
```

In this case, memory for **her_int** is set aside each time the function **my_func( )** is entered, so the program prints out:

```
The value of her_int is: 6.
The value of her_int is: 6.
```

Memory space on the stack is allocated for automatic variables when the program enters the code block in which they are declared; a code block is defined in C as a program statement(s) within curly braces. For example, we can add automatic variables to our earlier memory-use program like this:

```
        #include <malloc.h>

        int my_int, his_int = 3;

        main()
        {
→           int our_int;
            char *my_data;

            my_int = 5;
            my_int++;
            his_int -= 10;

            my_data = malloc(10);

            return(0);
        }
```

| TIP | Setting aside large arrays of automatic variables when a function is called can add significant amounts of overhead to a program. If you're looking for speed, keep that in mind. |

The space for **our_int** would then be set up in the stack when the program started (and the **main( )** code block was entered), like this:

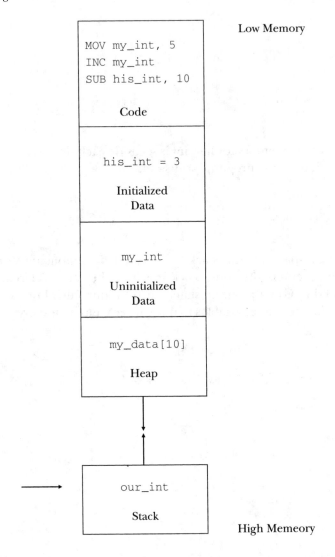

To review memory use, then: If we declare a variable static, a new copy of it is not made every time its function or block is entered. Instead, undisturbed space is set aside for it in the data area, not on the stack. Automatic variables are stored on the stack, static ones in the data area. If the static variables are initialized, as seen below,

```
static int i = 215;
```

then they are stored in the initialized part of the data area. If they are declared as uninitialized,

```
static int i;
```

then they are stored in the uninitialized data area. Since the data area is not reallocated whenever a function or block is entered, a static variable's value is just that, static.

All variables declared inside a code block are automatic by default. In fact, there is a keyword, **auto**, that you can use before a variable's declaration like this:

```
auto int j = 5;
```

This guarantees that a variable is automatic, but since automatic data types are the default, it is not necessary. The reason these variables are called automatic is that memory space for them is automatically allocated for them when needed. We can add the types of variables stored on the stack to our memory-use diagram:

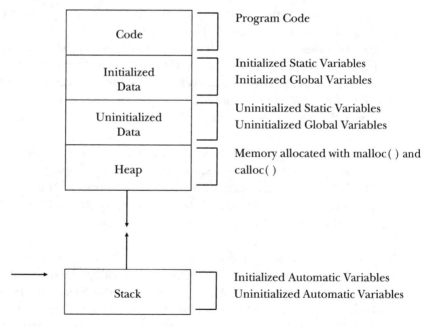

We can also add a few automatic variables to our data demonstration program like this:

```
int i;                  [Global → Uninitialized Data Area]
int j = 5;              [Global → Initialized Data Area]
```

```
        static int l = 5;        [Static Global → Initialized Data Area]
        static int m = 5;        [Static Global → Uninitialized Data Area]

        main()
        {
→           int n;               [Automatic → Stack]
→           int o = 5;           [Automatic → Stack]
            static int p;        [Static → Uninitialized Data Area]
            static int q = 5;    [Static → Initialized Data Area]
                :

        }
```

Now let's turn to a new topic, made possible by automatic variables. The fact that new memory space is allocated for all the variables in a block when that block is entered makes for a surprising fact in C: A function can call itself.

How Recursion Works

Because C makes a copy of all the data in a code block every time it enters that block, a function can call itself. The first time it is called, a function's data is allocated on the stack. Let's say that inside its own code the function calls itself again, which means that its data is allocated once again, further down the stack. This can keep going for many repetitions since these sets of data do not interfere with each other, there is no problem. There is a technique called **recursion** that makes use of this ability of functions to call themselves.

If we can break a problem up into a number of computationally identical levels, then we can use recursion. The traditional example is finding a number's factorial; a factorial is the product of a number multiplied by all the other positive integers down to 1. For instance, the factorial of 6, designated 6!, is equal to $6 \times 5 \times 4 \times 3 \times 2 \times 1 = 720$.

We can make this recursive by noticing that `n! = n * (n-1)!`. In other words, if our factorial function, **factorial( )**, is called **factorial(6)**, it can just return the value 6 * factorial(5). Of course, **factorial(5)** uses the function once again, and it returns 5 * **factorial(4)**. This process continues all the way down to **factorial(1)**. At this point, we know that 1! is 1, so we can simply return that value, 1. The returns then go back up the ladder of calls, and the answer is at last ready. In code, it looks like this:

```
#include <stdio.h>

int factorial(int the_number);
```

```
main()
{
    int my_int = 6;

    printf("The factorial of %d is %d.", my_int,\
    factorial(my_int));

    return(0);
}

int factorial(int the_number)
{
    if (the_number == 0) return 1;
    else return (the_number * factorial(the_number - 1));
}
```

That's all there is to it. We simply handle the final case explicitly:

```
#include <stdio.h>

int factorial(int the_number);

main()
{
    int my_int = 6;

    printf("The factorial of %d is %d.", my_int,\
    factorial(my_int));

    return(0);
}

int factorial(int the_number)
{
→   if (the_number == 0) return 1;
    else return (the_number * factorial(the_number - 1));
}
```

For all other cases, we use **factorial( )** again:

```
#include <stdio.h>

int factorial(int the_number);

main()
{
```

```
        int my_int = 6;

        printf("The factorial of %d is %d.", my_int,\
        factorial(my_int));

        return(0);
    }

    int factorial(int the_number)
    {
        if (the_number == 0) return 1;
→       else return (the_number * factorial(the_number - 1));
    }
```

That's it for recursion. However, we should also know that C does more interesting things than just use the stack for holding automatic variables. In addition, it passes parameters to functions using the stack. To see how that works, we have to first learn a few stack details (which will also be very useful to us when we connect C to assembly language).

How the Stack Works

The way the stack works will take a little examination. It is made up of a section of memory that is addressed as words (i.e., two bytes each), rather than as bytes. For example, let's say that this is part of the stack in memory:

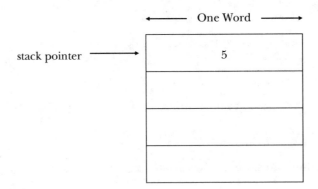

Notice the stack pointer, which points at a particular word called the **top** of the stack. When we put a word, such as 7, onto the stack, the stack pointer is **decremented** by 2 bytes to point to the previous word, and the 7 is placed at that location:

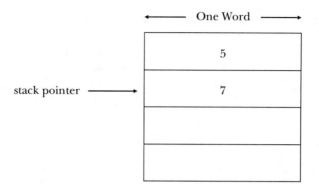

In this way, we **push** a value onto the stack (we can only push word values at a time). Next, we could push a value of, say, 12:

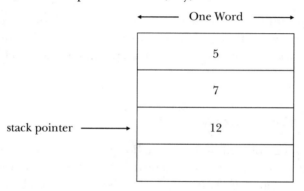

We can retrieve these values by **popping** them off the stack. If we pop one value from the stack, that will be the last value pushed, or 12, and the stack pointer moves up:

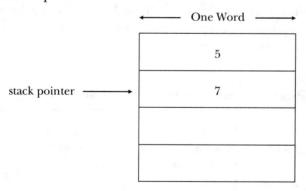

TIP A popular and useful way of thinking of the stack is with the abbreviation **FILO**, which means **FI**rst on, **L**ast **O**ff.

Popping the stack again yields a value of 7:

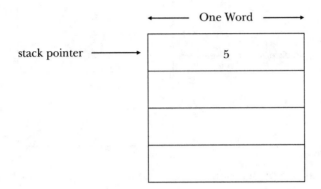

And so on until all the values have been popped. Note that they come off in the reverse order that they were put on. Now that we know how the stack actually works, we can see how C passes parameters to functions.

The C Calling Convention

The C calling convention indicates how parameters are pushed on the stack when a function is called. This convention, as shown in Table 7-4, holds for Microsoft C, Quick C, Turbo C, Turbo C++, and Turbo C++ Pro.

C parameters are passed by value (not as addresses as is the case with FORTRAN or BASIC), except for arrays, which are passed by reference (i.e., with a pointer). That reference is the address of the first element of the array, and it is either two or four bytes long. For near arrays, it will be two bytes; for far arrays it will be four bytes.

	Language	Parameters Pushed	Parameters Passed	Return Type
	BASIC	In order	As offset addresses	RET #
	FORTRAN	In order	As FAR addresses	RET #
→	C	In REVERSE order	As values	RET
	Pascal	In order	As values	RET #

Table 7-4. Calling Conventions.

The C calling convention also differs from other high-level languages in that it pushes the values to pass in **reverse** order (i.e., right-to-left). We will see this more clearly when we discuss the stack upon entering our assembly language procedures. For now, let's just see an example; we might want to pass two parameters to a function named **summer( )**, which adds those two numbers. Here is the way it might look:

```
int summer(int a, int b);

main()
{
    printf("3 + 2 = %d\n", summer(3, 2));

    return(0);
}
```

In most other languages, the 3 would be pushed (or its address), followed by the 2. However, C pushes parameters in reverse order, so the 2 will be pushed first, followed by the 3. Then it pushes the return address, the address C will return to when it is done with the function call and ready to proceed with the program.

When we invoke a function, C has to remember where it was before going off to that function, and it stores its current location (that is, its current address) on the stack. If it did not store its current location, we would not know where to return to after the function was executed. For that reason, this is what the stack will look like when we start to use it in **summer( )**:

In the case of large, medium, or huge memory models, the return address will be four bytes long, which means that the locations of all parameters will be shifted up by 2 bytes:

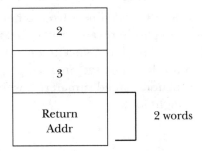

The function itself can now pick the parameters off the stack. In fact, we will do precisely that when we write a C function in assembly language later. Most of the time, C handles this process — taking parameters off the stack — for us, but we'll see how to do it ourselves towards the end of the book.

That's it, then, for the stack, as well as for the other parts of memory, the code area, the data areas, and the heap. We've seen all four in this chapter, so we're on the path to becoming memory experts. In fact, we'll have more to say about the way we use memory in the following chapter, when we cover advanced pointer use.

Advanced Pointers

We've seen how pointers work before, as far back as Chapter 3, and we've seen how useful they can be. However, there's a great deal about pointers that we haven't covered yet, much of which can add power and speed to our programs. In this chapter, we're going to go wild with pointers, becoming pointer experts and seeing how they can save us time, memory space, and a lot of trouble. We'll also see how pointers can be helpful when we're sorting records and setting up data lists in our programs. Once you become proficient in their use, you'll find that many programming tasks are made much easier and that pointers are natural to use. Let's start with a popular topic from the C programmer's pointer of view, seeing arrays as pointers.

From Arrays to Pointers

By now we're quite familiar with the use of arrays in C. If we want to use an array, we first have to declare it, like this:

```
      main()
      {
→         int array[10];
              :
              :
      }
```

We can refer to individual elements of this array with an index which we might call **i**:

```
main()
{
    int array[10], i=3;
        :
→       array[i] = 7;
        :
}
```

We mentioned earlier that the name of an array is really a pointer, and now it's time for a fuller explanation. What that means is that the word **"array"** in our program really stands for the address at which the array's data begins. That is to say, **array[0]** is equal to *__array__; the two expressions are interchangeable. This is an important fact, and much of this chapter is built on it.

It may make sense that array, as used in our program, is the name of a pointer pointing to the beginning of the array, but you may wonder how we might be able to access an element like **array[i]**. After all, what if the array is of a type where all elements are two bytes long?

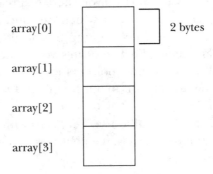

We can see that *__array__ might be **array[0]**:

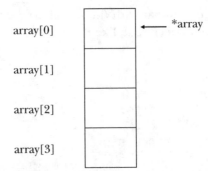

But then how do we reach **array[1]**? It turns out that we can add 1 to **array** and point to the next element like this:

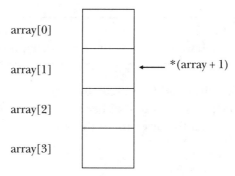

As we saw in Chapter 3, the compiler is smart enough to know how pointer addition should work. When we add 1 to **array**, C will check **array**'s type (let's say it's int) and realize that each element is two bytes long. It will then add two bytes to array, so we end up with the address of **array[1]**. In other words, when we add values to a pointer, the values are understood to be in units of elements, not bytes.

As we've seen, we can add numbers to pointers and even subtract two pointers from each other to find a relative offset. Let's take a look at an example showing how to subtract two pointers. After we subtract them, the result will be in units of the array's element size, not bytes. For instance, look at this program:

```
#include <stdio.h>

/* count number of array elements */

main()
{
    float array[] = {3.14, 2.13, 1.73, 1.44, 2.32}, \
          *begin_ptr, *end_ptr;

    begin_ptr = &array[0];
    end_ptr = &array[5];

    printf("Number of elements from beginning to end: %d",\
    end_ptr - begin_ptr);
}
```

Here we subtract two pointers to find the distance in elements between **end_ptr** and **begin_ptr**. The result of the program is 5, as it should be since pointer subtraction is done in terms of elements, not bytes. (If we had asked for **begin_ptr - end_ptr**, the result would have been -5.)

TIP   If you want to find distances in words, cast the pointers into integers first. (For far pointers, which we'll get to next chapter, use long ints.)

Now we know how to address **array[0]** in pointer notation: *array. And we've seen that **array[1]** is ***(array + 1)** because of the way pointer addition works. We can extend that to any element this way:

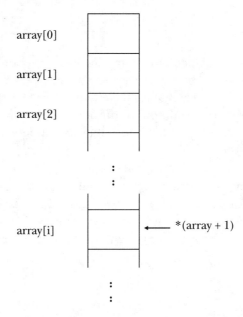

Which means that, in general, we can say this for **array[i]**:

array[i] = *(array + i)

In other words, we can substitute ***(array + i)** for **array[i]** in our programs. In the example we've just seen, that would produce this:

```
main()
{
    int array[10], i=3;
        :
→       *(array + i) = 7;
        :
}
```

Here's another example. In Chapter 3, we used this program to demonstrate the use of arrays:

```c
#include <stdio.h>

/* Record test scores. */

main()
{
    int loop_index, scores[5];

    scores[0] = 92;
    scores[1] = 73;
    scores[2] = 57;
    scores[3] = 98;
    scores[4] = 89;

    for (loop_index = 0; loop_index < 5; loop_index++)
        printf("Student's score: %d\n", scores[loop_index]);
}
```

We just set up a loop to fill the five elements of the array **scores[ ]** with integer test score values and then printed them out. Now we can change that from array to pointer notation like this:

```c
        #include <stdio.h>

        /* Record test scores using pointer notation. */

        main()
        {
          int loop_index, scores[5];

→         *(scores + 0) = 92;
:         *(scores + 1) = 73;
:         *(scores + 2) = 57;
          *(scores + 3) = 98;
          *(scores + 4) = 89;

          for (loop_index = 0; loop_index < 5; loop_index++)
→             printf("Student's score: %d\n", *(scores + \
                  loop_index));
        }
```

The two programs give the same result. At first, substituting ***(array + i)** for **array[i]** might seem like nothing more than an exercise in making programs more complex and difficult to read. It turns out, however, that there really is a good deal more here, both in terms of execution speed and memory-storage efficiency.

How to Make Your Programs Faster

For example, let's take a look at this program:

```
main()
{
    char array[] = "Hello, world.\n";
    int i;

    for(i = 0; i < 14; i++)
        putch(array[i]);
}
```

It prints out the string `"Hello, world\n"`. one character at a time. Each time through, we increment the index **i** and print the character **array[i]**. However, each time we make the reference to **array[i]**, the program is forced to find the location in memory at which that element is stored like this:

```
&array[0] + i*sizeof(char)
```

In other words, C starts at the base address of the array (**&array[0]**) finds the offset of the desired element into the array (**i * sizeof(char)**), and adds the two to get the element's address. In this simple case, **sizeof(char)** is just one byte and the multiplication is easy, but, if we had an array of floats or doubles, it would be different. Each time we reference an item in an array, a multiplication is performed, and multiplications are among the most time-consuming instructions in the 80×86. On the other hand, consider a change to the program like this:

```
        main()
        {
            char array[] = "Hello, world.\n",\
            *array_pointer = array;  ←
            int i;

            for(i = 0; i < 14; i++)
                putch(array[i]);

→           for(i = 0; i < 14; i++)
→               putch(*array_pointer++);
        }
```

Now we've added a pointer to the beginning of the array named **array_pointer** (note that we were able to initialize it when we declared it as well). Each time through the loop, we increment **array_pointer** and print out ***array_pointer**. The result is the same as before; the string `"Hello, world.\n"` is printed. However, even though we did the same thing (incremented through the elements of an array), no multiplications were involved. In other words, we're moving through the array simply by incrementing a pointer. We start like this:

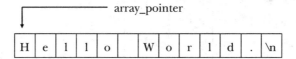

Every time through the loop, **array_pointer** points to the next element:

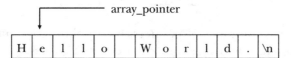

When the compiler sees an expression like **array_pointer++**, it simply encodes that as **array_pointer + sizeof(char)**. This is an improvement over arrays: We didn't have to find an element's address from scratch. Since hardware multiplications are very slow instructions, we've saved a good deal of time. Incrementing (or decrementing) a pointer through the elements of an array is far faster than generating a complete address for the item **array[i]**, and, using pointer notation, we can take advantage of that fact.

How to Save Memory Space

Besides frequently being faster, there are other reasons to consider pointer notation instead of array notation. Consider an array of character strings:

array[0][ ]	H	e	l	l	o	0					
array[1][ ]	W	o	r	l	d	.	0				
array[2][ ]	M	a	r	s	h	m	a	l	l	o	w	0
array[3][ ]	F	l	i	n	g	i	n	g	0			
array[4][ ]	r	e	d	0							
array[5][ ]	b	u	t	t	o	n	s	0			
array[6][ ]	w	i	l	d	l	y	0				

You can see that much space is wasted: The array has to have as many columns as there are characters in the longest string. With an array of pointers instead, however, we can do this:

array[0][ ] →	H	e	l	l	o	0					
array[1][ ] →	W	o	r	l	d	.	0				
array[2][ ] →	M	a	r	s	h	m	a	l	l	o	w	0
array[3][ ] →	F	l	i	n	g	i	n	g	0		
array[4][ ] →	r	e	d	0							
array[5][ ] →	b	u	t	t	o	n	s	0			
array[6][ ] →	w	i	l	d	l	y	0				

Here we have a number of pointers, each pointing to character strings. No space is wasted: The strings can be stored one right after the other. Frequently, memory is at a premium in programs, and using pointers instead of arrays can save much room. (In addition, we can also support variable-length fields this way.)

Two-Dimensional Arrays

Now let's go on to two-dimensional arrays. When the compiler sees a program like this:

```
main()
{
    int array[4][3], i=1, j = 2;
        :
    array[i][j] = 7;
        :
}
```

it makes up a formula to reference data items in **array[ ][ ]**. That kind of formula looks like this:

```
array[i][j] = *(&array[0][0] + 3*i + j)
```

In other words, the compiler knows where the array starts in memory (i.e., the address of **array[0][0]**). In order to find **array[i][j]**, it has to set up an equation like the one above, since the array is stored like this:

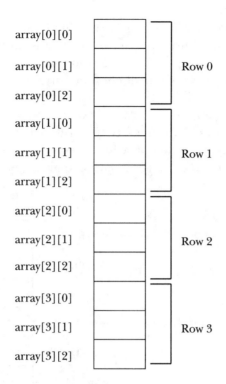

All three columns of row 0 are stored first, followed by all three columns of row 1, and so on. To find **array[i][j]**, C uses this formula: `array[i][j] = *(&array[0][0] + 3*i + j)`. To find an element, we only need to know the number of columns (three here), not the total number of rows. This is because C only needs the second index to know where to find a particular element; it has to skip over groups of numbers — three at a time — to get to the right location, so three is the only important number here.

TIP   There are a few tricks used by experienced C programmers worth mentioning here. As we saw earlier, C does not normally let you pass a whole array to a function. However, if we do want pass a copy of the whole array, it is worth knowing that you can make the array into a structure element. Paradoxically, C does let you pass whole structures to functions. In this same way, you can make array assignments. The statement `array2 = array1;` is illegal. However, if you make the arrays elements of a structure, there is no problem. The statement `struct2 = struct1;` works perfectly.

Now let's look at two-dimensional arrays in pointer notation. If a one-dimensional array name is just a pointer to the first element of an array, what is a two-dimensional array name? It turns out that a two-dimensional array name is a pointer to an array of one-dimensional arrays.

Let's take this step by step. Above, we saw how an array declared as **int array[4][3]** was stored in memory. It turns out that after we've made that declaration, expressions like **array[0]** or **array[1]** are legal in our program too. They are just pointers to one-dimensional arrays, each of which makes up a row:

```
array[0][0] ──────▶ array[0][0]  ┌──────────┐
                                  │          │
                      array[0][1] ├──────────┤
                                  │          │
                      array[0][2] ├──────────┤
                                  │          │
array[0][0] ──────▶ array[1][0]  ├──────────┤
                                  │          │
                      array[1][1] ├──────────┤
                                  │          │
                      array[1][2] ├──────────┤
                                  │          │
array[2][0] ──────▶ array[2][0]  ├──────────┤
                                  │          │
                      array[2][1] ├──────────┤
                                  │          │
                      array[2][2] ├──────────┤
                                  │          │
array[3][0] ──────▶ array[3][0]  ├──────────┤
                                  │          │
                      array[3][1] ├──────────┤
                                  │          │
                      array[3][2] └──────────┘
```

The name **array** is itself just a pointer to this one-dimensional array of pointers:

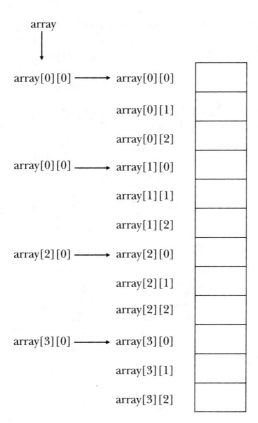

If we make the declaration int **array[4][3]**, then **array** is a pointer to an array whose elements are **array[0]**, **array[1]**, and **array[2]** (in other words, **array** is a pointer to a pointer). Also, **array[1]** is a pointer to an array whose elements are **array[1][0]**, **array[1][1]**, and **array[1][2]**:

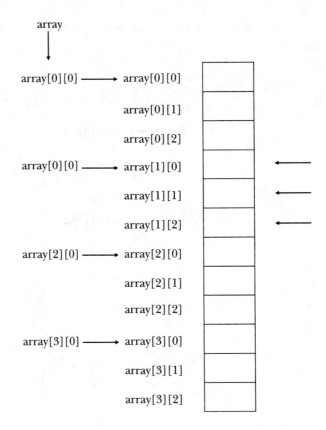

In general, an element can be reached like this:

```
*(array[m] + n) = array[m][n]
```

If we expand the expression **array[m]**, using the fact that **array[m] = *(array + m)**, we get this:

```
*(*(array + m) + n) = array[m][n]
```

Note that in the case of **array[0][0]**, this breaks down to ****array**, and this is exactly a pointer to a pointer (two indirection operators are used). Each time we increment the **m** in ***(*(array + m) + n)**, we move by one row through **array[ ][ ]**. To sum up our exploration of two-dimensional arrays, then, take a look at these expressions. They all refer to the same object:

```
array[m][n]
*(array[m] + n)
*(*(array + m) + n)
*(*array + m * column_size + n)
```

We can put these ways of looking at two-dimensional arrays together in this program, which prints out 7,7,7:

```
#include <stdio.h>

/* print out an array element three ways */

main()
{
    int array[4][3];

    array[2][1] = 7;
    printf("%d,%d,%d",array[2][1],*(*array + 2*3 + 1),\
    *(*(array + 2) + 1));
}
```

Now we've gotten experience in understanding arrays in pointer notation. It's not always advisable to use pointers instead of arrays, but they can be very helpful if we're incrementing through an array or if we have variable length elements (as in the case of an array of strings). C provides us with other powerful ways of using pointers as well, and one of those ways is using pointers to structures, which we'll take a look at next.

Pointers to Structures

Using pointers to structures is so popular a technique that a new operator, called the arrow operator by C programmers, was developed, and it looks like this: ->. In other words, if we set up a structure named **my_data** that looked like this:

```
struct large_data_struct{
    int key;
    int big_array[20];
} my_data;
```

Then we could declare a pointer named **my_pointer** to **my_data** like this:

```
struct large_data_struct *my_pointer;
```

And assign a value to it this way:

```
my_pointer = &my_data;
```

From now on, we can refer to the fields in **my_data**, like **my_data.key**, like this:

```
my_pointer->key = 5;   /* same as my_data.key */
```

In other words, **my_pointer** is a pointer to a structure; to reach a field in the structure it points to, use the arrow operator, **->**. That's the reason the **->** operator was developed: To let you pick the individual fields out of the structure you're pointing to. It was added to the * and & operators expressly for those cases when you point to a structure, because & or * alone can't access elements. That is, there is no such thing as ***my_pointer.key**; we have to use **my_pointer->key** instead.

One case in which pointers to structures are very useful is when you have a number of structures in an array, like this:

```
struct large_data_struct{
    int key;
    int big_array[20];
} my_data[10];            ←
```

In this case, each element of the array **my_data[ ]** is a structure that holds a considerable amount of data — both an integer named key and a twenty element array named **big_array[ ]**. Arrays of structures like this are frequently used to hold records, and operations that are frequently performed on such records involves moving them around in memory. For example, we might sort them, delete one and move the others up, or even add one and move the others down. However, moving the elements of an array of structures around in memory can be a very time consuming process; each time you move such a structure, you have to move the whole thing. There is, however, a faster way of doing things which moves only pointers around, not records. To see how that works, we'll make an exploration of record sorting next.

Fast Sorting Techniques

Professional database programs don't actually move records themselves, only pointers to the records. This method is a great deal faster. For example, imagine that the situation was as shown below, where we have three elements in the array **my_data[ ]**, each of which is a structure, and a pointer to each of those structures in the array **my_pointers[ ]**:

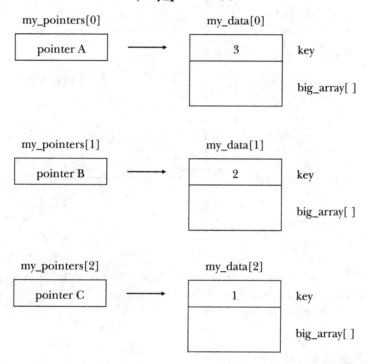

We can refer to the value of the field named key in record 0 like this: **my_pointers[0]->key**, and the value there is 3. The corresponding field in record 1 is **my_pointers[1]->key**, which holds 2, and so on:

```
my_pointers[0]->key: 3
my_pointers[1]->key: 2
my_pointers[2]->key: 1
```

Now let's say that we want to sort the records on the value in key. We can do that just by moving the pointers around (which keep pointing the same structure as they did before), like this:

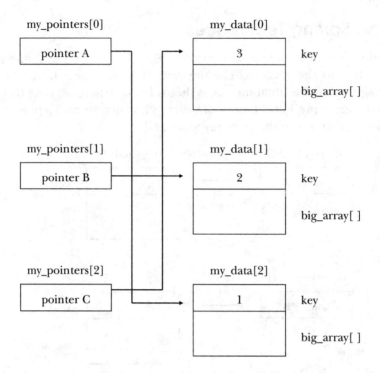

Now the pointer in **my_pointers[0]** points to **my_data[2]**, and so on. That means that **my_pointer[0]->key** has changed from 3 to 1, because that pointer is now pointing at the last record:

```
my_pointers[0]->key: 1
my_pointers[1]->key: 2
my_pointers[2]->key: 3
```

Of course, we can reach **big_array[ ]** using **my_pointers[ ]** also, so it would look to our program as if all the records have been moved around. In other words, we have changed the *apparent* ordering of the records, just by moving the pointers around used to reference them. This is a very quick way to sort when we have a lot of data. We can also see how this looks in code with an example. To do that, however, we have to learn how to sort data. For that reason, we'll take a look at how the shell sort works, which is itself a very useful topic in C.

How Shell Sorts Work

The standard shell sort is always popular among programmers. It works like this: Say you had a one-dimensional array with these values in it:

8 7 6 5 4 3 2 1

To sort this list into ascending order, divide it into two partitions like this:

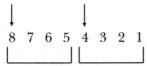

Then compare the first element of the first partition with the first element of the second:

8 7 6 5 4 3 2 1

In this case, 8 is greater than 4, so we switch the elements, and go on to compare the next pair:

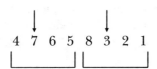

Again, 7 is greater than 3, so we switch and go on:

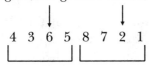

We also switch 6 and 2 and then look at the last pair:

After we switch them too, we get this as the new list:

4 3 2 1 8 7 6 5

While this is somewhat better than before, we're still not done. The next step is to divide each partition itself into two partitions, and repeat the process, comparing 4 with 2 and 8 with 6:

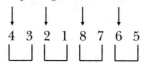

We switch both pairs and go on, comparing 3 with 1 and 7 with 5:

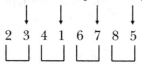

Again, we switch the second set of two pairs, leaving us with this:

2 1 4 3 6 5 8 7

This looks even closer. Now the partition size is down to one element, which means that this is the last time we'll need to sort the list. We need to compare the first, and only, element in each partition with the first, and only, element in the next partition. Here that means that we compare elements 2, 4, 6, and 8 with elements 1, 3, 5, and 7. When we swap them all, we get:

1 2 3 4 5 6 7 8

And that is how the standard shell sort works, at least if there's an even number of items to sort (in which case breaking them up into balanced partitions is easy). The case where we have an odd number of elements is slightly more difficult. For example, if we had a list of nine elements to sort, we would start by breaking them up into two partitions like this (note that there is no last element in the second partition):

Now we'd compare as before, switching as necessary, until we try to compare a value in the first partition to a value in the second partition that isn't there:

In this case, we just don't perform any comparison (i.e., there is no value in the x position that might have to be placed earlier in the array). Instead, we just continue on to the next smaller partition size. We keep going as before, working until the partition size becomes 1, perform the final switches, and then we're done.

TIP   Another sorting method is the Quicksort, which can be faster than shell sorts in certain cases. First find a key, or test, value to compare values to. The best value is the median value of the elements of the array, but usually a random entry is chosen. Then divide the array into two partitions: those less than the test value, and those greater. Move upward in the array until you come to the first value that is greater than the test value, and down the array (starting from the end) until you find a number less than the test value. Then swap them. Keep going until all the numbers in the first partition are less than the test value, and all the numbers in the second partition are greater. Then split each partition in two and repeat the process. Keep going in that way, splitting partitions continuously until there are just two numbers in a partition, at which point you can compare and switch them if necessary.

Let's see this in an example where we sort the pointers to an array of structures. We start off by setting up our data in the array **my_data[ ]**:

```
#include <stdio.h>

/* Example of sorting using pointers. */

main()
{
    struct large_data_struct{
        int key;
        int big_array[20];
    } my_data[10];               ←
        :
```

Next, we'll need a pointer to each structure in that array. In addition, we can load the descending values 10, 9, 8, ... 1 in the key fields at the same time and print them out like this:

```
#include <stdio.h>

/* Example of sorting using pointers. */

main()
{
    struct large_data_struct{
        int key;
        int big_array[20];
    } my_data[10];

    struct large_data_struct *my_pointers[10];
    int i;

    for(i = 0; i < 10; i++){
        my_data[i].key = 10 - i;
        my_pointers[i] = &my_data[i];
        printf("my_pointers[%d]->key: %d\n", i,\
        my_pointers[i]->key);
    }
        :
```

So far, our program has indicated that the key fields of the records are in exactly reverse order:

```
my_pointers[0]->key: 10
my_pointers[1]->key: 9
my_pointers[2]->key:  8
my_pointers[3]->key: 7
my_pointers[4]->key:  6
my_pointers[5]->key: 5
my_pointers[6]->key:  4
my_pointers[7]->key: 3
my_pointers[8]->key:  2
my_pointers[9]->key:  1
```

Now we have to sort the records by moving the pointers in the array **my_pointers[ ]** around. For example, when we're done, the pointer now in **my_pointers[0]** will be exchanged with the one in **my_pointers[9]**, so we'll get this:

```
my_pointers[0]->key: 1
            :
            :
            :
            :
my_pointers[9]->key: 10
```

Let's start developing the sorting part of the program. First, we have to decide on the partition size and set up the loop to loop over different partition sizes. In our case, that looks like this:

```
10  9  8  7  6  5  4  3  2  1
|_____|  |_____|
```

And we can do that this way, where we keep halving the partition size:

```
partition_size = number_items = 10;

do{
    partition_size = (partition_size + 1) / 2;
                :
                :
}while(partition_size > 1);
```

Note that our sorting code needs to know how many elements there are to sort (which you can find with **sizeof( )** if you need to). Next, we'll need to know the number of partitions so we can loop over each one, comparing the elements in it to the elements of the next partition. That number is not just **number_items** / **partition_size**, because **number_items** may not divide smoothly into **partition_size**, leaving us with an additional short partition on the end. Therefore, we set up **number_partitions** like this:

```
      partition_size = number_items = 10;

      do{
          partition_size = (partition_size + 1) / 2;
→         number_partitions = number_items / partition_size;
→         if (number_items%partition_size) number_partitions++;
                  :
      }while(partition_size > 1);
```

Now that we have **number_partitions** different partitions, we have to loop over them, comparing the elements of the current partition to the elements of the next. That means that we'll need an inner loop like this:

```
      partition_size = number_items = 10;

      do{
          partition_size = (partition_size + 1) / 2;
          number_partitions = number_items / partition_size;
          if (number_items%partition_size) number_partitions++;
→         for(i = 1; i < number_partitions; i++){
```

```
                :
                :
          }
     }while(partition_size > 1);
```

Because the current partition may be anywhere in the array, let's get the index of the first and last elements of the partition, and call them **first_index** and **last_index**:

```
                                              first_index
                                              last_index
partition_size = 5 ⟶ 10 9 8 7 6 5 4 3 2 1
```

That way, we can work from **first_index** to **last_index**, comparing the element at **first_index** to the one at **first_index + partition_size**, and so on up to **last_index**:

```
          partition_size = number_items = 10;

          do{
               partition_size = (partition_size + 1) / 2;
               number_partitions = number_items / partition_size;
               if (number_items%partition_size) number_partitions++;
→              first_index = 0;
               for(i = 1; i < number_partitions; i++){
→                   last_index = first_index + partition_size;
:                    if(last_index > number_items - partition_size)
:                         last_index = number_items - partition_size;
                     for(j = first_index; j < last_index; j++){
                          :
                          :
                          }
                    }
                    first_index += partition_size;
               }
          }while(partition_size > 1);
```

Here's where the real comparison is done. We have the location of the first element, **j**:

```
                       j
                       ↓
partition_size = 5     10 9 8 7 6 5 4 3 2 1
```

The element we want to compare it to is the corresponding element in the next partition, at location **j** + **partition_size**:

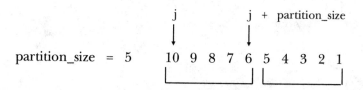

If we were using the array of **my_data[ ]**, we'd compare **my_data[j].key** to **my_data[j+partition_size].key**. However, we're using pointers, so we'll compare **my_pointers[j]->key** to **my_pointers[j+partition_size]->key** like this (including exchanging the pointers if we need to):

```
partition_size = number_items = 10;

do{
    partition_size = (partition_size + 1) / 2;
    number_partitions = number_items / partition_size;
    if (number_items%partition_size) number_partitions++;
    first_index = 0;
    for(i = 1; i < number_partitions; i++){
        last_index = first_index + partition_size;
        if(last_index > number_items - partition_size)
            last_index = number_items - partition_size;
        for(j = first_index; j < last_index; j++){
            if(my_pointers[j]->key >\
            my_pointers[j+partition_size]->key){
                temp = my_pointers[j+partition_size];\
                /* swap pointers */
                my_pointers[j+partition_size] =\
                my_pointers[j];
                my_pointers[j] = temp;
            }
        }
        first_index += partition_size;
    }
}while(partition_size > 1);
```

In this way, we compare each element in the current partition to the one in the next, then continue with the next partition, and so on. Then we divide the partition sizes in half and repeat the process, continuing until we're down to partition sizes of one. And that's it. Our pointer-sorting program is done. The whole program appears in Listing 8-1.

Listing 8-1. Example of Sorting with Pointers.

```c
#include <stdio.h>

/* Example of sorting using pointers. */

main()
{
    struct large_data_struct{
        int key;
        int big_array[20];
    } my_data[10];

    struct large_data_struct *temp, *my_pointers[10];
    int number_items, number_partitions, partition_size;
    int first_index, last_index, i, j;

    for(i = 0; i < 10; i++){
        my_data[i].key = 10 - i;
        my_pointers[i] = &my_data[i];
        printf("my_pointers[%d]->key: %d\n", i,\
        my_pointers[i]->key);
    }

    printf("Sorting.\n");

    partition_size = number_items = 10;

    do{
        partition_size = (partition_size + 1) / 2;
        number_partitions = number_items / partition_size;
        if (number_items%partition_size) number_partitions++;
        first_index = 0;
        for(i = 1; i < number_partitions; i++){
            last_index = first_index + partition_size;
            if(last_index > number_items - partition_size)
                last_index = number_items - partition_size;
            for(j = first_index; j < last_index; j++){
                if(my_pointers[j]->key >\
                my_pointers[j+partition_size]->key){
                    temp = my_pointers[j+partition_size];\
                    /* swap pointers */
                    my_pointers[j+partition_size] =\
                    my_pointers[j];
                    my_pointers[j] = temp;
                }
            }
            first_index += partition_size;
        }
```

Listing 8-1. *(continued)*

```
    }while(partition_size > 1);

    for(i = 0; i < 10; i++){
        printf("my_pointers[%d]->key: %d\n", i,
my_pointers[i]->key);
    }
}
```

C lets us do even more things with pointers, however, and there are some other very useful topics we should look at while we're on the subject. We'll start with pointers to functions.

Pointers to Functions

We can even define a pointer to a function in C, and this is occasionally useful. For example, it lets us treat functions almost like the elements of an array, allowing us, say, to read a menu response and dispatch the command off to the correct function. Another time to use pointers to functions is when you want one function to fill in for another. For example, let's say that you developed this software, which asks for today's date and the user's birthday:

```
#include <stdio.h>

void get_date(int *day, int *month, int *year);

/* Date-reading Example */

main()
{
    int birth_day, birth_month, birth_year;
    int this_day, this_month, this_year;

    printf("What is today? ");
    get_date(&this_day, &this_month, &this_year);

    printf("What is your birthday? ");
    get_date(&birth_day, &birth_month, &birth_year);
}

void get_date(int *day, int *month, int *year)
{
    scanf("%d/%d/%d", month, day, year);
}
```

In this way, the user can type in dates using the following format: 1/2/95. Now let's say that this program becomes so popular that you want to sell it in Europe as well. The date format there, however, is 2.1.95, where the day comes first, not the month. We can modify the program by first checking whether we're in America or Europe, and then calling the correct **get_date** function, **get_US_date( )** or **get_euro_date( )**. We start by adding the declaration of a function pointer named, appropriately, **function_pointer**:

```
#include <stdio.h>

/* Example showing pointers to functions. */

main()
{
    int birth_day, birth_month, birth_year;
    int this_day, this_month, this_year;
→   void (*function_pointer)();\
    /* declare function pointer */
        :
```

In general, the declaration of a pointer to a function looks like this:

```
type (*function_pointer_name)();
```

Here, type is return type of the function, and the parentheses around **function_pointer_name** are needed so that C can determine what the * operator is associated with. Next, we have to determine if we're in America or Europe, like this:

```
#include <stdio.h>
#include <ctype.h>

/* Example showing pointers to functions. */

main()
{
    int location;
    int birth_day, birth_month, birth_year;
    int this_day, this_month, this_year;
    void (*function_pointer)();\
    /* declare function pointer */
```

$\rightarrow$
```
        do{
            printf("Are we in (1) America or (2) Europe? ");
            scanf("%d", &location);
        }while(location != 1 && location != 2);
            :
```

If location is set to 1, we're in America; otherwise, we're in Europe. Now we can assign an address to **function_pointer**. It may surprise you to learn that, in C, the names of functions themselves are treated as pointers (that is, as addresses). In general, we assign the address of a function to a pointer just as we would any other pointer to pointer assignment. For example, we can assign **function_pointer** the address of **get_US_date( )** like this:

```
function_pointer = get_US_date;
```

TIP
In fact, you can even assign the addresses of C library functions to pointers, like this: **function_pointer = printf( );**, giving you considerable control over system resources.

That means that we can decide which date-getting function to use in our program like this:

```
#include <stdio.h>
#include <ctype.h>

void get_US_date(int *day, int *month, int *year);
void get_euro_date(int *day, int *month, int *year);

/* Example showing pointers to functions. */

main()
{
    int location;
    int birth_day, birth_month, birth_year;
    int this_day, this_month, this_year;
    void (*function_pointer)();\
    /* declare function pointer */

    do{
        printf("Are we in (1) America or (2) Europe? ");
        scanf("%d", &location);
```

```
      }while(location != 1 && location != 2);

→          function_pointer = location == 1 ? get_US_date :\
           get_euro_date;
              :
              :
```

All that remains is to use the function that's been assigned to **function_pointer**, and we can do that like this:

```
#include <stdio.h>
#include <ctype.h>

void get_US_date(int *day, int *month, int *year);
void get_euro_date(int *day, int *month, int *year);

/* Example showing pointers to functions. */

main()
{
    int location;
    int birth_day, birth_month, birth_year;
    int this_day, this_month, this_year;
    void (*function_pointer)();\
    /* declare function pointer */

    do{
        printf("Are we in (1) America or (2) Europe? ");
        scanf("%d", &location);
    }while(location != 1 && location != 2);

    function_pointer = location == 1 ? get_US_date :\
    get_euro_date;

    printf("What is today? ");
    (*function_pointer)(&this_day, &this_month,\
    &this_year);

    printf("What is your birthday? ");
    (*function_pointer)(&birth_day, &birth_month,\
    &birth_year);
}
```

That's it; the whole program, including **get_US_date( )** and **get_euro_date( )**, appears in Listing 8-2.

Listing 8-2. Example of Function Pointer Use.

```c
#include <stdio.h>
#include <ctype.h>

void get_US_date(int *day, int *month, int *year);
void get_euro_date(int *day, int *month, int *year);

/* Example showing pointers to functions. */

main()
{
    int location;
    int birth_day, birth_month, birth_year;
    int this_day, this_month, this_year;
    void (*function_pointer)(); /* declare function pointer */

    do{
        printf("Are we in (1) America or (2) Europe? ");
        scanf("%d", &location);
    }while(location != 1 && location != 2);

    function_pointer = location == 1 ? get_US_date :\
    get_euro_date;

    printf("What is today? ");
    (*function_pointer)(&this_day, &this_month, &this_year);

    printf("What is your birthday? ");
    (*function_pointer)(&birth_day, &birth_month, &birth_year);
}

void get_US_date(int *day, int *month, int *year)
{
    scanf("%d/%d/%d", month, day, year);
}

void get_euro_date(int *day, int *month, int *year)
{
    scanf("%d.%d.%d", day, month, year);
}
```

There are a few more topics to be covered while we're discussing data referencing with pointers, and they have to do with data organization. One of these topics is **linked lists**, which is a very popular programming construction that depends on the use of pointers. Let's explore that next.

Linked Lists

A linked list is an ideal way of storing data when you don't know in advance how many data items you'll have to store. It works this way: For each data item, there is also a pointer pointing to the next data item. At any time, you can add another data item to the list, as long as you update the last pointer to point to the new data item. If you start at the beginning of the list, you can work your way up by using the pointer in each item that points to the next item. The last pointer in the series is usually a NULL pointer (so you know the list is done when you reach it).

Schematically, a linked list looks like this:

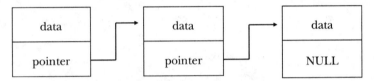

Note in particular that the last pointer is a NULL pointer. Here's what the structure type that makes up the elements of a linked list might look like:

```
struct list{
    char msg[20];
    struct list *ptr;
}
```

Note that it's legal to declare ptr as a pointer to the same type of structure that it's defined in; that is, structure type list. We can use that structure definition and set up a linked list with three elements, **item0**, **item1**, and **item2**:

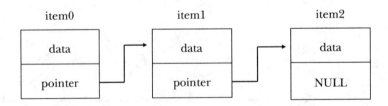

This is how it might look in code (note the initialization of each data structure — initializing with pointers this way only works in Microsoft products; in Borland products, you must assign these values in the program body, not when you declare the variables):

```c
#include <stdio.h>

/* Linked list example */

struct list{
    char msg[20];
    struct list *ptr;
};

main()
{
    struct list *pointer_to_next_item;
    struct list item2 = { " World.\n", NULL };
    struct list item1 = { " there,", &item2 };
    struct list item0 = { "Hello", &item1 };

    printf("%s", item0.msg);

    pointer_to_next_item = item0.ptr;
    printf("%s", pointer_to_next_item->msg);

    pointer_to_next_item = pointer_to_next_item->ptr;
    printf("%s", pointer_to_next_item->msg);
}
```

We work our way up the list by using the pointer in the present item, which points to the next item. In that way, the data items are chained together. The way to move up this chain is indicated in this line, where we update **pointer_to_the_next_item** to point to the one after that:

```c
pointer_to_next_item = pointer_to_next_item->ptr;
```

In addition to this kind of linked list, there are **doubly linked lists**. In this kind of list, there are two pointers, one to the next data item, and one to the last one. This way, we can move up and down the list.

Probably the most prominent example of a linked list in your computer is the File Allocation Table (FAT) on disks. This is a list of the clusters (the minimum size of disk storage allocation; on 360K diskettes, clusters are 1K long) allocated to files for storage, and since the files' size can grow, linked lists are appropriate. Each entry in the FAT, representing one cluster on the disk, holds the location of the next entry. To see what clusters a file is stored in, you work your way through the FAT until you come to the end-marker at the end of the list.

Circular Buffers

There is one other type of linked list, a list where the last item points to the first one so the whole thing forms a circle. This is called a **circular** or **ring buffer**. The most well-known circular buffer in your machine is the keyboard buffer.

What happens there is that while one part of the operating system is putting key codes into the keyboard buffer, another part is taking them out. The location in the buffer where they are put in is called the **tail** of the buffer, and the location where the next key code is read from is called the **head**.

When keys are typed in, the tail advances. When they are read, the head does. As you write to and read from the keyboard buffer, the head and tail march around. Note that any location in the circular buffer can be the head or the tail. When the buffer is filled, the tail comes up behind the head, and the buffer-full warning beeps.

Use circular buffers when some part of your program is reading data and some part is writing it, but at different rates. Store the location of the head and tail, and after you put data into the buffer, advance the tail. After you take data out, advance the head. This way, you can use the same memory space for reading and writing (as long as you keep taking out the data you put in and the buffer doesn't fill up).

We will have more to say about the keyboard buffer when we discuss assembly language. Before then, however, we will have more to say about the process of programming itself in the next chapter, when we debug our programs.

How to Debug C Programs

This is our debugging chapter. Even for the best programmers, errors still occur. This problem becomes more severe as programs become larger. The number of errors can increase, and they can become harder to find. Debugging becomes a fact of life for programmers, and, because it is, it is a topic we should cover.

Fortunately, we have some excellent debugging tools in C. The first one we'll cover is the **assertion statement**. Assertions are actually macros. They test statements you pass to them, and, if the statement turns out to be false, they halt the program and inform you that the assertion failed. After we cover assertions, we'll move on to the full screen debuggers that are available as we put debugging to work for us.

Using Assertions in Your Programs

Assertions can be very valuable. They can check whether certain conditions that you thought were true at some point in a program (e.g., `positive_number > 0`) are, in fact, true. Let's see an example with the following buggy program. This program is intended to read in a file named **file.dat** (if you're following along on your computer, you should create a text file named file.dat with random text in it at this point) and print out a character from the file on demand. Here it is:

```c
#include <malloc.h>     /* Borland products: #include <alloc.h> */
#include <stdio.h>

main()
{
    FILE *fptr;
    char *buffer;
    int i;

    fptr = fopen("files.dat", "rb");
    buffer = malloc(100);
    fread(buffer, 1, 100, fptr);
    fclose(fptr);

    printf("Character number to print:");
    scanf("%d",&i);

    printf("That character is %c.\n", buffer[i]);

    return(0);
}
```

When we run it, however, it generates a run time error and halts. What's wrong? We could start by checking the file pointer fptr with an assertion:

```c
#include <malloc.h>     /* Borland products: #include <alloc.h> */
#include <assert.h>
#include <stdio.h>

main()
{
    FILE *fptr;
    char *buffer;
    int i;

    fptr = fopen("files.dat", "rb");
    assert(fptr != NULL);                  ←
    buffer = malloc(100);
    fread(buffer, 1, 100, fptr);
    fclose(fptr);

    printf("Character number to print:");
```

```
    scanf("%d",&i);

    printf("That character is %c.\n", buffer[i]);

    return(0);
}
```

This new line, assert(fptr != NULL), checks the value of fptr. If there is something wrong with it, the assertion macro ends the program with an **exit(1)**. We can compile this program into, say, **assert.exe** and run it:

```
D>ASSERT
Assertion failed: fptr != NULL, file assert.c, line 13

Abnormal program termination
```

It appears that **fptr** was being left NULL. The assertion tells you what assertion failed (fptr != NULL), in what file (**assert.c**) and in what line (13). This makes debugging easier. You can fill your program with assertions and never see them unless there is an abnormal condition.

For example, we now know that **fopen( )** can't open **file.dat**. If we look at the **fopen( )** call, it's easy to see why. There was a error; we had been trying to open **files.dat**, not **file.dat**. We fix that and add another assertion for error checking:

```
#include <malloc.h>    /* Borland products: #include <alloc.h> */
#include <assert.h>
#include <stdio.h>

main()
{
    FILE *fptr;
    char *buffer;
    int i;

    fptr = fopen("file.dat", "rb");   ←
    assert(fptr != NULL);
    buffer = malloc(100);
    fread(buffer, 1, 100, fptr);
    fclose(fptr);

    printf("Character number to print:");
    scanf("%d",&i);
```

```
        assert(i >= 0);    ←

        printf("That character is %c.\n", buffer[i]);

        return(0);
    }
```

This new assertion checks whether the character we are requested to print out is always greater than or equal to 0. Assertions are frequently used for debugging, but they are usually left out of the final code. It's hard to see how much help the line: "Assertion failed: fptr != NULL, file assert.c, line 13" could be to an unsuspecting user.

C also has a much more powerful debugging tool: the interactive debugging environment provided by most compilers. After years of inadequate debuggers, powerful source-level debuggers are now available to us, and we will make use of them.

Interactive Debugging

Both Turbo and Microsoft Quick C have interactive editors with debugging features. Both debuggers function very similarly: you can set **breakpoints** or watch given values. In Quick C, you do this by selecting the Debug menu and then selecting **Breakpoints** or **Watch values**. In Turbo C, you select the **Break/Watch** menu and then work with **Breakpoints** or **Watch values** by pressing the indicated letter. Both menu systems are very easy to use.

Besides the menu system, there are a number of hotkeys that these debuggers use. Some important ones appear in Table 9-1.

Debugging Action	*Turbo*	*QuickC*
Execute program to cursor line	F4	F7
Trace (go through functions)	F7	F8
Trace (go around functions)	F8	F10
Display output screen	Alt-F5	F4
Select Watch menu	^F7	Alt-D Alt-W
Select Breakpoint menu	^F8	Alt-D Alt-B

Table 9-1. Debugging Hotkeys.

What is important, however, is not particular Alt key combinations or specific hotkeys, but debugging concepts. To illustrate, we'll use the Quick C debugger now, and the Turbo Debugger later in the chapter. Quick C supports the use of a mouse, so we won't need any Alt key combinations or hotkeys except F8 (Turbo: F7). Let's start off with a program named **bugs.c**. Here it is:

```c
#include <stdio.h>
#include <malloc.h>    /* Borland products: #include <alloc.h> */

main()
{
    FILE *fptr;
    int i, number;
    float answer;
    char *buffer;

    buffer = malloc(1000);
    fopen("file.dat", buffer);
    fread(buffer, 1, 20, fptr);

    for(i = 1; i < 20; i++){
        printf("%c", buffer[i]);
        if(buffer[i] == 'a') number++;
    }

    printf("Number of 'a's: %d", number);

    answer = addem(1.2, 3.1);
    printf("Answer: .2%f",answer);

}

addem(float param1, float param2)
{
    return (param1 + param2);
}
```

This program is intended to read in a small file named file.dat, whose contents are

```
This is a test.<cr>
```

The program, bugs.c is then supposed to print the file out, find the number of the character 'a's in the file, then use a function named **addem( )** to add 1.2

to 3.1, and print that result out. However, when we run it, it produces something like this:

```
i>@#t !^$5Number of 'a's: 2416Answer: .24.000000

run-time error R6001
- null-pointer assignment
```

There are obviously a few bugs here. Let's debug it; this is what the Quick C screen looks like:

```
 File   Edit   View   Search   Make   Run   Debug   Utility   Options      Help
 ────────────────────────────────── D:\BUGS.C ──────────────────────────────

 #include <stdio.h>
 #include <malloc.h>      /* Borland products: #include <alloc.h> */

 main()
 {                      ←
     FILE *fptr;
     int i, number;
     float answer;
     char *buffer;

     buffer = malloc(1000);
     fopen("file.dat", buffer);
     fread(buffer, 1, 20, fptr);

     for(i = 1; i < 20; i++){
         printf("%c", buffer[i]);
         if(buffer[i] == 'a') number++;
     }

 ──────────────────────────────────────────────────────────────────────────
 F1=Help   Enter   Esc=Cancel                                  00001:001
```

We're at the beginning of the program. We can trace through the program line by line. If we press F8 (Turbo: F7), we go to the next executable line:

```
 File   Edit   View   Search   Make   Run   Debug   Utility   Options      Help
─────────────────────────────── D:\BUGS.C ───────────────────────

#include <stdio.h>
#include <malloc.h>       /* Borland products: #include <alloc.h> */

main()
{
    FILE *fptr;
    int i, number;
    float answer;
    char *buffer;

    buffer = malloc(1000);       ←
    fopen("file.dat", buffer);
    fread(buffer, 1, 20, fptr);

    for(i = 1; i < 20; i++){
        printf("%c", buffer[i]);
        if(buffer[i] == 'a') number++;
    }
─────────────────────────────────────────────────────────
 F1=Help   Enter   Esc=Cancel                        00001:001
```

Since we are about to read from the file into buffer, we want to watch what is going on with the two variables **fptr** and **buffer**. We can watch variables in Quick C with the Debug (Turbo: Break/Watch) menu. If we choose it, we see these options:

```
 File   Edit   View   Search   Make   Run   Debug   Utility   Options      Help
─────────────────────────────────── D:\B │ Calls...
                                          │ Breakpoint...        F9
#include <stdio.h>                        │ Watchpoint...
#include <malloc.h>
                                          │ Quickwatch... Shift+F9
main()                                    │ Watch Value...
{                                         │ Modify Value...
    FILE *fptr;
    int i, number;                        │ History On
    float answer;                         │ Undo
    char *buffer;                         │ Replay
                                          │ Truncate User Input
    buffer = malloc(1000);          ←
    fopen("file.dat", buffer);
    fread(buffer, 1, 20, fptr);

    for(i = 1; i < 20; i++){
        printf("%c", buffer[i]);
        if(buffer[i] == 'a') number++;
    }


 F1=Help  Enter  Esc=Cancel                                    00001:001
```

We want to watch a variable, so we select the Watch Value... option. Quick C then asks for the name of the variable to watch, and we type **buffer**. We can do the same thing for the variable **fptr**. This is how the screen looks afterward:

```
 File   Edit   View   Search   Make   Run   Debug   Utility   Options     Help
 ───────────────────────────── D:\BUGS.C ─────────────────────────────
 buffer : ""    ←

 fptr : 0x51ce:0x0029              ←
 ──────────────────────────────────────────────────────────────────────
 #include <malloc.h>      /* Borland products: #include <alloc.h> */

 main()
 {
     FILE *fptr;
     int i, number;
     float answer;
     char *buffer;

     buffer = malloc(1000);       ←
     fopen("file.dat", buffer);
     fread(buffer, 1, 20, fptr);

     for(i = 1; i < 20; i++){
         printf("%c", buffer[i]);
         if(buffer[i] == 'a') number++;
 ──────────────────────────────────────────────────────────────────────
 F1=Help   Enter   Esc=Cancel                            00001:001
```

Note that two lines have been added. The program displays the values of **fptr** and **buffer**, and we can watch them change as the program progresses. (Turbo does the same thing with watched values.)

TIP Actually, you might notice that it is displaying the string pointed to by **buffer**, not **buffer** itself (which would be an address). This is very helpful if you want to watch what is going on in the buffer. If you want to see the value of the pointer **buffer**, however, and watch it as it changes, watch `&(*buffer)`.

Let's continue tracing through our program. We can trace through two more lines to the **fread( )** command:

```
  File  Edit  View  Search  Make  Run  Debug  Utility  Options    Help
  ───────────────────────────── D:\BUGS.C ─────────────────────────
  buffer : "*%-7 Dge (&JB(U +"    ←
  fptr : 0x51ce:0x0029            ←
  ─────────────────────────────────────────────────────────────────
  #include <malloc.h>      /* Borland products: #include <alloc.h> */

  main()
  {
      FILE *fptr;
      int i, number;
      float answer;
      char *buffer;

      buffer = malloc(1000);
      fopen("file.dat", buffer);
      fread(buffer, 1, 20, fptr);  ←

      for(i = 1; i < 20; i++){
          printf("%c", buffer[i]);
          if(buffer[i] == 'a') number++;
  ─────────────────────────────────────────────────────────────────
  F1=Help  Enter  Esc=Cancel                            00001:001
```

Already, something is wrong. The value of **fptr** has not changed since the beginning of the program, which means it hasn't been assigned. Maybe we used **fopen( )** incorrectly. To find the appropriate usage of any C keyword, all you have to do is position the cursor over the keyword and press F1 (Turbo: ^F1).

You can use the mouse, too. Move the mouse cursor over the keyword and press the right button. A definition comes up for the **fopen( )**, and we can see that we've used it incorrectly. We've used it like this:

```
fopen("file.dat", buffer);
```

But it should have been used like this:

```
fptr = fopen("file.dat", "rb");
```

We make the change to the program and try again:

```
#include <stdio.h>
#include <malloc.h>        /* Borland products: #include
<alloc.h> */

main()
{
    FILE *fptr;
    int i, number;
    float answer;
    char *buffer;

    buffer = malloc(1000);
    fptr = fopen("file.dat", "rb");    ←
    fread(buffer, 1, 20, fptr);

    for(i = 1; i < 20; i++){
        printf("%c", buffer[i]);
        if(buffer[i] == 'a') number++;
    }
    printf("Number of 'a's: %d",number);

    answer = addem(1.2, 3.1);
    printf("Answer: .2%f",answer);
}

addem(float param1, float param2)
{
    return (param1 + param2);
}
```

After compiling and linking, we get this:

```
D>bugs   ←
his is a test.
g$5Number of 'a's: 144Answer: .24.000000
```

This looks better, but there are still a number of errors. We are missing the first letter of the contents of the file **file.dat**. Let's debug again. This time, we will watch the character that is to be printed out, **buffer[i]**, directly. Simply use the **Watch Value...** option to watch **buffer[i]**, not just **buffer**. We trace through all the way to the `printf("%c", buffer[i])` line:

```
 File   Edit   View   Search   Make   Run   Debug   Utility   Options      Help
───────────────────────────────── D:\BUGS.C ─────────────────────────────
buffer : "This is a test\r\n"     ←
buffer[i] : 'h'                    ←
──────────────────────────────────────────────────────────────────────────
#include <malloc.h>      /* Borland products: #include <alloc.h> */

main()
{
    FILE *fptr;
    int i, number;
    float answer;
    char *buffer;

    buffer = malloc(1000);
    fptr = fopen("file.dat", "rb");
    fread(buffer, 1, 20, fptr);

    for(i = 1; i < 20; i++){
        printf("%c", buffer[i]);                      ←
        if(buffer[i] == 'a') number++;
──────────────────────────────────────────────────────────────────────────
F1=Help   Enter   Esc=Cancel                              00001:001
```

It's easy to see that although the whole buffer is there, **buffer[i]** is **'h'**, not **'T'**. We are about to print out the second character, not the first. The fault lies in our `printf("That character is %c.\n", )` loop:

```
for(i = 1; i < 20; i++){ ←
    printf("%c", buffer[i]);
    if(buffer[i] == 'a') number++;
}
```

We have started the array index with 1, not 0 (this is an error that is very common in C). We can change that line and check our output again:

```
D>bugs  ←
This is a test.
g$5Number of 'a's: 1024Answer: .24.000000
```

The full file is printed out, but some extra characters appear as well. That problem is easier to solve: Our printing loop seems to be typing out 20 characters, even though the file was only 17 characters long. We can change that by adding a **file_length** variable like this:

```c
#include <stdio.h>
#include <malloc.h>    /* Borland products: #include <alloc.h> */

main()
{
    FILE *fptr;
    int i, number, file_length;    ←
    float answer;
    char *buffer;

    buffer = malloc(1000);
    fptr = fopen("file.dat", "rb");
    file_length = fread(buffer, 1, 20, fptr);    ←

    for(i = 0; i < file_length; i++){    ←
        printf("%c", buffer[i]);
         if(buffer[i] == 'a') number++;
    }
    printf("Number of 'a's: %d",number);

    answer = addem(1.2, 3.1);
    printf("Answer: .2%f",answer);
}

addem(float param1, float param2)
{
    return (param1 + param2);
}
```

The output now looks like this:

```
D>bugs   ←
This is a test.
Number of 'a's: 1024Answer: .24.000000
```

The next problem is the number of 'a's. There should be only one 'a' counted in the file's data, not 1,024. We can debug the program again by tracing through it. Let's watch the number of 'a's, which is stored in the variable **number**:

```
 File  Edit  View  Search  Make  Run  Debug  Utility  Options     Help
 ─────────────────────── D:\BUGS.C ───────────────────────
 number : 38    ←
 ─────────────────────────────────────────────────────────
 #include <malloc.h>      /* Borland products: #include <alloc.h> */

 main()
 {
     FILE *fptr;
     int i, number;
     float answer;
     char *buffer;

     buffer = malloc(1000);
     fptr = fopen("file.dat", "rb");   ←
     fread(buffer, 1, 20, fptr);

     for(i = 0; i < 20; i++){
         printf("%c", buffer[i]);
         if(buffer[i] == 'a') number++;
     }
 ─────────────────────────────────────────────────────────
 F1=Help  Enter  Esc=Cancel                        00001:001
```

The variable **number** starts off at 38. By the time we trace all through to the point to print it out, we can take another look at it:

```
 File   Edit   View   Search   Make   Run  Debug   Utility  Options     Help
 ─────────────────────────────── D:\BUGS.C ───────────────────────────────
 number : 39     ←

 ─────────────────────────────────────────────────────────────────────────
 main()
 {
 FILE *fptr;
 int i, number;
 float answer;
 char *buffer;

 buffer = malloc(1000);
 fptr = fopen("file.dat", "rb");
 fread(buffer, 1, 20, fptr);

 for(i = 0; i < 20; i++)
         {
         printf("%c", buffer[i]);
         if(buffer[i] == 'a') number++;
         }
 printf("Number of 'a's: %d",number);    ←

 ─────────────────────────────────────────────────────────────────────────
 F1=Help  Enter  Esc=Cancel                               00001:001
```

Now it is 39, but it should be 1: We forgot to initialize it to zero (this mistake of forgetting to initialize counter variables to 0 is another very common one in C programming.) The next problem in the output is this:

```
D>bugs                           ↓↓
This is a test.
g$5Number of 'a's: 1024Answer: .24.000000
```

We've got the format specifier wrong:

```
                    ↓↓
       printf("Answer: .2%f",answer);
```

It should be **%.2f**, not **.2%f** (see Chapter 1). After fixing it, this is what the output looks like:

```
This is a test.
Number of 'a's: 1Answer: 4.00
```

The output has improved considerably. However, there is one last problem. We called **addem( )** with the values 1.2 and 3.1. It should have added them together to get 4.3. Instead, we got a result of 4.00. What's wrong? Here's what **addem( )** looks like:

```
addem(float param1, float param2)
{
    return (param1 + param2);
}
```

When we debug this time, let's watch the value of **param1** + **param2** to see what's happening:

```
 File  Edit  View  Search  Make  Run  Debug  Utility  Options    Help
───────────────────────── D:\BUGS.C ──────────────────────────
param1 + param2 : <unknown identifier>   ←
──────────────────────────────────────────────────────────────
#include <malloc.h>      /* Borland products: #include <alloc.h> */

main()
{
    FILE *fptr;
    int i, number;
    float answer;
    char *buffer;

    buffer = malloc(1000);
    fptr = fopen("file.dat", "rb");
    fread(buffer, 1, 20, fptr);

    for(i = 0; i < 20; i++){
        printf("%c", buffer[i]);
        if(buffer[i] == 'a') number++;
    }
──────────────────────────────────────────────────────────────
F1=Help  Enter  Esc=Cancel                          00001:001
```

These variables are not filled until we enter the function **addem( )**, since they are automatic variables. However, when we get to the end of **addem( )**, we see that **param1** + **param2** = 4.3:

```
 File   Edit   View   Search   Make   Run   Debug   Utility   Options      Help
                                    D:\BUGS.C
 param1 + param2 : 4.3   ←


     for(i = 0; i < file_length; i++){
         printf("%c", buffer[i]);
         if(buffer[i] == 'a') number++;
     }

     printf("Number of 'a's: %d",number);

     answer = addem(1.2, 3.1);
     printf("Answer: %.2f",answer);

 }


 addem(float param1, float param2)
 {
     return (param1 + param2);
 }                                   ←

 F1=Help   Enter   Esc=Cancel                                   00001:001
```

In other words, the addition **param1** + **param2** is being done correctly. The result must have been changed when we returned to **main( )**. When we check the program, we can see that we didn't declare a function prototype for **addem( )**, so C assumed that it would return an **int** (the default). However, **addem( )** doesn't return an **int**. It returns a floating point number.

Omitting the prototype is a very common error in C. Since C doesn't complain, it's hard to find the error. If your functions don't return integers, this is a source of possible errors. We can fix this one last problem by adding a prototype for **addem( )**:

```
#include <stdio.h>
#include <malloc.h>      /* Borland products: #include
<alloc.h> */
float addem(float param1, float param2)   ←

main()
{
    FILE *fptr;
    int i, number, file_length;
```

```
        float answer;
        char *buffer;

        buffer = malloc(1000);
        fptr = fopen("file.dat", "rb");
        file_length = fread(buffer, 1, 20, fptr);
        number = 0;

        for(i = 0; i < file_length; i++){
            printf("%c", buffer[i]);
            if(buffer[i] == 'a') number++;
        }

        printf("Number of 'a's: %d",number);

        answer = addem(1.2, 3.1);
        printf("Answer: %.2f",answer);
    }

    float addem(float param1, float param2)
    {
        return (param1 + param2);
    }
```

And this is what the output looks like now:

```
This is a test.
Number of 'a's: 1Answer: 4.30
```

Except for the minor formatting problems, the output is accurate. The program has been debugged.

Dedicated C Debuggers

There is both a dedicated Turbo debugger (**TD.EXE**) and a dedicated Microsoft debugger (CodeView — **CV.EXE**). Both debuggers do not edit your code, nor do they compile it. However, they are powerful debuggers, and they function similarly. Most capabilities of either can be found in the other. For example, what CodeView calls breakpoints, watchpoints, and tracepoints, the Turbo Debugger groups into breakpoints and conditional breakpoints.

The Turbo Debugger has some features that CodeView does not. For example, the Turbo Debugger can log debugging sessions, while CodeView cannot. Also, the Turbo Debugger can debug **remotely**, where only a fraction of the whole code (15K) is in memory. The entire CodeView program must be in memory to use it.

Let's put together a program to debug with the Turbo Debugger, **TD.EXE**. In this example, we'll present a print formatter, a program to print files on the printer. We can embed special codes in the file to change the format of the printed text. Let's use these codes to turn printing features on or off:

@d → double spacing
@s → single spacing
@u → underlining on
@v → underlining off
@b → bold on
@c → bold off
@# → indent # spaces

For example, if we sent this file (**file.dat**) to the printer program:

```
This is a test.
This is a test.@d
And this is a test of double spacing.
And this is a test of double spacing.@s
Sometimes, @bbold is better@c. But
not always. Now we can try @5indenting. Is
this working? Let's give it a
few lines to try it out. @0Now we should return
to no indent? Did we? How about a little
@uunderlining@v?
```

Then this is the output we'd expect:

```
This is a test.
This is a test.

And this is a test of double spacing.

And this is a test of double spacing.
Sometimes, <esc>Gbold is better<esc>H. But
not always. Now we can try indenting. Is
     this working? Let's give it a
     few lines to try it out. Now we should return
to no indent? Did we? How about a little
<esc>-1underlining<esc>-0?
```

Where <esc> is the escape character, ASCII 27. We want the program to put in certain escape codes that the printer uses (universal printer codes include: <esc>G/<esc>H = turn on/off bold, <esc>-1/<esc>-0 = turn on/off underlining). In addition, let's make the program capable of redirecting output to a file, not the printer. For example, if our program was called **printer.c**, this would print file.dat on the printer:

```
printer file.dat
```

And this would send the output to **file.prt** instead:

```
printer file.dat file.prt
```

With all this in mind, then, our first attempt at **printer.c** appears in Listing 9-1.

Listing 9-1. Buggy Version of printer.c.

```c
/* Printer.c formats and prints files. Codes:    */
/*                                                */
/* @d → double spacing                           */
/* @s → single spacing                           */
/* @u → underlining on                           */
/* @v → underlining off                          */
/* @b → bold on                                   */
/* @c → bold off                                  */
/* @# → indent # spaces                           */

#include <stdio.h>
#include <malloc.h>        /* Borland products:\
                              #include <alloc.h> */

main(int argc, char **argv)
{
    FILE *in_file_ptr = NULL;
    FILE *out_file_ptr = NULL;
    char *data_ptr, *end_of_data_ptr, thischar;
    int num_bytes_read, spacing = 1, padding = 0, i = 0;

    switch (argc){
        case 0:
            printf("Usage: printer file.ext [file.prt]");
            exit(1);
            break;
```

Listing 9-1 *(continued)*

```
        case 1:
            if((in_file_ptr = fopen(*argv, "r")) == NULL){
                printf("Could not open input file");
                exit(1);
            }
            else
                out_file_ptr = stdprn;
            break;
        case 2:
            if((in_file_ptr = fopen(*argv, "r")) == NULL){
                printf("Could not open input file");
                exit(1);
            }
            else if((in_file_ptr = fopen(*(argv + 1), "w"))\
            == NULL){
                printf("Could not open output file");
                exit(1);
            }
            else break;
        default:
                break;
    }

data_ptr = malloc(20000);
num_bytes_read = fread(data_ptr, 1, 20000, in_file_ptr);
end_of_data_ptr = data_ptr + num_bytes_read;
*(data_ptr + num_bytes_read) = '\0';

while(data_ptr < end_of_data_ptr){
    if(*data_ptr != '@' && *data_ptr != '\n')
        putc(*data_ptr++, out_file_ptr);
    else if(*data_ptr == '@'){
        data_ptr++;
        switch (*data_ptr = thischar){
            case 'd':
                spacing = 2;
                break;
            case 's':
                spacing = 1;
                break;
            case 'u':
                putc(27,out_file_ptr);
                putc('-',out_file_ptr);
                putc('1',out_file_ptr);
                break;
```

(continued)

Listing 9-1 *(continued)*

```
                 case 'v':
                      putc(27,out_file_ptr);
                      putc('-',out_file_ptr);
                      putc('0',out_file_ptr);
                      break;
                 case 'b':
                      putc(27,out_file_ptr);
                      putc('G',out_file_ptr);
                   case 'c':
                      putc(27,out_file_ptr);
                      putc('H',out_file_ptr);
                      break;
                 default:
                      if(thischar <= '9' && thischar >= '1')
                           padding = thischar - '0';
                      break;
             }
          data_ptr++;
       }
       else{
          data_ptr++;
           putc('\n',out_file_ptr);
           if(spacing == 2){
               putc('\r',out_file_ptr);
               putc('\n',out_file_ptr);
           }
           for(i = 0; i < padding; i++)
               putc(' ',out_file_ptr);
       }
    }
 }
```

The idea here is to first use a switch statement to read command line arguments. The switch statement checks **argc** (the parameter in which C passes the number of command-line arguments). If there were no command-line arguments, **printer** exits:

```
        switch (argc){
 →          case 0:
 →              printf("Usage: printer file.ext [file.prt]");
 →              exit(1);
 →              break;
```

If there was one command-line argument, **printer.c** assumes that it is the name of the file to format and send to the printer. It opens the file and calls the file pointer to this file **in_file_ptr**. We will be writing to the file pointer

out_file_ptr, and in this case, **out_file_ptr** is set to the predefined pointer **stdprn**, which is the way we send output to the printer in C:

```
            switch (argc){
            case 0:
                printf("Usage: printer file.ext [file.prt]");
                exit(1);
                break;
→           case 1:
→               if((in_file_ptr = fopen(*argv, "r")) == NULL){
→               printf("Could not open input file");
→               exit(1);
→           }
→           else
→               out_file_ptr = stdprn;
→           break;
```

Finally, if there were two command-line arguments, we open the input file and the output file like this:

```
            switch (argc){
                    case 0:
                      printf("Usage: printer file.ext [file.prt]");
                      exit(1);
                      break;
                    case 1:
                      if((in_file_ptr = fopen(*argv, "r")) == NULL){
                          printf("Could not open input file");
                          exit(1);
                      }
                      else
                          out_file_ptr = stdprn;
                          break;
→                   case 2:
→                     if((in_file_ptr = fopen(*argv, "r")) == NULL){
→                         printf("Could not open input file");
→                         exit(1);
→                     }
→                     else if((in_file_ptr = fopen(*(argv + 1),\
                      "w")) == NULL){
→                         printf("Could not open output file");
→                         exit(1);
→                     }
→                   else break;
                    default:
                        break;
            }
```

Now that **in_file_ptr** and **out_file_ptr** are set, we allocate memory, point to it with a pointer called **data_ptr**, and read the file in. The number of characters we read goes into a variable named **num_bytes_read**:

```
        data_ptr = malloc(20000);
  →     num_bytes_read = fread(data_ptr, 1, 20000, in_file_ptr);
        end_of_data_ptr = data_ptr + num_bytes_read;
        *(data_ptr + num_bytes_read) = '\0';
```

Characters are printed by sending them to **out_file_ptr** with the **putc( )** function. We use this function because it ends individual characters to a stream of our choosing (we've seen its counterpart, **getc( )**, in Chapter 5). In our case, that stream will be **out_file_ptr** (i.e., the printer or another file). As we print, we check every character, looking for embedded codes that begin with the '@' symbol. If we find one, we examine the next character, which is the format character.

Format characters turn formatting options on or off, and, depending on what the character is, we set or reset a flag. Every time we print a newline character, '**\n**', we check the flags. If double-spacing is on, for example, we print out a second '**\n**'. If indenting is on, we print out the required extra characters after the '**\n**'.

Unfortunately, although it compiles, it doesn't work. This version of the program doesn't even produce an output file that we can print. Let's use the Turbo Debugger to debug **printer.c**. To do that, we have to compile **printer.c** with the **-v** option with the command line compiler **tcc.exe**:

```
tcc -v printer.c
```

Using the **-v** (use **-Zi** under Microsoft C to prepare a file for CodeView) option makes the compiler keep the symbolic names in the program so they can be used for symbolic debugging.

TIP   It is a good idea to use the **-Od** switch if you are using the Microsoft C compiler, which turns off optimization. If your code is optimized, Codeview may not be able to match commands in the **.EXE** file with source code statements.

Now we use the Turbo Debugger, **TD.EXE**, like this:

```
D:\> TD printer
```

This is what the TD screen looks like this:

```
 File    View    Run   Breakpoints    Data   Window    Options      READY
 Module:  PRINTER   File: printer.c  1 ══════════════════════════════════
  /* Printer.c formats and prints files. Codes:   */
  /*                                               */
  /* @d → double spacing                           */
  /* @s → single spacing                           */
  /* @u → underlining on                           */
  /* @v → underlining off                          */
  /* @b → bold on                                  */
  /* @c → bold off                                 */
  /* @# → indent # spaces                          */
  #include <stdio.h>
  #include <stdlib.h>
  main(int argc, char **argv)
  char **argv;
  {
      FILE *in_file_ptr = NULL;

 Watches ───────────────────────────────────────────────────────────────


 F2-Bkpt F3-Close F4-Here F5-Zoom F6-Next F7-Trace F8-Step F9-Run F10-Menu
```

The commands here are much like those in Quick C or Turbo C. To select a menu option using the keyboard, press Alt and that letter. We can scroll the screen up and down just by using the PgUp, PgDn, and the up or down arrows. The area on the bottom of the screen is the watch box, and we will watch the value of certain variables there.

We can even view the registers of the computer in **TD.EXE** by selecting the **View** menu (press Alt-V) and then choosing **Registers** in that menu. A window **pane** opens up, and you can see the contents of all the registers:

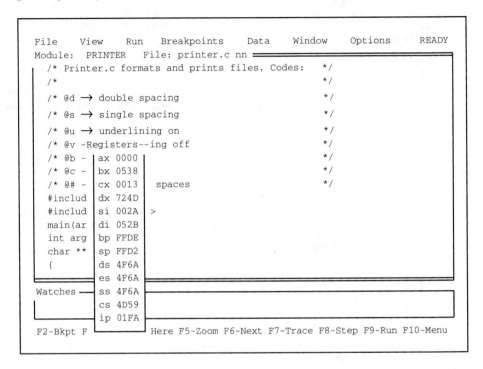

```
 File    View    Run    Breakpoints    Data    Window    Options    READY
 Module:  PRINTER    File: printer.c nn
 /* Printer.c formats and prints files. Codes:    */
 /*                                                */
 /* @d → double spacing                           */
 /* @s → single spacing                           */
 /* @u → underlining on                           */
 /* @v -Registers--ing off                        */
 /* @b - ┌ax 0000┐                                */
 /* @c - │bx 0538│                                */
 /* @# - │cx 0013│   spaces                       */
 #includ │dx 724D│
 #includ │si 002A│ >
 main(ar │di 052B│
 int arg │bp FFDE│
 char ** │sp FFD2│
 {       │ds 4F6A│
         │es 4F6A│
 Watches─┤ss 4F6A├
  ┌      │cs 4D59│
  │      └ip 01FA┘
 F2-Bkpt F           Here F5-Zoom F6-Next F7-Trace F8-Step F9-Run F10-Menu
```

To close a window pane like this one, press Escape. Let's debug **printer.c**. Press F7 to trace through one command at a time. **TD** will indicate where we are:

```
 File    View    Run    Breakpoints    Data    Window    Options    READY
 Module:  PRINTER    File: printer.c nn ═══════════════════════════════
│  /* Printer.c formats and prints files. Codes:   */                  │
│  /*                                               */                 │
│  /* @d → double spacing                           */                 │
│  /* @s → single spacing                           */                 │
│  /* @u → underlining on                           */                 │
│  /* @v → underlining off                          */                 │
│  /* @b → bold on                                  */                 │
│  /* @c → bold off                                 */                 │
│  /* @# → indent # spaces                          */                 │
│  #include <stdio.h>                                                  │
│  #include <stdlib.h>                                                 │
│  main(int argc, char **argv)  ←                                      │
│  char **argv;                                                        │
│  {                                                                   │
│      FILE *in_file_ptr = NULL;                                       │
│                                                                      │
 Watches ──────────────────────────────────────────────────────────────
│                                                                      │
│                                                                      │

 F2-Bkpt F3-Close F4-Here F5-Zoom F6-Next F7-Trace F8-Step F9-Run F10-Menu
```

When the program starts, it examines the command-line arguments with the **switch** statement. Use F7 to trace a few times until you reach line 22 (the line number appears at the top of the screen, right after the file name):

```
File     View    Run    Breakpoints    Data    Window    Options      READY
Module:  PRINTER    File: printer.c 22 ═══════════════════════════════
  main(int argc, char **argv)
  {
      FILE *in_file_ptr = NULL;
      FILE *out_file_ptr = NULL;
      char *data_ptr, *end_of_data_ptr, thischar;
      int num_bytes_read, spacing = 1, padding = 0, i = 0;
→ switch (argc){
        case 0:
            printf("Usage: printer file.ext [file.prt]");
            exit(1);
            break;
        case 1:
            if((in_file_ptr = fopen(*argv, "r")) == NULL){
                printf("Could not open input file");
                exit(1);
Watches _____


F2-Bkpt F3-Close F4-Here F5-Zoom F6-Next F7-Trace F8-Step F9-Run F10-Menu
```

This is the **switch** statement. Here, we are checking the value of **argc**. If it is 0, we exit. If it is 1, we read in the file. We can examine the value of **argc** by selecting the **View** menu, and then the **Variables** option. The variables that have already been defined in the program are displayed in two windows. On the left are the internal (Turbo C) variables, and on the right, the ones we have defined. Switch to the set of variables that we have defined by pressing Shift Right Arrow, and it will look something like this:

```
 File    View    Run   Breakpoints   Data   Window   Options      READY
 Module:  PRINTER   File: printer.c 22 ═════════════════════════════
   main(int argc, char **argv)
    {                        Variables ──────
        FILE *in_file_ptr num_bytes_read     9089 (0x2381)
        FILE *out_file_pt thischar           '\x03' 3 (0x03)
        char *data_ptr, * end_of_data_ptr  ds:4F6A "   \r\
        int num_bytes_rea data_ptr             ds:052B ""
        switch (argc){    out_file_ptr         ds:0000
           case 0:        in_file_ptr          ds:0000
              print("Us argv                   ds:FFE6
              exit(1) argc                    1 (0x1)
              break;
           case 1:
           if((in_file_ptr = fopen(*argv, "r")) == NULL){
              printf("Could not open input file");
              exit(1);
 ───────────────────────────────────────────────────────────────────
 Watches ──────────────────────────────────────────────────────────


 ───────────────────────────────────────────────────────────────────
 F2-Bkpt F3-Close F4-Here F5-Zoom F6-Next F7-Trace F8-Step F9-Run F10-Menu
```

We can scroll through this list, and we see that **argc** (at the bottom) is 1. Let's examine that command line argument with the watch box. Select the **Data** menu, and the **Watch** option in it. **TD** will prompt you for an expression to examine. Simply type ***argv** and a carriage return. The watch box displays that string, like this (at the bottom of the screen):

```
File    View    Run    Breakpoints    Data    Window    Options    READY
Module: PRINTER    File: printer.c 22 ══════════════════════════════════
  main(int argc, char **argv)
  {
      FILE *in_file_ptr = NULL;
      FILE *out_file_ptr = NULL;
      char *data_ptr, *end_of_data_ptr, thischar;
      int num_bytes_read, spacing = 1, padding = 0, i = 0;
      switch (argc){    ←
          case 0:
              printf("Usage: printer file.ext [file.prt]");
              exit(1);
              break;
          case 1:
              if((in_file_ptr = fopen(*argv, "r")) == NULL){
                  printf("Could not open input file");
                  exit(1);

Watches ─────────────────────────────────────────────────────────────
   *argv                         char * ds:FFEA "C:\\TC\\PRINTER.EXE"

F2-Bkpt F3-Close F4-Here F5-Zoom F6-Next F7-Trace F8-Step F9-Run F10-Menu
```

As you can see, the string at **argv** is simply the name of the program, **printer.exe**. Unfortunately, **argc** is 1 if there are no command-line arguments, not 0 as we have been assuming. The name of the program itself always counts as one command-line argument. We can see that all the cases in our switch statement are off by one. We should exit if **argc** is 1, not 0, and so forth. This line must be changed:

```
      switch (argc){
→         case 0:
              printf("Usage: printer file.ext [file.prt]");
              exit(1);
              break;
```

Instead, this is really case 1 (i.e., no file names were typed):

```
        switch (argc){
→           case 1:
                printf("Usage: printer file.ext [file.prt]");
                exit(1);
                break;
```

We can add 1 to each case in the **switch** statement and compile again. This time, we will pass command-line arguments to **printer.exe**. To do that, we have to invoke **TD** this way:

```
    C:\>TD printer file.dat file.prt
```

When we supply command-line arguments this way, they will be passed directly to **printer.exe**. In our case, there will be 3 command-line arguments, **printer**, **file.dat**, and **file.prt**. We work through case 3 of the switch statement by tracing a few times with F7. After case 3 is completed, let's check the values of **in_file_ptr** and **out_file_ptr** (**in_file_ptr** is for **file.dat**; **out_file_ptr** is for **file.prt**) to make sure they were assigned:

```
 File    View    Run   Breakpoints    Data   Window    Options     READY
 Module:  PRINTER   File: printer.c 50
        case 3:
            if((in_file_ptr = fopen(*(argv+1), "r")) == NULL){
                printf("Could not open input file");
                exit(1);
            }
            else if((in_file_ptr = fopen(*(argv + 2), "w")) == NULL){
                printf("Could not open output file");
                exit(1);
            }
            else break;
        default:
                break;
    }                        ←

    data_ptr = malloc(20000);

 Watches
  out_file_ptr              →         struct  * ds:0000
  in_file_ptr                         struct  * ds:02D4

 F2-Bkpt F3-Close F4-Here F5-Zoom F6-Next F7-Trace F8-Step F9-Run F10-Menu
```

The pointer **out_file_ptr** is a null pointer. It was never assigned. Let's look at case 3 of the **switch** statement, where we open the files:

```
    case 3
        if((in_file_ptr = fopen(*(argv + 1), "r")) == NULL){
            printf("Could not open input file");
            exit(1);
        }
→       else if((in_file_ptr = fopen(*(argv + 2), "w"))\
        == NULL){
            printf("Could not open output file");
            exit(1);
        }
        else break;
    default:
            break;
```

Here we should open the output file, but we have mistakenly assigned the file pointer to **in_file_ptr**. This line should be changed to this:

```
    else if((out_file_ptr = fopen(*(argv + 2), "w")) == NULL){
```

This time, the program does produce an output file for the printer. However, it looks like this:

```
This is a test.
This is a test.
And this is a test of double spacing.
And this is a test of double spacing.
Sometimes, bold is better. But
not always. Now we can try indenting. Is
this working? Let's give it a
few lines to try it out. Now we should return
to no indent? Did we? How about a little
underlining?
```

All the control codes have been neatly stripped out, but ignored. Our file isn't formatted at all. What's wrong? Let's watch as the data in the file is processed. The line after the **switch** statement is line 55:

```
49:          }
50:          else break;
51:      default:
52:              break;
53: }
54:
55: data_ptr = malloc(20000);     ←
56: num_bytes_read = fread(data_ptr, 1, 20000, in_file_ptr);
```

Let's set a *breakpoint* here. When we run the program, execution will automatically stop at this line; the files will be open, and we'll be ready to read data. That means that we'll actually be able to watch as the data is read in and formatted.

Breakpoints

Scroll down to line 55, and press F2. The line turns red to indicate that a breakpoint has been set there. Now simply let the program execute with the Go, F9, key. Execution halts at line 55 automatically:

```
 ┌──────────────────────────────────────────────────────────────────┐
 │ File   View   Run   Breakpoints   Data   Window   Options   READY │
 │ Module:  PRINTER   File: printer.c 55 ════════════════════════    │
 │ ┌──────────────────────────────────────────────────────────────┐ │
 │ │          printf("Could not open output file");               │ │
 │ │          exit(1);                                            │ │
 │ │      }                                                        │ │
 │ │      else break;                                             │ │
 │ │   default:                                                   │ │
 │ │          break;                                              │ │
 │ │ }                                                            │ │
 │ │                                                              │ │
 │ │  data_ptr = malloc(20000);     ←                             │ │
 │ │  num_bytes_read = fread(data_ptr, 1, 20000, in_file_ptr);    │ │
 │ │  end_of_data_ptr = data_ptr + num_bytes_read;                │ │
 │ │  *(data_ptr + num_bytes_read) = '\0';                        │ │
 │ │                                                              │ │
 │ │  while(data_ptr < end_of_data_ptr){                          │ │
 │ │      if(*data_ptr != '@' && *data_ptr != '\n')               │ │
 │ └──────────────────────────────────────────────────────────────┘ │
 │ Watches ────────────────────────────────────────────────────     │
 │ ┌──────────────────────────────────────────────────────────────┐ │
 │ │                                                              │ │
 │ └──────────────────────────────────────────────────────────────┘ │
 │ F2-Bkpt F3-Close F4-Here F5-Zoom F6-Next F7-Trace F8-Step F9-Run F10-Menu │
 └──────────────────────────────────────────────────────────────────┘
```

At line 55, we are about to allocate 20,000 bytes of memory pointed to by **data_ptr**, and then read in the data from the file. The number of bytes we read will go into **num_bytes_read**. Let's trace through a few lines and then check the values of **data_ptr** and **num_bytes_read** afterward:

```
File    View    Run   Breakpoints    Data   Window    Options     READY
Module:  PRINTER   File: printer.c 57
                break;
    }

    data_ptr = malloc(20000);
    num_bytes_read = fread(data_ptr, 1, 20000, in_file_ptr);
    end_of_data_ptr = data_ptr + num_bytes_read;          ←
    *(data_ptr + num_bytes_read) = '\0';

    while(data_ptr < end_of_data_ptr){
        if(*data_ptr != '@' && *data_ptr != '\n')
            putc(*data_ptr++, out_file_ptr);
        else if(*data_ptr == '@'){
            data_ptr++;
            switch (*data_ptr = thischar){
```

```
Watches
 data_ptr   char * ds:0972 "This is a test.\nThis is a test.@d\nAnd this
 num_bytes_read              int 328 (0x148)
```

```
F2-Bkpt F3-Close F4-Here F5-Zoom F6-Next F7-Trace F8-Step F9-Run F10-Menu
```

As you can see in the watch window at the bottom, **num_bytes_read** (the number of bytes read in) is 328, and **data_ptr** does indeed point to the file's data. We have gotten this far without error. Let's watch the characters we're interpreting from the file as we step through the program:

```
File    View    Run   Breakpoints    Data    Window    Options     READY
Module:  PRINTER   File: printer.c 60 ═══════════════════════════════
               break;
     }

     data_ptr = malloc(20000);
     num_bytes_read = fread(data_ptr, 1, 20000, in_file_ptr);
     end_of_data_ptr = data_ptr + num_bytes_read;          ←
     *(data_ptr + num_bytes_read) = '\0';

     while(data_ptr < end_of_data_ptr){
         if(*data_ptr != '@' && *data_ptr != '\n')
             putc(*data_ptr++, out_file_ptr);
         else if(*data_ptr == '@'){
             data_ptr++;
             switch (*data_ptr = thischar){
                 case 'd':
─ Watches ─────────────────────────────────────────────────────────
  data_ptr  char * ds:0972 "This is a test.\nThis is a test.@d\nAnd this

F2-Bkpt F3-Close F4-Here F5-Zoom F6-Next F7-Trace F8-Step F9-Run F10-Menu
```

We keep looping over the characters in the buffer with our `while(data_ptr < end_of_data_ptr)` loop until we come to a newline character or a '@'. Let's continue tracing until we can see that the first format code, **@d**, is about to be interpreted:

```
This is a test.
This is a test.@d    ←
And this is a test of double spacing.
And this is a test of double spacing.@s
Sometimes, @bbold is better@c. But
not always. Now we can try @5indenting. Is
this working? Let's give it a
few lines to try it out. @0Now we should return
to no indent? Did we? How about a little
@uunderlining@v?
```

Now the character at ***data_ptr** is the @ in our format code **@d** (see the display of **data_ptr** at the bottom):

```
File     View     Run    Breakpoints    Data     Window     Options     READY
Module:  PRINTER    File: printer.c 60
              break;
    }

    data_ptr = malloc(20000);
    num_bytes_read = fread(data_ptr, 1, 20000, in_file_ptr);
    end_of_data_ptr = data_ptr + num_bytes_read;
    *(data_ptr + num_bytes_read) = '\0';

    while(data_ptr < end_of_data_ptr){
        if(*data_ptr != '@' && *data_ptr != '\n')      ←
            putc(*data_ptr++, out_file_ptr);
        else if(*data_ptr == '@'){
            data_ptr++;
            switch (*data_ptr = thischar){
                case 'd':

Watches
 data_ptr   char * ds:0991 "@d\nAnd this is a test of double spacing.\nAn

F2-Bkpt F3-Close F4-Here F5-Zoom F6-Next F7-Trace F8-Step F9-Run F10-Menu
```

Since ***data_ptr** is '@', the program traces through these lines:

```
63:     else if(*data_ptr == '@'){      ←
64:         data_ptr++;
65:     switch (*data_ptr = thischar){
66:         case 'd':
67:             spacing = 2;
```

Here, we increment **data_ptr** to point to the format command which follows @. In this case, the **d** in **@d**:

```
63:     else if(*data_ptr == '@'){
64:         data_ptr++;                     ←
65:     switch (*data_ptr = thischar){
66:         case 'd':
67:             spacing = 2;
```

And then enter a **switch** statement designed to check which format code (now at ***data_ptr**) is being used:

```
63:        else if(*data_ptr == '@'){
64:            data_ptr++;
65:            switch (*data_ptr = thischar){      ←
66:                case 'd':
67:                    spacing = 2;
```

Inside this new **switch** statement, we interpret the various printing formats and set the necessary flags. You can see the double-spacing case in line 68 above, where spacing is set to 2. We enter the default case of the switch statement if the format code was not a letter, in which case we assume it was a single digit number meant to set indenting.

In that default case, we use a variable named **thischar** (line 93, below). That variable will hold a copy of the current character in the buffer, ***data_ptr**, so we have been assigning it in the beginning of the **switch** statement, line 65:

```
63:        else if(*data_ptr == '@'){
64:            data_ptr++;
65:            switch (*data_ptr = thischar){      ←
66:                case 'd':
67:                    spacing = 2;
                        :
                        :
92:                default:
93:                    if(thischar <= '9' && thischar >= '1')   ←
94:                        padding = thischar - '0';
95:                    break;
96:            }
```

Unfortunately, the assignment in line 65 is backwards. This line in the code is wrong:

```
63:        else if(*data_ptr == '@'){
64:            data_ptr++;
65:            switch (*data_ptr = thischar){      ←
66:                case 'd':
67:                    spacing = 2;
```

It should be: switch (thischar = *data_ptr){. The program has been overwriting the control code in the buffer with the uninitialized variable **thischar**, and then examining a control code that was meaningless. We can fix that by making `*data_ptr = thischar` into `thischar = *data_ptr`. Here's the way the output of the program looks now:

```
This is a test.
This is a test.

And this is a test of double spacing.

And this is a test of double spacing.
Sometimes, <esc>G<esc>Hbold is better<esc>H. But
not always. Now we can try indenting. Is
        this working? Let's give it a
        few lines to try it out. Now we should return
        to no indent? Did we? How about a little
<esc>-1underlining<esc>-0?
```

There has been considerable improvement. However, one thing we see immediately is that instead of turning **bold** on (with <esc>G), we've turned it both on and off (with <esc>G<esc>H). This type of error is the sure mark of leaving out the **break** in a case statement. We check our code:

```
case 'b':
    putc(27,out_file_ptr);
    putc('G',out_file_ptr);
                                    ← missing break;
case 'c':
    putc(27,out_file_ptr);
    putc('H',out_file_ptr);
    break;
default:
    if(thischar <= '9' && thischar >= '1')
        padding = thischar - '0';
    break;
```

And see that that is indeed what is happening. Control just passes on to the next case, where we turn **bold** off. This type of error, also very common in C programming, can cause many problems unless you catch it. We add the missing **break**, yielding this:

```
This is a test.
This is a test.

And this is a test of double spacing.

And this is a test of double spacing.
Sometimes, <esc>Gbold is better<esc>H. But
not always. Now we can try indenting. Is
    this working? Let's give it a
    few lines to try it out. Now we should return
    to no indent? Did we? How about a little
    <esc>-1underlining<esc>-0?
```

This looks much better, but we still have trouble turning off the **indent**. Let's see what's wrong. The number of spaces to indent is stored in a variable named **padding**. We can watch when **padding** is set back to zero with a **watchpoint**.

A watchpoint is a special kind of breakpoint. Unlike a simple breakpoint, a watchpoint is line-independent. A watchpoint is triggered when a certain **condition** becomes true.

First, select the **View** menu, and the **Breakpoints** option in it. Next, press Alt-F10 to pop up the Breakpoints local menu. To create a breakpoint, select the option named **Global**. A breakpoint named **Global_1** will be added to the list of breakpoints. Next, in the same local Breakpoints menu, select **Condition**, and then the **Expression True** option. TD prompts you for an expression; type "padding = 0". The watchpoint is set. Now, when **padding** is set to 0, we'll be alerted.

We run the program with the F9 key, but the watchpoint is never triggered. In other words, **padding** must never be set to zero. Let's see what's going on with a breakpoint at the line (94) where **padding** is set, and then let the program run. We stop at line 94:

```
File    View    Run    Breakpoints    Data    Window    Options    READY
Module:  PRINTER    File: printer.c 94 ═══════════════════════════════
                    putc('0',out_file_ptr);
                    break;
              case 'b':
                    putc(27,out_file_ptr);
                    putc('G',out_file_ptr);
              case 'c':
                    putc(27,out_file_ptr);
                    putc('H',out_file_ptr);
                    break;
              default:
                    if(thischar <= '9' && thischar >= '1')
        →             padding = thischar - '0';
                    break;
              }
          data_ptr++;

  Watches ─────────────────────────────────────────────────────────


  F2-Bkpt F3-Close F4-Here F5-Zoom F6-Next F7-Trace F8-Step F9-Run F10-Menu
```

Here, **padding** is set to the value of **thischar** - '0'. We can check the value of **thischar** by watching it (see the window at the bottom):

```
 File    View    Run    Breakpoints    Data    Window    Options    READY
 Module:  PRINTER    File: printer.c 94 ═══════════════════════════════
                     putc('0',out_file_ptr);
                     break;
                case 'b':
                     putc(27,out_file_ptr);
                     putc('G',out_file_ptr);
                case 'c':
                     putc(27,out_file_ptr);
                     putc('H',out_file_ptr);
                     break;
                default:
                     if(thischar <= '9' && thischar >= '1')
        →                 padding = thischar - '0';
                     break;
                }
            data_ptr++;
─────────────────────────────────────────────────────────────────────
 Watches ──────────────────────────────────────────────────
  thischar                        char '5' 53 (0x35)

 F2-Bkpt F3-Close F4-Here F5-Zoom F6-Next F7-Trace F8-Step F9-Run F10-Menu
```

The answer is '5'. This is the point where **padding** is set to 5 in the test file:

```
This is a test.
This is a test.@d
And this is a test of double spacing.
And this is a test of double spacing.@s
Sometimes, @bbold is better@c. But
not always. Now we can try @5indenting. Is  ←
this working? Let's give it a
few lines to try it out. @0Now we should return
to no indent? Did we? How about a little
@uunderlining@v?
```

Now we want to see it set back to 0. We type F9 to continue, and the program ends. We never reach line 94 again to set **padding** back to 0. The fault must lie in the test we make on **thischar** before setting the variable **padding**. If we look at that test, we can see what's wrong:

```
92:                    default:
93:        →          if(thischar <= '9' && thischar >= '1')
94:                        padding = thischar - '0';
95:                    break;
96:            }
97:        data_ptr++;
```

When we check to make sure **thischar** is a single digit, we check whether it is less than or equal to '9' and greater than or equal to '1', but the test should be whether it is greater than or equal to '0'. The way the program is now, we can never set **padding** back to 0. To solve this problem, we change this to:
if(thischar <= '9' && thischar >= '0'):

```
92:                    default:
93:        →          if(thischar <= '9' && thischar >= '0')
94:                        padding = thischar - '0';
95:                    break;
96:            }
97:        data_ptr++;
```

This time, the output file looks like this:

```
This is a test.
This is a test.

And this is a test of double spacing.

And this is a test of double spacing.
Sometimes, <esc>Gbold is better<esc>H. But
not always. Now we can try indenting. Is
     this working? Let's give it a
     few lines to try it out. Now we should return
to no indent? Did we? How about a little
<esc>-1underlining<esc>-0?
```

And at last it is correct. We've gotten all the bugs out (as far as our test file goes, anyway). For reference, the debugged version of printer.c appears in Listing 9-2.

Listing 9-2. Debugged Version of printer.c.

```
/* Printer.c formats and prints files. Codes:   */
/*                                               */
/* @d → double spacing                           */
/* @s → single spacing                           */
/* @u → underlining on                           */
/* @v → underlining off                          */
/* @b → bold on                                  */
/* @c → bold off                                 */
/* @# → indent # spaces                          */

#include <stdio.h>
#include <stdlib.h>

main(int argc, char **argv)
{
    FILE *in_file_ptr = NULL;
    FILE *out_file_ptr = NULL;
    char *data_ptr, *end_of_data_ptr, thischar;
    int num_bytes_read, spacing = 1, padding = 0, i = 0;

    switch (argc){
       case 1:
            printf("Usage: printer file.ext [file.out]");
            exit(1);
            break;
       case 2:
            if((in_file_ptr = fopen(*(argv+1), "r")) == NULL){
                printf("Could not open input file");
                exit(1);
            }
             else
                out_file_ptr = stdprn;
           break;
       case 3:
            if((in_file_ptr = fopen(*(argv+1), "r")) == NULL){
               printf("Could not open input file");
               exit(1);
            }
            else  if((out_file_ptr = fopen(*(argv+2), "w"))\
            == NULL){
                printf("Could not open output file");
                exit(1);
            }
             else break;
         default:
```

(continued)

Listing 9-2. *(continued)*

```
                break;
    }

data_ptr = malloc(20000);
num_bytes_read = fread(data_ptr, 1, 20000, in_file_ptr);
end_of_data_ptr = data_ptr + num_bytes_read;
*(data_ptr + num_bytes_read) = '\0';

while(data_ptr < end_of_data_ptr){
    if(*data_ptr != '@' && *data_ptr != '\n')
        putc(*data_ptr++, out_file_ptr);
    else if(*data_ptr == '@'){
        data_ptr++;
        switch (thischar = *data_ptr){
            case 'd':
                spacing = 2;
                break;
            case 's':
                spacing = 1;
                break;
            case 'u':
                putc(27,out_file_ptr);
                putc('-',out_file_ptr);
                putc('1',out_file_ptr);
                break;
            case 'v':
                putc(27,out_file_ptr);
                putc('-',out_file_ptr);
                putc('0',out_file_ptr);
                break;
            case 'b':
                putc(27,out_file_ptr);
                putc('G',out_file_ptr);
                break;
            case 'c':
                putc(27,out_file_ptr);
                putc('H',out_file_ptr);
                break;
            default:
                if(thischar <= '9' && thischar >= '0')
                    padding = thischar - '0';
                break;
        }
        data_ptr++;
    }
    else{
```

Listing 9-2. *(continued)*

```
            data_ptr++;
            putc('\n',out_file_ptr);
            if(spacing == 2){
                putc('\r',out_file_ptr);
                putc('\n',out_file_ptr);
             }
            for(i = 0; i < padding; i++)
                putc(' ',out_file_ptr);
        }
    }
 }
```

That's it for debugging C. The range and power of the options available today are impressive. In fact, debugging techniques can take up an entire book by themselves. Now, though, it's time to turn to another very powerful topic, the extension of C into C++.

Welcome to C++

——

In 1983, Bjarne Stroustrup developed C++. In essence, C++ is the same as C, but with a number of important extensions. In other words, all that we've learned about C still applies, but C++ offers us even more power and we'll get a tour of what's available in this chapter. Primary among the additions C++ brings to C is the idea of an **object**.

An object is really just like a new kind of structure except that it can hold both data and functions. The driving force behind objects is **modularity**, a concept that we've already stressed. C++ was originally written to be used when C programs got very long, over 2,500 lines (now, however, programmers use it as soon as new versions come out; it's become much more flexible than standard C). In programs that long, it's often hard to remember all the details about all the parts. It's much easier if you can somehow connect associated functions and the data they need into some kind of object, which we can then think of as a single entity. That way, we can think of the whole object in terms of its overall function, without having to remember all the details of its internal data handling.

For instance, one example of an object we'll develop in this chapter is a stack. We've already seen that you can push and pop values onto a stack to store them, and that the values are popped off a stack in the reverse order in which they were pushed.

To make your own stack, you'd need both the memory space used for storage as well as the functions that do the pushing and the popping. The stack may even have some internal functions that some of its functions use to monitor the stack. All these details can be distracting if you've got a lot of other things on your mind, and it's easier if you can wrap them all into one logical idea: a stack. In fact, **encapsulation** is a C++ term meaning just that: the wrapping of functions and the data they need into an easy concept — an object — like a stack.

NOTE   In this chapter we'll use the package that's become the standard C++ implementation for the IBM compatibles, Turbo C++, Turbo C++ Pro (which adds the Turbo Assembler and other tools to C++) or Borland C++.

Screen Output in C++

We can begin our tour of C++ by seeing how to manage normal I/O in C++, such as printing on the screen and reading from the keyboard. Even though we can still use **printf( )** or **scanf( )** (because C++ includes all of standard ANSI C, and Turbo C++ or Borland C++ includes all of standard Turbo C), there are even easier ways available to us now. And, because they are easier to use, C++ programs are often distinctive for their use of them, even when objects are not involved.

The C++ Predefined I/O Streams

We already know about the standard streams, **stdin**, **stdout**, **stderr**, **stdlog**, and **stdprn**. In C++, there are some additional predefined streams named **cin**, **cout**, **cerr**, and **clog**; they are tied to the same devices, but we use them in a different way. Let's see an example, showing how to print on the screen using **cout**. Here's how to print `"Hello, world.\n"` on the screen using the typically C++ method of sending output to **cout**:

```
#include <iostream.h>

/* Hello, World. */

main()
{
    cout << "Hello, world.\n";\
    // Put "Hello, world.\n" on screen.

    return(0);
}
```

> **NOTE**   **cin**, **cout**, **cerr**, and **clog** are actually special cases of what are called C++ I/O class libraries, which are a whole topic in themselves. They make up a series of **predefined** objects that you can use for powerful I/O.

We should notice a number of things here. First, to use any of the predefined C++ streams, we had to include the header file **iostream.h**. Next, we sent our string to the screen with this operator:

```
cout << "Hello, world.\n";   // Put "Hello, world.\n" on screen.
```

This terminology is reminiscent of the DOS redirection commands. In this case, we're sending `"Hello, world.\n"` to **cout** using `<<`. In normal C, this is a bitwise **left shift operator**, and it works on integer values by shifting their bits left by a specified number of places. For example, if we had an integer value stored in a variable named **my_bits** whose binary representation was 0101010101010101, then this statement:

```
my_bits << 1;
```

would leave a value of 1010101010101010 in **my_bits**. Every bit has been shifted left one place. Similarly, there is a **right shift operator**, `>>`, which shifts bits right (we'll see more about bitwise shifts in the next chapter, Chapter 11). However, in C++, `<<` and `>>` do more than just shift the bits of operands.

That is, the `<<` and `>>` operators still function as the left and right shift operators, but, in C++, operators can have more than one meaning. In this case, `<<` may also be used to send output to cout, and `>>` may also be used to read input from **cin**. This is called **operator overloading**, and it's an important part of C++.

Say, for example, that you define some complex data structure, and that you want to be able to define the operation of addition on such structures. In C++, you can overload the + operator to handle it without problem. In fact, almost any of the usual C operators (except for some special ones like ?: or the dot operator, .) can be overloaded in C++.

Next, you might notice a new method of using comments. We were able to put a one-line comment into our program (`// Put "Hello, world.\n" on screen.`) by prefacing it with the symbol `//`. This is a new addition in C++, and it only works for one-line comments; C++ ignores the rest of the line following `//`. The older `/* */` method is still available, of course, but C++

programmers usually use the // one-line comments, reserving the /* */ method for multiline ones.

We can also use << with a number of arguments, as in the following case:

```
#include <iostream.h>

/* Hello, World. */

main()
{
    cout << "Hello, " << "world.\n";

    return(0);
}
```

We can stack up as many data items to send to the screen as we want, like this:

```
cout << "Hello, " << "world.\n";
```

In fact, we can also print numbers too, without even having to use a formatting string. As we'll see, C++ is smart enough to recognize the type of data it is working on, and to take the appropriate action:

```
#include <iostream.h>

/* Print out numbers using cout */

main()
{
    int my_int = 5;
    float my_float = 5.333;

    cout << "The value of my_int is: " << my_int << "\n";
    cout << "The value of my_float is: " << my_float << "\n";

    return(0);
}
```

TIP
There are special formatting words that we can send to the predefined I/O streams that will do formatting for us, giving us a good deal of control. These words are called **manipulators**. For example, `cout << hex` sets the output format of numbers to hexadecimal, and `cout << dec` sets it to decimal. You can also set the width of a particular numerical field on the screen with **setw( )**. For example, `cout << setw(5)` sets the field width to 5.

In fact, the ability to handle different data types in the manner that they require is the basis of operator overloading, as well as **function overloading**, which we'll see later. We'll be able to define the same function over and over for different data types, ints, floats, or whatever. When we actually use the function, C++ will know what data type we're using it on, and select the appropriate definition of the function to match. This will turn out to be extraordinarily powerful, allowing us, among other things, to define our stack for chars, ints, and floats. In C++, this data type flexibility is called **polymorphism**, and it's one of the reasons that C++ is so popular.

Besides printing numbers on the screen, we can read them as well, and we won't need any formatting strings then either. Let's see how that works next.

Keyboard Input in C++

Let's develop an example that reads an integer from the keyboard using **cin**. We start by printing a prompt:

```
#include <iostream.h>

/* Read and print out a number */

main()
{
    cout << "Please type an integer: ";
      :
```

Then we use **cin** in a manner you might expect, like this:

```
#include <iostream.h>

/* Read and print out a number */

main()
```

```
        {
            int my_int;

            cout << "Please type an integer: ";
→           cin >> my_int;
                :
```

Here we just use the >> operator to read from the keyboard. Note that even though we are assigning a value to **my_int**, it appears on the right hand side of the statement. Finally, we can type the result out:

```
        #include <iostream.h>

        /* Read and print out a number */

        main()
        {
            int my_int;

            cout << "Please type an integer: ";
            cin >> my_int;
→           cout << "The value of that integer is: " << my_int;

            return(0);
        }
```

Just as with **cout** and <<, so we can handle multiple arguments with **cin** and >>, as in this example, where we read two integers and print their values on the screen:

```
        #include <iostream.h>

        /* Read and print out two numbers */

        main()
        {
            int my_first_int, my_second_int;

            cout << "Please type two integers: ";
            cin >> my_first_int >> my_second_int;
            cout << "Those were: " << my_first_int << " and " <<\
            my_second_int;

            return(0);
        }
```

To run this program, type it into a file named, say, **input.cpp**; C++ files end with the extension **.cpp**, not just **.c**. If you wish your file to be compiled as a normal C file, use the **.c** extension. If you want to treat it as a C++ file, use the **.cpp** extension. Then just select the **Run** option in the **Run** menu of Turbo C++, and **input.exe** will be produced. When you run that, the screen looks like this:

```
E:\>input
Please type two integers:
```

Since the program wants two integers, we can type 5 and 6, separating them with a space. The program responds this way:

```
E:\>input
Please type two integers: 5 6 ←
Those were: 5 and 6

E:\>
```

Besides **cin**, **cout**, <<, and >>, don't forget that we still have **printf( )**, **scanf( )**, and all the others. By themselves, << and >> are not what make C++ different. The real difference comes when we define classes and objects and use them. Let's turn to that now, and get to the heart of C++.

How to Use C++ Classes

The important part of C++ is that it can use **classes**. In fact, C++ was originally called C with Classes. To put it briefly, a class is just like a structure in C, except that a class can be defined to hold functions as well as data. A class makes up a formal type, just as when you define the fields of a structure. When you actually declare variables of that type, those are the objects. That's how it works in C++; you set up a class just as you might a structure with **struct**, except that a class definition can also hold function prototypes:

```
      class our_first_class {
          int my_array[100];
          public:
          int my_int;
→         void init(void);
→         int my_func(int my_param);
      };
```

Then, when you declare variables of this type, those are your objects. In the above case, we're setting up a class named **our_first_class**. This class includes some data, **my_int** and **my_array[ ]**, and it also includes two functions, **init( )** and **my_func( )**. If this had been a structure, we could only have included data:

```
struct some_struct {
    int my_int;
    int my_array[100];
};
```

Then we could have declared variables of this structure type like this:

```
struct some_struct {
    int my_int;
    int my_array[100];
} my_struct;                    ←
```

We could then reach the members of **my_struct** with the dot operator, like this:

```
my_struct.my_int = 5;
```

In fact, it works the same way with classes. When we declare a variable of class **our_first_class**, it is an object:

```
class our_first_class {
    int my_array[100];
public:
    int my_int;
    void init(void);
    int my_func(int my_param);
} my_object;                    ←
```

And now we can reach the member data of **my_object** like this, just as we could with **my_struct**:

```
my_object.my_int = 5;
```

However, we can also refer to functions the same way:

```
my_object.my_func(5);
```

This is something new, and it's what C++ programmers mean by encapsulation. We've associated not only data with **my_object**, but also functions. We did that simply by including their prototypes in the definition of **our_first_class**:

```
    class our_first_class {
        int my_array[100];
    public:
        int my_int;
→       void init(void);
→       int my_func(int my_param);
    };
```

You may notice the keyword **public** here. There are two ways of including member data and functions in a class, as **private** or as **public**. By default, all members of a class are **private**, which is why we don't include that keyword. If something is **private**, that means that no part of the program can refer to it outside the object. In **our_first_class**, **my_array[ ]** is **private**, so it cannot be reached by any part of the program except by those functions associated with the objects of that class (i.e., the member functions). Functions can be **private** as well as data, and it is good to remember the spirit of C++ here. In most cases, as much of the object should be made **private** as possible to increase the modularity of programs. This is an important part of the C++ style, and it's the reasons all member data and functions are **private** by default (that's the whole idea behind encapsulation).

However, if everything in an object was **private**, no part of it could be reached from the outside, making it useless. Here, we've declared the variable **my_int** **public**, as well as the functions **init( )** and **my_func( )**. That means that we can reach them from other places in the program like this:

```
my_object.my_int = 5;  // Set my_int
my_object.init();      // Initialize internal my_object routines
my_object.my_func(3);  // Use my_func()
```

In particular, you might notice that we have included an initialization function named **my_object.init( )** here. The data in objects often needs some kind of initialization performed (we'll have to initialize our stack pointer in a moment), and it's not uncommon to see an initialization function. (In fact, C++ provides for some automatic initialization of objects, but that's beyond the scope of this book.) That's the kind of function you need to declare **public**: those that must be reached from the rest of the program in order to make the object function properly. The functions that should be left **private** are those that are purely internal to the object, and they're usually used only by other member functions.

Now that we have some background, let's see it in action and develop our working example: a stack object, capable of pushing and popping data onto and off of its internal (**private**) data stack.

A Stack — An Object Example

Let's review how a stack works. We can push, say, an int with the value 6 onto a stack, when we do, the stack pointer, which points at the next item to be popped, is set like this:

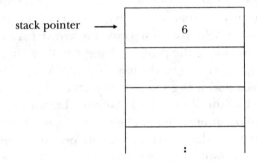

Next, we might push 5. The stack pointer is moved and that value is placed on the stack like this:

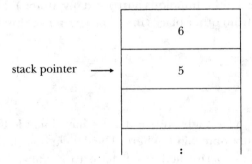

When we pop the stack, we get 5 back, and the stack pointer moves to the last item pushed:

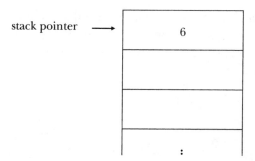

That's the way our stack will work. It's easy to design our stack class. We can do that right away. First, we'll need some space for the stack itself:

```
        class stack_type {
→           int data_buffer[100];
                :
        };
```

Note that we have left it private; that is, only member functions will have access to the stack. This way, the rest of the program doesn't have to bother with it. In addition, we'll have to store the value of the stack pointer, which will be our index in this array, pointing at the element that will be popped next:

```
        class stack_type {
            int data_buffer[100];
→           int stack_ptr;      // stack_ptr = -1 → stack is empty
        };
```

This too is **private**, since only member functions will worry about the value of the stack pointer. The rest of the program only needs to push and pop values, not to worry about the stack pointer itself. Note that in the comment we indicate that when **stack_ptr** holds -1, the stack is empty. When we push a value, it will go into the first element of the array, **data_buffer[0]**, and **stack_ptr** will become 0. The next time we push a value, it will go into **data_buffer[1]**, and **stack_ptr** will become 1 also. When we pop a value, **stack_ptr** will go back to 0. After we pop that value too, **stack_ptr** becomes -1 and there is nothing left on the stack, which means that we can't pop any more values off.

Next, let's set up the prototypes for the two functions that will actually do the pushing and popping. They should be public so the rest of the program can use them. In addition, we should notice that some stack operations ought to generate an error, such as popping an empty stack, or attempting to push data onto a full stack. For that reason, let's have **push( )** and **pop( )** return integer values, 0 for failure and 1 for success:

```
class stack_type {
    int data_buffer[100];
    int stack_ptr;     // stack_ptr = -1 → stack is empty
public:
→       int pop(int *pop_to);
→       int push(int push_this);
};
```

We should also include an initialization function to set the stack pointer to -1 (i.e., an empty stack) at the beginning of the program:

```
class stack_type {
    int data_buffer[100];
    int stack_ptr;     // stack_ptr = -1 → stack is empty
public:
→       void init(void);
        int pop(int *pop_to);
        int push(int push_this);
};
```

Our class is now ready. That was all there was to it (except, of course, for writing the member functions). Now that our class, **stack_type**, is set up, let's declare an object of that type named **my_stack**:

```
class stack_type {
    int data_buffer[100];
    int stack_ptr;     // stack_ptr = -1 → stack is empty
public:
    void init(void);
    int pop(int *pop_to);
    int push(int push_this);
} my_stack;                        ←
```

When we want to push data onto the stack, we can do it like this:

```
my_stack.push(my_data);
```

Conversely, when we want to pop it, we can use **pop( )**:

```
my_stack.pop(&my_data);
```

TIP It's a good idea to have your functions return a value of 0 (i.e., FALSE) for failure because it's easy to use them in loops and if statements. For example, we'll be able to keep popping values off the stack until we have them all with a simple `while(my_stack.pop(&my_data))` loop.

Now all we need to do is to define the member functions **init( )**, **push( )**, and **pop( )**. The **init( )** function is particularly easy because all it does is prime the stack by setting the **stack_ptr** to indicate an empty stack. Let's begin with it:

```
class stack_type {
    int data_buffer[100];
    int stack_ptr;      // stack_ptr = -1 → stack is empty
public:
    void init(void);
    int pop(int *pop_to);
    int push(int push_this);
} my_stack;

→    void stack_type::init(void)
→    {
→    stack_ptr = -1;
→    }
```

Note that the definition of **init( )** follows the definition of the class. To indicate that this is a member function of the class **stack_type**, we use the **scope resolution operator**, ::, this way:

```
void stack_type::init(void)
```

This informs C++ that **init( )** is a member function **stack_type**. Note also that we're defining **init( )** before reaching the **main( )** function. This is not technically necessary. As long as you use the scope resolution operator, ::, you can define member functions anywhere in a program. However, the C++ style is to define them in the beginning of the program, before **main( )**.

In fact, C++ programmers usually place class and member function definitions both into header files. That way, you only have to include the header
files — and thus the classes — that you want. C++ will compile the member
functions that it finds in header files like this automatically (C will not).

Now that **init( )** is defined, we can use it in the beginning of our program
once, **my_stack.init( )**, to initialize the stack. Next, let's define the function
pop( ). If the stack is empty, popping is an error, and we should return a value
of 0 to indicate that:

```
#include <stdio.h>

/* Stack implemented as an object  */

class stack_type {
    int data_buffer[100];
    int stack_ptr;      // stack_ptr = -1 → stack is empty
public:
    void init(void);
    int pop(int *pop_to);
    int push(int push_this);
} my_stack;

void stack_type::init(void)
    {
    stack_ptr = -1;
    }

int stack_type::pop(int *pop_to)
    {
    if(stack_ptr == -1) // Stack is empty -- return error
        return 0;
            :
```

Otherwise, we have to take data off the stack; that is, the array named
data_array. Notice that we've passed a pointer to **pop( )**. This is because we
want to be able to change the value of the parameter passed to it. In this case,
our pointer is named **pop_to**, and the data it refers to is ***pop_to**, so we can
send the contents of the current stack location there. That stack location is
pointed to by **stack_ptr**, which we've set up as the location where the next int
will be popped. We can place the popped int at memory address **pop_to** and
decrement the stack pointer all in the same statement (recall that the **postfix**

decrement operator means that **stack_ptr** will not be decremented until after the statement has been executed):

```
#include <stdio.h>

/* Stack implemented as an object  */

class stack_type {
    int data_buffer[100];
    int stack_ptr;      // stack_ptr = -1 → stack is empty
public:
    void init(void);
    int pop(int *pop_to);
    int push(int push_this);
} my_stack;

void stack_type::init(void)
{

    stack_ptr = -1;
}

int stack_type::pop(int *pop_to)
{
    if(stack_ptr == -1)  // Stack is empty -- return error
        return 0;
    else                 // Else return data
    *pop_to = data_buffer[stack_ptr--];
    return 1;
    }
    :
```

Note also that we're returning a nonzero value — 1 in this case — to indicate success. That's it for **pop( )**. The only error condition that we had to handle was when there was nothing left to pop from the stack, and we checked that simply by checking the value of **stack_ptr**.

We can check for error conditions when we write **push( )** in the same way. Our stack in memory, **data_buffer[100]**, has enough room for 100 integers, and **stack_ptr** can range from -1 for an empty stack to 99 for a completely full one. When we try to push an integer, it's an error if the stack is full, and we can check that by comparing **stack_ptr** to its maximum possible value, 99. If it's greater than or equal to this value, we should return 0. Otherwise, we have to increment the stack pointer and place the incoming int onto the stack. Note that since the stack pointer points to the next integer to be popped, we have to increment it *before* placing an integer on the stack. We can do that this way:

```c
#include <stdio.h>

/* Stack implemented as an object  */

class stack_type {
    int data_buffer[100];
    int stack_ptr;      // stack_ptr = -1 → stack is empty
public:
    void init(void);
    int pop(int *pop_to);
    int push(int push_this);
} my_stack;

void stack_type::init(void)
{
stack_ptr = -1;
}

int stack_type::pop(int *pop_to)
{
if(stack_ptr == -1)       // Stack is empty -- return error
    return 0;
    else                  // Else return data
        *pop_to = data_buffer[stack_ptr--];
        return 1;
}

int stack_type::push(int push_this)
{
if(stack_ptr >= 99)       // Stack is full -- return error
    return 0;
    else                  // Else store data
    data_buffer[++stack_ptr] = push_this;
    return 1;
}
```

Again, we return 0 if there was an error, 1 otherwise. Now our class — **stack_type** — is completely set up, and we've defined an object of that class named **my_stack**. We're ready to use this object because we've defined everything it needs, including the member functions. To use it in a program, we simply need to use the dot operator, like this:

```c
my_stack.push(5);
```

This statement pushes a value of 5 onto our stack. Let's continue with our program, seeing our object at work. To do that, we have to define the **main( )** function, and we can do that next. The first thing to do in **main( )** is to initialize the stack with **my_stack.init( )**:

```
#include <stdio.h>

/* Stack implemented as an object  */

class stack_type {
    int data_buffer[100];
    int stack_ptr;       // stack_ptr = -1 → stack is empty
public:
    void init(void);
    int pop(int *pop_to);
    int push(int push_this);
} my_stack;

void stack_type::init(void)
    {
    stack_ptr = -1;
    }

int stack_type::pop(int *pop_to)
{
if(stack_ptr == -1)        // Stack is empty -- return error
    return 0;
    else                   // Else return data
        *pop_to = data_buffer[stack_ptr--];
    return 1;
}

int stack_type::push(int push_this)
{
    if(stack_ptr >= 99)  // Stack is full -- return error
        return 0;
    else                 // Else store data
        data_buffer[++stack_ptr] = push_this;
        return 1;
}

main()
{
→     my_stack.init();
         :
```

Now that we've initialized the stack, we're free to push and pop values. Let's try it out with a loop. Here we can push, say, the numbers from 0 to 9 and print them out at the same time:

```
#include <stdio.h>

/* Stack implemented as an object  */

class stack_type {
    int data_buffer[100];
    int stack_ptr;      // stack_ptr = -1 → stack is empty
public:
    void init(void);
    int pop(int *pop_to);
    int push(int push_this);
} my_stack;

void stack_type::init(void)
{
    stack_ptr = -1;
}

int stack_type::pop(int *pop_to)
{
    if(stack_ptr == -1)   // Stack is empty -- return error
        return 0;
    else                  // Else return data
        *pop_to = data_buffer[stack_ptr--];
        return 1;
}

int stack_type::push(int push_this)
{
    if(stack_ptr >= 99)  // Stack is full -- return error
        return 0;
    else                  // Else store data
        data_buffer[++stack_ptr] = push_this;
        return 1;
}

main()
{
    int loop_index;

    my_stack.init();

    printf("Pushing values now...\n");
```

```
      for(loop_index = 0; loop_index < 10; loop_index++){
→         my_stack.push(loop_index);
          printf("Pushed value--> %d\n", loop_index);
      }
      :
```

That's it, we've placed ten numbers on the stack like this:

Now when we pop a value, the first integer that comes off will be 9, and **pop( )** will move the stack pointer back one element:

We can do that in our program with another loop. This time, we have to use **my_stack.pop( )**, and we have to pass it a pointer so it can return a value like this:

```
#include <stdio.h>

/* Stack implemented as an object  */

class stack_type {
    int data_buffer[100];
    int stack_ptr;       // stack_ptr = -1 → stack is empty
public:
    void init(void);
    int pop(int *pop_to);
    int push(int push_this);
} my_stack;

void stack_type::init(void)
{
    stack_ptr = -1;
}

int stack_type::pop(int *pop_to)
{
    if(stack_ptr == -1) // Stack is empty -- return error
        return 0;
```

```
        else                    // Else return data
            *pop_to = data_buffer[stack_ptr--];
            return 1;
    }

    int stack_type::push(int push_this)
    {
        if(stack_ptr >= 99)   // Stack is full -- return error
            return 0;
        else                    // Else store data
            data_buffer[++stack_ptr] = push_this;
            return 1;
    }

    main()
    {
        int loop_index, popped_value;

        my_stack.init();

        printf("Pushing values now...\n");

        for(loop_index = 0; loop_index < 10; loop_index++){
            my_stack.push(loop_index);
            printf("Pushed value--> %d\n", loop_index);
        }

        printf("Popping values now...\n");

        for(loop_index = 0; loop_index < 10; loop_index++){
→           my_stack.pop(&popped_value);
→           printf("Popped value--> %d\n", popped_value);
        }
        return(0);
    }
```

That's it. When we pop a value, it is placed in the integer variable
popped_value, and then we print it out. On the screen, the output of our
program looks like this:

```
Pushing values now...
Pushed value→ 0
Pushed value→ 1
Pushed value→ 2
Pushed value→ 3
Pushed value→ 4
Pushed value→ 5
```

```
Pushed value→ 6
Pushed value→ 7
Pushed value→ 8
Pushed value→ 9
Popping values now...
Popped value→ 9
Popped value→ 8
Popped value→ 7
Popped value→ 6
Popped value→ 5
Popped value→ 4
Popped value→ 3
Popped value→ 2
Popped value→ 1
Popped value→ 0
```

Our stack is a success. The numbers are coming off in reverse order. We've put together a functioning C++ object. The next step is to break through another boundary. Usually, stacks can only push and pop integer values, but, under C++, we can redefine our member functions to take all sorts of different data types. When we use them on a particular data type, that will automatically tell C++ which function definition to apply. This is called **function overloading**, and it's one of the big attractions of C++.

Function Overloading in C++

The flexibility that C++ brings to programming tasks has made it a programmer's favorite, and that flexibility is very evident in **function overloading**. Rather than the restrictive data typing we might find in other languages, where if you use the wrong data type at the wrong time, your program might crash, C++ is smart enough to check the data type you want to use and to see whether that function has been defined with that type or not. That means that we'll be able to define, say, **pop( )** a number of times. The only thing that will differentiate our definitions is the data types used for the parameters. For example, we can expand our stack to work on floating point values, not just on integers. When we're done, both of these will be legal in our program:

```
my_stack.push(my_int);      // Push an integer value
my_stack.push(1.3333);      // Push a float value
```

By itself, C++ will select the correct definition of **push( )**, the one for floats or the one for ints. This means that we'll have to have two internal stacks, however, one for floats and one for ints. We can begin the new, expanded class definition with the new arrays, **int_data_buffer[ ]** and **float_data_buffer[ ]** (to avoid using up too much memory on C++'s own stack, let's limit those arrays to 50 elements each):

```
#include <stdio.h>

/* Overloading stack functions */

class stack_type {
→       int int_data_buffer[50];
→       float float_data_buffer[50];
            :
```

Two stacks also mean that we'll have to have two stack pointers:

```
#include <stdio.h>

/* Overloading stack functions */

class stack_type {
    int int_data_buffer[50];
    float float_data_buffer[50];
→       int int_stack_ptr;       // int_stack_ptr = -1
                                 // →stack is empty
→       int float_stack_ptr;     // float_stack_ptr = -1
                                 // → stack is empty
        :
```

Now let's write the functions. We'll have to modify **init( )** to initialize both stack pointers, but we'll still only need one **init( )** function. However, we'll need two **pop( )**s and two **push( )**es, one to handle ints and one to handle floats. We can include their prototypes in the class definition like this:

```
#include <stdio.h>

/* Overloading stack functions */

class stack_type {
    int int_data_buffer[50];
    float float_data_buffer[50];
    int int_stack_ptr;       // int_stack_ptr = -1
                             // → stack is empty
```

```
        int float_stack_ptr;    // float_stack_ptr = -1
                                // → stack is empty
    public:
→       void init(void);
:       int pop(int *pop_to);
:       int pop(float *pop_to);
        int push(int push_this);
        int push(float push_this);
    } my_stack;
        :
```

This is the way function overloading works: C++ makes no complaint about the duplicated prototypes as long as the parameter list has the same number of items but includes some different data types. Now we can define the member functions themselves. Once again, we use the :: scope resolution operator to let C++ know which class these functions belong to. The **init( )** function has to initialize both **int_stack_ptr** and **float_stack_ptr**, and that can be done easily (-1 indicates an empty stack):

```
#include <stdio.h>

/* Overloading stack functions */

class stack_type {
    int int_data_buffer[50];
    float float_data_buffer[50];
    int int_stack_ptr;      // int_stack_ptr = -1
                            // → stack is empty
    int float_stack_ptr;    // float_stack_ptr = -1
                            // → stack is empty
public:
    void init(void);
    int pop(int *pop_to);
    int pop(float *pop_to);
    int push(int push_this);
    int push(float push_this);
} my_stack;

void stack_type::init(void)
{
→   int_stack_ptr = -1;
→   float_stack_ptr = -1;
}
    :
```

Next, as before, we can define the **pop( )** function this way:

```
#include <stdio.h>

/* Overloading stack functions */

class stack_type {
    int int_data_buffer[50];
    float float_data_buffer[50];
    int int_stack_ptr;      // int_stack_ptr = -1
                            // → stack is empty
    int float_stack_ptr;    // float_stack_ptr = -1
                            // → stack is empty
public:
    void init(void);
    int pop(int *pop_to);
    int pop(float *pop_to);
    int push(int push_this);
    int push(float push_this);
} my_stack;

void stack_type::init(void)
{
    int_stack_ptr = -1;
    float_stack_ptr = -1;
}
```
→
```
    int stack_type::pop(int *pop_to)
{

    if(int_stack_ptr == -1)         // Stack is empty
                                    // -- return error
        return 0;
    else                            // Else return data
        *pop_to = int_data_buffer[int_stack_ptr--];
    return 1;
}
    :
```

This is the integer version. We also have to include the floating point version, which uses **float_data_buffer[ ]** and **float_stack_ptr**. We can do that like this:

```
#include <stdio.h>

/* Overloading stack functions */

class stack_type {
```

```
        int int_data_buffer[50];
        float float_data_buffer[50];
        int int_stack_ptr;      // int_stack_ptr = -1
                                 // → stack is empty
        int float_stack_ptr;    // float_stack_ptr = -1
                                 // → stack is empty
    public:
        void init(void);
        int pop(int *pop_to);
        int pop(float *pop_to);
        int push(int push_this);
        int push(float push_this);
    } my_stack;

    void stack_type::init(void)
        {
        int_stack_ptr = -1;
        float_stack_ptr = -1:
    }

    int stack_type::pop(int *pop_to)
    {
        if(int_stack_ptr == -1)      // Stack is empty
                                     // -- return error
            return 0;
        else                         // Else return data
            *pop_to = int_data_buffer[int_stack_ptr--];
            return 1;
    }
```

→
:
:

```
    int stack_type::pop(float *pop_to)
    {
        if(float_stack_ptr == -1)      // Stack is empty
                                       // -- return error
            return 0;
        else                           // Else return data
            *pop_to = float_data_buffer[float_stack_ptr--];
            return 1;
    }
```
:

And that's how function overloading looks. We can also do the same for
push( ):

```
    #include <stdio.h>

    /* Overloading stack functions */
```

```
class stack_type {
    int int_data_buffer[50];
    float float_data_buffer[50];
    int int_stack_ptr;      // int_stack_ptr = -1
                            // → stack is empty
    int float_stack_ptr;    // float_stack_ptr = -1
                            // → stack is empty
public:
    void init(void);
    int pop(int *pop_to);
    int pop(float *pop_to);
    int push(int push_this);
    int push(float push_this);
} my_stack;

void stack_type::init(void)
    {
    int_stack_ptr = -1;
    float_stack_ptr = -1;
}

int stack_type::pop(int *pop_to)
{
    if(int_stack_ptr == -1)     // Stack is empty
                                // -- return error
        return 0;
    else                        // Else return data
        *pop_to = int_data_buffer[int_stack_ptr--];
        return 1;
}

int stack_type::pop(float *pop_to)
{
    if(float_stack_ptr == -1)    // Stack is empty
                                 // -- return error
        return 0;
    else                         // Else return data
        *pop_to = float_data_buffer[float_stack_ptr--];
        return 1;
}

int stack_type::push(int push_this)
{
    if(int_stack_ptr >= 49)     // Stack is full
                                // -- return error
        return 0;
    else                        // Else store data
        int_data_buffer[++int_stack_ptr] = push_this;
        return 1;
}
```

```
int stack_type::push(float push_this)
{
    if(float_stack_ptr >= 49)        // Stack is full
                                     // -- return error
        return 0;
    else                             // Else store data
        float_data_buffer[++float_stack_ptr] = push_this;
        return 1;
}
:
```

Now our object **my_stack** is ready to be used with either integers or floats. That's all there is to it. We can modify our loops to push and pop floating point values with a type cast this way:

```
      for(loop_index = 0; loop_index < 10; loop_index++){
→         my_stack.push((float) loop_index);
          printf("Pushed value--> %f\n", (float) loop_index);
      }
```

The new program appears in Listing 10-1. This time, the program output looks like this:

```
Pushing values now...
Pushed value→ 0.000000
Pushed value→ 1.000000
Pushed value→ 2.000000
Pushed value→ 3.000000
Pushed value→ 4.000000
Pushed value→ 5.000000
Pushed value→ 6.000000
Pushed value→ 7.000000
Pushed value→ 8.000000
Pushed value→ 9.000000
Popping values now...
Popped value→ 9.000000
Popped value→ 8.000000
Popped value→ 7.000000
Popped value→ 6.000000
Popped value→ 5.000000
Popped value→ 4.000000
Popped value→ 3.000000
Popped value→ 2.000000
Popped value→ 1.000000
Popped value→ 0.000000
```

Listing 10-1. Function Overloading Example.

```c
#include <stdio.h>

/* Overloading stack functions */

class stack_type {
    int int_data_buffer[50];
    float float_data_buffer[50];
    int int_stack_ptr;        // int_stack_ptr = -1
                              // → stack is empty
    int float_stack_ptr;      // float_stack_ptr = -1
                              // → stack is empty
public:
    void init(void);
    int pop(int *pop_to);
    int pop(float *pop_to);
    int push(int push_this);
    int push(float push_this);
} my_stack;

void stack_type::init(void)
{
    int_stack_ptr = -1;
    float_stack_ptr = -1;
}

int stack_type::pop(int *pop_to)
{
    if(int_stack_ptr == -1)        // Stack is empty
                                   // -- return error
        return 0;
    else                           // Else return data
        *pop_to = int_data_buffer[int_stack_ptr--];
        return 1;
}

int stack_type::pop(float *pop_to)
{
    if(float_stack_ptr == -1)      // Stack is empty
                                   // -- return error
        return 0;
    else                           // Else return data
        *pop_to = float_data_buffer[float_stack_ptr--];
        return 1;
}

int stack_type::push(int push_this)
```

Listing 10-1. *(continued)*

```
{
    if(int_stack_ptr >= 49)        // Stack is full
                                   // -- return error
        return 0;
    else                    // Else store data
        int_data_buffer[++int_stack_ptr] = push_this;
        return 1;
}

int stack_type::push(float push_this)
{
    if(float_stack_ptr >= 49)      // Stack is full
                                   // -- return error
        return 0;
    else                    // Else store data
        float_data_buffer[++float_stack_ptr] = push_this;
        return 1;
}

main()
{
    int loop_index;
    float popped_value;

    my_stack.init();

    printf("Pushing values now...\n");

    for(loop_index = 0; loop_index < 10; loop_index++){
        my_stack.push((float) loop_index);
        printf("Pushed value--> %f\n", (float) loop_index);
    }

    printf("Popping values now...\n");

    for(loop_index = 0; loop_index < 10; loop_index++){
        my_stack.pop(&popped_value);
        printf("Popped value--> %f\n", popped_value);
    }
    return(0);
}
```

We've developed a useful programming tool so far in C++: an integer or floating point stack that maintains and manipulates its own internal data. We've already seen how to use that tool in our programs, but there is a new way of using tools like this as well in C++. We can use them in other classes. In other words, we can set up certain foundation classes that have a number of desirable attributes and then derive others from them, adding additional attributes each time. This is called **inheritance**.

C++ Inheritance

When you're working in C++, you'll frequently find that some of your defined classes share many of the same things. For example, you could define a number of classes: **tiger**, **lion**, **elephant**, **snake**, and **antelope**. While each of these have obvious differences, they may include many of the same member functions, such as **eat( )**, **sleep( )**, **breathe( )**, and so on. In C++, we can handle this by setting up certain generic classes we call **base classes**. A base class includes the members that all the subsequent **derivedclasses** have in common. For example, the base class here could be called **animal**, and it may include the member functions **eat( )**, **sleep( )**, and **breathe( )**.

Then, when we wanted to define, say, the class **elephant**, we could include the class **animal** to get the basics, adding such functions as **trumpet( )** and **stampede( )**. In general, then, a class definition looks like this:

```
class class_name : access base_class {
    private data and function list
public:
    public data and function list
} object_list;
```

We include a base class in the definition of a derived class, in our example, that would look like this:

```
→    class elephant : public animal {
     public:
         int trumpet(void);
         int stampede(void);
     } jumbo;
```

The **access** keyword in front of the base class can be either **public** or **private**, and we make it **public** here so that the class **elephant** can have access to all of the member functions and data of **animal**.

Let's see an example. Our stack provides us with a useful base class since many computational operations can use a stack. For example, you may remember the example in which we read a decimal integer, converted it to hex and printed it out:

```c
#include <stdio.h>

/* Convert decimal to hex. */

main()
{
    unsigned int i = 0, index = 0, hexdig = 0;
    char out_string[10];

    printf("Type a positive integer please ");
    scanf("%d", &i);

    do{
        out_string[index++] = (i%16 > 9 ? i%16 - 10 + 'a' :\
        i%16 + '0');
    }while(i /= 16);

    printf("That number in hexadecimal is ");
    while(index) printf("%c", out_string[--index]);
}
```

In this case, we set up an array named **out_string** in which we placed the successive digits. Since we stripped them off and stored them in reverse order, however, we had to take them out of the array backwards. This would be easier if we just used a stack, pushing the characters on until there were no more to push, and then popping and printing them. Let's use our class **stack_type** as a base class to provide stack support. From it, we can derive a new class, say **derived_type**, which might include the function **print_number_in_hex( )**. In other words, we can use **stack_type** as the base class for **derived_type** like this:

```c
→    class derived_type : public stack_type {
        public:
        void print_number_in_hex(int i);
    } derived_object;
```

As you can see, we add the function **print_number_in_hex( )** to **stack_type** in order to form **derived_type**. In addition, we declare an object of that type named **derived_object**. If we had a decimal number to print out in hex, we could do that like this in our **main( )** function:

```c
derived_object.print_number_in_hex(number);
```

Because of inheritance, the **print_number_in_hex( )** function has access to both the **push( )** and **pop( )** functions, and it can use them freely. For example, that function might look like this:

```
void derived_type::print_number_in_hex(int i)
{
    char the_char;

    do{
        derived_object.push( (char) (i%16 > 9 ? i%16-10+'a' :\
        i%16+'0'));
    }while(i /= 16);

    printf("That number in hexadecimal is ");

    while(derived_object.pop(&the_char)) printf("%c",\
    the_char);
}
```

We should note two things here. First, **push( )** and **pop( )** are now members of the object we've defined, **derived_object**, so we use them like this: **derived_object.push( )** and **derived_object.pop( )**. In other words, the only object in this program is **derived_object**, and **push( )** and **pop( )** have become member functions of it. Second, we are pushing a char here, so we had to use a char type cast in front of the integer expression (`i%16 > 9 ? i%16+10+'a' : i%16+'0'`). That also means that we'll have to add a char stack to the base class stack type. We can do that like this in the class definition:

```
#include <stdio.h>

/* Example showing inheritance */

class stack_type {
    char char_data_buffer[50];
    int int_data_buffer[50];
    float float_data_buffer[50];
    int char_stack_ptr;      // char_stack_ptr = -1
                             // → stack is empty
    int int_stack_ptr;       // int_stack_ptr = -1
                             // → stack is empty
    int float_stack_ptr;     // float_stack_ptr = -1
                             // → stack is empty
public:
    void init(void);
    int pop(char *pop_to);
```

```
        int pop(int *pop_to);
        int pop(float *pop_to);
→       int push(char push_this);
        int push(int push_this);
        int push(float push_this);
    };
    :
```

Through function overloading, our class **stack_type** can now handle chars, ints, and floats. The next step is to set up the class **derived_type** and declare **derived_object**:

```
#include <stdio.h>

/* Example showing inheritance */

class stack_type {
    char char_data_buffer[50];
    int int_data_buffer[50];
    float float_data_buffer[50];
    int char_stack_ptr;        // char_stack_ptr = -1
                               // → stack is empty
    int int_stack_ptr;         // int_stack_ptr = -1
                               // → stack is empty
    int float_stack_ptr;       // float_stack_ptr = -1
                               // → stack is empty
public:
    void init(void);
    int pop(char *pop_to);
    int pop(int *pop_to);
    int pop(float *pop_to);
    int push(char push_this);
    int push(int push_this);
    int push(float push_this);
};

→   class derived_type : public stack_type {
    public:
        void print_number_in_hex(int i);
    } derived_object;
    :
```

Following this are the definitions of all the member functions, including **print_number_in_hex( )**:

```
#include <stdio.h>

/* Example showing inheritance */

class stack_type {
    char char_data_buffer[50];
    int int_data_buffer[50];
    float float_data_buffer[50];
    int char_stack_ptr;     // char_stack_ptr = -1
                            // → stack is empty
    int int_stack_ptr;      // int_stack_ptr = -1
                            // → stack is empty
    int float_stack_ptr;    // float_stack_ptr = -1
                            // → stack is empty
public:
    void init(void);
    int pop(char *pop_to);
    int pop(int *pop_to);
    int pop(float *pop_to);
    int push(char push_this);
    int push(int push_this);
    int push(float push_this);
};

class derived_type : public stack_type {
public:
    void print_number_in_hex(int i);
} derived_object;

void stack_type::init(void)
{
    char_stack_ptr = -1;
    int_stack_ptr = -1;
    float_stack_ptr = -1;
}

int stack_type::pop(char *pop_to)
{
    if(char_stack_ptr == -1)        // Stack is empty
                                    // -- return error
        return 0;
    else                            // Else return data
        *pop_to = char_data_buffer[char_stack_ptr--];
        return 1;
}

int stack_type::pop(int *pop_to)
{
```

```
    if(int_stack_ptr == -1)     // Stack is empty
                                // -- return error
        return 0;
    else                        // Else return data
        *pop_to = int_data_buffer[int_stack_ptr--];
        return 1;
}

int stack_type::pop(float *pop_to)
{
    if(float_stack_ptr == -1)     // Stack is empty
                                  // -- return error
        return 0;
    else                          // Else return data
        *pop_to = float_data_buffer[float_stack_ptr--];
        return 1;
}

int stack_type::push(char push_this)
{
    if(char_stack_ptr >= 49)     // Stack is full
                                 // -- return error
        return 0;
    else                         // Else store data
        char_data_buffer[++char_stack_ptr] = push_this;
        return 1;
}

int stack_type::push(int push_this)
{
    if(int_stack_ptr >= 49)     // Stack is full
                                // -- return error
        return 0;
    else                        // Else store data
        int_data_buffer[++int_stack_ptr] = push_this;
        return 1;
}

int stack_type::push(float push_this)
{
    if(float_stack_ptr >= 49)     // Stack is full
                                  // -- return error
        return 0;
    else                          // Else store data
        float_data_buffer[++float_stack_ptr] = push_this;
        return 1;
}
```

```
void derived_type::print_number_in_hex(int i)
{
    char the_char;

    do{
        derived_object.push( (char)\
        (i%16 > 9 ? i%16+10+'a' : i%16+'0'));
    }while(i /= 16);

    printf("That number in hexadecimal is ");

    while(derived_object.pop(&the_char))\
    printf("%c", the_char);
}
    :
```

Now the object we've called derived_object is ready. We can use that in our **main( )** function like this:

```
main()
{
    unsigned int number = 0;

    derived_object.init();

    printf("Type a positive integer please ");
    scanf("%d", &number);

→   derived_object.print_number_in_hex(number);

    return(0);
}
```

And that's all there is to it. The entire program appears in Listing 10-2.

Listing 10-2. C++ Inheritance Example.

```
#include <stdio.h>

/* Example showing inheritance */

class stack_type {
    char char_data_buffer[50];
    int int_data_buffer[50];
    float float_data_buffer[50];
    int char_stack_ptr;     // char_stack_ptr = -1
                            // → stack is empty
```

Listing 10-2. *(continued)*

```
        int int_stack_ptr;        // int_stack_ptr = -1
                                  // → stack is empty
        int float_stack_ptr;      // float_stack_ptr = -1
                                  // → stack is empty
public:
    void init(void);
    int pop(char *pop_to);
    int pop(int *pop_to);
    int pop(float *pop_to);
    int push(char push_this);
    int push(int push_this);
    int push(float push_this);
};

class derived_type : public stack_type {
public:
void print_number_in_hex(int i);
} derived_object;

void stack_type::init(void)
{
    char_stack_ptr = -1;
    int_stack_ptr = -1;
    float_stack_ptr = -1;
}

int stack_type::pop(char *pop_to)
{
    if(char_stack_ptr == -1)      // Stack is empty
                                  // -- return error
        return 0;
    else                          // Else return data
        *pop_to = char_data_buffer[char_stack_ptr--];
        return 1;
}

int stack_type::pop(int *pop_to)
{
    if(int_stack_ptr == -1)       // Stack is empty
                                  // -- return error
        return 0;
    else                          // Else return data
        *pop_to = int_data_buffer[int_stack_ptr--];
        return 1;
}
```

(continued)

Listing 10-2. *(continued)*

```
int stack_type::pop(float *pop_to)
{
    if(float_stack_ptr == -1)        // Stack is empty
                                     // -- return error
        return 0;
    else                         // Else return data
        *pop_to = float_data_buffer[float_stack_ptr--];
        return 1;
}

int stack_type::push(char push_this)
{
    if(char_stack_ptr >= 49)     // Stack is full
                                 // -- return error
        return 0;
    else                         // Else store data
        char_data_buffer[++char_stack_ptr] = push_this;
        return 1;
}

int stack_type::push(int push_this)
{
    if(int_stack_ptr >= 49)      // Stack is full
                                 // -- return error
        return 0;
    else                         // Else store data
        int_data_buffer[++int_stack_ptr] = push_this;
        return 1;
}

int stack_type::push(float push_this)
{
    if(float_stack_ptr >= 49)    // Stack is full
                                 // -- return error
        return 0;
    else                         // Else store data
        float_data_buffer[++float_stack_ptr] = push_this;
        return 1;
}

void derived_type::print_number_in_hex(int i)
{
    char the_char;
```

Listing 10-2. *(continued)*

```
    do{
        derived_object.push( (char)\
        (i%16 > 9 ? i%16+10+'a' : i%16+'0'));
    }while(i /= 16);

    printf("That number in hexadecimal is ");

    while(derived_object.pop(&the_char))\
        printf("%c", the_char);
}

main()
{
    unsigned int number = 0;

    derived_object.init();

    printf("Type a positive integer please ");
    scanf("%d", &number);

    derived_object.print_number_in_hex(number);

    return(0);
}
```

That's it for inheritance, and that's it for our discussion of C++. As we've seen, it provides some powerful techniques. Of course, we've only touched on the subject here. A complete treatment would take a book in itself.

So far, we've seen a great deal about C, from the simplest programs up until now to the very large ones, where programmers use self-contained objects to keep things straight. Paradoxically, the next C topic that we'll cover isn't C at all. It's assembly language. That is because connecting assembly language and C has always been very popular with C programmers. In fact, the most common environment for application programmers today is a combination of C and assembly language. In addition, the interface is an easy one, and assembly language resembles C in many ways. For these reasons, we'll spend a little time dipping into assembly language next in order to give some real speed and power to our C programs.

Welcome to Assembly Language

We'll begin our tour of assembly language in this chapter. Here, we're going to start working with the machine on the lowest levels. This is where we'll boost C's speed and capabilities enormously. This chapter is going to be about the essentials of assembly language, and in the next chapter we'll interface it to C. We'll see how to write our own C functions entirely in assembly language for unprecedented power. However, the most important thing right now is to get a good base to start from, and we'll start that process immediately.

Machine Language

To get a computer to do something, we have to supply machine language instructions, and these bytes are really only comprehensible to the microprocessor. Often, only part of the machine language instruction will be used to tell the computer what to do, and the rest of the instruction is data. For example, we can write an instruction to put the byte 0xff into a certain memory location. Part of the instruction will be to tell the microprocessor that we want to store a number, part of the instruction will be to tell it the location in memory we want to store the number at, and part of it will be the number itself, 0xff.

Although machine language instructions can be many bytes long, data and the instruction codes never mix across byte boundaries. For example, some machine language instructions may be all instruction to the microprocessor:

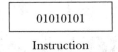

| 01010101 |

Instruction

And some will be a mix of both instruction and data:

| 01010101 | 10111010 |

Instruction   Data used by the instruction

or even mostly data:

| 01010101 | 10111010   10010101   001010100 |

Instruction   Data used by the instruction

The data used by the instruction is either memory address(es) or data, like the 0xff we wanted to store in a memory location earlier. However, reading this kind of binary code is extremely difficult. Imagine yourself confronted with a page of numbers, all 0's or 1's. Even if such instructions were to be converted to hex, you'd have to look up the meaning of each byte before understanding what was going on (there are tables in the manuals that accompany assemblers listing what binary instructions mean what). Mostly, however, what means everything to the microprocessor means nothing to us.

Assembly Language

This is where assembly language enters. It is the direct intermediary between machine language and English. For every machine language instruction, there is one assembly language instruction. Rather than using a byte like **10101010B** (we'll place a B for Binary at the end of binary numbers), an English-language mnemonic is used, such as **MOV AX,5**.

This instruction, **MOV AX,5**, may be terse, but it is still an improvement over the corresponding machine code: **0xB8 0x00 0x05**. What this instruction does is to direct the machine to move (the "**MOV**" part of **MOV AX,5**) the value of 5 into the **AX** register.

Instruction	Assembly Language		Machine Language
MOV	DI,00B0	→	BF B0 00
MOV	COUNTER,00B0	→	C7 06 C3 01 B0 00
MOV	BX,0080	→	BB 80 00
CMP	INDEX,00	→	80 3F 00
JZ	0670	→	74 12
CMP	[SI],0D	→	80 3C 0D
JZ	0666	→	74 03
MOVSB		→	A4
JMP	065E	→	EB F8

Table 11-1. What an Assembler Does.

What an assembler does is simple: It takes the program we've written in assembly language, and converts it, instruction by instruction, directly into machine language.

The machine language is then run by the microprocessor. Let's see some assembly language examples. Table 11-1 shows some examples of assembly language instructions that were assembled — converted into machine language — and the corresponding machine language for each instruction (all numbers are in hex).

Sometimes assembly language is hard to write, sometimes it's hard to debug. There is no escaping the fact. It has to follow the design of the microprocessor, and as we'll see, assembly language for the PC has many quirks.

The MOV Instruction

The most fundamental assembly language instruction is **MOV**, the instruction that moves data between registers and memory, or between registers and registers. The **MOV** format is this: **MOV destination, source**. The data gets moved from the **source** into the **destination**. If we have something stored in memory and want to work with it, we can use MOV. Here's how it works:

```
MOV    AX, 0FFFFH
```

Here we are putting the number 0FFFFH (65,535) into **AX**. This is the biggest number any register can hold (all are 16 bits except in the 80386, and we'll use them in their 16-bit mode): 0FFFFH. Note that in assembly language, the **H** for **Hex** goes at the end of the number (0FFFFH) not at the beginning as in C (0xffff). In addition, if any number begins with a letter, like FFFFH, we have to preface it with a 0 — 0FFFFH — to let the assembler know it's really a number and not a name. Now we can take the 0FFFFH in the register **AX** and move it into the **DX** register:

```
MOV    DX, AX    (Move the data from AX into DX)
```

And now **DX** and **AX** hold the same value. We could also work one byte at a time. We're already familiar with the idea of breaking registers into upper and lower bytes:

```
MOV    DL, AL    (Move the data from AL into DL)
```

Data can also be moved into registers from memory. Let's say we have a memory location with 0 in it: This can be moved into, say, **CX**, this way:

```
MOV    CX, [Memory Location]
```

Or, we can move whatever is in **DX** into the memory location this way:

```
MOV    [Memory Location], DX
```

However, data cannot be moved from memory directly to memory. This is one of the peculiarities of the 80×86: Data cannot go directly from memory location to memory location in one instruction. If we wanted to, we could move data from memory location 1 to **AX**, and then to memory location 2 like this:

```
MOV AX, [Memory Location 1]
MOV [Memory Location 2], AX
```

But it cannot go like this:

```
MOV [Memory Location 2], [Memory Location 1]
```

An Assembly Language Example

It's always better to see an example. There is an excellent program that comes with all DOS versions named **DEBUG.COM**. **DEBUG** has had the ability to assemble small programs that we write on the spot: A mini-assembler is built into the program. We'll use this mini-assembler to convert our instruction **MOV AX,5** into machine language, and then run it, watching the value stored in **AX** change from 0 to 5. Start the **DEBUG** program. It gives us its hyphen prompt:

```
C:\>DEBUG
```

The command "**R**" in **DEBUG** stands for **Register**, and it lets us see the contents of all the 80×86's registers. In fact, we can pick out the registers **AX**, **BX**, **CX**, and **DX** readily. (Note that all numbers displayed in **DEBUG** are in hexadecimal, which is standard for assembly language debuggers):

```
C:\>DEBUG
-R
AX=0000  BX=0000  CX=0000  DX=0000  SP=FFEE BP=0000  SI=0000  DI=0000
DS=0EF1  ES=0EF1  SS=0EF1  CS=0EF1  IP=0100   NV UP EI PL NZ NA PO NC
0EF1:0100 9AEC04020F    CALL    0F02:04EC
```

In addition to the registers shown:

```
C:\>DEBUG
-R
AX=0000  BX=0000  CX=0000  DX=0000  SP=FFEE BP=0000  SI=0000  DI=0000

DS=0EF1  ES=0EF1  SS=0EF1  CS=0EF1  IP=0100  NV UP EI PL NZ NA PO NC
0EF1:0100 9AEC04020F    CALL    0F02:04EC
```

The settings of the internal flags of the 80×86 are shown:

```
C:\>DEBUG
-R
AX=0000  BX=0000  CX=0000  DX=0000  SP=FFEE BP=0000  SI=0000  DI=0000

DS=0EF1  ES=0EF1  SS=0EF1  CS=0EF1  IP=0100  NV UP EI PL NZ NA PO NC
0EF1:0100 9AEC04020F    CALL    0F02:04EC
```

Flags are used in conditional jumps, and we'll work with them later in this chapter. **DEBUG** also tells us the current memory location. Here, we are at memory location 0EF1:0100:

```
C:\>DEBUG
-R
AX=0000  BX=0000  CX=0000  DX=0000  SP=FFEE BP=0000  SI=0000  DI=0000
DS=0EF1  ES=0EF1  SS=0EF1  CS=0EF1  IP=0100    NV UP EI PL NZ NA PO NC

 0EF1:0100   9AEC04020F     CALL     0F02:04EC
```

The final part of the **DEBUG** "**R**" display indicates what is to be found at the current memory location. In our case, those are the bytes following the address in the "**R**" display:

```
C:\>DEBUG
-R
AX=0000  BX=0000  CX=0000  DX=0000  SP=FFEE  BP=0000  SI=0000  DI=0000
DS=0EF1  ES=0EF1  SS=0EF1  CS=0EF1  IP=0100    NV UP EI PL NZ NA PO NC

0EF1:0100   9AEC04020F     CALL     0F02:04EC
```

DEBUG tries to group bytes together, starting at the current memory location (which only holds one byte), into what would be a valid machine language instruction. It then provides us with an assembly language translation of that (assumed) machine language instruction.

When there is in reality no machine language instruction there (as frequently there is not), the translation is meaningless. That is the case here: Having just started **DEBUG**, there is as yet no program to look at. It is just taking leftover bytes in the computer's memory and trying to make sense out of them. In fact, **DEBUG**'s supplied translation means nothing:

```
C:\>DEBUG
-R
AX=0000  BX=0000  CX=0000  DX=0000  SP=FFEE BP=0000  SI=0000  DI=0000
DS=0EF1  ES=0EF1  SS=0EF1  CS=0EF1  IP=0100    NV UP EI PL NZ NA PO NC

0EF1:0100   9AEC04020F → CALL     0F02:04EC
```

We'll use the **A** (for **Assemble**) command to put our own program in, consisting of only one line: **MOV AX,5**. The **A** command needs an address at which to start depositing the machine language instructions it will generate in memory. Our current address is 0EF1:0100, and we will tell it to assemble the machine language right there, using the shorthand **A100**:

```
C:\>DEBUG
-R
AX=0000  BX=0000  CX=0000  DX=0000  SP=FFEE BP=0000  SI=0000  DI=0000
DS=0EF1  ES=0EF1  SS=0EF1  CS=0EF1  IP=0100    NV UP EI PL NZ NA PO NC
0EF1:0100 9AEC04020F    CALL    0F02:04EC
-A100                          ← Here is the A100 command.
0EF1:0100                      ← DEBUG's response.
```

Following the **A100** command, **DEBUG** returned with the line: 0EF1:0100, showing the current address at which it will deposit assembled code. We simply type **MOV AX,5** and then a carriage return:

```
C:\>DEBUG
-R
AX=0000  BX=0000  CX=0000  DX=0000  SP=FFEE BP=0000  SI=0000  DI=0000
DS=0EF1  ES=0EF1  SS=0EF1  CS=0EF1  IP=0100    NV UP EI PL NZ NA PO NC
0EF1:0100 9AEC04020F    CALL    0F02:04EC
-A100
0EF1:0100 MOV     AX,5          ← Type "MOV AX,5<cr>"
0EF1:0103
```

DEBUG then prompts for the next instruction we wish to give with the address 0EF1:0103. There are no more instructions to assemble at this time, so we give **DEBUG** a carriage return. It interprets the blank line to mean that we are through assembling, and returns to its normal prompt.

That's all there is to it. We've just assembled our first line of assembly language. To see what occurred, remember that the **R** command displays the current memory location and instruction. Since we assembled **MOV AX, 5** at the current memory location, let's give the **R** command and take a look:

```
C:\>DEBUG
-R
AX=0000  BX=0000  CX=0000  DX=0000  SP=FFEE BP=0000  SI=0000  DI=0000
DS=0EF1  ES=0EF1  SS=0EF1  CS=0EF1  IP=0100    NV UP EI PL NZ NA PO NC
0EF1:0100 9AEC04020F    CALL    0F02:04EC
-A100
0EF1:0100 MOV     AX,5
0EF1:0103
-R                              ←
AX=0000  BX=0000  CX=0000  DX=0000  SP=FFEE  BP=0000  SI=0000  DI=0000
```

```
DS=0EF1  ES=0EF1  SS=0EF1  CS=0EF1  IP=0100     NV UP EI PL NZ NA PO NC
0EF1:0100 B80500        MOV    AX,0005
```

We can see that our instruction is there (note the machine language bytes corresponding to **MOV AX,5** in **DEBUG**'s display). Executing this instruction is simple. **DEBUG** has a trace command, and typing **T** once will execute the current instruction, and increment us to the next memory location:

```
C:\>DEBUG
-R
AX=0000  BX=0000  CX=0000  DX=0000  SP=FFEE BP=0000  SI=0000  DI=0000
DS=0EF1  ES=0EF1  SS=0EF1  CS=0EF1  IP=0100     NV UP EI PL NZ NA PO NC
0EF1:0100 9AEC04020F    CALL    0F02:04EC
-A100
0EF1:0100 MOV    AX,5
0EF1:0103
-R
AX=0000  BX=0000  CX=0000  DX=0000  SP=FFEE  BP=0000  SI=0000 DI=0000
DS=0EF1  ES=0EF1  SS=0EF1  CS=0EF1  IP=0100     NV UP EI PL NZ NA PO NC
0EF1:0100 B80500        MOV    AX,0005

-T                              ←   This will execute our MOV instruction.

AX=0005  BX=0000  CX=0000  DX=0000 SP=FFEE  BP=0000  SI=0000  DI=0000
DS=0EF1  ES=0EF1  SS=0EF1 CS=0EF1  IP=0103    NV UP EI PL NZ NA PO NC
0EF1:0103 020F        ADD    CL,[BX]                    DS:0000=CD
```

After the **T** command, **DEBUG** displays what the register contents and flags are now. **AX** holds 5. All the flags remain unchanged. On the other hand, the memory location *has* changed, from 0EF1:0100 to 0EF1:0103. This is because the machine language instruction corresponding to **MOV AX,5** is three bytes long in memory (0B8H 05H 00H). The instruction following it will begin three bytes later, which means that the 100H has changed to 103H.

Our First Program

DEBUG not only allows us to assemble programs, but to write them out to the disk as well. Let's use **DEBUG** to assemble our first assembly language program. This program will simply type out the character 'Z' and then exit. We'll start with the **A** command. As before, we will put our machine language code starting at location 0100H:

```
C:\>DEBUG
-A100            ←
0EF1:0100
```

We're going to use interrupt 21H, service 2, to print out a letter. Just type in the following assembly language instructions verbatim, followed by a carriage return after the prompt 0EF1:010A to stop assembling:

```
C:\>DEBUG
-A100
1CE1:0100 MOV AH,2
1CE1:0102 MOV DL,5A
1CE1:0104 INT 21
1CE1:0106 INT 20
1CE1:0108        ← Just type a <cr> here.
-
```

Our program loads the registers **AH** and **DL** with the **MOV** instruction. We're invoking service 2 of interrupt 21H, and that service prints out the ASCII code in **DL**. We place the ASCII code for '**Z**' there, 5AH.

Then we issue an interrupt 21H instruction directly (INT 21H) followed by INT 20H. Interrupt 20H is used to end programs at the assembly language level and return to the DOS prompt. It's much like a **return(0)** statement at the end of a C program. That's how we'll end our assembly language programs with INT 20H. We can call the program **PRINTZ.COM**, and name it this way:

```
C:\>DEBUG
-A100
1CE1:0100 MOV AH,2
1CE1:0102 MOV DL,5A
1CE1:0104 INT 21
1CE1:0106 INT 20
1CE1:0108
-NPRINTZ.COM    ←
```

Now let's write it out (**DEBUG** will write this file in the current directory). **DEBUG** needs the number of bytes to write out, and in our case, the program goes from locations 0100H to 0107H. Each memory location holds a byte, so that makes 8 bytes.

The **DEBUG W** command, **Write**, reads the number of bytes to write as a file directly out of the **CX** register. This means that to write our 8 byte program **PRINTZ.COM**, we will have to load the **CX** register with 8. To move 8 into **CX**, we can use the **R** (**Register**) command again. If we use the **R** command without any arguments, **DEBUG** gives us its standard display. On the other hand, giving the command **RCX** indicates to **DEBUG** that we wish to change the value in **CX** (this will work with any register). **DEBUG** displays the current value in **CX** (which will be 0000) and gives us a colon prompt, after which we will type our new value for **CX**, 8, and a carriage return. Then we can write **PRINTZ.COM** by giving the **W** command:

```
C:\>DEBUG
-A100
1CE1:0100 MOV AH,2
1CE1:0102 MOV DL,5A
1CE1:0104 INT 21
1CE1:0106 INT 20
1CE1:0108
-NPRINTZ.COM
-RCX              ←
CX 0000           ←
:8                ←
-W                ← The W command
Writing 0008 bytes
-Q
```

Now we've written a functional 8-byte program to disk. Let's run it:

```
C:\>PRINTZ
Z
C:\>
```

And **PRINTZ** does what it's supposed to do: It types out 'Z' and exits. For the first time, we've reached interrupt 21H directly, without **int86( )**. We've simply used interrupt 21H, service 2, to print out a character on the screen. Table 11-2 shows some other interrupt 21H character I/O services we'll find useful in this chapter.

Service #	Name	Set These	What Happens
1	Keyboard Input	AH = 1	ASCII code of typed key returned in AL
2	Character Output	AH = 2 DL = ASCII Code	The character corresponding to the ASCII code in DL is put on the screen
9	String Output	AH=9 DS:DX = Address of string of characters to print	Prints a string of bytes from memory on the screen (we will use this service in this chapter)

Table 11-2. Some Interrupt 21H Character I/O Services.

Now that we have some experience, we can start putting together assembly language programs without using **DEBUG**. To do that, we'll have to review the way memory is accessed by the 80×86 chips. Memory usage as important in assembly language as it is in C. In fact, knowing our way around is essential.

A Review of Memory Segmentation

The address 0EF1:0100 is made up of two hex numbers, each 16 bits long. As we've seen in Chapter 7, this is usual for addresses. Two words are involved for a full address. This is the way it works: We move the segment address *left* by one hex place and add it to the offset address to get the real 20-bit address:

```
    0EF1      ← Note: shifted left one place
+   0100
    -----
    0F010     ← Real 20-bit address
```

In other words, byte 0EF1:0100 really means byte 0F010H, or byte 61,456, in memory. The lowest address is 0000:0000, byte 0 in memory, and the highest address is F000:FFFF, which corresponds to byte 0FFFFFH, or 1048575. Using these 20-bit addresses, we can refer to 1 megabyte, 1,024K:

	Segmented Address		Real Address	
	F000:FFFF	1 Byte	FFFFFH	← The top of memory
				(FFFFFH = 1 MByte - 1)
	F000:FFFE	1 Byte	FFFFEH	
	F000:FFFD	1 Byte	FFFFDH	
	F000:FFFC	1 Byte	FFFFCH	
		:		
One Megabyte	C000:AAAA	1 Byte	CAAAAH	
	C000:AAA9	1 Byte	CAAA9H	
	C000:AAA8	1 Byte	CAAA8H	
	C000:AAA7	1 Byte	CAAA7H	
		:		
	0000:0003	1 Byte	00003H	
	0000:0002	1 Byte	00002H	
	0000:0001	1 Byte	00001H	
	0000:0000	1 Byte	00000H	← The bottom of memory

Segments in Memory

A segment is the memory space that can be addressed with one particular segment address, and a segment can go from xxxx:0000 to xxxx:FFFF, 64K. For example, the segment that starts at the bottom of memory, segment 0000, can extend from 0000:0000 to 0000:FFFF (keeping the segment address, 0000, unchanged). Once we choose a segment address, like 0000, we have a 64K workspace we can use without having to change the segment address again.

On the other hand, even though segments can describe such a large area, they can overlap. The next possible segment after segment 0000 is segment 0001. This segment extends from 0001:0000 to 0001:FFFF. Converting these numbers to 20-bit addresses gives 00010H to 1000FH.

Segment 0001 starts just 16 bytes (called a **paragraph**) after segment 0000. Segment 0002 starts just 16 bytes after segment 0001, and so on. Choosing a segment gives us a 64K work space, but that 64K work space overlaps with many other segments too:

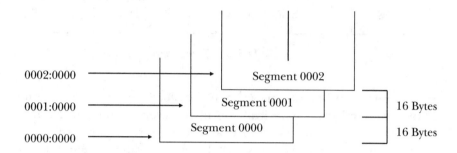

To let us set the segment that we want to choose as our work area, the 80x86 provides four **segment registers**. We usually set these segment registers at the beginning of a program, or let them be set automatically for us. Keep in mind, however, that they only define a 64K area. If we want something outside that area, we'll have to take care of setting them as required.

Table 11-3 shows the four segment registers: **CS**, **DS**, **ES**, and **SS**. They stand for code segment, data segment, extra segment, and stack segment.

The code segment is where the instructions of our program will be stored. When our program is loaded, the code segment is chosen for it by the program loader. We will not have to set this segment register, **CS**, for the things we are going to do in this book:

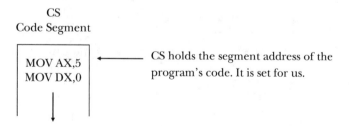

The **DS** register holds the value of the data segment. Anything that we want to store as data, and not let the computer execute (cell entries in a spreadsheet, for example, or text in a word processor), can be stored here.

Segment Register	Means	Used With
CS	Code Segment	The program's instructions.
DS	Data Segment	The data we want to work on.
ES	Extra Segment	Auxiliary data segment register.
SS	Stack Segment	Set by DOS; holds the stack.

Table 11-3. The Four Segment Registers.

You usually set **DS**, the data segment register (if ever) at the beginning of the program and then leave it alone. If, however, we want to read bytes from faraway places in memory, to examine the screen buffer, or the keyboard buffer, for example, we can set DS before we address them. Using DS as the high word of our addresses, we can reach and read — or write — any byte in memory. Let's say that our program code is in the segment 2000H, and that our data is in the segment at 3000H:

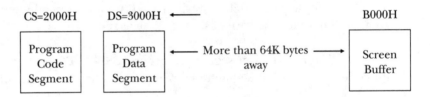

Now let's say that we wanted to change data in a CGA's video buffer (i.e., the characters that appear on the screen), which starts at segment B800H. We'd have to change the data segment that we're using, in DS, to B800H:

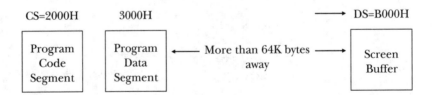

And then we could reference any data there with our instructions. Whenever we read data from memory, the 80×86 checks the value of **DS** for the segment part of the address. Instructions that reference memory locations (like the **MOV** we used earlier) automatically mean that **DS** will be used as the segment address.

The extra segment can be used as another data segment, and we won't make much use of it here. There's also a stack segment: DOS stores data and return addresses on the stack, and C passes parameters to us using the stack.

Segment Registers in Use: .COM Files

The first full programs that we write in assembly language will be .COM files. The default for .COM files is to set all four segment registers to the same value, the code segment. (We will do this so that we don't have to worry about the segment registers just at the time when we are being introduced to our first programs.)

Everything that goes on in a .COM file will be limited to one 64K workspace. In fact, when the program is loaded, DOS sets that segment address for us. In practice, that means that we will not have to be careful about how the segment registers are set; here, **CS = DS = ES = SS**, and DOS will set them for us.

A .COM file is the simplest working program we can write on the PC (although the .COM format is no longer supported under OS/2). This file is, quite literally, just machine language instructions, ready to be executed. Setting these files up is going to give us the expertise we need to link assembly language into C.

Assembler Directives

When we write an assembly language source file (which ends with the letters **.ASM**), we have to specify where we want the code to be placed in the code segment, whether we will have a separate data segment, and other things. Here, we set up our segments with **assembler directives**, much like compiler directives in C. These directives do not generate any code. They only give directions to the assembler.

We can set up either code or data segments when we are writing a program, and we will use assembler directives to do it. If we are setting up a code segment, the program instructions themselves will go there. If we are setting up a data segment, we'll declare some variables or constants for our program to use. The assembler will make sure that this information is loaded into the correct segments in memory if we use the correct segment directives.

The .CODE Directive

Everything we put into our .ASM files will be enclosed inside a segment definition. We can add the code segment definition to the source code for the program **PRINTZ** we wrote earlier:

```
.CODE     ←

        MOV     AH,2
        MOV     DL,5AH
        INT     21H
        INT     20H
          :
```

From this point on, everything we write will be put into the code segment until the file ends, or until the assembler finds another segment directive such as **.DATA** (which starts a data segment and which we'll explore later in this chapter). However, since there is only one segment in .COM files, everything goes into the code segment.

Labels

We can label our data byte by byte, or word by word; labels are also directives. And, as in C, we can label an instruction in our program itself so that we can jump from the current instruction to the labeled one, which may be some distance away. For example, the machine language instruction for **MOV AH, 2** is three bytes long. We can give a label to that instruction — let's call it **Start** — and we can also give a label to the last instruction (INT 20H), which we can call **Exit**:

```
.CODE

Start:  MOV     AH,2      ←
        MOV     DL,5AH
        INT     21H
Exit:   INT     20H       ←
```

To label an instruction, we just use a name followed by a colon, as in C. If, during our program, we wanted to leave quickly, we could just go to the label **Exit**, and the INT 20H instruction would be executed, causing us to finish and quit. If we did decide to go there, the assembler would have to know the address of the **Exit** instruction, and it finds this by counting the number of machine language bytes it has produced from the beginning of the code segment (the position we have labeled **Start**).

TIP We can make labels as long as we want. However, only the first 31 characters count. That's all the assembler reads.

Positioning Code in the Code Segment

When .EXE files are loaded, they are placed at the beginning of the code segment (i.e., at CS:0000), and their first instruction can start right there. On the other hand, .COM files are supplied with a header that is loaded in before they are, and the header is put at CS:0000, not the first instruction of the .COM file. This header is 100H — 256 decimal — bytes long, which means that the header runs from CS:0000 to CS:00FF, and the .COM file, now loaded into memory, starts exactly at CS:0100:

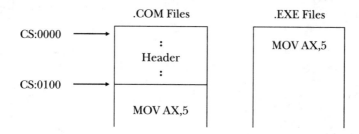

This means that we are going to have to start the code in **PRINTZ.ASM** at offset 0100H in the code segment. That's why we started assembling at 0100H in our **DEBUG** example (using A100). In a .COM file, machine language instructions must start at offset 0100H inside the program. We can set our location in the code segment with the directive ORG (for origin):

```
.CODE
          ORG      100H    ←
  Start:  MOV      AH,2
          MOV      DL,5AH
          INT      21H
  Exit:   INT      20H

          END      Start
```

This tells the assembler to make the offset of **Start** (the line immediately after the ORG directive) 0100H. The assembler now treats the instruction **MOV**

AH, 2 as though it will be placed at CS:0100, and not at CS:0000 (and everything to follow gets treated as though it were placed after this instruction). In this way, we have made the correct allowance for the .COM file header that is automatically created for the .COM file.

The END Directive

The last thing we must do is set an **entry point** for the program. In C, the entry point is set when we define **main( )**; control is always passed there first. In assembly language, we can set the entry point anywhere in our program with the **END** directive. Every **.ASM** file needs to end with **END** so the assembler knows when to stop. At the same time, we can set the entry point by placing its label after **END**.

In our case, we want the entry point to be at 0100H in the code segment. We have labeled that instruction as **Start** already, so we can simply use the directive END Start:

```
.CODE

        ORG     100H
Start:  MOV     AH,2
        MOV     DL,5AH
        INT     21H
Exit:   INT     20H

        END     Start    ←
```

Finally, we have to declare the memory model with the **.MODEL** directive, and we do that like this:

```
.MODEL SMALL            ←
.CODE

        ORG     100H
Start:  MOV     AH,2
        MOV     DL,5AH
        INT     21H
Exit:   INT     20H

        END     Start    ←
```

And that's it. Our program **PRINTZ.ASM** is finished.

Assembling PRINTZ.ASM

If you have a word processor or editor, use it to type our program into a file named **PRINTZ.ASM**; now we're ready to use an assembler. If you have the Microsoft assembler (we will be using Microsoft MASM version 5.1), type this command:

```
R:\>MASM PRINTZ;   ←
```

And the macro assembler will do this:

```
R:\>MASM PRINTZ;
Microsoft (R) Macro Assembler Version 5.10
Copyright (C) Microsoft Corp 1981, 1988.  All rights reserved.

  50144 + 31277 Bytes symbol space free

      0 Warning Errors
      0 Severe  Errors
```

We've assembled the program, but, so far, all we have is an .OBJ file. The next step is to strip off some information left by the assembler in that object file, and we'll use the linker to do it. Among other things, the linker checks every segment. In our case, it's going to give us a warning that we have no stack segment. Stack segments are necessary for all executable files, *except* .COM files, which use DOS's own stack. However, the linker doesn't know that we are creating a .COM file, and it issues this warning:

```
R:\>LINK PRINTZ;
Microsoft (R) Overlay Linker Version 3.64
Copyright (C) Microsoft Corp 1983-1988.  All rights reserved.

LINK : warning L4021: no stack segment   ←
```

Now we are almost ready. The linker has taken the .OBJ file, **PRINTZ.OBJ**, and produced an .EXE file, **PRINTZ.EXE**. We did not set this up as a .EXE file, however. It's a .COM file. For the final step, we must strip off the header that the linker left in the .EXE file. To do that, we run a DOS program called **EXE2BIN** (which comes with DOS) on the output from **LINK**. This is the last step in the process, and it converts the .EXE file into .COM format:

```
R:\>EXE2BIN PRINTZ PRINTZ.COM
```

Finally, our .COM file is there, ready to go. Give **PRINTZ.COM** a try. It does indeed print out 'Z', just as our **DEBUG** version did. Now we've made another advancement. We've got a working .ASM file. If you're using the Turbo assembler, **TASM**, type this:

```
R:\>TASM PRINTZ;  ←

Assembling file:    PRINTZ.ASM
Error messages:     None
Warning messages:   None
Remaining memory:   272k
```

Then link it with TLINK:

```
R:\>TLINK PRINTZ;  ←
Turbo Link Version 2.0  Copyright (c) 1987, 1988 Borland
International
Warning: no stack
```

Finally, run it through exe2bin, and that's it:

```
R:\>EXE2BIN PRINTZ PRINTZ.COM
```

When you run **PRINTZ**, you'll get the same result as under the Microsoft assembler. And that's it. We've created our own assembly language program.

Adding Data

On the other hand, this is really only half the story. As it stands, **PRINTZ.ASM** is a working program, but it is very primitive. Some data will be stored in almost all .COM files. Every variable used in a program is data. We might want to read a file from the disk and store it in the data area, treating it as data. Or we might have program messages like "Hello, world." in the data area.

Let's look at an example. It turns out that we can use variables in assembly language — just as in C — and we'll use the **DB**, **define byte**, and **DW**, **define word** directives to set them up.

The DB and DW Data Directives

We use the **DB** directive to name bytes in memory (i.e., the char type in C) so that we can store data in them. To define a byte named, say, **VALUE**, use **DB** like this:

```
VALUE DB 5
```

If we wanted to put this data into a data segment, the code might look like this:

```
        .CODE
        MOV     AL,VALUE
                :

        .DATA
→       VALUE   DB 5
                :
```

We ended the code segment and began the data segment by using the **.DATA** directive. We can't use **.DATA** in .COM files, but we can when designing .EXE files. Everything that follows **.DATA** will go into the data segment. In memory, the code and data segments might then look something like this:

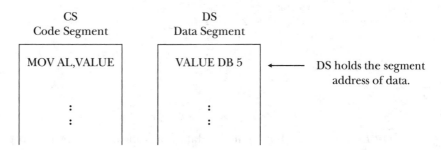

Now we are free to read the data in **VALUE** in the program:

```
MOV AL, VALUE
```

This is the way to use memory in the PC. Set aside locations for variables with **DB** and give names to them. Then, we can use these names just like variables in C. We can also store data a word at a time (like the C int) with the **DW**, or **define word** directive like this:

```
        .CODE
        MOV      AX,WORD_VALUE
                 :


        .DATA
  →     WORD_VALUE   DW 0x1234
                 :
```

In this case, we could work with **WORD_VALUE** like this:

```
   MOV      AX, WORD_VALUE
```

Let's see how all this works by adding data to **PRINTZ.ASM**. In this case, we'll have to put it into the code segment, because there is only one segment available. The only data we have is the character we're going to print out, 'Z', so let's store that in memory:

```
.MODEL SMALL
.CODE

        ORG      100H
        Our_Character   DB 'Z'   ←
Start:  MOV      AH,2
        MOV      DL,5AH
        INT      21H
Exit:   INT      20H

        END      Start
```

DB tells the assembler that the data that follows is to be put in the program without interpretation; it is data. We have set aside a location, one byte, that we've called **Our_Character**, and then we initialized it by putting the character 'Z' in it. The assembler will translate the 'Z' for us into the ASCII code that the machine needs: 5AH (we could also have said `Our_Character DB 5AH` — it is the same thing to the assembler). Here are some **DB** examples:

```
Flag7   DB 0
Char_Z  DB 'Z'
Numbers DB 1,2,3,4,5,0 ← 6 bytes are put aside.
Prompt  DB "How long has it been since you called "
        DB "your mother?"
```

When we refer to the names **Flag7**, **Char_Z**, **Numbers**, or **Prompt**, we are actually referring to the first byte that follows **DB**. For example, if we were to say:

```
MOV      AH, Numbers
```

The 1 (i.e., the first number after **DB**), would be loaded into **AH**. In **PRINTZ.ASM**, here is how we load our character into **DL**, just before printing it out:

```
.MODEL SMALL
.CODE

        ORG      100H
        Our_Character   DB 'Z'
Start:  MOV      AH, 2
        MOV      DL, Our_Character   ←
        INT      21H
Exit:   INT      20H

        END      Start
```

Now we've been able to label and use a memory location; however, we've left ourselves with a problem. The label **Start** is supposed to be at 100H in the code segment, and now that we've added one byte of memory space just before it, it will be at the wrong location (specifically, 101H). To solve this problem, we do what most .COM files with data do. We set aside a data area at the beginning of the program, and add a **jump** instruction, so that when things start at 100H, the first thing the microprocessor will do is jump *over* the data area and to the first instruction. It looks like this:

```
.MODEL SMALL
.CODE

        ORG      100H
Start:  JMP      PrintZ   ←
        Our_Character   DB 'Z'
PrintZ: MOV      AH,2
        MOV      DL,Our_Character
        INT      21H
Exit:   INT      20H

        END      Start
```

We've moved the label **Start** to a new instruction that is at 100H, but that instruction says, **JMP PrintZ**. This instruction lets us jump over the data area to the label **PrintZ** and then continue; **JMP** is an assembly language instruction that is exactly like **goto** in C. To use **JMP**, just provide it with a label to jump to, as we've done here (JMP PrintZ).

And that's it; **PRINTZ.ASM** — updated to hold data — is done. It's ready to be assembled and run. If we want to fit in more data, we can insert it right after **Our_Character**. That's it for setting up .COM files; in general, this is how a .COM file shell looks:

```
.MODEL SMALL
.CODE

        ORG     100H
Start:  JMP     PROG
        _____
        This is the data area. Use DB here
        _____
PROG:
        _____
        And this is where the program goes.

Exit:   INT     20H

        END     Start
```

There is an area set aside for data (using **DB** or **DW**) and a part for the program code. Now let's develop a few more skills that we'll need.

Strings in Memory

We still have not resolved how to store character strings in memory. A character string — like a string in C — is just a number of characters, one after the other, that makes sense to us but not to the computer. We want to keep them together: The computer only sees a number of bytes with no apparent relation.

Strings in assembly language are just stored as bytes, as they are in C. And, as in C, they have a terminator to mark the end of the string. Although strings usually end with 0, which is called ASCIIZ format, this is not always the case. Strings are stored like **PROMPT** above, and if we want the string to end with a 0 byte, it is our responsibility to put it in:

```
Prompt   DB "How long has it been since you called "
         DB "your mother?", 0
```

The assembler lets us store strings this way, using the quotation marks as shorthand (otherwise, we'd have to use **DB** for each letter).

INT 21H, Service 9 — Print a String

The string printing service, service 9, of interrupt 21H prints out strings; it's the **printf( )** of assembly language. To terminate the string here, we add a '$' (not a 0 byte) as the last character. This indicates to service 9 that it should stop printing, and it is one of the times strings that are not terminated with a 0 byte. Here's how it might look if we wanted to start changing our program to **PRINTXYZ**:

```
.MODEL SMALL
.CODE

        ORG     100H
Start:  JMP     PrintZ
        Our_Characters  DB "XYZ$"  ←
PrintZ: MOV     AH,2
        MOV     DL,Our_Characters
        INT     21H
Exit:   INT     20H

        END     Start
```

Notice the '$' terminating character, the last byte in the string. We still have to tell service 9 where to find this string in memory, and to change the call from service 2 to service 9. Service 9 reads the address of the string from **DS:DX**. If the address was 0EF1:0105, for example, we'd have to load 0EF1H into **DS** and 0105H into **DX**. Since we are dealing with a .COM file, the value of **DS** never changes, so it is already set. To get the offset address of **Our_Characters** into **DX**, we use the **OFFSET** directive like this:

```
.MODEL SMALL
.CODE
        ORG     100H
Start:  JMP     PrintZ
        Our_Characters  DB "XYZ$"
PrintZ: MOV     AH,9
        MOV     DX, OFFSET Our_Characters       ←
```

```
            INT    21H
  Exit:     INT    20H

            END    Start
```

The **OFFSET** directive gives us a label's offset value from the beginning of the data segment (which is the same as the code segment here). We can think of it as returning a pointer to that object, much like the address operator, &. For example, our line

```
  MOV    DX, OFFSET Our_Characters
```

will load the offset of the first byte of **Our_Characters** into **DX**. **OFFSET** is a handy directive that we'll use often (especially in the next chapter), since many interrupt services need the address of our data, not the data itself. That's all there is to it; now we have a working .ASM file that prints out "XYZ" instead of just 'Z'.

Using Comments

Before we leave **PRINTXYZ**, let's discuss commenting our code. Comments can be added in assembly language by preceding them with a semicolon (;) as is similar to the // one-line comments in C++:

```
.MODEL SMALL
.CODE

          ORG    100H               ;Set up for a .COM file.
  Start:  JMP    PrintZ             ;JMP over data area.
          Our_Characters DB "XYZ$"  ;We will print out this string.
  PrintZ: MOV    AH,9               ;Request INT 21H service 9.
          MOV    DX, OFFSET Our_Characters   ;Point to our string.
          INT    21H                ;And print it out here.
  Exit:   INT    20H                ;End the program.

          END    Start              ;Set entry point to label Start.
```

By reading the comments, we can see what was intended in each line. Comments are often more important in assembly language that in C, and they can be a great help.

Now that we have the fundamentals of program-writing down, let's broaden our library of instructions and start to read some keys from the keyboard. Working with keyboard input will give us some experience in a vital assembly language topic: Conditional jumps (the if...else statements of assembly language).

Accepting Keyboard Input

The most basic of the interrupt 21H services is service 1, which reads keyboard input. This is assembly language's **scanf( )**. When a key is typed, it is echoed on the screen and its ASCII code is returned in the **AL** register. Let's put this service to use.

An Example Program — CAP.COM

The example program that we're about to develop will accept a letter that we type, capitalize it, and print it on the screen. For the first time, we will get our assembly language program to accept input from us. Let's start with the .COM file shell:

```
.MODEL SMALL
.CODE

        ORG 100H
Start:  JMP CAP
        ;Data Area
CAP:
        ;Program will go here.

Exit:   INT     20H

        END Start
```

And add the instructions that will let us accept input:

```
.MODEL SMALL
.CODE

        ORG 100H
Start:  JMP CAP
        ;Data Area
CAP:    MOV     AH,1    ;Request keyboard input  ←
        INT     21H     ;From INT 21H            ←

Exit:   INT     20H

        END Start
```

Uppercase	Code		Lowercase	Code
A	65	←subtract 32 —	a	97
B	66	←subtract 32 —	b	98
C	67	←subtract 32 —	c	99
:	:		:	:
:	:		:	:
Z	90	←subtract 32 —	z	122

Table 11-4. Capitalizing

After the INT 21H instruction is executed, the ASCII code of the typed character is in **AL**. The program's job is to capitalize the letter and print it out. The ASCII codes for 'A' to 'Z' run from 65 to 90; for 'a' to 'z' from 97 to 122. To capitalize a letter we just have to subtract a number from its ASCII code to move the code from its place in the a...z part of the table to its corresponding place in the A...Z part:

The number we have to subtract, then, is just equal to ASCII('a') - ASCII('A'), which is 97 - 65 = 32, the distance between the two parts of the table. With that in mind, here's how we capitalize the ASCII value in **AL**, introducing a new instruction, **SUB**, for subtract:

```
        .MODEL SMALL
        .CODE

                ORG 100H
        Start:  JMP CAP
                ;Data Area
        CAP:    MOV     AH,1      ;Request keyboard input
        INT     21H               ;From INT 21H
→               SUB     AL,'a'- 'A'      ;Capitalize the typed key
        :
        :
        Exit:   INT     20H

                END Start
```

The SUB and ADD Instructions

The **SUB** instruction is used this way:

```
SUB     AL, 5
```

Here, 5 is subtracted from the contents of **AL**; **AL** is changed. In the same way, we could do this:

```
SUB     AX, DX
```

This subtracts the contents of **DX** from **AX**; **AX** is changed, and **DX** is not. Besides the **SUB** instruction, there is also **ADD**, the built-in add instruction. **ADD** works like this:

```
ADD     AL, 5
ADD     AX, DX
```

We will use **ADD** and **SUB** frequently. In addition, the assembler lets us use expressions like 'a' - 'A'. For instance, we can use a line like this:

```
SUB     AL, 'a'-'A'
```

As in C, this makes what we are doing much clearer than if we simply said:

```
SUB     AL, 32
```

Similarly, expressions like 'a'+'A' are allowed. Now that we've read a character and capitalized it by subtracting 'a'-'A', we have to print it out. Interrupt 21H service 2, which prints a character on the screen, expects the ASCII code of the character in **DL**. In **CAP.ASM** so far, the ASCII code is still in the **AL** register (because service 1 returned it there); we can move that code from **AL** to **DL** and then print the character out:

```
.MODEL SMALL
.CODE

        ORG 100H
Start:  JMP Cap
        ;Data Area
Cap:    MOV     AH,1      ;Request keyboard input
        INT     21H       ;From INT 21H
        SUB     AL, 'a'-'A'     ;Capitalize the typed key
        MOV     DL, AL    ;Set up for service 2.     ←
        MOV     AH, 2     ;Request character output  ←
        INT     21H       ;Type out character.       ←
Exit:   INT     20H

        END Start
```

And that's it; **CAP.ASM** is complete. We read a key with INT 21H service 1, capitalize it ourselves, and then print it out with INT 21H service 2. Give **CAP.COM** a try. When we run it, we see this:

```
D:\>CAP
```

The program waits for a key to be typed. As soon as we type a letter, say 's', it echoes it and prints out a capital 'S'. Then it simply exits:

```
D:\>CAP
sS        ←
D:\>
```

Although it is gratifying to get the result we expected, there are a number of problems with this program. Perhaps the most serious one is what happens if we type in some character other than a lowercase letter? Odd characters will be printed, since we are only ready to handle small letters.

This problem may be fixed if we check the incoming ASCII code to make sure that it actually represents a lowercase letter; in other words, we have to check that the ASCII code is between the values for 'a' and 'z'. This type of checking brings us to the topic of conditional jumps, which are extremely important in assembly language, since they are almost the only branching instructions available.

Conditional Jumps

We want to augment **CAP.ASM** to check that the incoming ASCII code is between 'a' and 'z'. If it is not, we exit. To make this check, we divide the process into two steps. First, we check whether the character is greater than or equal to 'a', and, next, we check whether it's less than or equal to 'z'. If both tests pass, we capitalize the letter, print it, and exit.

The CMP Instruction

Checking a value against some other value can be done with the assembly language instruction compare, **CMP**. To branch on the results of the comparison, we then use a **conditional jump** immediately after the **CMP** instruction. Unlike C, comparisons are a two-step process in assembly language. For example, here is the code to check whether the value in **AL** (i.e., the ASCII code read from the keyboard) is above or equal to 'a'. **JB** means **jump if below**:

```
        .MODEL SMALL
        .CODE

                ORG 100H
        Start:  JMP  Cap
                ;Data Area
        Cap:    MOV  AH,1       ;Request keyboard input
                INT  21H        ;From INT 21H
→               CMP  AL,'a'     ;Compare the incoming ASCII code to 'a'.
→               JB   Exit       ;If the letter is not lower case, exit.
                :
                :
                SUB  AL,'a'-'A'     ;Capitalize the typed key
                MOV  DL,AL      ;Set up for service 2.
                MOV  AH,2       ;Request character output
                INT  21H        ;Type out character.
        Exit:   INT  20H

        END Start
```

Here, we've compared **AL** to the ASCII value for 'a' and then immediately followed with a **JB**, Jump if Below, instruction:

```
CMP    AL,'a'  ;Compare the incoming ASCII code to 'a'.
JB     Exit    ;If the letter is not lower case, exit.
```

If the comparison indicates that the value in **AL** was below 'a' in value, we will jump to the label **Exit** at the end of the program and leave without capitalizing it. What actually happens is this: First, the microprocessor's flags are set by the **CMP** instruction, and then the **JB** instruction checks these internal flags and acts accordingly:

```
CMP    AL,'a'    ← Sets Flags
JB     Exit      ← Reads Flags
```

The next step is to check whether the ASCII code is below or equal to 'z'. This can be done with an instruction named, as you could probably guess, **JA**, Jump if Above:

```
        .MODEL SMALL
        .CODE
```

```
            ORG 100H
    Start:  JMP Cap
            ;Data Area
    Cap:    MOV    AH,1    ;Request keyboard input
            INT    21H     ;From INT 21H
            CMP    AL,'a'  ;Compare the incoming ASCII code to 'a'.
            JB     Exit    ;If the letter is not lower case, exit.
→           CMP    AL,'z'  ;Compare the incoming ASCII code to 'z'.
→           JA     Exit    ;If the letter is not lower case, exit.
            SUB    AL,'a'-'A'        ;Capitalize the typed key
            MOV    DL,AL   ;Set up for service 2.
            MOV    AH,2    ;Request character output
            INT    21H     ;Type out character.
    Exit:   INT    20H

            END Start
```

That completes the program **CAP.ASM**, our first, real assembly language program. It both accepts input and generates output, and it even checks for errors.

More Conditional Jumps

At this point, we've seen the two instructions **JA** and **JB**. These follow a **CMP** — compare — instruction, and, depending on the result, a jump may be made. There are actually many conditional jumps. In fact, there are even variations of **JA** and **JB**. In addition to these two, there are JAE (Jump if Above or Equal), **JBE** (Jump if Below or Equal), **JNA** (Jump if Not Above), **JNB** (Jump if Not Below), **JNAE** (Jump if Not Above or Equal), and **JNBE** (Jump if Not Below or Equal). All of these can be used after a **CMP** instruction. Table 11-5 shows a number of conditional jumps and their meanings.

We can see that there is a rich selection of jump instructions. Without such a selection of conditional jumps, assembly language would be very difficult to use. As it is, there are conditional jumps that meet most needs. Now let's put our assembly language expertise to work with the final example of the chapter, a program that converts hex numbers to decimal numbers.

DEHEXER.ASM

The next step will be to write program that's slightly more substantial, and will let us convert four digit hex numbers to decimal numbers. We can call this program **DEHEXER.COM**, and we'll start with the .COM file shell:

Conditional Jump	Means
JA	Jump if Above
JB	Jump if Below
JAE	Jump if Above
JBE	Jump if Below
JNA	Jump if Not Above
JNB	Jump if Not Below
JNAE	Jump if Not Above
JNBE	Jump if Not Below
JE	Jump if Equal
JNE	Jump if Not Equal
JZ	Jump if result was Zero
JNZ	Jump if result was Not Zero
JCXZ	Jump if CX = 0 (Used at end of loops)

Table 11-5. Conditional Jumps.

```
.MODEL SMALL
.CODE

        ORG 100H
ENTRY:  JMP DEHEXER

        ;Data will go here.

DEHEXER:

        ;Program will go here.

        INT     20H
        END     ENTRY
```

First, we'll have to read the hex number from the keyboard. DOS provides special input services to read strings, and we can use them by setting up a buffer in memory with the **DB** directive like this:

```
BUFFER DB #, 0, 0, 0, 0, 0, 0, 0, 0, 0, 0, 0
```

To fill this buffer, we will use INT 21H, service 0AH — get string, the **gets( )** of assembly language. We set the number (# above) in the beginning of the buffer to the length of the buffer. (Service 0AH needs that number so it won't return too many bytes). This service always sets the last byte of the buffer to ASCII 13 (a carriage return) as an end-of-string marker, so we set # to one more than the number of characters we expect as input.

Service 0AH fills the second byte in the buffer with the number of bytes actually typed. If we're careful, we can set up our buffer with some foresight by expressly labeling the important bytes in it:

```
        .MODEL SMALL
        .CODE

                ORG 100H
ENTRY: JMP DEHEXER
→               BUFFER          DB 5
→               NUM_TYPED       DB 0
→               ASCII_NUM       DB 3 DUP (0)
→               END_NUM         DB 0
→               CRLF            DB 0
     DEHEXER:MOV     AH,9
             MOV     DX,OFFSET PROMPT
             INT     21H
             MOV     AH,0AH
             MOV     DX,OFFSET BUFFER
             INT     21H

             INT     20H
```

You might notice the use of the directive *DUP.*

```
        BUFFER          DB 5
        NUM_TYPED       DB 0
→       ASCII_NUM       DB 3 DUP (0)
        END_NUM         DB 0
        CRLF            DB 0
```

This directive stands for **duplicate**, and it saves us time. This expression: ASCII_NUM DB 3 DUP(0) is equal to ASCII_NUM DB 0, 0, 0, not such a big saving for 3 bytes, but it would be if we needed to reserve space for 32,000. Now we've set up and labeled our buffer like this:

```
BUFFER DB  5, 0, 0, 0, 0, 0, 0
```

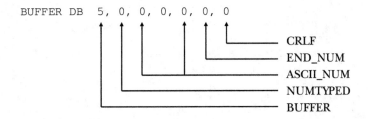

We can also add a prompt to the code — "Type in a 4 digit hex number:$" —
which we can print out with service 9, the string printing service. To print out
our prompt, we have to pass service 9 an offset address in **DX**:

```
        .MODEL SMALL
        .CODE

                ORG 100H
        ENTRY:  JMP DEHEXER
→           PROMPT              DB "Type in a 4 digit hex number:$"
            BUFFER          DB 5
            NUM_TYPED       DB 0
            ASCII_NUM       DB 3 DUP (0)
            END_NUM         DB 0
            CRLF            DB 0
        DEHEXER:MOV     AH,9
→           MOV     DX,OFFSET PROMPT
→           INT     21H
            :
```

This is what the prompt will look like on the screen:

```
Type in a 4 digit hex number:
```

Next, we can use service 0AH to read the four-digit hex number from the
keyboard. This is the number that we'll convert to decimal and print out. We
just have to pass the offset of the beginning of the buffer to service 0AH in **DX**,
and that looks like this:

```
        .MODEL SMALL
        .CODE

                ORG 100H
        ENTRY:  JMP DEHEXER
```

```
                    PROMPT            DB "Type in a 4 digit hex number:$"
                    BUFFER            DB 5
                    NUM_TYPED         DB 0
                    ASCII_NUM         DB 3 DUP(0)
                    END_NUM           DB 0
                    CRLF              DB 0
         DEHEXER:MOV      AH,9
                 MOV      DX,OFFSETPROMPT
                 INT      21H
                 MOV      AH,0AH
   →             MOV      DX,OFFSET BUFFER
   →             INT      21H
                  :
                  :
                 INT      20H
```

Next we issue an INT 21H instruction and accept the hex number.

NOTE If you try to type more than the number of characters we can accept in the buffer, the computer will beep; this is the same beep that DOS uses, and for that matter, the same internal service (0AH) that it uses to accept keyboard input at the DOS prompt.

After the buffer has been filled with input from the keyboard, the ASCII string extends from the locations **ASCII_NUM** to **END_NUM**. The <cr> — ASCII 13 — at the end of the returned string will go into the byte marked **CRLF**, and we can ignore it. The first step is to convert our character string into a number. If the number typed was 1234H, then the buffer now looks like this:

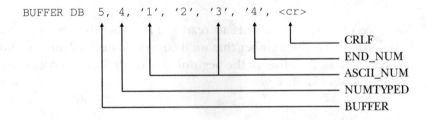

We can just point to the last number, 4, convert it from ASCII to binary, then point to the previous number, 3, convert it to binary, multiply by 16, add it to the 4 we already have, and keep going to higher places. In this way, we will loop over all characters.

We have labeled the last ASCII digit as **END_NUM**, so we can read the ASCII character at that location with the instruction MOV AL, END_NUM. But how do we point to the previous digits?

It turns out that we can use a register as a pointer. In assembly language, the **BX** register was designed explicitly to be used as a pointer; let's examine how that's done. We'll need a loop to read all four digits, so we start off by loading BX with the offset address of **END_NUM**:

```
        .MODEL SMALL
        .CODE

            ORG 100H
ENTRY:  JMP DEHEXER
            PROMPT              DB "Type in a 4 digit hex number:$"
            BUFFER          DB 5
            NUM_TYPED       DB 0
            ASCII_NUM       DB 3 DUP(0)
            END_NUM         DB 0
            CRLF        DB 0
DEHEXER:MOV     AH,9
            MOV     DX,OFFSET PROMPT
            INT     21H
            MOV     AH,0AH
            MOV     DX,OFFSET BUFFER
            INT     21H

            MOV     CX, 0
            MOV     AX,0
            MOV     BX, OFFSET END_NUM
        LOOP1:
                :
                :
            JB      LOOP1

            INT     20H
            END     ENTRY
```

Now we'll load the ASCII character into the **DL** register. We can do that like this:

```
.MODEL SMALL
.CODE

        ORG 100H
ENTRY:  JMP DEHEXER
```

```
                PROMPT          DB "Type in a 4 digit hexnumber:$"
                BUFFER          DB 5
                NUM_TYPED       DB 0
                ASCII_NUM       DB 3 DUP (0)
                END_NUM         DB 0
                CRLF            DB 0
      DEHEXER:MOV     AH,9
              MOV     DX,OFFSET PROMPT
              INT     21H
              MOV     AH,0AH
              MOV     DX,OFFSET BUFFER
              INT     21H

              MOV     BX, OFFSET END_NUM
      LOOP1:  MOV     DL, [BX]                    ←
              DEC     BX                          ←
                :
                :

              JB      LOOP1

              INT     20H
              END     ENTRY
```

Putting **BX** inside square brackets — [BX] — means that the microprocessor will use the value in **BX** as a pointer; that is, as an address. This is called **indirect addressing** in assembly language, and it's going to be important in Chapter 12. [BX] stands for the byte at location **END_NUM** now, because **BX** holds that byte's offset address:

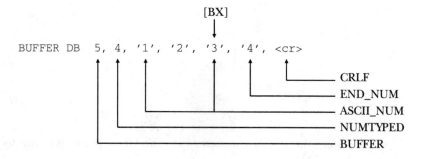

We can move that byte into **DL** like this: MOV DL, [BX] (i.e., [ ] in assembly language works much like * in C). After moving the byte into **DL**, we decrement the pointer BX by 1 with the **DEC** instruction, which is just like both SUB BX, 1 and the decrement operator in C. (The corresponding instruction for incrementing by 1 is **INC**.) This points us to the previous ASCII character in preparation for the next time through the loop:

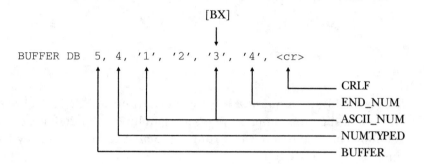

And that is how indirect addressing, [BX], works — **BX** holds a pointer to the byte or word that we want to locate. Now that the last ASCII character ('4') is in **DL**, we have to convert it into binary. If it's in the range '0' to '9', we have to subtract the ASCII value for '0' from it (i.e., '0' will become 0, '1' will become 1, and so on). If it's in the range 'A' to 'F', we have to subtract 'A' and add 10 to it. We do that this way:

```
.MODEL SMALL
.CODE

        ORG 100H
ENTRY:  JMP DEHEXER
        PROMPT          DB "Type in a 4 digit hex number:$"
        BUFFER          DB 5
        NUM_TYPED       DB 0
        ASCII_NUM       DB 3 DUP (0)
        END_NUM         DB 0
        CRLF            DB 0
DEHEXER:MOV     AH,9
        MOV     DX,OFFSET PROMPT
        INT     21H
        MOV     AH,0AH
        MOV     DX,OFFSET BUFFER
        INT     21H

        MOV     BX, OFFSET END_NUM
LOOP1:  MOV     DX,0
        MOV     DL, [BX]
        DEC     BX
        CMP     DL,'9'                        ←
```

```
              JBE     UNDER_A                ←
              SUB     DL, 'a' - '0' - 10     ←
     UNDER_A: SUB     DL, '0'                ←
              :
              JB      LOOP1

              INT     20H
              END     ENTRY
```

DL now holds the numerical value of the current hex digit. To interpret the entire four-digit hex number, we have to multiply each digit by the appropriate power of 16 and add it to a running total. And, to multiply by 16, we can shift the value in **DL** left.

There is an assembly language instruction called **SHL**, for shift left, just like the C operator << (and there's also **SHR** for shift right). We can use it to shift all the bits of an operand to the left (**SHR** shifts them to the right) like this:

```
  ←    01010101
       :
  becomes
       :
       10101010
```

Every time we shift an operand left by one binary place, it's the same as multiplying by 2. To use this instruction, we must load the number of places to shift left into **CL**; that is, we could shift the value in **DL** left like this:

```
  SHL      DL, CL
```

For example, if **CL** held 2 and DL held 00000001B, then after the SHL DL, CL instruction was executed, **DL** would hold 00000100B. Shifting left by four binary places is the same as multiplying by 16, and each time through our loop, we'll add 4 to **CL** so that we SHL DL, CL will produce the next hex digit. Note that when we shift **DL** left by more than two hex places, however, the result will be bigger than a byte can hold. Instead, we will use the whole **DX** register, not just **DL**:

```
  SHL      DX, CL
```

After it is shifted, we have to add this current next digit to the running total. Let's keep the running total in, say, **AX**, and add **DX** to it each time we loop through. In code, it looks like this:

```
            .MODEL SMALL
            .CODE

            ORG 100H
   ENTRY:   JMP DEHEXER
            PROMPT              DB "Type in a 4 digit hex number:$"
            BUFFER              DB 5
            NUM_TYPED           DB 0
            ASCII_NUM           DB 3 DUP (0)
            END_NUM             DB 0
            CRLF                DB 0
   DEHEXER:MOV     AH,9
            MOV     DX,OFFSET PROMPT
            INT     21H
            MOV     AH,0AH
            MOV     DX,OFFSET BUFFER
            INT      21H

→          MOV     CX, 0
→          MOV     AX,0
            MOV     BX, OFFSET END_NUM
   LOOP1:   MOV     DX,0      ←
            MOV     DL, [BX]
            DEC     BX
            CMP     DL,'9'
            JBE     UNDER_A
            SUB     DL, 'a' - '0' - 10
   UNDER_A:SUB      DL, '0'
→          SHL     DX, CL
→          ADD     AX, DX
→          ADD     CL,4
→          CMP     CL,16
            JB      LOOP1

            INT     20H
            END     ENTRY
```

Every time through the loop, we load the ASCII value into **DL**, make it into a binary number, shift it to the left, and add it to the running total in **AX**. We only loop four times, one for each digit.

At this point, the ASCII string has been converted to a numerical value in **AX**. However, we now have to convert it to decimal ASCII digits. To do that, we can peel successive decimal digits off by dividing the number in **AX** by 10. Each time we divide by 10, the **remainder** is the current decimal digit. For example, if we divided the number 21 by 10, the result would be 2 with a remainder of 1. Let's see how to divide by 10 next.

The DIV and MUL Instructions

There is a divide instruction in assembly language, named **DIV**. If we load the number to divide into **AX** and divide by a byte-long register like this:

```
DIV BL
```

then the value in **AX** is divided by the value in **BL**; that is, **AX** is assumed to hold the number to divide when we divide by a byte. Note that this is not floating point arithmetic; the quotient is returned in **AL**, and the remainder in **AH**. For example, 5 / 3 = 1 with a remainder of 2. On the other hand, if we execute this instruction (i.e., using a 16-bit register):

```
DIV BX
```

then the microprocessor assumes that we are dividing the double-word number in **DX:AX** by the specified register, **BX**.

NOTE   The terminology **DX:AX** is an unfortunate way of specifying double words, since addresses are also specified with a colon; however, when segment registers are used, we can be sure it's an address.

Similarly, MUL BL will multiply **AL** by **BL** and leave the result in **AX**. MUL BX will multiply **BX** by **AX** and leave the result in **DX:AX**. If we use the DIV BX instruction, the number in **DX:AX** will be divided by **BX**, so let's load **DX** with 0 and **BX** with 10. **AX** already holds the number to convert. After the division is through, **AX** will hold the quotient (ready to be divided by 10 again in the next pass to peel the next decimal digit off) and **DX** holds the remainder:

```
.MODEL SMALL
.CODE

        ORG 100H
ENTRY:  JMP DEHEXER
        PROMPT          DB "Type in a 4 digit hex number:$"
        BUFFER          DB 5
        NUM_TYPED       DB 0
```

```
            ASCII_NUM       DB 3 DUP (0)
            END_NUM         DB 0
            CRLF            DB 0
DEHEXER:MOV     AH,9
        MOV     DX,OFFSET PROMPT
        INT     21H
        MOV     AH,0AH
        MOV     DX,OFFSET BUFFER
        INT     21H

        MOV     CX, 0
        MOV     AX,0
        MOV     BX, OFFSET END_NUM
LOOP1:  MOV     DX,0
        MOV     DL, [BX]
        DEC     BX
        CMP     DL,'9'
        JBE     UNDER_A
        SUB     DL, 'a' - '0' - 10
UNDER_A:SUB     DL, '0'
        SHL     DX, CL
        ADD     AX, DX
        ADD     CL,4
        CMP     CL,16
        JB      LOOP1

        MOV     CX,0      ←
        MOV     BX, 10    ←
LOOP2:  MOV     DX,0      ←
        DIV     BX        ← After this, DX holds current decimal digit.
          :
        INT     20H
        END     ENTRY
```

The remainder in **DX** is what we want: It's the current decimal digit. Note that we are peeling the digits off in backwards order. For example, if we had the number 4,321 (decimal) in **AX**, the first time we divided by 10 we would get a remainder of 1, the next time a remainder of 2, and so on.

To store these decimal digits, we push them on the stack, using the instruction **PUSH DX**. After we push a value, we can also pop it. **POP CX** would pop the value from the stack into **CX**, and the stack would be empty. As we've seen, pushing and then popping values reverses their order, which is just what we want here.

In our program, we'll strip each decimal digit off the value now in **AX** and **PUSH** it onto the stack. A decimal value of 8,573 would be pushed onto the stack as 3, 7, 5, and 8 (we'll also keep track of how many numbers we've pushed so we can **POP** them later; a four-digit hex number can give from 1 to 5 decimal digits). Here, then, is the way we load each decimal digit onto the stack:

```
        .MODEL SMALL
        .CODE

                ORG 100H
        ENTRY:  JMP DEHEXER
                PROMPT          DB "Type in a 4 digit hex number:$"
                BUFFER          DB 5
                NUM_TYPED       DB 0
                ASCII_NUM       DB 3 DUP (0)
                END_NUM         DB 0
                CRLF            DB 0
        DEHEXER:MOV     AH,9
                MOV     DX,OFFSET PROMPT
                INT     21H
                MOV     AH,0AH
                MOV     DX,OFFSET BUFFER
                INT     21H

                MOV     CX, 0
                MOV     AX,0
                MOV     BX, OFFSET END_NUM
        LOOP1:  MOV     DX,0
                MOV     DL, [BX]
                DEC     BX
                CMP     DL,'9'
                JBE     UNDER_A
                SUB     DL, 'a' - '0' - 10
        UNDER_A:SUB     DL, '0'
                SHL     DX, CL
                ADD     AX, DX
                ADD     CL,4
                CMP     CL,16
                JB      LOOP1

                MOV     CX,0
                MOV     BX, 10
        LOOP2:  MOV     DX,0
                DIV     BX
                PUSH    DX              ←
                INC     CX              ← ;CX holds the number of digits pushed
```

```
        CMP     AX,0            ← ;Anything left to strip digits off of?
        JA      LOOP2           ← ;If yes, loop again
        :
        INT     20H
        END     ENTRY
```

At this point, we're almost done. The decimal digits are on the stack, and the number of digits is in **CX**. Let's print out a message saying "That number in decimal is:" with service 9 of INT 21H:

```
        .MODEL SMALL
        .CODE
            ORG 100H
ENTRY:  JMP DEHEXER
            PROMPT          DB "Type in a 4 digit hex number:$"
            BUFFER          DB 5
            NUM_TYPED       DB 0
            ASCII_NUM       DB 3 DUP (0)
            END_NUM         DB 0
            CRLF            DB 0
→           ANS_STRING      DB 13, 10, "That number in decimal is: $"
DEHEXER:MOV     AH,9
        MOV     DX,OFFSET PROMPT
        INT     21H
        MOV     AH,0AH
        MOV     DX,OFFSET BUFFER
        INT     21H

        MOV     CX, 0
        MOV     AX,0
        MOV     BX, OFFSET END_NUM
LOOP1:  MOV     DX,0
        MOV     DL, [BX]
        DEC     BX
        CMP     DL,'9'
        JBE     UNDER_A
        SUB     DL, 'a' - '0' - 10
UNDER_A:SUB     DL, '0'
        SHL     DX, CL
        ADD     AX, DX
        ADD     CL,4
        CMP     CL,16
        JB      LOOP1

        MOV     CX,0
        MOV     BX, 10
LOOP2:  MOV     DX,0
        DIV     BX
```

```
          PUSH    DX
          INC     CX
          CMP     AX,0
          JA      LOOP2

→         MOV     AH,9
→         MOV     DX,OFFSET ANS_STRING
→         INT     21H
          :
          INT     20H

          END     ENTRY
```

And now we can just print out the digits using service 2 of INT 21H and **POP DX**. Note that since we peeled the digits off in reverse order, and that, since using the stack has reversed that order once again, we can just print digits as we pop them. In other words, if the number was 1,234, we would have peeled the digits off and pushed them in the order: 4, 3, 2, and 1, so the stack looks like this now:

```
┌───────────────┐
│               │
│       4       │
│               │
├───────────────┤
│               │
│       3       │
│               │
├───────────────┤
│               │
│       2       │
│               │
├───────────────┤
│               │
│       1       │
│               │
└───────────────┘
```

The first digit to be popped, and printed, is 1, followed by 2, and so on, meaning that we'll print 1234. Each digit still has to be converted to ASCII. For example, if we pop 1 off the stack, that's still not ASCII '1'. To convert them to ASCII, we have to add the ASCII value for '0' to them; i.e., 0 will become '0', 1 will become '1', and so on.

Here's the loop where we pop the digits. We'll pop them into **DX** since service 2 expects the ASCII character to print to be in **DL**, and we'll use the new **LOOP** instruction:

```
        .MODEL SMALL
        .CODE


                ORG 100H
ENTRY:  JMP DEHEXER
                PROMPT          DB "Type in a 4 digit hex number:$"
                BUFFER          DB 5
                NUM_TYPED       DB 0
                ASCII_NUM       DB 3 DUP (0)
                END_NUM         DB 0
                CRLF            DB 0
                ANS_STRING      DB 13, 10, "That number in decimal is: $"
DEHEXER:MOV     AH,9
        MOV     DX,OFFSET PROMPT
        INT     21H
        MOV     AH,0AH
        MOV     DX,OFFSET BUFFER
        INT     21H


        MOV     CX, 0
        MOV     AX,0
        MOV     BX, OFFSET END_NUM
LOOP1:  MOV     DX,0
        MOV     DL, [BX]
        DEC     BX
        CMP     DL,'9'
        JBE     UNDER_A
        SUB     DL, 'a' - '0' - 10
UNDER_A:SUB     DL, '0'
        SHL     DX, CL
        ADD     AX, DX
        ADD     CL,4
        CMP     CL,16
        JB      LOOP1


        MOV     CX,0
        MOV     BX, 10
LOOP2:  MOV     DX,0
        DIV     BX
        PUSH    DX
        INC     CX
        CMP     AX,0
        JA      LOOP2


        MOV     AH,9
        MOV     DX,OFFSET ANS_STRING
        INT     21H
```

```
        MOV     AH,2                ←
LOOP3:  POP     DX                  ←
        ADD     DX,'0'              ←
        INT     21H                 ←
        LOOP    LOOP3               ←

        INT     20H
        END     ENTRY
```

The LOOP Instruction

In this case, we use the **LOOP** instruction to loop over the pushed digits, pop them, and print them out. The **LOOP** instruction is very much like a **for** loop in C; in order to use it, we just fill **CX** with the number of times we want to loop, define a label, and then loop like this:

```
        MOV     CX,5
LOOP_1:
        :
        :
        LOOP    LOOP_1
```

Here, the body of **LOOP_1** will be executed five times. In **DEHEXER**, the previous loop (where we stripped the decimal digits off the value in **AX**) left the number of digits in **CX** already, so the loop index, **CX**, is all set. All we have to do is to use **LOOP**, printing out each digit as we pop it off the stack:

```
        MOV     AH, 2
LOOP3:  POP     DX
        ADD     DX, '0'
        INT     21H
        LOOP    LOOP3
```

And that's it. We've read in a hex number, converted it to binary by multiplying each digit by a power of 16, peeled decimal digits off by successively dividing it by 10, reversed their order, and now printed them out. We've made a great deal of progress in assembly language.

The program works. Give it a try. It accepts four-digit hex numbers and prints out the correct decimal version. On the other hand, there is still one difference between it and most .ASM files. Most .ASM files have at least one procedure defined inside them. This will be the final topic of this chapter, and it's crucial to know about procedures for the next chapter (where we connect assembly language to C).

Assembly Language Procedures

In C, we write functions. In assembly language, we write procedures. We can make **DEHEXER** into a single procedure by adding the **PROC** and **ENDP** directives so that they straddle our code like this:

```
        .MODEL SMALL
        .CODE

              ORG 100H
        ENTRY: JMP DEHEXER
              PROMPT           DB "Type in a 4 digit hex number:$"
              :
        DEHEXER PROC
              MOV     AH,9
              MOV     DX,OFFSET PROMPT          The DEHEXER Procedure
              :
              INT     20H
        DEHEXER ENDP

              END     ENTRY
```

Here's how the whole program looks now:

```
        .MODEL SMALL
        .CODE

              ORG 100H
        ENTRY: JMP DEHEXER
              PROMPT           DB "Type in a 4 digit hex number:$"
              BUFFER           DB 5
              NUM_TYPED        DB 0
              ASCII_NUM        DB 3 DUP (0)
              END_NUM          DB 0
              CRLF             DB 0
              ANS_STRING       DB 13, 10, "That number in decimal is: $"
        DEHEXER PROC           ←
              MOV     AH,9
              MOV     DX,OFFSET PROMPT          ;Print prompt
              INT     21H
              MOV     AH,0AH
```

```
            MOV     DX,OFFSET BUFFER          ;Get number
            INT     21H

            MOV     CX, 0
            MOV     AX,0
            MOV     BX, OFFSET END_NUM
LOOP1:      MOV     DX,0                      ;Get digit by digit into AX
            MOV     DL, [BX]
            DEC     BX
            CMP     DL,'9'
            JBE     UNDER_A
            SUB     DL, 'a' - '0' - 10
UNDER_A:SUB        DL, '0'
            SHL     DX, CL
            ADD     AX, DX
            ADD     CL,4
            CMP     CL,16
            JB      LOOP1

            MOV     CX,0                      ;Strip off onto stack
            MOV     BX, 10
LOOP2:      MOV     DX,0
            DIV     BX
            PUSH    DX
            INC     CX
            CMP     AX,0
            JA      LOOP2

            MOV     AH,9
            MOV     DX,OFFSET ANS_STRING
            INT     21H

            MOV     AH,2                      ;Strip off from stack
LOOP3:      POP     DX
            ADD     DX,'0'
            INT     21H
            LOOP    LOOP3

            INT     20H
DEHEXER ENDP                                  ←

            END     ENTRY
```

We have added the **PROC** and **ENDP** directives, which define procedures. The **PROC** directive lets the assembler know that we want to define a procedure, and the **ENDP** directive indicates that the procedure definition is finished.

Unless we are in the main procedure, we have to end the procedure with a return, or **RET** instruction. Let's break **DEHEXER** into two procedures to see how this is done. We can, for example, print out the decimal answer in a new procedure called **PRINT_NUM**.

As soon as we've decoded the typed hex number into a binary value in **AX**, we can call **PRINT_NUM** to do the job of stripping decimal digits from **AX**, placing them on the stack, and then printing them out. We call **PRINT_NUM** with the instruction **CALL Print_Num**, and return at the end with a **RET** instruction (just as we can use **return( )** at the end of a C function):

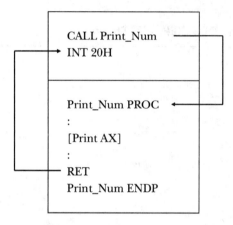

Here's how it looks in outline:

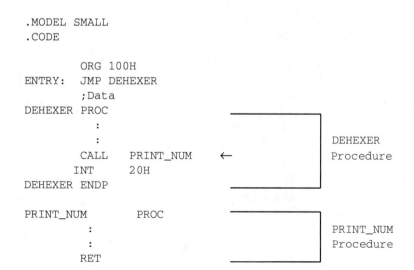

```
.MODEL SMALL
.CODE

        ORG 100H
ENTRY:  JMP DEHEXER
        ;Data
DEHEXER PROC
           :
           :
            CALL    PRINT_NUM    ←
            INT     20H
DEHEXER ENDP

PRINT_NUM       PROC
           :
           :
            RET
```

```
PRINT_NUM        ENDP

        END      ENTRY
```

This works as you'd expect it to: When we CALL PRINT_NUM, control is transferred to the first line there. Execution continues until the return instruction, **RET**, is reached, and then we return to the line just after the CALL PRINT_NUM instruction in the main procedure. In assembly language, we do not call procedures with arguments (like CALL PRINT_NUM(AX)); instead, we pass values in the registers. We can find the final version of the program in Listing 11-1.

Listing 11-1. The DEHEXER.ASM Program.

```
.MODEL SMALL
.CODE

        ORG 100H
ENTRY:  JMP DEHEXER
        PROMPT          DB "Type in a 4 digit hex number:$"
        BUFFER          DB 5
        NUM_TYPED       DB 0
        ASCII_NUM       DB 3 DUP (0)
        END_NUM         DB 0
        CRLF            DB 0
        ANS_STRING      DB 13, 10, "That number in decimal is: $"
DEHEXER PROC
        MOV     AH,9
        MOV     DX,OFFSET PROMPT
        INT     21H
        MOV     AH,0AH
        MOV     DX,OFFSET BUFFER
        INT     21H

        MOV     CX, 0
        MOV     AX,0
        MOV     BX, OFFSET END_NUM
LOOP1:  MOV     DX,0
        MOV     DL, [BX]
        DEC     BX
        CMP     DL,'9'
        JBE     UNDER_A
        SUB     DL, 'a' - '0' - 10
UNDER_A:SUB     DL, '0'
        SHL     DX, CL
        ADD     AX, DX
```

Listing 11-1. *(continued)*

```
            ADD     CL,4
            CMP     CL,16
            JB      LOOP1

            CALL    PRINT_NUM               ←

            INT     20H
DEHEXER ENDP

PRINT_NUM       PROC                        ←
            MOV     CX,0
            MOV     BX, 10
LOOP2:  MOV     DX,0
            DIV     BX
            PUSH    DX
            INC     CX
            CMP     AX,0
            JA      LOOP2

            MOV     AH,9
            MOV     DX,OFFSET ANS_STRING
            INT     21H

            MOV     AH,2
LOOP3:  POP     DX
            ADD     DX,'0'
            INT     21H
            LOOP    LOOP3
            RET                             ←
PRINT_NUM       ENDP                        ←

            END     ENTRY
```

Procedures in assembly language don't specifically return any values, as functions can in C. Instead, information is returned in the registers, or, in some cases, in the flags.

NOTE Also, there is no such thing as a formal local variable in assembly language, unless the variable is in another file. All variables in the same module are shared; that is, they are global.

That's how **PROC** and **ENDP** work, and we'll see much more of them soon. And that's it for our assembly language primer. Now that we've reached this point, we're up to speed in assembly language and we're ready to press on. We can start putting all our knowledge to work when we interface C to assembly language, and we'll do that next.

Connecting Assembly Language to C

We've gotten our start in assembly language in the last chapter. In this chapter, we'll start putting C and assembly language together for the first time. There are two main ways of doing this, by using in-line assembly language and by linking assembly language modules into our program. Both have their uses, and we'll explore both of them in this chapter, beginning with in-line assembly language.

Using In-Line Assembly Language

In-line assembly language used to be very primitive. In fact, in some languages, you had to type the actual bytes of machine code in (this was called **in-line code**). However, as speed became more and more important, languages started to improve their support of in-line assembly language. Now, in the Microsoft or Turbo C series, you can do practically anything that you can do in normal assembly language.

> **NOTE** There is one notable exception: You can't use the data directives like **DB** or **DW** in Microsoft C (you can in Turbo). Besides that, however, you are free to do most things.

In Turbo C, you have to include this line in your program:

```
#pragma inline
```

before you can use assembly language. In addition, you have to have TASM, Turbo's assembler on your disk. The Turbo C compiler actually creates a file out of your assembly language instructions, assembles it with TASM.EXE, and links the .OBJ file in. When writing in-line assembly language with Turbo, you have to preface every assembly language line with the letters **asm**, like this:

```
#pragma inline
main()
{
    asm mov dl, 90
    asm mov ah, 2
    asm int 21h

    return(0);
}
```

This is our earlier program **PRINTZ**. That's all there is to it. We can create the file **PRINTZ.EXE** with the command:

```
F:\>tcc printz.c
```

When we run it, **printz.exe** prints 'Z', just as the straight assembly language version did. Using in-line assembly language is as easy as that. All we have to do is to put the assembly code in our C source file and mark it appropriately. Under Microsoft C, we can preface a whole block with the keyword **_asm**, like this:

```
main()
{
    _asm{              ←
        mov dl, 90
        mov ah, 2
        int 21h
    }

    return(0);
}
```

Then we just use the C compiler as usual. For example, to create **printz.exe** in this case, we can use Quick C this way:

```
F:\>qcl printz.c
```

Turbo and Microsoft C are very close when it comes to in-line code, except that Microsoft C doesn't allow us to use define data directives (like **DB** and **DW**). However, in both compilers, we can define data in the normal C fashion, as C variables, and then refer to it in the assembly language code. Let's see how to do that next.

Using Data in In-Line Assembly Language

Here we will write an example program to print out the line: "Hello, world.\n" using in-line assembly language. Let's start this way:

```
main()
{
    char *MSG "Hello, world.\n$";
        :
}
```

We are just setting up a string of type **char** in memory (recall that a string is just a char array and that a pointer can be substituted for an array). Notice that we end it with '$' so we can use it with the string-printing DOS service, service 9. Now we can set up our in-line code (under Microsoft C here):

```
main()
{
    char *MSG "Hello, world.\n$";

    _asm{
        mov dx, MSG
        mov ah, 9
        int 21h
    }

    return(0);
}
```

That's it. Note that, since MSG is a pointer (that is, the address of the beginning of MSG in memory), we should omit the directive **OFFSET** when using it. In other words, we did not use the instruction mov dx, offset MSG, as we would have in an assembly language program. The normal assembly language program would have looked like this:

```
        .MODEL SMALL
        .CODE
        ORG 100H
ENTRY:  JMP HELLO
        MSG DB "Hello, world.",13,10,"$"
HELLO   PROC NEAR
        MOV DX, OFFSET MSG  ←
        MOV AH, 9
        INT 21H
        INT 20H
HELLO   ENDP

        END ENTRY
```

With that understanding, using character strings is easy. Here, for example, is our entire program **DEHEXER.ASM** (which doesn't use any data except for character strings), written as **DEHEXER.C** under Microsoft C:

```
main()
{
    char *PROMPT = "Type in a 4 digit hex number:$";
    char *BUFFER = "\5        ";
    char *ANS_STRING = "\nThat number in decimal is: $";
    char *END_NUM = BUFFER + 5;

    _asm{
    DEHEXER:MOV     AH,9
            MOV     DX, PROMPT
            INT     21H
            MOV     AH,0AH
            MOV     DX, BUFFER
            INT     21H

            MOV     CX, 0
            MOV     AX,0
            MOV     BX, END_NUM
    LOOP1:  MOV     DX,0
            MOV     DL, [BX]
            DEC     BX
            CMP     DL,'9'
            JLE     UNDER_A
            SUB     DL, 'A' - '0' - 10
    UNDER_A:SUB     DL, '0'
            SHL     DX, CL
            ADD     AX, DX
            ADD     CX,4
            CMP     CX,16
```

```
            JL      LOOP1

            MOV     CX,0
            MOV     BX, 10
    LOOP2:  MOV     DX,0
            DIV     BX
            PUSH    DX
            INC     CX
            CMP     AX,0
            JA      LOOP2

            MOV     AH,9
            MOV     DX, ANS_STRING
            INT     21H

            MOV     AH,2
    LOOP3:  POP     DX
            ADD     DX,'0'
            INT     21H
            LOOP    LOOP3
        }
    return(0);
}
```

You can compile this as you would any normal C program. Here's the same thing in Turbo C (notice that we must define the labels in the code as normal C labels, without the keyword asm):

```
main()
{
    char *PROMPT = "Type in a 4 digit hex number:$";
    char *BUFFER = "\5        ";
    char *END_NUM = BUFFER + 5;
    char *ANS_STRING = "\n\rThat number in decimal is: $";
    #pragma inline

    asm MOV     AH,9
    asm MOV     DX, PROMPT
    asm INT     21H
    asm MOV     AH,0AH
    asm MOV     DX, BUFFER
    asm INT     21H
    asm
    asm MOV     CX, 0
    asm MOV     AX,0
    asm MOV     BX, END_NUM
    LOOP1:
```

```
        asm MOV        DX,0
        asm MOV        DL, [BX]
        asm DEC        BX
        asm CMP        DL,'9'
        asm JLE        UNDER_A
        asm SUB        DL, 'A' - '0' - 10
        UNDER_A:
        asm SUB        DL, '0'
        asm SHL        DX, CL
        asm ADD        AX, DX
        asm ADD        CX,4
        asm CMP        CX,16
        asm JL         LOOP1
        asm
        asm MOV        CX,0
        asm MOV        BX, 10
        LOOP2:
        asm MOV        DX,0
        asm DIV        BX
        asm PUSH       DX
        asm INC        CX
        asm CMP        AX,0
        asm JA         LOOP2
        asm
        asm MOV        AH,9
        asm MOV        DX, ANS_STRING
        asm INT        21H
        asm
        asm MOV        AH,2
        LOOP3:
        asm POP        DX
        asm ADD        DX,'0'
        asm INT        21H
        asm LOOP       LOOP3
        asm

        return(0);
    }
```

The way we would use other types of data is similar. The usual method is to simply declare it in C format so the C part of the code can use it as well, and then refer to it in our in-line assembly language as we would if we had declared it with **DB** or **DW**.

Understanding the Internal C Data Formats

However, we must know the internal data format that C uses for its variables if we want to connect to C at this level; that is, we have to know how to read and work with C data on a byte-by-byte basis to interface with assembly language. Let's take a look at the internal representation of C data next.

Integers

A short int, for example, is simply a 16-bit word, so we can write the following program:

```
main()
{
    int apples = 5;              ←
    int oranges = 3;            ←
    char *msg2 = "Total fruit: $";
    _asm{
            MOV        DX, msg2
            MOV        AH, 9
            INT        21H
            MOV        DX, apples
            ADD        DX, oranges
            ADD        DX, '0'
            MOV        AH, 2
            INT        21H
    }
        return(0);
}
```

Here we have defined two ints, **apples** and **oranges**. Since they are just two one-word variables, those declarations are just the same as they would be if we had used the DW directive. We can read the value in apples like this: MOV DX, apples. We add this value to the value in the variable **oranges** and print out the sum.

The result of the program is the output, Total fruit: 8. Our in-line assembly language code can use the variables just as the C part of the code can — if we know the data format. If we wished, we could use byte-long values instead of word-long ones (note the use of **DL**, not **DX**):

```
main()
{
    char apples = 5;            ←
    char oranges = 3;           ←
    char *msg2 = "Total fruit: $";
    _asm{
            MOV        DX, msg2
            MOV        AH, 9
```

```
        INT     21H
        MOV     DL, apples        ←
        ADD     DL, oranges       ←
        ADD     DL, '0'           ←
        MOV     AH, 2
        INT     21H
    }
    return(0);
}
```

Here we have declared **apples** and **oranges** as variables of type **char**, which is the same as declaring them with **DB**.

Long Integers

We can also look at unsigned long int format. Because of the peculiarities of the 80×86 data storage methods, long (two-word) numbers like 12345678H are stored with high and low words reversed *and* high and low bytes reversed. In other words, 12345678H would be stored as 78H 56H 34H 12H.

This means that our number of apples, stored as a long double, would look like this: 05 00 00 00. Since that's the case, we can just load **apples** into **DX** again because 05 00 (the low word) is the word that we are interested in, and that is the first word in memory (if we had wanted the high word, we could have used a pointer to it):

```
main()
{
    long apples = 5;              ←
    long oranges = 3;             ←
    char *msg2 = "Total fruit: $";
    _asm{
        MOV     DX, msg2
        MOV     AH, 9
        INT     21H
        MOV     DX, apples        ←
        ADD     DX, oranges       ←
        ADD     DX, '0'
        MOV     AH, 2
        INT     21H
    }
    return(0);
}
```

For signed integers, C uses **two's complement notation**, and that's what we must learn next. Up to this point, all the numbers we've been using in assembly language have been unsigned whole numbers. A number could range from 0000H to FFFFH and that was it. Here, unsigned means, really, positive, and positive numbers are only half the story. Temperatures run negative as well as positive, as do budgets or voltages or any number of categories. To keep track of these, any modern computer has to be able to use signed numbers.

The Sign Bit

The highest bit — the leftmost bit — in a byte or word can be used as the sign bit. In fact, what determines whether or not a number is signed is whether or not we pay attention to this bit. In unsigned bytes or words, this bit was always there, certainly, but it was only the highest bit and had no other significance. To make a number signed, we just have to treat it as signed, which means starting to pay attention to the sign bit. A 1 in the highest bit will mean that the number, if thought of as signed, is negative:

```
      ┌───── Highest Order Bit (Treating this byte as unsigned)
      ▼
┌───┬───┬───┬───┬───┬───┬───┬───┐
│ 1 │ 1 │ 0 │ 0 │ 1 │ 1 │ 1 │ 0 │
└───┴───┴───┴───┴───┴───┴───┴───┘


      ┌───── Sign Bit (Treating this byte as signed)  → Negative number
      ▼
┌───┬───┬───┬───┬───┬───┬───┬───┐
│ 1 │ 1 │ 0 │ 0 │ 1 │ 1 │ 1 │ 0 │
└───┴───┴───┴───┴───┴───┴───┴───┘
```

How Signed Numbers Work

The whole scheme of signed numbers in the 80x86 comes from the simple fact that $1 + (-1) = 0$. We realize that if we want to do any calculation with negative numbers in the PS/2 or PC, the number we choose to be -1, when added to 1, has to give 0. Yet this seems impossible. Can you think of an eight bit number which, when added to 1, will give a result of 0? It seems as though the result must always be 1 or greater.

In fact, if we limit ourselves to the eight bits of the byte, there is an answer. If we add 255 (= 11111111B) and 1, as seen below,

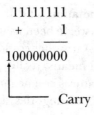

Carry

it yields 100000000B. The eight bit register is left holding 00000000, or 0, and there is a carry, since the 1 is in the 2^8 place (256), more than the register's capacity to hold. This carry means that the **carry flag** will be set. If we ignore this carry, and only look at the eight bits that fit into the byte, we are left with 00000000B; in other words, FFH + 1 = 0.

Finding a Two's Complement

As a practical matter, how are these negative numbers found? For instance, if we wanted to know what -109 was, how could we find it? To find -109, we would start with 109 and find what is called its two's complement. Two's complement math is the math used in computers for dealing with negative numbers. We already know one two's complement: The two's complement of 1 is FFFFH.

We can find any number's two's complement easily. We begin by noting that if you take a number like 5, which is 00000101B in binary, then flip all its bits, 11111010B (= FAH), and add the two together, you get all 1s:

$$
\begin{array}{rl}
00000101 & \leftarrow\ 5 \\
+\quad 11111010 & \leftarrow\ 5 \text{ with bits flipped [FAH]} \\
\hline
11111111 & =\ \text{FF}
\end{array}
$$

That is, 5 + FAH = 11111111B. This is close to what we want. Adding 1 to this sum gives us 0 with a carry. If we ignore the carry, we can see that 5 + FAH + 1 = 0. In other words, adding 5 to (FAH + 1) gives 0 with the (ignored) carry:

$$
\begin{array}{r}
5 \\
+\quad (\text{FAH} + 1) \\
\hline
0)
\end{array}
$$

We know that 5 plus -5 equals zero:

$$
\begin{array}{r}
5 \\
+ \quad -5 \\
\hline
0
\end{array}
$$

And this means that -5 must equal (**FAH** + 1), which is **FBH**. This is how negative numbers are found; the rule is simple — to find any number's two's complement (and therefore to change its sign), just flip the bits and add 1. Thus we see that **-1 = Flip(1)** + 1 = 11111110B + 1 = 11111111B = FFH (in byte form; it would be FFFFH in word form).

The NOT and NEG Instructions

To flip the bits in a word or byte in assembly language, you can use the **NOT** instruction. For example, if **AX** was equal to 00000000, then **NOT AX** would make **AX** equal to 11111111. If **BX** was equal to 01010101, then **NOT BX** would make it 10101010. This is just like the bitwise **NOT** operator in C, ~.

If you use **NOT** on a word or byte, and then add 1 to the result, you will have that word or byte's two's complement. In fact, there is a special 80×86 instruction that does just this: **NEG**. **NEG** is the same as **NOT**, except that it adds 1 at the end to make a two's complement of the number. If **AX** held 1, then **NEG AX** would give it 1111111111111111 or FFFF.

NOTE	**NEG** flips signs. It does not always make signs negative. For example, **NEG -1 = 1**.

Let's see how to use two's complement when interfacing to C. See the example below:

```
main()
{
    int apples = -1;              ←
    int oranges = 3;
    char *msg2 = "Total fruit: $";
    _asm{
        MOV     DX, msg2
        MOV     AH, 9
        INT     21H
```

```
        MOV     DX, apples
        ADD     DX, oranges
        ADD     DX, '0'
        MOV     AH, 2
        INT     21H
    }
    return(0);
}
```

In this program, the number of apples, -1, is stored as FFFFH. Since we already know how to use two's complement, we are prepared for this format. That's all there is to negative numbers.

Floating Point Format

As you can see, working with integer formats is not too difficult. We can read from memory and write to it without problem.Floating point formats, however, will be more difficult to decipher. We can store a floating point number like this:

```
main()
{
    float val = 10.5;        ←
        :
        :
}
```

That looks easy enough, but what is the internal representation of such a floating point number?

If we dig into the .EXE file, we will find that our number 10.5 has been stored as 41280000H. Where did it come from? The format for floating point numbers is complex, and takes a little getting used to. A number like 32.1 is just 3×10^1 plus 2×10^0 and 1×10^{-1}. On the other hand, the computer is a binary machine, which means it uses base 2, so a number like 10.5 must be stored as 1×2^3 plus 1×2^1 plus 1×2^{-1}, which is 1010.1, where the point is a binary point. It is possible to store any number in binary that can be stored in decimal, it just might take more places. For instance, 0.75 can be broken down into 1/2 + 1/4, or $2^{-1} + 2^{-2}$, so 0.75 = .11B.

The numbers stored as floats are all **normalized**, which means they appear with the binary point near the beginning, so 1010.1 would appear like this: 1.0101×2^3. To expand this, just move the binary point three places to the right, giving 1010.1 again. You can see that the first digit in any normalized binary number is always one. Under C floating point format, the leading 1 is **implicit**. In other words, all that is stored of the **significand** is 0101. The exponent is still three, but, to make matters even more complex, all exponents are stored after being added to some offset or **bias**.

For a float, this bias is 7FH, or 127. For doubles, this number is 3FFH, or 1,023. In other words, if our number, 1010.1B, is going to be stored as a float, the exponent will be 3 + 127 = 130 = 82H. Finally, the first bit of any floating point number is the sign bit. Floating point numbers are not stored in two's complement notation. If the sign bit is 1, the number is negative. If it is 0, the number is positive. That's the only distinction between positive and negative numbers. The float format looks like this:

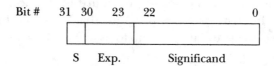

So 10.5 = 1010.1B will look like this:

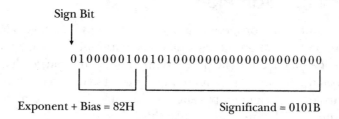

This can be made into Hex by grouping every four binary digits together:

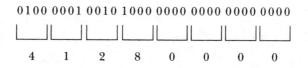

That is, 10.5 is stored as 41280000H. In fact, because the 80×86 actually stores low bytes first inside a word and then low words first, 10.5 actually shows up in memory as 00H 00H 28H 41H. These bytes are far indeed from 10.5.

TIP   If you are going to work with floating point numbers, probably the first thing you should do is write a function to translate floating point format into something you can use, or let C do the translation for you.

The format for doubles is this:

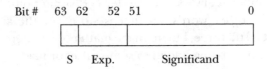

> **TIP**
>
> It's worth noting that this floating point format is the same format used by the 80x87 coprocessors, so you can interface with them easily.

Working directly with variables as we have been doing provides one way of communicating with a C program, but, in some cases, we won't know the actual names of the variables we're supposed to use. For example, we might be writing an assembly language procedure to replace a ponderous C library function. In that case, the program that calls our function will only pass parameters to us, and it will be up to us to pick them off the stack. Let's do that next.

Passing Parameters

So far, our entire program has been in assembly language. However, it's more common to write only a few functions in assembly language (i.e., that part of the code that needs to be speeded up), and, to do that, we'll have to learn how to read the parameters that might be passed to us in a function. We'll start our discussion of parameter passing with a simple function that doesn't accept any parameters. That might look like this:

```c
char *MSG "Hello, world.\n$";

main()
{
    print_msg();        ←

    return(0);
}

print_msg()             ←
{
    _asm{
    MOV DX, MSG
    MOV AH, 9
    INT 21H
    }
}
```

Language	Parameters Pushed	Parameters Passed	Return Type
BASIC	In order	As offset addresses	RET #*
FORTRAN	In order	As FAR addresses	RET #
→ C	In REVERSE order	As values	RET
Pascal	In order	As values	RET #

*Where RET # is used, # equals the total size in bytes of all pushed parameters.

Table 12-1. C's Calling Conventions.

In other words, the whole program can still be written in C, except for the function(s) which we choose to write in assembly language. As you can see, it's easy to write a C function in assembly language, as long as we don't pass any parameters to it. (Note that we made MSG a global variable here so that **print_msg( )** could have access to it.)

Now let's say that we wanted to pass a parameter to our function. We could change our function to, say, **print_char( )**, and we could call **print_char( )** with an argument like this: print_char('Z'). The question becomes this: What happens to the function's argument? To answer this question, we have to take a look at C's calling convention (see Table 12-1).

That is (as we saw in Chapter 7), parameters are pushed onto the stack in reverse order in C. In addition, C parameters are always passed by value (not as addresses as is the case with FORTRAN or BASIC), except for arrays, which are passed by reference (i.e., with a pointer). The array reference is the address of the first element of the array, and will be either two or four bytes long, depending on the pointer size in the memory model used. Even structures are passed by value. The last word is pushed first, and so on down to the first. Let's give all this a try. Our example with the **print_msg( )** function didn't use any passed parameters:

```
char *MSG "Hello, world.\n$";

main()
{
    print_msg();      ←

    return(0);
}
```

```
print_msg()              ←
{
    _asm{
        MOV DX, MSG
        MOV AH, 9
        INT 21H
    }
}
```

That means that when we arrive at **print_msg( )**, the stack will look like this, depending on memory model:

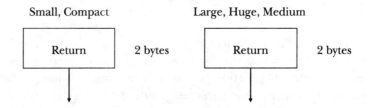

The size of the return address pushed on the stack depends on the memory model used in the C program. In the Large, Huge, and Medium models, code can be more that one segment long, so the return address is four bytes (two words).

Now, however, let's change our example so that we pass two char parameters:

```
main()
{
    print_2_char('A','Z');        ←

    return(0);
}

print_2_char(char a, char b)       ←
{
    _asm{
        :
        :
    }
}
```

This time, we are passing two parameters, ASCII 65 ('A') and 90 ('Z'). The way the stack looks when we arrive at **print_2_char( )** is like this:

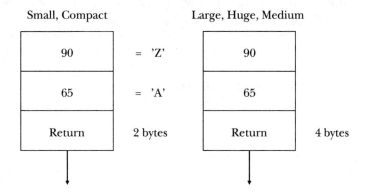

Note that the parameters were pushed in reverse order. First, the 'Z' was pushed, and then 'A'. Notice also that each parameter takes up a full word. We cannot push byte values onto the C stack (unlike our C++ example). Now we need to access the parameters that were passed to us, and that turns out to be easy. We can simply refer to our variables as a C function would:

```
main()
{
    print_2_char('A','Z');

    return(0);
}

print_2_char(char a, char b)
{
    _asm{
        MOV     AH, 2
        MOV     DX, 0
        MOV     DL, a    ←
        INT     21H
        MOV     DX, 0
        MOV     DL, b    ←
        INT     21H
    }
}
```

Here, C picks parameters off the stack for us. In other words, the instruction MOV DL, b moves the value passed as b into the **DL** register.

> **NOTE**   To give us access to the parameters that were passed, C actually substitutes the appropriate memory reference for our variables **a** and **b**. That is, since the variables are on the stack, and the stack is part of memory, their names can simply be replaced with memory addresses.

Here's the same program in Turbo:

```
main()
{
    print_2_char('A','Z');

    return(0);
}

print_2_char(char a, char b)
{
    #pragma inline
        asm MOV     AH, 2
        asm MOV     DX, 0
        asm MOV     DL, a      ←
        asm INT     21H
        asm MOV     DX, 0
        asm MOV     DL, b      ←
        asm INT     21H
}
```

Passing Longs

It makes sense that we can pass one-byte or one-word parameters easily by pushing them. But what if we need to push more than one word? For example, look at the function **my_func( )** here:

```
main()
{
    long numb = 0xaaaabbbb;

    my_func(numb);
}

my_func(long a)
{
}
```

The number passed to our function is a long value. However, we can convert it to two one-word values for use in our assembly language code like this:

```
main()
{
    long numb = 0xaaaabbbb;

    my_func(numb);

    return(0);
}

my_func(long a)
{
    int ahigh, alow;

    alow = (int) a;             ←
    ahigh = (int) a >> 16;      ←

    _asm{
        MOV     DX, ahigh       ←
        MOV     AX, alow        ←
        :
        :
    }
}
```

All we did was to put the low word into the variable **alow** by using a typecast of **int**, and then we loaded the high word by first shifting the long variable a down by 16 places (so the high word becomes the low word). Then we referred to those variables in our in-line code. We can do the same in Turbo:

```
main()
{
    long numb = 0xaaaabbbb;

    my_func(numb);

    return(0);
}

my_func(long a)
{
    int ahigh, alow;

    alow = (int) a;
    ahigh = (int) a >> 16;
```

```
      #pragma inline
      asm MOV    DX, ahigh      ←
      asm MOV    AX, alow       ←
           :
           :
      }
  }
```

In other words, we should let C handle the details of manipulating the stack if we can. Now that we've gained some expertise with passing parameters, how about returning values? We can read the parameters that the calling function passes to us, but we know that real functions can return values as well. That's something we can do too, and it's as easy as reading passed parameters.

Returning Values from Functions

Returning values is unexpectedly easy. The convention (Microsoft C, Turbo C, etc.) is to use these registers to return values from functions (see Table 12-2).

It's very simple. Depending on the return value expected from the function (set in the function prototype), C just reads return values from **AL**, **AX**, or **DX:AX**. To return a byte-long value, just leave the value in **AL** when you exit the function. If the calling function is expecting a byte-long return value, it will read that byte from **AL**. Word values (like short integers) are returned in

Returning	*Use*
char	AL
short	AL
int	AX
long	DX:AX (high word in DX
float	AX = Address (DX:AX for far)
double	AX = Address (DX:AX for far)
struct	AX = Address (DX:AX for far)
near pointer	AX
far pointer	DX:AX

Table 12-2.   Register Return Values.

AX. Doubleword values are simply returned in **DX:AX** (**DX** = high word, **AX** = low word).

Let's put this to use by writing a function named **summer( )**. This function will just add two integers; that is, we'll accept two ints and return an int value (in **AX**). Here's what it looks like under the small model:

```
main()
{
    printf("3 + 2 = %d",summer(3,2));

    return(0);
}

int summer(int a, int b)
{
    _asm{
        MOV       AX, a
        ADD       AX, b
    }
}
```

This program just leaves the result in **AX**, and this value therefore becomes the function's returns value. When we return to the calling function, we type out a message and the return value of **summer( )**. Here, the program types out "3 + 2 = 5." Returning values is that simple. Here's the same program under Turbo C:

```
main()
{
    printf("3 + 2 = %d",summer(3,2));

    return(0);
}

int summer(int a, int b)
{
    #pragma inline
    asm MOV       AX, a
    asm ADD       AX, b
}
```

However, if we add two integers together, the result could be a long integer. We should adjust **summer( )** to allow for such a result by returning a long integer in **DX:AX**. That looks like this under Microsoft C:

```
unsigned long summer(int a, int b);

main()
{
    unsigned int x = 50000, y = 60000;
    printf("%u + %u = %lu", x, y, summer(x,y));

    return(0);
}

unsigned long summer(int a, int b)
{
    _asm{
        MOV     DX, 0
        MOV     AX, a
        ADD     AX, b
        ADC     DX, 0
    }
}
```

and this under Turbo:

```
unsigned long summer(int a, int b);

main()
{
    unsigned int x = 50000, y = 60000;
    printf("%u + %u = %lu", x, y, summer(x,y));

    return(0);
}

unsigned long summer(int a, int b)
{
    #pragma inline
        asm MOV     DX, 0
        asm MOV     AX, a
        asm ADD     AX, b
        asm ADC     DX, 0
}
```

Here we're anticipating the next chapter with the use of the instruction ADC
DX, 0. This instruction places a 1 in **DX** if there was a carry from the addition,
and 0 otherwise. The output of this program is "50,000 + 60,000 = 110,000."

Now we have considerable expertise in writing in-line assembly language. We
can use data that has been declared in C format, we can read parameters

passed to us in a function—and now we can even return values. This means that we can write whole functions in pure assembly language, taking advantage of the improved speed and shortened size that such functions can offer.

However, there is much more to interfacing assembly language to C than in-line assembly language. The second half of this chapter will cover the other, more common technique: writing files in assembly language and linking them in as modules. This is the first step in the process of building your own library of assembly language C functions.

Linking in External Assembly Language Files

We have to learn about linking under assembly language before we can link our own streamlined code into C. Let's use a simple example: We'll look at a small program that uses INT 21H service 9 (the string printer) to print out the message, "Hello, world." Just to make sure we are on solid ground, the first method of printing out "Hello, world." will be familiar to us. We already know how to write a program this way:

```
.MODEL  SMALL
.CODE
ORG     100H
ENTER:  JMP     PRINT
ALL_OK  DB "Hello, world.$"
PRINT   PROC    NEAR            ←
MOV     DX, OFFSET ALL_OK
MOV     AH, 9
INT     21H
INT     20H
PRINT   ENDP                    ←
END     ENTER
```

This works well, and it's a method we're familiar with. We might even divide the task up by calling a procedure to do the printing for us:

```
.MODEL  SMALL
.CODE
ORG     100H
ENTER:
PRINT   PROC    NEAR
CALL    SUB_PRINT
INT     20H
PRINT   ENDP
```

```
SUB_PRINT        PROC NEAR
JMP      GO
ALL_OK   DB "Hello, world.$"          ←
GO:      MOV     DX,OFFSET ALL_OK
MOV      AH,9
INT      21H
RET
SUB_PRINT        ENDP
END      ENTER
```

When we call **SUB_PRINT**, the first instruction we encounter is **JMP GO**, which means that we pass over the data and move on to the instructions. Storing data in the procedure that uses it makes sense, and, if you have a lot of procedures, it's a good idea.

Linking

Now we can start working with two files and linking them together. Let's break our example up into separate files:

File 1

```
.MODEL SMALL
.CODE
        ORG     100H
ENTER:
PRINT   PROC    NEAR
        CALL    SUB_PRINT
        INT     20H
PRINT   ENDP
        END     ENTER
```

File 2

```
.MODEL SMALL
.CODE
SUB_PRINT        PROC NEAR
        JMP     GO
        ALL_OK  DB "Hello, world.$"
GO:     MOV     DX,OFFSET ALL_OK
        MOV     AH,9
        INT     21H
        RET
SUB_PRINT        ENDP
        END
```

In order to link the files, we have to inform the assembler that the procedure **SUB_PRINT** will not be found in **file 1**; instead, it will be linked in later. We can do that with an **EXTRN** directive (just like the corresponding **extern** keyword in C). To declare a label as **EXTRN**, we have to tell the assembler what kind of label it is, **NEAR** or **FAR**. This way, it can leave the proper length in the code for the address — one word or two — which the linker fills in later. An **EXTRN** statement might look like this, for example:

```
EXTRN    LABEL_1:NEAR, LABEL_2:FAR
```

In addition, we have to do something we would not have to do in C. We have to declare **SUB_PRINT** as **PUBLIC** in **file 2**. The assembler does not save the actual labels used in the program as C does. If we want to save a label for the linker's use later, we have to explicitly do so. Here is how our new files look:

File 1

```
EXTRN    SUB_PRINT:NEAR    ←
.MODEL SMALL
.CODE
         ORG      100H
ENTER:
PRINT    PROC     NEAR
         CALL     SUB_PRINT
         INT      20H
PRINT    ENDP
         END      ENTER
```

File 2

```
PUBLIC   SUB_PRINT    ←
.MODEL SMALL
.CODE
SUB_PRINT        PROC NEAR
         JMP     GO
         ALL_OK  DB "Hello, world.$"
GO:      MOV     DX,OFFSET ALL_OK
         MOV     AH,9
         INT     21H
         RET
SUB_PRINT        ENDP
         END
```

They're all set to be linked. Let's link them into one .COM file. First we assemble **FILE1.ASM** and **FILE2.ASM**:

```
C>MASM FILE1;

Microsoft (R) Macro Assembler Version 5.10
Copyright (C) Microsoft Corp 1981, 1988.  All rights reserved.

  50106 + 31315 Bytes symbol space free

      0 Warning Errors
      0 Severe  Errors

C>MASM FILE2;

Microsoft (R) Macro Assembler Version 5.10
Copyright (C) Microsoft Corp 1981, 1988.  All rights reserved.

  50260 + 31161 Bytes symbol space free

      0 Warning Errors
      0 Severe  Errors
```

Then we link them together with LINK:

```
C>LINK FILE1+FILE2;

Microsoft (R) Overlay Linker  Version 3.64
Copyright (C) Microsoft Corp 1983-1988.  All rights reserved.

LINK : warning L4021: no stack segment
```

This generates an .EXE file named **FILE1.EXE**; we can take that .EXE file and run it through EXE2BIN to create the .COM file, which we run:

```
C>EXE2BIN FILE1 FILE1.COM

C>FILE1
Hello, world.
```

We've linked two files together. Using the Turbo assembler, the process is identical, except for one small detail: The label **ENTER**, which we've used in **file 1**, is a reserved keyword in TASM. Instead of **ENTER**, we can rename the label **ENTER_1**:

File 1

```
EXTRN    SUB_PRINT:NEAR
.MODEL SMALL
.CODE
         ORG      100H
ENTER_1:                              ←
PRINT    PROC     NEAR
         CALL     SUB_PRINT
         INT      20H
PRINT    ENDP
         END      ENTER_1           ←
```

File 2

```
PUBLIC   SUB_PRINT
.MODEL SMALL
.CODE
SUB_PRINT        PROC NEAR
         JMP      GO
         ALL_OK   DB "Hello, world.$"
GO:      MOV      DX,OFFSET ALL_OK
         MOV      AH,9
         INT      21H
         RET
SUB_PRINT        ENDP
         END
```

And we're all set. We just use TASM on both files:

```
C>TASM FILE1;

Assembling file:    FILE1.ASM
Error messages:     None
Warning messages:   None
Remaining memory:   381k

C>TASM FILE2;

Assembling file:    FILE2.ASM
Error messages:     None
Warning messages:   None
Remaining memory:   381k
```

Then we use TLINK (using the same syntax that we used with LINK):

```
C>TLINK FILE1+FILE2;

Turbo Link  Version 2.0  Copyright (c) 1987, 1988 Borland
International
Warning: no stack
```

Finally, we use EXE2BIN as before and run the program:

```
C>EXE2BIN FILE1 FILE1.COM

C>FILE1
Hello, world.
```

Now that we've seen how to link assembly language to assembly language, let's begin to take a look at the process of linking assembly language to C.

Linking Assembly Language Functions to C

Here's a program that calls a function named **vidmode( )**, which returns the current video mode (and which we are going to write in assembly language):

```
extern int vidmode();

main()
{
    printf("The video mode is: %d\n", vidmode());

    return(0);
}
```

We declare **vidmode( )** external this way, `extern int vidmode`. This tells C that **vidmode** is in a different file, and that it will return an integer value. Now let's write **vidmode( )** itself. It turns out that we can't just write an assembly language procedure for **vidmode( )**. The C naming convention for external functions is to use an underscore before the name of the procedure to be linked in like this: **_vidmode**. To cover that and other details (including the reverse parameter pushing and stack conventions on return), we indicate to the assembler that we're interfacing to C like this:

```
.MODEL  SMALL, C  ←
         :
         :
```

| TIP | Other languages you could use here include PASCAL, FORTRAN, and BASIC. |

And here's how **vidmode( )** itself looks:

```
.MODEL   SMALL, C
.CODE
    PUBLIC  vidmode           ;For C Interface
vidmode          PROC

    MOV     AH, 0FH  ←
    INT     10H      ←
    MOV     AH, 0    ←

    RET
vidmode          ENDP
    END
```

We find the video mode with service 0FH of INT 10H, as described in the appendix. The details of this service are unimportant here. It just returns the video mode information in AX, and we can return that information in the same register.

You may also notice that we left the word **vidmode** in small letters. That's because C is case sensitive, and it will expect to find the **vidmode** label in small letters. The assembler, however, makes all **PUBLIC** labels into capital letters by default, unless we use the **-mx** switch (with both the Microsoft and Turbo assemblers). If we use this switch, the assembler will not change the case of **PUBLIC** labels. To see how that works, let's link **videmode.obj** into our C program. For example, under Microsoft Quick C and MASM, the process would look like this:

```
F:\>qcl -c vid.c;
Microsoft (R) Quick C Compiler Version 2.00
Copyright (c) Microsoft Corp 1987-1989. All rights reserved.

F:\>masm -mx vidmode;
Microsoft (R) Macro Assembler Version 5.10
Copyright (C) Microsoft Corp 1981, 1988.  All rights reserved.

  50020 + 336953 Bytes symbol space free

      0 Warning Errors
      0 Severe  Errors
```

Here we have given our files different names — **vid.c** and **vidmode.asm** — so the .obj files will not have the same name. First, we compiled with the **-c** option so that Quick C would not call the linker. Next, we assembled **vidmode** with the **-mx** option; finally, we can link them together to create the .EXE file:

```
F:\>link vid+vidmode;
Microsoft (R) QuickC Linker  Version 4.06
Copyright (C) Microsoft Corp 1984-1989.  All rights reserved.
```

That's all we need to do. The linker fills the CALL instruction in **vid.c** with the address of **vidmode** in **vidmode.obj**. When run, the program calls **vidmode**, which returns the video mode, and the program prints it out. Under Turbo, the process is the same. Let's combine the compiling and linking into one step with tcc.exe. First, we have to assemble **vidmode**:

```
F:\>tasm -mx vidmode;

Assembling file:    VIDMODE.ASM
Error messages:     None
Warning messages:   None
Remaining memory:   381k
```

Then we compile **vid.c** and link **vidmode.obj** in at the same time:

```
F:\>tcc vid.c vidmode.obj
Turbo C  Version 2.0  Copyright (c) 1987, 1988 Borland
International
vid.c:
Turbo Link  Version 2.0  Copyright (c) 1987, 1988 Borland
International

        Available memory 330906
```

And that's all there is to it.

Passing Parameters in Action

However, the **vidmode** example is less than realistic. Usually, we will want to pass some parameters to our external functions. For example, if we wanted to link in our function **summer( )** to add two integers, this is the way it might look:

```
extern int SUMMER(int a,int b);

main()
{
    printf("3 + 2 = %d\n", SUMMER(3,2));

    return(0);
}
```

Here, we're writing the function name in capital letters to show that we don't have to use the **-mx** option when assembling. We start the assembly code like this:

```
.MODEL   SMALL, C

.CODE
        PUBLIC   SUMMER   ←      ;For C Interface
           :
           :
```

Now we declare the procedure with PROC:

```
.MODEL   SMALL, C

.CODE
        PUBLIC   SUMMER            ;For C Interface
SUMMER PROC NEAR USES DI SI, VALUE1:WORD, VALUE2:WORD ←
    :
    :
```

This will save us a lot of time: We're indicating that **SUMMER** is a **NEAR** procedure which uses the registers **DI** and **SI** (note that there are no commas separating **DI** and **SI**). MASM or TASM will automatically add the needed pushes and pops to our function to save and restore those registers. Next, we list the arguments passed to us, indicating the names that we want to use for them.

In this case, we're specifying that two parameters will be passed to our function. Both are **WORDs**, and we'll refer to them as **VALUE1** and **VALUE2**. Other variable types that we could use instead of WORD here include **BYTE**, **DWORD** (for double word), and **QWORD** (quad word). The assembler will generate the correct expression (i.e., a memory reference) to take these parameters off the stack whenever we refer to **VALUE1** or **VALUE2** from now on. That means that the rest of our procedure looks like this:

```
        .MODEL   SMALL, C

        .CODE
             PUBLIC   SUMMER              ;For C Interface
        SUMMER PROC NEAR USES DI SI, VALUE1:WORD, VALUE2:WORD

  →         MOV      AX, VALUE1
  →         ADD      AX, VALUE2

            RET
        SUMMER ENDP
            END
```

That's all there is to it. After we give names to the parameters passed to us, we can simply use those names in our program. In other words, picking parameters off the stack this way is easy. The assembler handles the details for us. (Note that although we specified that we were using **SI** and **DI**, that specification was for demonstration purposes only. We did not in fact use them in our program, so we did not have to save them.)

How about Data?

That approach is fine if, like **SUMMER( )**, we don't have any data in our linked-in functions. If we do, however, we can use one of two approaches. We can bury the data in the code segment as we did in **file 2** above:

        File 2

```
 PUBLIC   SUB_PRINT
 .MODEL SMALL
 .CODE
 SUB_PRINT         PROC NEAR
         JMP       GO
         ALL_OK  DB "Hello, world.$"   ←
 GO:     MOV       DX,OFFSET ALL_OK
         MOV       AH,9
         INT       21H
         RET
 SUB_PRINT         ENDP
        END
```

In that case, we jumped over the data. However, that is a little clumsy, and it limits us to the use of the code segment for our data. On the other hand, Microsoft or Turbo C programs use a data segment, and we can put our data into their data segment with the **.DATA** directive. When linked this way, all the data goes into the same area.

For example, let's assume that we want to link in a function written in assembly language which we can call **PRINT( )**. This function just prints "Hello, world.", and here's how the C code might look:

```
extern PRINT();

main()
{
    PRINT();

    return(0);
}
```

This is what the assembly language function PRINT might look like. We're using two segments now, one for code and one for the data used in **PRINT:**

```
PUBLIC   PRINT
.MODEL SMALL, C
.DATA                                    ←
    ALL_OK  DB "Hello, world.$"

.CODE                                    ←
PRINT  PROC     NEAR
    MOV     DX, OFFSET ALL_OK
    MOV     AH,9
    INT     21H
    RET
PRINT  ENDP
    END
```

We've used the **.DATA** directive to place our data in the data segment of the final .EXE file. Beyond that, nothing special is required; we just assemble, compile, and link as before (under both Microsoft or Turbo C), and the program runs correctly. That's the way we store data in the data segment; we just use the .DATA segment directive, and then refer to our data as normal.

Let's try another example. Here we can set up a function named **MAX( )**, which just returns the maximum of two integers. This is what the C code might look like:

```
extern MAX(int x, int y);

main()
{
    int a = 12, b = 27;

    printf("The larger of %d and %d is %d", a, b, MAX(a, b));

    return(0);
}
```

And the corresponding assembly language procedure might look like this:

```
.MODEL   SMALL, C

.DATA
    INT1    DW      0         ←
    INT2    DW      0         ←

.CODE
        PUBLIC   MAX
MAX     PROC NEAR USES BX, PARAM1:WORD, PARAM2:WORD

    MOV     AX, PARAM1
    MOV     INT1, AX
    MOV     AX, PARAM2
    MOV     INT2, AX

    MOV     AX, INT1
    CMP     AX, INT2
    JA      OVER
    MOV     AX, INT2

OVER:   RET
MAX     ENDP
    END
```

Here we're moving integers in and out of the data segment. We refer to the two parameters passed to us as **PARAM1** and **PARAM2**, then we load them into the data segment variables **INT1** and **INT2** like this:

```
.MODEL   SMALL, C

.DATA
    INT1    DW      0
    INT2    DW      0
```

```
        .CODE
                PUBLIC  MAX
        MAX     PROC NEAR USES BX, PARAM1:WORD, PARAM2:WORD

                MOV     AX, PARAM1
  →             MOV     INT1, AX
                MOV     AX, PARAM2
  →             MOV     INT2, AX

                MOV     AX, INT1
                CMP     AX, INT2
                JA      OVER
                MOV     AX, INT2

        OVER:   RET
        MAX     ENDP
            END
```

Next, we just compare those two variables and return the larger one in **AX**. In other words, using data is easy. All we have to do is to put it into the data segment, and then we use it as we have been using data in our previous assembly language programs. And that's it. That's all there is to linking assembly language procedures into our programs as C functions. We've made the C to assembly language connection.

Linking C into Assembly Language

Besides linking assembly language subroutines into C, we can go the other way too. Let's develop an example to print out our phrase "Hello, world." using **printf( )**, but calling it from an assembly language program.

As it turns out, most C functions expect some initialization to have been done before they are called. That means that we will have to make a preliminary call to C before taking over in our assembly language program. We'll set up a main C routine:

```
main()
{
    real_main();

    return(0);
}
```

This program just calls **real_main( )**, the assembly language program that makes up the real main module. Here's what **REALMAIN.ASM** looks like. Note that we push the parameters we want to pass (i.e., pointers to the format string and the message we want to print) onto the stack ourselves:

```
        .MODEL SMALL, C
            PUBLIC real_main
            EXTRN  printf:NEAR

        .DATA
            MSG DB "Hello, world.",0
            FORMAT_STRING DB "%s",0

        .CODE
            real_main PROC NEAR
→               MOV     AX, OFFSET MSG
→               PUSH    AX
→               MOV     AX, OFFSET FORMAT_STRING
→               PUSH    AX
→               CALL    printf
                POP     BX
                POP     BX

                RET
            real_main ENDP
        END
```

Note also that we do something very important after the call to **printf( )**: We pop the stack twice. That is because, in C, the calling procedure is responsible for resetting the stack after a call was made. In other words, we pushed two words, pointers to **MSG** and **FORMAT_STRING**, before calling **printf( )**. After the call, those words were still on the stack, and we remove them by popping them harmlessly into the **BX** register (where they're ignored).

In order to use **printf( )** like this, we first have to link it in. And, since C is case-sensitive, we have to use lower case letters, as well as declaring it **EXTRN**:

```
        .MODEL SMALL, C
            PUBLIC real_main
→           EXTRN  printf:NEAR

        .DATA
            MSG DB "Hello, world.",0
            FORMAT_STRING DB "%s",0
```

```
        .CODE
            real_main PROC NEAR
                MOV    AX, OFFSET MSG
                PUSH   AX
                MOV    AX, OFFSET FORMAT_STRING
                PUSH   AX
  →             CALL   printf
                POP    BX
                POP    BX

                RET
            real_main ENDP
        END
```

As mentioned, the assembler normally converts all labels to capital letters. If we did nothing else, we wouldn't find **printf( )** in the C library when we linked. However, we tell the assembler not to convert the labels with the **-mx** switch:

```
    E:\>masm -mx realmain;
```

After we compile the C module, which we might name **my_func.c**, we can link the files together. To pick up the function **printf( )**, we have to link in the library of small model C functions (under Microsoft C, for example, that is called **slibce.lib**):

```
    E:\>link my_func+realmain

    Microsoft (R) QuickC Linker  Version 4.06
    Copyright (C) Microsoft Corp 1984-1989.  All rights reserved.

    Run File [MY_FUNC.EXE]:
    List File [NUL.MAP]:
    Libraries [.LIB]:slibce.lib     ←
```

And now we can run it:

```
    E:\>my_func
    Hello, world.
```

It works. Now we can go both ways. In other words, we could already write C library functions in assembly language. Now we can also *use* C library functions from our assembly language programs. These techniques, of course, take practice. However, if speed and size are any issue, they can be invaluable.

We've established the C to assembly language connection in this chapter. In the next chapter, we will start augmenting our assembly language knowledge by adding some useful routines, routines which were specially designed for the C programmer.

Assembly Language Routines for C Programmers

Now that we've gotten a grip both on the basics of assembly language and how to connect it to C, we're going to see some assembly language routines of interest to the C programmer in this chapter. In other words, we'll see what assembly language is good for. You can also build **libraries** of your assembly language routines, and we'll see how to do that here.

Some Fast Math

The largest capacity of any register in the PC is 16 bits (unless you have a 80386 or 80486), which can hold unsigned numbers up to 65,535. In other words, 16 bits will only give us mathematical accuracy to four decimal places. This level of accuracy is far too low for most programs. If, on the other hand, we were to use two words, 32 bits, we could handle numbers up to 4,294,967,299. Since this is the kind of accuracy that makes computers useful, we'll work with some 32-bit math in this chapter.

The 80×86 has provisions for handling 32 bits in both addition and subtraction. Even multiplication can be handled by breaking the number into partial products, and we will do that below. Division, though, will be more difficult. There is no easy way to break a division operation up into smaller sections.

481

Instead, when we come to high precision division, we'll develop a fast bit-by-bit algorithm.

High Precision Adding

If we wanted to add the number held in **DX:AX** to the number held in **BX:CX**, and if both were unsigned (or could be made so by finding their two's complements), we might use these instructions:

```
ADD     AX, CX          [Add DX:AX + BX:CX]
ADC     DX, BX
JC      ERROR
```

We first add the lower 16 bits of both numbers, held in **AX** and **CX**. The result is stored in **AX**. If this answer is too large to hold in 16 bits, there will be a carry, and the **carry flag** will be set. To include that carry in the subsequent addition of the top 16 bits, we use the **Add with Carry instruction**, **ADC**:

```
        ADD     AX, CX          [Add DX:AX + BX:CX]
  →     ADC     DX, BX
        JC      ERROR
```

ADC includes the carry from the first addition, if there was one, in the second addition. The final result is stored in **DX:AX**. In this calculation, we are not prepared for answers longer than 32 bits (although that can be handled with an additional **ADC** to as many stages as you desire), so if there was a carry after the second addition, we jump to a location marked **ERROR** using **JC**, the jump if carry flag set instruction.

High Precision Subtracting

Subtraction follows this plan as well. If we subtract a big number from a small one, we have to borrow from higher order places. The 80x86's designers included the **SBB**, **Subtract with Borrow**, instruction for expressly this use:

```
        SUB     AX, CX          [Sub DX:AX - BX:CX]
   →    SBB     DX, BX
        JC      ERROR
```

Here we are figuring out what **DX:AX - BX:CX** is. Again, if there is a carry after the **SBB** instruction, we consider it an error and jump to **ERROR**.

High Precision Multiplying

The **MUL** instruction requires us to use the **AX** register. If we execute the instruction MUL BX, the 80×86 multiplies **AX** by **BX** and leaves the 32-bit result in **DX:AX**. If we wanted to multiply **AX:DX** by **BX:CX**, we must be prepared for a 64 bit result, using up all our registers.

In this case, it would be better to use memory locations. We could, for instance, multiply the number **Y1:Y0**, held in 16-bit words we've named Y1 and **Y0**, by the number held in locations **Z1:Z0**. And we could store our result in four memory locations as, say, **A:B:C:D**. To do that we might use this code:

```
        MOV     B, 0
        MOV     A, 0
        MOV     AX, Z0
        MUL     Y0
        MOV     D, AX
        MOV     C, DX
        MOV     AX, Z0
        MUL     Y1
        ADD     C, AX
        ADC     B, DX
        ADC     A, 0
        MOV     AX, Z1
        MUL     Y0
        ADD     C, AX
        ADC     B, DX
        ADC     A, 0
        MOV     AX, Z1
        MUL     Y1
        ADD     B, AX
        ADC     A, DX
```

All it does is this calculation:

$$
\begin{array}{r}
Y1 \ : \ Y0 \\
\times \ \ Z1 \ : \ Z0 \\
\hline
Z0*Y0 \\
+ \quad Z0*Y1 \\
+ \quad Z1*Y0 \\
+ \quad Z1*Y1 \\
\hline
2^{32} \, Z1*Y1 + 2^{16} \, Z0*Y1 + 2^{16} \, Z1*Y0 + Z0*Y0
\end{array}
$$

The algorithm here is nothing more than long multiplication. On occasions, however, multiplying with this kind of accuracy is necessary. To use this algorithm, just set aside space for your data like this:

```
Y1        DW  0
Y0        DW  0
Z1        DW  0
Z0        DW  0
A         DW  0
B         DW  0
C         DW  0
D         DW  0
```

Then load your 32-bit multiplicands into **Y1:Y0** (i.e., high word in **Y1**; low word in **Y0**) and **Z1:Z0**, and execute the above algorithm. The result of **Y1:Y0** $\times$ **Z1:Z0** will be left in **A:B:C:D**.

High Precision Dividing

In division, unfortunately, our path is not as smooth. In all three of the previous cases we were able to divide our calculations into sub-parts and then join the results together from those parts. Unfortunately, division cannot be dissected that way. We are reduced to dividing on a bit-by-bit level if we want 32-bit accuracy. In this case, we will use an actual hardware divide algorithm. This algorithm, usually expressed in cryptic computer design language, is not the fastest available, but it is at least intelligible using the model of long division, and it expresses a wonderful economy in the use of registers that is something of an art in itself.

As we have seen, the 80×86 has an internal **DIV** instruction that will divide 32 bits (held in the two registers **DX:AX**) by a 16 bit number (`DIV BX`, which divides **DX:AX** by **BX**). This process returns a 16-bit result and a 16-bit remainder. However, we want to maintain our 32-bit accuracy, so let's develop a bit-by-bit divide algorithm that divides a 64 number by a 32-bit number, giving powerful 32-bit results and remainders.

To refresh our memories concerning long division, let's work through a short example. Here we will divide 14 by 6. Our answer will come out in whole numbers as an answer and a remainder (as will all integer division in the 80×86). In particular, 14/6 will yield an answer of 2 and a remainder of 2. We start here:

$$A \ \overline{| \ B} \quad \longrightarrow \quad 6 \ \overline{| \ 14} \quad \longrightarrow \quad 0110 \ \overline{| \ 1110}$$

To keep the example short we'll only use four bits and leave using 64 up to the imagination. Our first move is to compare 6, that is, 0110B, against progressively more of the number being divided (B above):

$$0110 \ \overline{| \ 1 \ 1 \ 1 \ 0}$$
$$\uparrow$$

Since 0110B is bigger than 1, we place a 0 above it and subtract 0 from it:

$$0110 \ \overline{| \ \begin{matrix} 0 \ \longleftarrow \\ 1 \ 1 \ 1 \ 0 \\ \underline{0} \\ 1 \end{matrix}}$$

Then we bring down the next digit of B:

$$0110 \ \overline{| \ \begin{matrix} 0 \\ 1 \ 1 \ 1 \ 0 \\ \underline{0} \downarrow \\ 1 \ 1 \end{matrix}}$$

We're now comparing **A**, 0110B, against the first two digits of **B**, 11B. Since 0110B is also bigger than 11B we put in another 0 up on top, subtract 0 from 11B and bring down another digit, a 1:

```
        0 0   ←————
0110 | 1 1 1 0
   ⎺  0  |
   ⎺  11 |
      00 ↓
      1 1 1
```

Now we are comparing **A** to the first three digits of **B**, 111, and 0110 goes smoothly into 111 once, so we put a 1 on top, subtract 0110 from 111 and bring down another digit:

```
        0 0 1   ←————
0110 | 1 1 1 0
   ⎺  0  |
   ⎺  11 |
      00 |
   ⎺  1 1 1|
      1 1 0↓
      0 0 1 0
```

Now we have to compare 0110 to what is left on the bottom, 0010. Since 0110 is greater than 0010, another 0 goes on top:

```
        0 0 1 0    Answer
0110 | 1 1 1 0
   ⎺  0
   ⎺  11
      00
   ⎺  1 1 1
      1 1 0
      0 0 1 0
      0 0 0 0
      0 0 1 0    Remainder
```

And this leaves us with a 4-bit answer, 0010B (2) and a 4-bit remainder, 0010B (also 2). To make an algorithm out of this, we have to mimic what we did at each stage in assembly language. If the problem looked like this:

```
A | B
```

then we would have compared **A** to progressively more and more of **B**, the number being divided. If **A** was bigger than **B**, we would have entered a 0 in the answer, but if **A** was smaller than **B**, we would have entered a 1 and subtracted **A**. We kept going until we had done this four times, once for every place in **B**.

Computerizing Our Example

To compare **A** to progressively more of **B**, we can use the **CMP** instruction. All we have to do is to use `CMP AX, BX` where **AX** holds A and **BX** holds B. To get more and more of **B** into **BX**, we can simply shift **B** into it one bit at a time. We'll compare **A** to more and more of **B** as more and more of **B** appears in **BX**. If **A** is bigger than what we have of **B**, we put 0 in the answer. If **A** is smaller, then we subtract **B** - **A** and put a 1 into the answer. In other words, if we start off with **AX**, **BX**, and **CX** loaded like this for 14/6 (and we treat them as only 4-bit registers),

AX=6	BX	CX=14
0110	0000	1110

then we would start by shifting the first digit into **BX** this way:

AX=6	BX	CX=14
0110	0001	← 110

Since we've got a new **BX**, we compare **AX** to it and see immediately that **AX** > **BX**. This means that the first bit of the answer is 0. Our algorithm will not waste any space whatsoever; we can slip this first bit into the newly vacated rightmost bit of **CX**. When we are all done, the answer will be fully in **CX**:

AX=6	BX	CX=14
0110	0001	110 0 ←
		↑

With the first bit of the answer ready, we shift **CX** again to the left:

```
AX=6         BX          CX=14
----         ----        ----
0110         0011   ←   10 0
                          ↑
```

and again compare **AX** to the new part of **B** we have in **BX**. Since again **AX** > **BX**, another 0 goes into the answer in **CX**:

```
AX=6         BX          CX=14
----         ----        ----
0110         0011        10 00        ←
                           ↑
```

Now we have to get a new value in **BX**, and so we shift **CX** left again:

```
AX=6         BX          CX=14
----         ----        ----
0110         0111   ←   0 00
                          ↑
```

Now when we compare **AX** to **BX**, we have enough bits in **BX** to make **AX** < **BX**. As in our long division example, this means that we subtract **A** (in **AX**) from what we have of **B** (in **BX**) and put a 1 into the answer this way:

```
AX=6         BX          CX=14
----         ----        ----
0110         0111        0 001        ←
           – 0110          ↑
             ----
             0001
```

That leaves a 1 in **BX**:

```
AX=6         BX          CX=14
----         ----        ----
0110         0001        0 001
                          ↑
```

so we shift the final 0 from **CX** into **BX**;

```
AX=6         BX          CX=14
----         ----        ----
0110         0010   ←   001
                         ↑
```

Since 0110 > 10, we have to finish by putting a 0 into **CX**:

AX=6	BX	CX=14
0110	0010	0010 ←
	Remainder	Answer

Now we've done our comparison four times (one for each place), so we're done. The leftover bits of **B** that **A** didn't divide evenly are the remainder, now in **BX**, and the final answer that we built bit by bit is in **CX**. In a direct way, this algorithm has provided a translation of long division into the language of registers and left shifts.

Dividing in Code

To get this into code that you can use, let's suppose that we want to divide **A:B:C:D** by **Z1:Z0**, 64 bits by 32. The actual divison code is relatively small, and here it is:

```
;64 Bit By 32 Bit Division (memory locations A:B:C:D by Z1:Z0)

MOV        COUNT, 64
XOR        AX, AX  ;Going to divide A:B:C:D by BX:CX
XOR        DX, DX  ; End up with quotient in A:B:C:D
MOV        BX, Z1
MOV        CX, Z0
SHIF:
       ...CALL     SHL_BIG ;SHL DX:AX:A:B:C:D by 1 place (96 bits !)
       :  CMP      DX, BX
       :  JB       NOT_YET
       :  JA       HIT
       :  CMP      AX, CX   ;DX = BX, Check AX,CX
       :  JB       NOT_YET
HIT: :  SUB      AX, CX
       :  SBB      DX, BX
       :  ADD      D, 1     ;Put in a 1 since divisor went\
                              into dividend once
NOT_YET:
       :  DEC      COUNT
       :  CMP      COUNT, 0
       :..JNE      SHIF     ;Keep going all 64 times
```

The variable **COUNT** will serve as a loop index. We begin by clearing the registers **AX** and **DX** and loading **BX:CX** with **Z1:Z0**:

```
MOV     COUNT, 64
XOR     AX, AX   ;Going to divide A:B:C:D by BX:CX
XOR     DX, DX   ; End up with quotient in A:B:C:D
MOV     BX, Z1
MOV     CX, Z0
```

XOR AX, AX is a method used by professional programmers to clear the **AX** register, and you can often find it in listings. **AX** may be set to zero with MOV AX, 0, of course, but you often see the instruction XOR AX, AX instead. When you **XOR** a number with itself, all ones are sure to meet ones and all zeroes sure to meet zeros, so the result is zero.

We will gradually shift more and more of **A:B:C:D** into **DX:AX** and compare it to **BX:CX**. As we shift **A:B:C:D** into **DX:AX** we gradually leave zeroes behind in **D**. Every time that **DX:AX** is greater than **BX:CX**, however, we will put a 1 there instead.

The whole process begins by shifting a bit from **A:B:C:D** into **DX:AX**. In other words, we'd like to execute an instruction like, SHL DX:AX:A:B:C:D, 1. In the absence of such a handy instruction, though, we have to make one for ourselves. Ours will be called **SHL_BIG**, and can be found here:

TIP   Note that we can use immediate values when we shift such as SHL DX, 1. We can also use immediate shifts larger than 1 with microprocessors after the 8088 this way: SHL DX, 3. However, we should write our code to work on all machines, including ones that use 8088s, so we'll use **CL** for immediate shifts larger than 1; e.g., MOV CL, 3 SHL DX, CL.

```
;SHL_BIG, a subroutine to shift 96 bits at once

SHL_BIG PROC
        ;Shifts left 96 (!!) bits of DX:AX:A:B:C:D by 1
        PUSH    BX
        PUSH    CX
        MOV     BX, 0
        MOV     CX, 0
        SHL     D, 1                ;Start with rightmost
        ADC     BX, 0               ;Overflow in BX
        SHL     C, 1
        ADC     CX, 0               ;New overflow in CX, old in BX
        ADD     C, BX
        MOV     BX, 0
```

```
        SHL     B, 1
        ADC     BX, 0    ;BX has new overflow, old in CX
        ADD     B, CX
        MOV     CX, 0
        SHL     A, 1
        ADC     CX, 0    ;CX has new overflow, old in BX
        ADD     A, BX
        MOV     BX, 0
        SHL     AX, 1
        ADC     BX, 0    ;BX has new overflow, old in CX
        ADD     AX, CX
        SHL     DX, 1    ;Disregard overflow here
        ADD     DX, BX
        POP     CX
        POP     BX
        RET
SHL_BIG ENDP
```

When we shift a 16-bit word to the left one place and end up shifting a 1 out
to the left, the carry bit gets set. **SHL_BIG** follows all those carries up the line
with **ADC**, Add with Carry, adding the carry into successive words, and that
accounts for the majority of its length.

After we've shifted the first part of **A:B:C:D** into **DX:AX**, we have to compare
it to the number we're dividing by, BX:CX. It would be nice to have a CMP
DX:AX, BX:CX instruction here. Instead, we'll have to do the same thing 16
bits at a time, starting with the highest bits.

DX>BX: If **DX** is greater than **BX**, then **DX:AX** is definitely greater than
BX:CX and we have a "hit," so we move 1 into **A:B:C:D**.

DX<BX: If **DX** is less than **BX**, then **DX:AX** is less than **BX:CX**, and we will
leave the 0 that was shifted into the end.

DX=BX: If, though, **DX** equals **BX**, then we must check **AX** and **CX**. The entire
process goes this way:

```
SHIF:   CALL    SHL_BIG          ;SHL DX:AX:A:B:C:D by 1 place (96 bits !)
  →             CMP     DX, BX
                JB      NOT_YET
                JA      HIT
  →             CMP     AX, CX   ;DX = BX, Check AX,CX
                JB      NOT_YET
```

```
HIT:      SUB      AX, CX
          SBB      DX, BX
          ADD      D,1    ;Put in a 1 since divisor went into\
                                dividend once
NOT_YET: [Shift more of A:B:C:D into DX:AX]
```

Notice the use of two conditional jumps, one right after the other:

```
SHIF:     CALL     SHL_BIG ;SHL DX:AX:A:B:C:D by 1 place (96 bits !)
          CMP      DX, BX
→         JB       NOT_YET
→         JA       HIT
                   :
```

Since conditional jumps do not affect the flags that are set, this will work (check your assembler's documentation to learn which instructions affect which flags). If the part we have of **A:B:C:D** is bigger than what we're dividing by, we want to subtract it by subtracting **DX:AX** from **BX:CX**. This is done at the label **HIT**:

```
HIT:   SUB      AX, CX
SBB    DX, BX
ADD    D, 1     ;Put in a 1 since divisor went into dividend once
```

And we also put a 1 into the end of **A:B:C:D**. After we've either let the shifted-in 0 stand or put in a 1, we have to go back and shift more of the number we're dividing into **DX:AX** (and decrement the count using the **DEC** instruction):

```
SHIF:
    ...[Shift to the left and compare]
    :      :
    :      :
    :  DEC     COUNT
    :  CMP     COUNT, 0
    :..JNE     SHIF     ;Keep going all 64 times
```

And that's it. We're done. When you use this algorithm, load the 64-bit number to divide into **A:B:C:D**, load the number to divide it by into **Z1:Z0**. The quotient will be left in **A:B:C:D**, and the remainder in **Z1:Z0**.

That's it for our heavy math. We've gone through addition, subtraction, multiplication, and now division. Let's take a look at some low-level graphics now.

For example, we can set some pixels on the screen directly from assembly language.

Pixel Graphics in Assembly Language

Regrettably, there is no real graphics support in assembly language. You cannot draw ellipses with an easy call, for example. What services there are are under INT 10H (see the appendix at the end of the book), and all they can do is turn a pixel on the screen on. However, they can do that much faster than C can, and we can even do it ourselves much faster than INT 10H can if we know something about the way the video buffer is set up. If you do all your graphics work on such a low level, this will save you a lot of time. Let's take a look at the way the CGA buffer is set up as an example.

In high-resolution CGA mode, 640×200 pixels, you can only choose to turn a pixel on or off, 0 or 1. The computer only needs to save one bit per pixel in this case. Since there are 200 lines down (on graphics monitors characters are 8 scan lines high, and 8×25 lines = 200) and 640 columns across, there are $640 \times 200 = 128,000$ bits needed. This makes 16,000 bytes, rounded up in the PC's graphics video buffer to 16K.

In medium resolution, 320×200, we can specify one of four colors for each pixel, so we need two bits to hold the possible values for each pixel. Since there are only half as many pixels (320 across versus 640 across), but each needs twice as many bits, we still use the same size video buffer, 16K.

In high resolution mode, it seems natural that if you wanted to turn the pixel on at location (0, 0), the top left corner of the screen, you would set the first bit in the video buffer to 1. That is actually how it works. To turn the next pixel in the top row (row 0) on, you would set the next bit to 1, and so forth to the end of the first line on the screen, the first 640 pixels (numbers 0 – 639).

It also seems natural that if you wanted to turn on the first pixel of the second row (row 1), you would set bit 640 in the video buffer to 1, since the first line goes from 0 to 639. Unfortunately, that is not how it works.

Instead, the graphics video buffer is divided into two blocks of 8K each. The first block, starting at location B800:0000, holds the even scan lines on the screen; the second block, starting at B800:2000, holds the odd scan lines. This is because the CGA video controller scans over all the even lines on the screen first, and then all the odd ones. To facilitate its operation, we give it the bits in the order needed. This is an added complication for any program; now it has to split up its image between two blocks in memory.

TIP   In practice this is not very hard if you have a subroutine to put pixels on the screen that keeps track of which block they go into, or if you use INT 10H, Service 12, which also sets pixels on the screen.

The scheme in medium resolution is similar, but here there can be four colors, not just two. Four colors demand two bits, so every two bits in the screen buffer can be grouped together into one pixel. Since there are only one-half as many pixels on a line, but twice as many bits per pixel, there are the same number of memory bits corresponding to each screen line, 640.

The Program PUT_PIXEL

As an example of some fairly tight code, here's a small program, **PUT_PIXEL**, that will turn high resolution CGA pixels on. Just supply the screen row (0 – 199) of the pixel in **DX** and its column (0 – 639) in **CX**:

```
PUT_PIXEL       PROC
        ;SUPPLY DX=ROW,CX=COLUMN. ASSUMES ES=B800H and screen in High
        ; Resolution mode (Use INT 10H Service 0).
        XOR     BX, BX
        SHR     DX, 1
        JNC     CALC
        ADD     BX, 8*1024
CALC:   MOV     AX, DX          ;Get 80*DX
        SHL     DX, 1
        SHL     DX, 1
        ADD     DX, AX
        MOV     AX, CX
        MOV     CL, 4
        SHL     DX, CL          ;DX now multiplied by 80 (16*5)
        ADD     BX, DX          ;Add to index
        MOV     DX, AX
        AND     DX, 7           ;Get X3 into DX
        MOV     CL, 3
        SHR     AX, CL          ;CX/8
        ADD     BX, AX          ;Find byte along row
        NEG     DL
```

```
        ADD     DL, 7
        MOV     CL, DL          ;Get bit to turn on
        MOV     AL, 1
        SHL     AL, CL
        OR      ES:[BX], AL
        RET
PUT_PIXEL       ENDP
```

PUT_PIXEL is about three times as fast as the equivalent INT 10H service call. If you really want to work with graphics on the PC, you should know how to address individual pixels on the screen; for that reason we'll work through **PUT_PIXEL** in a little detail. This example will also give us some experience with code written expressly for speed.

Let's start immediately. **PUT_PIXEL**'s first job is to determine which 8K block the pixel goes into, the first or the second one. The first 8K of the video buffer holds screen lines 0, 2, 4, 6, 8, etc.; the second 8K holds screen lines 1, 3, 5, 7, 9; etc. (see Table 13-1).

The pixel's screen coordinates are passed to **PUT_PIXEL** in **DX** (= screen row, 0 — 199) and **CX** (= screen column, 0 — 639). That means that if **DX** is even, the pixel is in the first block; if odd, in the second. Let's use [**BX**] to point to the pixel's location in the video buffer. To start **PUT_PIXEL**, then, we can place an offset of 0 into **BX** if the pixel is in the first 8K block, and an offset of 8K if it is in the second. We can determine which block the pixel is in by checking the last bit of **DX** to see if the screen row is odd or even. It turns out that when we shift **DX** right by one place, that last bit is placed into the carry flag, and we can check its value with **JNC**, **Jump if No Carry**:

Screen Row # (in DX)	First or Second 8K	Line inside 8K Block
0	1	0
1	2	0
2	1	1
3	2	1
4	1	2

Table 13-1. Video Buffer 8K Blocks.

```
       PUT_PIXEL        PROC
                        ;SUPPLY DX=ROW,CX=COLUMN.  ASSUMES ES=B800H
                        XOR     BX, BX
    →                   SHR     DX, 1
    →                   JNC     CALC
    →                   ADD     BX, 8*1024
       CALC:   MOV      AX, DX              ;Get 80*DX        ←
```

Now we've decided which 8K block the pixel is in (and placed the offset of that block, 0 or 8K, into **BX**). Let's say that it was the first one:

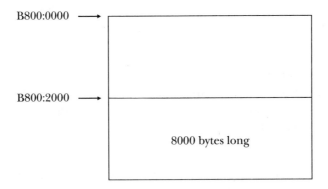

B800:0000 ⟶

B800:2000 ⟶

8000 bytes long

The next job is to find the pixel's row in that block. To do that, we just divide the pixel's screen row (the number originally passed in **DX**) by two and disregard the remainder (e.g., a pixel in screen row 0 will be in memory row 0 of its 8K block, a pixel in screen row 3 will be in memory row 1 of its 8K block, and so on as outlined above). Note that dividing by two is the same as shifting **DX** to the right once, which we've already done, so **DX** already holds the pixel's row number in the correct 8K block.

To find the byte offset of that row from the beginning of its 8K block, we just have to multiply it by 640 bits per row / 8 bits per byte = 80 bytes per row. In other words, multiplying the value now in **DX** (the pixel's row number in its 8K block) by 80 (the number of bytes per row) gives us the byte offset of the pixel's row from the beginning of its block:

B800:0000 →

B800:(SHR DX,1)×80 →

B800:2000 →

```
. . . . . . . . . . . 80 Bytes . . . . . . . . . . .
. . . . . . . . . . . 80 Bytes . . . . . . . . . . .
. . . . . . . . . . 80 Bytes . . . . . . . . . . .



                   8000 bytes long
```

DX=Row Number on Screen.
Low Bit(DX) → 8K Block Number
SHR DX,1=Row Number in its 8K Block.
(SHR DX,1)x80=Offset of correct line in 8K Block.

Here, then, is how we multiply **DX** by by 80 and add the result to **BX** (so that **BX** now points to the beginning of the pixel's row in memory):

TIP   The 80×86 has a multiply instruction, of course, but it is very slow. We should try to avoid using it when speed is of the essence, as it is here. To multiply by 80, we could just multiply by 5 and then by 16, or, even better, we could multiply **DX** by 4, add **DX** to it again to make five times, and then multiply by 16. Multiplying by powers of two, of course, is done by shifting to the left.

```
PUT_PIXEL        PROC
          ;SUPPLY DX=ROW,CX=COLUMN. ASSUMES ES=B800H and screen
          ;in High Resolution mode (Use INT 10H Service 0).
          XOR     BX, BX
          SHR     DX, 1
          JNC     CALC
          ADD     BX, 8*1024
CALC:     MOV     AX, DX    ←        ;Get 80*DX
          SHL     DX, 1     ←
          SHL     DX, 1     ←
          ADD     DX, AX    ←
          MOV     AX, CX    ←
          MOV     CL, 4     ←
          SHL     DX, CL    ←        ;DX now multiplied by 80 (16*5)
          ADD     BX, DX    ←        ;Add to index
```

BX now holds the offset of the pixel's row in memory. Next, we have to find which individual byte in the row to work on, and that depends on the column required, 0 – 639, which was passed in **CX**. Since each of these 640 places is a bit, we have to divide **CX** by 8 to get a byte offset which we add to **BX**:

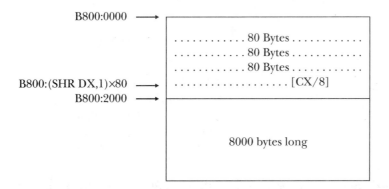

After we add **CX** / 8 (the offset of the pixel's byte in its row) to **BX** (the offset of the row itself from the beginning of the screen segment, B800), **BX** will point to the byte which holds the pixel in memory. Here's how that looks in code:

```
PUT_PIXEL         PROC
                  ;SUPPLY DX=ROW,CX=COLUMN. ASSUMES ES=B800H and
                  ; screen in High Resolution mode (Use INT 10H
                  ; Service 0).
                  XOR     BX, BX
                  SHR     DX, 1
                  JNC     CALC
                  ADD     BX, 8*1024
        CALC:     MOV     AX, DX       ;Get 80*DX
                  SHL     DX, 1
                  SHL     DX, 1
                  ADD     DX, AX
                  MOV     AX, CX
                  MOV     CL, 4
                  SHL     DX, CL       ;DX now multiplied by 80 (16*5)
                  ADD     BX, DX       ;Add to index
  →               MOV     DX, AX
                  AND     DX, 7        ;Get X3 into DX
  →               MOV     CL, 3
  →               SHR     AX, CL       ;CX/8
  →               ADD     BX, AX       ;Find byte along row
```

At the same time, we can calculate which bit in that byte to turn on. If the screen column number in **CX** (which can range from 0 to 639) was 0, we would want to turn on the leftmost bit of the 0th byte of that line, bit 7. In general, the bit we want to turn on is **7 - (CX % 8)**, where **CX % 8** is the remainder of dividing **CX** by 8. In fact, **CX % 8** is just **AND(CX, 7)**, where **AND** is the 80×86 bitwise **AND** instruction (just like the C version, &). That means that we want bit number **7 - AND(CL, 7)** in the byte at [**BX**].

To work on that bit, we put a 1 into, say, **AL** and shift it left **7 - AND(CL, 7)** times, then **OR** the result with whatever byte is in the screen buffer at location [**BX**]. And that, finally, turns the pixel on. It's pretty clear that working with graphics directly in the PC is not a job that's especially easy. The whole procedure may be seen in Listing 13-1.

Listing 13-1. CGA_PIXEL — Turns a CEGA Pixel On.

```
PUT_PIXEL         PROC
                  ;SUPPLY DX=ROW,CX=COLUMN. ASSUMES ES=B800H and
                  ; screen in High Resolution mode (Use INT 10H
                  ; Service 0).
                  XOR     BX,BX
                  SHR     DX,1
                  JNC     CALC
                  ADD     BX,8*1024
        CALC:     MOV     AX,DX          ;GET 80*DX
                  SHL     DX,1
                  SHL     DX,1
                  ADD     DX,AX
                  MOV     AX,CX
                  MOV     CL,4
                  SHL     DX,CL          ;DX now multiplied by 80 (16*5)
                  ADD     BX,DX          ;Add to index
                  MOV     DX,AX
    →             AND     DX,7           ;Get X3 into DX
                  MOV     CL,3
                  SHR     AX,CL          ;CX/8
                  ADD     BX,AX          ;Find byte along row
    →             NEG     DL
    →             ADD     DL,7
    →             MOV     CL,DL          ;Get bit to turn on
                  MOV     AL,1
                  SHL     AL,CL
                  OR      ES:[BX],AL
                  RET
        PUT_PIXEL         ENDP
```

Note that **PUT_PIXEL** requires **ES** to already have a value of B800H in it. That's because **PUT_PIXEL** uses the **ES** segment, and it would slow the program down to have to load **ES** with B800H (the segment address of the CGA video buffer) every time it was called to turn a pixel on. However, to load segment registers, we cannot simply say:

```
MOV    ES, B800H
```

Instead, we have to go through the intermediate step of loading a direct value into a general purpose register like **AX**:

```
MOV    AX, B800H MOV    ES, AX
```

TIP   In 80286 and later microprocessors, you can push immediate values, so this is often accomplished this way: `PUSH B800H, POP ES`. These instructions take up less memory and execute faster.

This is just a fact of the 80×86's internal architecture. The same is true of any segment register: None of them may be loaded with immediate values. In this case, use these two lines in your program and leave **ES** set to that value while you work with **PUT_PIXEL**.

We can also do for the 16-color EGA modes what **PUT_PIXEL** does for the two-color CGA high resolution mode. However, developing that procedure is considerably more complex (we have to allow for a color value, 0 – 15, in the **BX** register, and other details). Even so, that shouldn't deter you from actually using such a routine, so we present **EGA_PIXEL** in Listing 13-2, ready for you to use.

Listing 13-2.   EGA_PIXEL — Turns an EGA Pixel On.

```
            AND_OR_REG      EQU   3CEH       ;Like #define in C.
            PLANE_REG       EQU   3C4H

EGA_PIXEL PROC
        ;SUPPLY BX=COLOR VALUE, DX=ROW, CX=COLUMN. ASSUMES ES=A0000H

            PUSH    AX
            PUSH    BX
            PUSH    CX
            PUSH    DX
            XOR     DI, DI
```

Listing 13-2. *(continued)*

```
        MOV     AX, DX    ;GET 80*DX
        SHL     DX, 1
        SHL     DX, 1
        ADD     DX, AX
        MOV     AX, CX
        MOV     CL, 4
        SHL     DX, CL    ;DX now multiplied by 80 (16*5)
        PUSH    DX        ;Put into index.
        POP     DI
        MOV     DX, AX    ;Get column no.
        AND     DX, 7     ;Find col. no. MOD 7
        MOV     CL, 3
        SHR     AX, CL    ;CX/8
        ADD     DI, AX    ;DI now holds byte addr in video buffer.
        NEG     DL
        ADD     DL, 7
        MOV     CL, DL    ;Get bit to turn on.
        MOV     AL, 1
        SHL     AL, CL
        MOV     CL, AL    ;Bit set in CL is bit to turn on (for ORing).
        MOV     CH, 0FFH
        SUB     CH, CL    ;CH has same bit turned off (for ANDing).

BLUE:   MOV     DX, PLANE_REG   ;Enable plane 0 (blue)
        MOV     AH, 1           ;Plane 0
        MOV     AL, 2
        OUT     DX, AX

        TEST    BX, 1
        JZ      BLU_OFF

BLU_ON: MOV     DX, AND_OR_REG          ;Select OR function
        MOV     AH, 16
        MOV     AL, 3
        OUT     DX, AX

        OR      BYTE PTR ES:[DI], 0FFH  ;Load latch
        MOV     BYTE PTR ES:[DI], CL    ;Turn bit on.
        JMP     SHORT GREEN

BLU_OFF:MOV     DX, AND_OR_REG          ;Select AND function
        MOV     AH, 8
        MOV     AL, 3
        OUT     DX, AX
```

(continued)

Listing 13-2. *(continued)*

```
                OR      BYTE PTR ES:[DI], 0FFH    ;Load latch
                MOV     BYTE PTR ES:[DI], CH      ;Turn bit off.

      GREEN:    MOV     DX, PLANE_REG    ;Enable plane 1 (green)
                MOV     AH, 2               ;Plane 1
                MOV     AL, 2
                OUT     DX, AX

                TEST    BX, 2
                JZ      GRN_OFF

      GRN_ON:   MOV     DX, AND_OR_REG           ;Select OR function
                MOV     AH, 16
                MOV     AL, 3
                OUT     DX, AX

                OR      BYTE PTR ES:[DI], 0FFH    ;Load latch
                MOV     BYTE PTR ES:[DI], CL      ;Turn bit on.
                JMP     SHORT RED

      GRN_OFF:  MOV     DX, AND_OR_REG           ;Select AND function
                MOV     AH, 8
                MOV     AL, 3
                OUT     DX, AX

                OR      BYTE PTR ES:[DI], 0FFH    ;Load latch
                MOV     BYTE PTR ES:[DI], CH      ;Turn bit off.

      RED:      MOV     DX, PLANE_REG    ;Enable plane 2 (red)
                MOV     AH, 4               ;Plane 2
                MOV     AL, 2
                OUT     DX, AX

                TEST    BX, 4
                JZ      RED_OFF

      RED_ON:   MOV     DX, AND_OR_REG           ;Select OR function
                MOV     AH, 16
                MOV     AL, 3
                OUT     DX, AX

                OR      BYTE PTR ES:[DI], 0FFH    ;Load latch
                MOV     BYTE PTR ES:[DI], CL      ;Turn bit on.
                JMP     SHORT INTENSE

      RED_OFF:  MOV     DX, AND_OR_REG           ;Select AND function
                MOV     AH, 8
```

Listing 13-2. *(continued)*

```
            MOV     AL, 3
            OUT     DX, AX

            OR      BYTE PTR ES:[DI], 0FFH    ;Load latch
            MOV     BYTE PTR ES:[DI], CH      ;Turn bit off.

INTENSE:MOV     DX, PLANE_REG    ;Enable plane 3 (intensity)
            MOV     AH, 8                     ;Plane 3
            MOV     AL, 2
            OUT     DX, AX

            TEST    BX, 8
            JZ      INT_OFF

INT_ON: MOV     DX, AND_OR_REG            ;Select OR function
            MOV     AH, 16
            MOV     AL, 3
            OUT     DX, AX

            OR      BYTE PTR ES:[DI], 0FFH    ;Load latch
            MOV     BYTE PTR ES:[DI], CL      ;Turn bit on.
            JMP     SHORT DONE

INT_OFF:MOV     DX, AND_OR_REG            ;Select AND function
            MOV     AH, 8
            MOV     AL, 3
            OUT     DX, AX

            OR      BYTE PTR ES:[DI], 0FFH    ;Load latch
            MOV     BYTE PTR ES:[DI], CH      ;Turn bit off.

DONE:   POP     DX
            POP     CX
            POP     BX
            POP     AX
            RET
EGA_PIXEL ENDP
```

Let's turn now from turning pixels on to a way of making our assembly language routines easier to use and easier to link into our C programs. In particular, we will cover the use of libraries next. This method of organizing our assembly language routines will be, appropriately, our final assembly language topic.

How to Create Assembly Language Libraries

If you work with many files, there comes a point where the use of libraries is almost necessary. Once you develop routines, you usually want to forget them and have them automatically linked in. That's the idea of a library. When we link .OBJ files, the whole thing becomes part of the .EXE file (stripped of the .OBJ file header). When we link in a library, however, the linker looks for **unresolved externals** (that is, labels that have been declared **EXTRN** but not yet found in an .OBJ file) and takes only those it needs. Although the library could contain a thousand commonly used procedures, only the ones that the linker needs to complete your file will be taken.

We can create such libraries with the program LIB.EXE. If we take the two files below, for example, then we can start by making a library out of the second file, which holds the procedure **PRINT**.

```
———————— File 1 ————————
.MODEL   SMALL
         EXTRN    PRINT:NEAR
.CODE
         ORG      100H

PROG     PROC     NEAR
         CALL     PRINT
         INT      20H
PROG     ENDP

         END      PROG

———————— File 2 ————————
.MODEL SMALL
.CODE
         PUBLIC   PRINT
         HELLO_MSG  DB "Hello, world.$"

PRINT    PROC     NEAR
         MOV      DX,OFFSET HELLO_MSG
         MOV      AH,9
         INT      21H
         RET
PRINT    ENDP

         END
```

NOTE For our discussion of libraries: if you're using the Turbo or Borland (e.g., Borland C++) series, just substitute TASM for MASM, TLINK for LINK, and TLIB for LIB. All the examples developed here work exactly the same way for Turbo and Borland products.

Let's call this library **PRINT.LIB**; whenever we wanted to use the procedure **PRINT**, all we would have to do is to tell the linker to search **PRINT.LIB**. LINK would then find **PRINT** in this library and link it in. Here's how to take **FILE2.ASM** and make it into the library file **PRINT.LIB**:

```
C:\>MASM FILE2;
Microsoft (R) Macro Assembler Version 5.10
Copyright (C) Microsoft Corp 1981, 1988.  All rights reserved.


  50192 + 31229 Bytes symbol space free

       0 Warning Errors
       0 Severe  Errors


C:\>LIB PRINT.LIB+FILE2.OBJ;
Microsoft (R) Library Manager  Version 3.10
Copyright (C) Microsoft Corp 1983-1988.  All rights reserved.
```

The **LIB** command — `LIB PRINT.LIB+FILE2.OBJ;` — creates a library file named **PRINT.LIB**, made up of the second file's object code. Note that we could also have used this command: `LIB PRINT+FILE2;` the **.LIB** extension is assumed for the first file and **.OBJ** for the second (and any following ones).

If **PRINT.LIB** already existed, however, this command would not create it, but would add the code in **FILE2.OBJ** to it. (We'll see this when we add new routines to **PRINT.LIB**.) Now that we have **PRINT.LIB**, let's use it. First, assemble **FILE1.ASM**, and then link it, including **PRINT.LIB** (Turbo and Borland: TLINK FILE1,,,PRINT):

```
C:\>LINK
Microsoft (R) Overlay Linker  Version 3.64
Copyright (C) Microsoft Corp 1983-1988.  All rights reserved.

Object Modules [.OBJ]:FILE1  ← Type this.
Run File [TA.EXE]:
```

```
List File [NUL.MAP]:
Libraries [.LIB]:PRINT          ← And this.

LINK : warning L4021: no stack segment
```

Now we can use EXE2BIN on the created file, FILE1.EXE, and run it:

```
C:\>EXE2BIN FILE1 FILE1.COM

C:\>FILE1
Hello, world.
C:\>
```

Adding a Second Module to Our Library

So far, there has been no advantage to using the library file **PRINT.LIB**. We could just as well have linked in **FILE1.OBJ** entirely. On the other hand, we can also add a second procedure to **PRINT.LIB**. Everything that comes from an .OBJ file and goes into a library is referred to as a **module**. So far, all we have is the **FILE2** module. But we could write another .ASM file, which we might call **file 3**, and which is identical to **FILE2.ASM** except for the name of the procedure and its message:

```
———————— File 3 ————————

.MODEL SMALL
.CODE
        PUBLIC  PRINT2
        HOW_MSG      DB "How are you?$"  ←

PRINT2  PROC    NEAR
        MOV     DX,OFFSET HOW_MSG              ←
        MOV     AH,9
        INT     21H
        RET
PRINT2  ENDP

        END
```

Here we define the procedure **PRINT2**, which prints out `How are you?`. We can assemble this file and add it to the already existing library file **PRINT.LIB** this way:

```
C:\>MASM FILE3;
Microsoft (R) Macro Assembler Version 5.10
Copyright (C) Microsoft Corp 1981, 1988.  All rights reserved.


  50192 + 31229 Bytes symbol space free

      0 Warning Errors
      0 Severe  Errors


C:\>LIB PRINT.LIB+FILE3.OBJ;        ← This adds PRINT2 to
PRINT.LIB
Microsoft (R) Library Manager  Version 3.10
Copyright (C) Microsoft Corp 1983-1988.  All rights reserved.
```

This time, **PRINT.LIB** is not created since it already exists; instead, **FILE3.OBJ** is added to it. Now the **PRINT** library holds both PRINT ("Hello, world.") and PRINT2 ("How are you?"). We can still link **FILE1.OBJ** with **PRINT.LIB** this way:

```
C:\>LINK
Microsoft (R) Overlay Linker  Version 3.64
Copyright (C) Microsoft Corp 1983-1988.  All rights reserved.

Object Modules [.OBJ]:FILE1  ← Type this.
Run File [TA.EXE]:
List File [NUL.MAP]:
Libraries [.LIB]:PRINT        ← And this again.

LINK : warning L4021: no stack segment
```

In this case, the linker will only take **PRINT** from **PRINT.LIB**, since there is no call to **PRINT2**. Theoretically, there could be hundreds of procedures in **PRINT.LIB**, and we'd only take the one(s) we needed. Of course, we could add a call to **PRINT2** (in addition to **PRINT**) in our main file, **FILE1**, like this:

```
.MODEL    SMALL
          EXTRN    PRINT:NEAR, PRINT2:NEAR
.CODE
          ORG      100H

PROG      PROC     NEAR
          CALL     PRINT
```

```
        CALL    PRINT2                  ←
        INT     20H
PROG    ENDP

        END     PROG
```

Note that we also added **PRINT2** to our declaration of external labels:

```
.MODEL  SMALL
        EXTRN   PRINT:NEAR, PRINT2:NEAR  ←
.CODE
        ORG     100H

PROG    PROC    NEAR
        CALL    PRINT
        CALL    PRINT2
        INT     20H
PROG    ENDP

        END     PROG
```

This new version of **FILE1** can now be assembled, linked, and run:

```
C:\>MASM FILE1;
Microsoft (R) Macro Assembler Version 5.10
Copyright (C) Microsoft Corp 1981, 1988.  All rights reserved.


  50202 + 31219 Bytes symbol space free

      0 Warning Errors
      0 Severe  Errors


C:\>LINK
Microsoft (R) Overlay Linker  Version 3.64
Copyright (C) Microsoft Corp 1983-1988.  All rights reserved.

Object Modules [.OBJ]:FILE1  ←
Run File [TA.EXE]:
List File [NUL.MAP]:
Libraries [.LIB]:PRINT       ←

LINK : warning L4021: no stack segment

C:\>EXE2BIN FILE1 FILE1.COM
```

```
C:\>FILE1
Hello, world.How are you?
```

As we can see, both calls were made; that is, both **PRINT** and **PRINT2** have been found in the library **PRINT.LIB**. (We didn't provide a space in our strings between messages, so they came out right next to each other.)

NOTE   Notice that LINK only asks for the names of library files after you've given it a full list of .OBJ files to include. If a version of **PRINT** was in one of them, it would not be taken from the file **PRINT.LIB**, since the **EXTRN** had already been satisfied.

If we want to delete a module from a library file like PRINT.LIB, we could use the - sign instead of +. We can do that easily enough. For example, let's delete **PRINT2** from **PRINT.LIB** like this:

```
C:\>LIB PRINT-FILE3;
Microsoft (R) Library Manager  Version 3.10
Copyright (C) Microsoft Corp 1983-1988.  All rights reserved.
```

PRINT.LIB no longer includes **PRINT2**. Note that, when we subtract modules this way, we have to supply the name of the original .OBJ file (**FILE3.OBJ**), not the name of the procedure we want to subtract (**PRINT2**). Also, we cannot subtract individual procedures, only whole .OBJ modules.

There is also a provision for **extracting** modules, not just deleting them from a library; this is useful if you want to reorganize your libraries. For example, you could extract **FILE3.OBJ** from **PRINT.LIB**, and then add it to another library file, **BADNEWS.LIB**. Extraction is done with the * symbol; for example, this is how we could take **PRINT2** (that is, **FILE3.OBJ**) out of **PRINT.LIB** and place it into **BADNEWS.LIB**:

```
C:\>LIB PRINT*FILE3;
Microsoft (R) Library Manager  Version 3.10
Copyright (C) Microsoft Corp 1983-1988.  All rights reserved.

C:\>LIB BADNEWS+FILE3;
Microsoft (R) Library Manager  Version 3.10
Copyright (C) Microsoft Corp 1983-1988.  All rights reserved.
```

Once again, we have to extract the entire .OBJ file, not just individual procedures. Let's see what would happen if we were to link **FILE1** with **PRINT.LIB** after now that we've extracted **PRINT2** from **PRINT.LIB**:

```
C:\>LINK
Microsoft (R) Overlay Linker  Version 3.64
Copyright (C) Microsoft Corp 1983-1988.  All rights reserved.

Object Modules [.OBJ]:FILE1
Run File [TA.EXE]:
List File [NUL.MAP]:
Libraries [.LIB]:PRINT

LINK : warning L4021: no stack segment

LINK : error L2029: Unresolved externals:

PRINT2 in file(s):
 FILE1.OBJ(FILE1.ASM)

There was 1 error detected
```

As you can see, LINK is unable to satisfy the call to **PRINT2**, and gives us an error message calling **PRINT2** an "Unresolved external."

Updating Library Files

In time, you may create new versions of certain library modules; for example, you may debug some code, or there may be changes in what the program is supposed to do. To handle these changes, you could subtract the module and then add a new one. For example, if an old module in one of your libraries was named **ALERT.OBJ**, and you wanted to change it to a new version, you could do this:

```
C:\>LIB PRINT-ALERT;
Microsoft (R) Library Manager  Version 3.10
Copyright (C) Microsoft Corp 1983-1988.  All rights reserved.

C:\>LIB PRINT+ALERT;
Microsoft (R) Library Manager  Version 3.10
Copyright (C) Microsoft Corp 1983-1988.  All rights reserved.
```

Actually, the library manager lets us do both operations at once, with the combined operation -+ (which stands for replace). If there is an .OBJ file on the disk, then -+ will delete the current module in the specified library and add the new one from the disk file. For example, to update **ALERT** in **PRINT.LIB** in one step, just type:

```
C:\>LIB PRINT-+ALERT;
Microsoft (R) Library Manager  Version 3.10
Copyright (C) Microsoft Corp 1983-1988.  All rights reserved.
```

NOTE Keep in mind that if a procedure in one of your .LIB files calls a procedure in some other .LIB file, link the one with the call in first. LINK won't know that it is supposed to include a particular procedure until that procedure is called. If it has already searched the correct library before you make the call, it won't be able to find the called procedure when you finally do call it.

Libraries can be very useful at helping you to manage your programs, and they can help when programs become very large. On the other hand, you should keep your library up to date. If the library contains old versions of particular modules, they will be linked in. That's it, then, for our coverage of libraries, and that's all for our exploration of assembly language.

We've come far in C; from the very beginning up through graphics, files, the mouse, pointers, C++, and now all the way up to linking in assembly language. Our survey is done now, our tour is over. At this point, we have a good deal of experience, and we've seen many tricks of the trade. We've seen the power of C in its own environment, and we've learned what it has to offer. We've even put it to work for ourselves. In fact, we've gone from novices to true C programmers. All that remains now is the important part: putting it to work! (Happy programming.)

BIOS and DOS Reference

This appendix is intended for use as a reference. We will work through all the interrupts that are available, from 0 to FFH, reviewing the ones that are useful. BIOS uses interrupts 0 to 1FH, and DOS continues from 20H upward.

BIOS Interrupts

INT 0 — Divide By 0

Interrupt 0 is the divide by zero routine; if a divide by zero occurs, then this interrupt is called. It prints out its message, "Divide Overflow," and usually stops program execution.

INT 1 — Single Step

No one, except a debugger, uses this interrupt. It is used to single step through code, with a call to this interrupt between executed instructions.

INT 2 — NonMaskable Interrupt (NMI)

This is a hardware interrupt. This interrupt cannot be blocked off by using STI and CLI. It always gets executed when called.

INT 3 — Breakpoint

This is another debugger interrupt. DEBUG uses this interrupt with the Go command. If you want to execute all the code up to a particular address and then stop, DEBUG will insert an INT 3 into the code at that point and then give control to the program. When the INT 3 is reached, DEBUG can take control again.

INT 4 — Overflow

This is similar to INT 0. If there is an overflow condition, this interrupt is called. Usually, though, no action is called for, and BIOS simply returns.

INT 5 — Print Screen

This interrupt was chosen by BIOS to print the screen out. If you use the PrtSc key on the keyboard, this is the interrupt that gets called. Needless to say, your program can also issue an INT 5 by just including that instruction in the program. There are no arguments to be passed.

INT 6 and 7 — Reserved

INT 8 — Time of Day

This is another hardware interrupt. This interrupt is called to update the internal time of day (stored in the BIOS data area) 18.2 times a second. If the date needs to be changed, this interrupt will handle that too.

This interrupt calls INT 1CH as well. If you want to intercept the timer and do something 18.2 times a second, it is recommended you intercept INT 1CH instead of this one.

INT 9 — Keyboard

This hardware interrupt may be intercepted by memory-resident programs.

INT 0AH — Reserved

INT 0BH – 0FH

These interrupts point to the BIOS routine D_EOI, which is BIOS' End of Interrupt routine. All this routine does is to reset the interrupt handler at port 20H and return.

INT 10H, Service 0 — Set Screen Mode

Input

AH = 0
AL = Mode

Mode (in AL)	Display Lines	Number of Colors	Adapters	Maximum Pages
0	40×25	B&W text	CGA, EGA, VGA	8
1	40×2,5	Color text	CGA, EGA, VGA	8
2	80×25	B&W text	CGA, EGA, VGA	4 (CGA) 8 (EGA, VGA)
3	80×25	Color text	CGA, EGA, VGA	4 (CGA) 8 (EGA, VGA)
4	320×200	4	CGA, EGA, VGA	1
5	320×200	B&W	CGA, EGA, VGA	1
6	640×200	2	(on or off) CGA, EGA, VGA	1
7	80×25	Monochrome	MDA, EGA, VGA	1 (MDA) 8 (EGA, VGA)
8	160×200	16	PCjr	1
9	320×200	16	PCjr	1
A	640×200	1	PCjr	1
B	Reserved for future use			
C	Reserved for future use			
D	320×200	16	EGA	VGA
E	640×200	16	EGA	VGA
F	640×350	monochrome	EGA, VGA	2
10H	640×350	16	EGA, VGA	2
11H	640×480	2	VGA	1
12H	64x×480	16	VGA	1
13H	320×200	256	VGA	1

INT 10H, Service 1 — Set Cursor Type

Input

```
AH  = 1
CH  = Cursor start line
CL  = Cursor end line
```

Output

New cursor

INT 10H, Service 2 — Set Cursor Position

Input

```
DH,DL = Row, column
BH  = Page number
AH  = 2
```

Output

Cursor position changed

Note: DH,DL = 0,0 = upper left

INT 10H, Service 3 — Find Cursor Position

Input

```
BH  = Page Number
AH  = 3
```

Output

```
DH,DL = Row, column of cursor
CH,CL = Cursor mode currently set
```

INT 10H, Service 4 — Read Light Pen Position

Input

```
AH  = 4
```

Output

```
AH  = 0  → Light pen switch not down
AL  = 1  → DH,DL = Row, column of Light Pen position
```

$$
\begin{aligned}
\text{CH} &= \text{Raster line (vertical; 0 - 199)} \\
\text{BX} &= \text{Pixel column (horizontal; 0 - 319, 639)}
\end{aligned}
$$

INT 10H, Service 5 — Set Active Display Page

Input

AL   = 0 – 7 (Screen modes 0, 1)
      0 – 3 (Screen modes 2, 3)
AH   = 5

Output

Active page changed

Note: Different pages available in alphanumeric modes only (graphics adapters).

INT 10H, Service 6 — Scroll Active Page Up

Input

AL   = # lines blanked at bottom (0→blank whole area)
CH,CL = Upper-left row,column of area to scroll
DH,DL = Lower-right row,column of area to scroll
BH   = Attribute used on blank line
AH   = 6

INT 10H, Service 7 — Scroll Active Page Down

Input

AL   = # lines blanked at bottom (0→blank whole area)
CH,CL = Upper-left row,column of area to scroll
DH,DL = Lower-right row,column of area to scroll
BH   = Attribute used on blank line
AH   = 7

INT 10H, Service 8 — Read Attribute and Character at Cursor Position

Input

BH   = Page number
AH   = 8

Output

AL   = Character read (ASCII)
AH   = Attribute of character (alphanumerics only)

INT 10H, Service 9 — Write Attribute and Character at Cursor Position

Input

BH   = Page number
BL → Alpha modes = Attribute
        Graphics modes = Color
CX   = Count of characters to write
AL   = IBM ASCII code
AH   = 9

Output

Character written on screen at cursor position

INT 10H, Service A — Write Character ONLY at Cursor Position

Input

BH   = Page number
CX   = Count of characters to write
AL   = IBM ASCII code
AH   = 0AH

Output

Character written on screen at cursor position

INT 10H, Service B — Set Color Palette

Input

BH   = Palette Color ID
BL   BH = 0 → BL = Background color
        BH = 1 → BL = Palette number
                         0 = green/red/yellow
                         1 = cyan/magenta/white
AH   = 11

INT 10H, Service C — Write Dot

Input

DX = Row number(0 – 199) — [0,0] is upper-left
CX = Column number(0 – 319, 639)
AL = Color value (0 – 3)
AH = 12

Note: If bit 7 of AL is 1, the color value is XORed with the current value of the dot.

INT 10H, Service D — Read Dot

Input

DX = Row number(0 – 199) — [0,0] is upper-left
CX = Column number(0 – 319 ,639)
AH = 13

Output

AL = Color value (0 – 3)

Note: If bit 7 of AL is 1, the color value is XORed with the current value of the dot.

INT 10H, Service E — Teletype Write to Active Page

Input

AL = IBM ASCII code.
BL = Foreground color (graphics mode)
AH = 14

INT 10H, Service FH — Return Video State

Input

AH = 15

Output

AH = Number of alphanumeric columns on screen
AL = Current mode (see INT 10H, Service 0)
BH = Active display page

INT 10H, Service 10H — Set Palette Registers

Default Palette Colors (0 – 15) on EGA.

Color Value	Color	rgbRGB
0	Black	000000
1	Blue	000001
2	Green	000010
3	Cyan	000011
4	Red	000100
5	Magenta	000101
6	Brown	010100
7	White	000111
8	Dark gray	111000
9	Light blue	111001
10	Light green	111010
11	Light cyan	111011
12	Light red	111100
13	Light magenta	111101
14	Yellow	111110
15	Intense white	111111

INT 10H, Service 10H, Function 0 — Set Individual Palette Register

Input

```
AH  =  10H
AL  =  0
BL  =  Palette register to set (0 – 15)
BH  =  Value to set (0 – 63)
```

INT 10H, Service 10H, Function 1 — Set Overscan (Border) Register

Input

```
AH  =  10H
BH  =  Value to set (0 – 63)
```

INT 10H, Service 10H, Function 2 — Set All Palette Registers

Input

```
AH    = 10H
AL    = 2
ES:BX = Address of a 17-byte table holding color selections (0 – 63)
        Bytes 0 – 15 hold color selections for palette registers 0 – 15
        Byte 16 holds the new overscan (border) color
```

INT 10H, Service 10H, Function 7 — Read Individual Palette Register

Input

```
AH    = 10H
AL    = 7
BL    = Register to read (color value)
```

Output

```
BH    = Register setting
```

INT 10H, Service 10H, Function 8 — Read Overscan (Border) Register

Input

```
AH    = 10H
AL    = 8
```

Output

```
BH    = Overscan setting
```

INT 10H, Service 10H, Function 10H — Set DAC Register

Input

```
AH    = 10H
AL    = 10H
BX    = Register to set (0 – 255)
CH    = Green intensity
CL    = Blue intensity
DH    = Red intensity
```

INT 10H, Service 10H, Function 12H — Set DAC Registers

Input

```
AH    = 10H
AL    = 12H
BX    = First register to set (0 – 255)
CX    = Number of registers to set (1 – 256)
ES:DX = Address of a table of color intensities. Three bytes are used
        for each DAC register (use only lower 6 bits of each byte).
        Table is set as red, green, blue, red, green, blue, . . . .
```

INT 10H, Service 10H, Function 13H — Select Color Page Mode

Input

```
AH    = 10H
AL    = 13H
BL    = 0 Select color paging mode
        BH  = 0 Selects 4 DAC register pages of 64 registers each
        BH  = 1 Selects 16 DAC register pages of 16 registers each
BL    = 1 Select active color page
For use with 4-page mode:
        BH  = 0 Selects the first block of 64 DAC registers
        BH  = 1 Selects the second block of 64 DAC registers
        BH  = 2 Selects the third block of 64 DAC registers
        BH  = 3 Selects the fourth block of 64 DAC  egisters
For use with 16-page setting:
        BH  = 0 Selects the first block of 16 DAC regist
        BH  = 1 Selects the second block of 16 DAC registei s
                :
                :
        BH  = 15 Selects the 15th block of 16 DAC registers
        BH  = 16 Selects the 16th block of 16 DAC registers
```

INT 10H, Service 11H — Character Generator

INT 10H, Service 12H — Alternate Select

Input

```
AH    = 12H
BL    = 30H
```

$$AL = 0 \rightarrow 200 \text{ screen scan lines}$$
$$= 1 \rightarrow 350 \text{ screen scan lines}$$
$$= 2 \rightarrow 400 \text{ screen scan lines}$$

INT 11H — Equipment Determination

Output

Bits of AX:

15, 14	Number of printers
13	Not used
12	Game adapter attached
11, 10, 9	Number of RS232 cards installed
8	Unused
7, 6	Number of diskette drives
	($00 \rightarrow 1; 01 \rightarrow 2; 10 \rightarrow 3; 11 \rightarrow 4$ If Bit 0=1)
5, 4	Video mode (00 unused, 01=40×25 color card,
	10=80×25 color card, 11=80×25 monochrome)
3, 2	Motherboard RAM (00=16K, 01=32K, 10=48K, 11=64K)
1	Not used.
0	1 if there are diskette drives attached

INT 12H — Determine Memory Size

Output

AX= Number of contiguous 1K memory blocks

INT 13H, Service 0 — Reset Disk

Input

AH = 0

Output

No Carry $\rightarrow$ AH=0, success
Carry $\rightarrow$ AH=Error code (see Service 1)   DL=81H $\rightarrow$ reset

Note: On hard disk systems, DL=80H $\rightarrow$ reset d'
hard disk.

INT 13H, Service 1 — Read Status of Last Operation

Input

AH   =   1

Output

Disk error codes:

AL   =   00 No error
AL   =   01 Bad command passed to controller
AL   =   02 Address mark not found
AL   =   03 Diskette is write-protected
AL   =   04 Sector not found
AL   =   05 Reset failed
AL   =   07 Drive parameters wrong
AL   =   09 DMA across segment end
AL   =   0BH Bad track flag seen
AL   =   10H Bad error check seen
AL   =   11H Data is error corrected
AL   =   20H Controller failure
AL   =   40H Seek operation has failed
AL   =   80H No response from disk
AL   =   0BBH Undefined error
AL   =   0FFH Sense operation failed

Note: DL=Drive number; set bit 7 to 1 for hard disks. For hard disks, drive number in DL can range from 80H to 87H.

IN Service 2 — Read Sectors into Memory

out

AH   =   2
DL   =   Drive number
H   =   Head number
    =   Cylinder or track (floppies) number
    =   Bits 7 and 6 are the high two bits of the 10-bit cylinder number
    =   Sector number (bits 0 − 5)
    =   Number of sectors to read (floppies, 1 − 8; hard disks, 1 − 80H; hard disks read/write long, 1 − 79H)
    =   Address of buffer for reads and writes

Output

No Carry → AL = Number of sectors read (diskette)
Carry → AH = Disk error code (see Service 1)

Note: DL=Drive number; set bit 7 to 1 for hard disks. For hard disks, drive number in DL can range from 80H to 87H.

INT 13H, Service 3 — Write Sectors to Disk

Input

AH	=	3
DL	=	Drive number
DH	=	Head number
CH	=	Cylinder or track (floppies) number
CL	=	Bits 7 and 6 are the high two bits of the 10-bit cylinder number
CL	=	Sector number (bits 0 – 5)
AL	=	Number of sectors to write (floppies, 1 – 8; hard disks, 1 – 80H; hard disks read/write long, 1 – 79H)
ES:BX	=	Address of buffer for reads and writes

Output

No Carry → AL = Number of sectors written (diskette)
Carry → AH = Disk error code (see Service 1)

Note: DL = Drive number; set bit 7 to 1 for hard disks. For hard disks, drive number in DL can range from 80H to 87H.

INT 13H, Service 4 — Verify Sectors

Input

AH	=	4
DL	=	Drive number
DH	=	Head number
CH	=	Cylinder or track (floppies) number
CL	=	Bits 7 and 6 are the high two bits of 10-bit cylinder number
CL	=	Sector number (bits 0 – 5)
AL	=	Number of sectors (floppies, 1 – 8; hard disks, 1 – 80H; hard disks read/write long, 1 – 79H)

Output

> No Carry → AH = 0, success.
>
> Carry → AH = Disk error code (see Service 1)

Note: DL = Drive number; set bit 7 to 1 for hard disks. For hard disks, drive number in DL can range from 80H to 87H.

INT 13H, Service 8 — Return Drive Parameters

This service works only on hard disks and PS/2s.

Input

> AH   = 8
> DL   = Drive number (0 based)

Output

> DL   = Number of drives attached to controller
> DH   = Maximum value for head number
> CH   = Maximum cylinder value
> CL   = Bits 7 and 6 are the high two bits of the 10-bit cylinder number
> CL   = Maximum value for sector number (bits 0 – 5)
> BL (for PS/2 diskettes only):
> > = 1 → 360K drive
> > = 2 → 1.2 M drive
> > = 3 → 720K drive
> > = 4 → 1.44 M drive

Note: DL = Drive number; set bit 7 to 1 for hard disks. For hard disks, drive number in DL can range from 80H to 87H.

INT 13H, Services 0AH, and 0BH — Reserved

INT 13H, Service 0CH — Seek

This service works ONLY on hard disks.

Input

> AH   = 0CH
> DH   = Head number
> DL   = Drive number (80H – 87H allowed)

CH   = Cylinder number

CL   = Sector number; bits 7 and 6 of CL are the high two bits of 10-bit cylinder number

Output

No Carry $\rightarrow$ AH = 0, success

Carry $\rightarrow$ AH = Disk error code (see Service 1)

Note: DL = Drive number; set bit 7 to 1 for hard disks. For hard disks, drive number in DL can range from 80H to 87H.

INT 13H, Service 0DH — Alternate Disk Reset

INT 13H, Services 0EH and 0FH — Reserved

INT 13H, Service 10H — Test Drive Ready

INT 13H, Service 11H — Recalibrate Hard Drive

This service works ONLY on hard disks.

Input

AH   = 11H (read)

DL   = Drive number (80H – 87H allowed)

Output

No Carry $\rightarrow$ AH = 0, success

Carry $\rightarrow$ AH = Disk error code (see Service 1)

Note: DL = Drive number; set bit 7 to 1 for hard disks. For hard disks, drive number in DL can range from 80H to 87H.

INT 13H — Diagnostic Services

These services work ONLY on hard disks.

Input

AH   = 12H (RAM diagnostic)

AH   = 13H (drive diagnostic)

AH   =   14H (controller diagnostic)

DL   =   Drive number (80H – 87H allowed)

Output

No Carry $\rightarrow$ AH = 0, success

Carry $\rightarrow$ AH = Disk error code (see Service 1)

Note: DL = Drive number; set bit 7 to 1 for hard disks. For hard disks, drive number in DL can range from 80H to 87H.

INT 13H, Service 19H — Park Heads PS/2 Only

Input (PS/2)

DL=   Drive number

Output

Carry   = 1 $\rightarrow$ Error, AH = error code

        = 0 $\rightarrow$ success

Note: DL = Drive number; set bit 7 to 1 for hard disks. For hard disks, drive number in DL can range from 80H to 87H.

INT 14H, AH = 0 — Initialize RS232 Port

Input

AH   =   0

Bits of AL:

     0, 1   Word length (01 $\rightarrow$ 7 bits, 11 $\rightarrow$ 8 bits)

     2   Stop bits (0 $\rightarrow$ 1, 1 $\rightarrow$ 2 stop bits)

     3, 4   Parity (00 $\rightarrow$ none, 01 $\rightarrow$ odd, 11 $\rightarrow$ even)

     5, 6, 7   Baud rate (000 $\rightarrow$ 110, 001 $\rightarrow$ 150, 010 $\rightarrow$ 300, 011 $\rightarrow$ 600,

                 100 $\rightarrow$ 1,200, 101 $\rightarrow$ 2,400, 110 $\rightarrow$ 4,800, 111 $\rightarrow$ 9,600)

INT 14H, AH = 1 — Send Character through Serial Port

Input

AH   =   1

AL   =   Character to send

Output

If bit 7 of AH is set, failure

If bit 7 is not set, bits 0 – 6 hold status (see INT 14H, AH = 3).

INT 14H, AH = 2 — Receive Character from Serial Port

Input

AH   = 2

Output

AL   = character received

AH   = 0, success, otherwise, AH holds an error code
         (see INT 14H, AH = 3)

INT 14H, AH = 3 — Return Serial Port's Status

Input

AH   = 3

Output

AH bits set:

$7 \rightarrow$ Time out

$6 \rightarrow$ Shift register empty

$5 \rightarrow$ Holding register empty

$4 \rightarrow$ Break detected

$3 \rightarrow$ Framing error

$2 \rightarrow$ Parity error

$1 \rightarrow$ Overrun error

$0 \rightarrow$ Data ready

AL bits set:

$7 \rightarrow$ Received line signal detect

$6 \rightarrow$ Ring indicator

$5 \rightarrow$ Data set ready

$4 \rightarrow$ Clear to send

$3 \rightarrow$ Delta receive line signal detect

$2 \rightarrow$ Trailing edge ring detector

$1 \rightarrow$ Delta data set ready

$0 \rightarrow$ Delta clear to send

INT 15H — Cassette I/O

Input

AH = 0 → Turn cassette motor on
AH = 1 → Turn cassette motor off
AH = 2 → Read one or more 256-byte blocks; store data at ES:BX;
           CX = count of bytes to read
AH = 3 → Write one or more 256-byte blocks from ES:BX; count of
           bytes to write in CX

Output

DX = Number of bytes
Carry flag set if error
If carry, AH = 01 → CRC error
          = 02 → Data transitions lost
          = 04 → No data found

In recent BIOS versions, new items have been added to this interrupt, such as joystick support, the ability to switch processor mode (protected or not), mouse support, and some BIOS parameters.

INT 16H, Service 0 — Read Key from Keyboard

Input

AH = 0

Output

AH = Scan code
AL = ASCII code

INT 16H, Service 1 — Check if Key Ready to be Read

Input

AH = 1

Output

Zero flag = 1 → Buffer empty
Zero flag = 0 → AH = Scan Code
                 AL = ASCII Code

INT 16H, Service 2 — Find Keyboard Status

Input

AH = 2

Output

AL = Keyboard status byte

INT 17H, Service 0 — Print character in AL

Input

AH = 0
AL   = Character to be printed
DX = Printer number (0, 1, 2)

Output

AH = 1 → Printer time out

INT 17H, Service 1 — Initialize Printer Port

Input

AH = 1
DX = Printer Number (0, 1, 2)

Output

AH = Printer status
Bits set of AH:
     7 → Printer not busy
     6 → Acknowledge
     5 → Out of paper
     4 → Selected
     3 → I/O error
     2 → Unused
     1 → Also unused
     0 → Time out

INT 17H, Service 2 — Read Printer Status into AH

Input

AH = 2
DX = Printer number (0, 1, 2)

Output

AH set to status byte as in INT 17H, AH = 1

INT 18H — Resident BASIC

This interrupt starts up ROM-resident BASIC in the PC.

INT 19H — Bootstrap

This interrupt is the one that boots the machine (try it with DEBUG).

INT 1AH, Service 0 — Read Time of Day

Input

AH   = 0

Output

CX   = High word of timer count
DX   = Low word of timer count
AL   = 0 if timer has not passed 24 hours since last read

Note: Timer count increments by 65,536 in one hour.

INT 1AH, Service 1 — Set Time of Day

Input

AH   = 1
CX   = High word of timer count
DX   = Low word of timer count

Note: Timer count increments by 65,536 in one hour.

INT 1BH — Keyboard Break Address

INT 1CH — Timer Tick Interrupt

INT 1DH — Video Parameter Tables

INT 1EH — Diskette Parameters

INT 1FH — Graphics Character Definitions

DOS Interrupts

Interrupt 1FH is the last BIOS Interrupt, and DOS starts with INT 20H.

INT 20H — Terminate

Programs are usually ended with an INT 20H.

INT 21H

Interrupt 21H is the DOS service interrupt. To call one of these services, load AH with the service number, and the other registers as shown.

INT 21H, Service 0 — Program Terminate

Input

AH   = 0

INT 21H, Service 1 — Keyboard Input

Input

AH   = 1

Output

AL   = ASCII code of struck key; does echo on screen

Checks for ^C or ^Break.

INT 21H, Service 2 — Character Output on Screen

Input

```
AH  = 2
DL  = Character's ASCII code
```

INT 21H, Service 3 — Standard Auxiliary Device Input

Input

```
AH  = 3
```

Output

```
Character in AL
```

INT 21H, Service 4 — Standard Auxiliary Device Output

Input

```
AH  = 4
DL  = Character to output
```

INT 21H, Service 5 — Printer Output

Input

```
AH  = 5
DL  = Character to output
```

INT 21H, Service 6 — Console I/O without Echo

Input	Output
AH = 6	
DL = FFH →	Zero flag set if no character was ready; otherwise, AL holds character's ASCII code
DL< FFH →	Type ASCII code in DL on screen

Does NOT check for ^C or ^Break.

INT 21H, Service 7 — Console Input without Echo

Input

AH = 7

Output

AL = ASCII code of struck key; no echo on screen

Does NOT Check for ^C or ^Break.

INT 21H, Service 8 — Console Input without Echo with ^C Check

Input

AH = 8

Output

AL = ASCII code of struck key; does NOT echo the typed key

Checks for ^C or ^Break.

INT 21H, Service 9 — String Print

Input

DS:DX point to a string that ends in '$'
AH = 9

INT 21H, Service A — String Input

Input

AH = 0AH
[DS:DX] = Length of buffer

Output

Buffer at DS:DX filled; echos the typed keys

Checks for ^C or ^Break.

INT 21H, Service OBH — Check Input Status

Input

    AH   = 0BH

Output

    AL   = FF $\rightarrow$ Character ready. AL=00 $\rightarrow$ Nothing to read in

^Break is checked for.

INT 21H, Service OCH — Clear Keyboard Buffer and Invoke Service

Input

    AH   = 0CH
    AL   = Keyboard function number

Output

    Standard output from the selected service.

^Break is checked for.

INT 21H, Service ODH — Disk Reset

Input

    AH   = 0DH

INT 21H, Service OEH — Select Disk

Input

    AH   = 0EH
    DL   = Drive number (DL = 0 $\rightarrow$ A, DL = 1 $\rightarrow$ B, and so on)

INT 21H, Service OFH — Open Preexisting File

Input

    DS:DX points to an FCB
    AH   = 0FH

Output

> AL = 0 → Success
>
> AL = FF → Failure

INT 21H, Service 10H — Close File

Input

> DS:DX points to an FCB
>
> AH = 10H

Output

> AL = 0 → Success
>
> AL = FF → Failure

INT 21H, Service 11H — Search for First Matching File

Input

> DS:DX points to an unopened FCB
>
> AH = 11H

Output

> AL = FF → Failure
>
> AL = 0 → Success; DTA holds FCB for match

Note: DTA is at CS:0080 in .COM files on startup.

INT 21H, Service 12H — Search for Next Matching File

Input

> DS:DX points to an unopened FCB
>
> AH = 12H

Output

> AL = FF → Failure
>
> AL = 0 → Success; DTA holds FCB for match

Use this service after Service 11H.

INT 21H, Service 13H — Delete Files

Input

DS:DX points to an unopened FCB

AH   = 13H

Output

AL   = FF $\rightarrow$ Failure

AL   = 0 $\rightarrow$ Success

INT 21H, Service 14H — Sequential Read

Input

DS:DX points to an opened FCB

AH   = 14H

Current block and record set in FCB

Output

Requested Record put in DTA.

AL = 0 Success:

    1 End of file; no data in record

    2 DTA segment too small for record

    3 End of file; record padded with 0

Record address incremented.

INT 21H, Service 15H — Sequential Write

Input

DS:DX points to an opened FCB

AH   = 15H

Current block and record set in FCB.

Output

One record read from DTA and written

AL = 0 Success:

    1 Disk full

    2 DTA segment too small for record

Record address incremented.

INT 21H, Service 16H — Create File

Input

>> DS:DX points to an unopened FCB
>> AH   = 16H

Output

>> AL   = 0 Success
>>   = FF Directory full

INT 21H, Service 17H — Rename File

Input

>> DS:DX points to a MODIFIED FCB
>> AH   = 17H

Output

>> AL   = 0 Success
>>   = FF Failure

Modified FCB → Second file name starts six bytes after the end of the first file name, at DS:DX+11H.

INT 21H, Service 18H — Internal to DOS

INT 21H, Service 19H — Find Current Disk

Input

>> AH   = 19H

Output

>> AL   = Current disk (0 = A, 1 = B, and so on)

INT 21H, Service 1AH — Set the DTA Location

Input

>> DS:DX points to new DTA address
>> AH   = 1AH

Note: DTA = Disk Transfer Address, the data area used with FCB services. Default DTA is 128 bytes long, starting at CS:0080 in the PSP.

INT 21H, Service 1BH — FAT Information for Default Drive

Input

> AH   = 1BH

Output

> DS:BX points to the "FAT byte"
> DX   = Number of clusters
> AL   = Number of sectors/cluster
> CX   = Size of a sector (512 bytes)

Note: Files are stored in clusters — the smallest allocatable unit on a disk.

INT 21H, Service 1CH — FAT Information for Specified Drive

Input

> AH   = 1CH
> DL   = Drive number (0 = Default, 1 = A, ...)

Output

> DS:BX points to the "FAT byte"
> DX   = Number of clusters
> AL   = Number of sectors/cluster
> CX   = Size of a sector (512)

Note: Files are stored in clusters — the smallest allocatable unit on a disk.

INT 21H, Services 1DH – 20H Internal to DOS

INT 21H, Service 21H — Random Read

Input

> DS:DX points to an opened FCB
> Set FCB's random record field at DS:DX+33 and DS:DX+35
> AH   = 21H

Output

> AL = 00 Success
>   = 01 End of file, no more data
>   = 02 Not enough space in DTA segment
>   = 03 End of file, partial record padded with 0s

INT 21H, Service 22H — Random Write

Input

> DS:DX points to an opened FCB
> Set FCB's random record field at DS:DX+33 and DS:DX+35
> AH = 21H

Output

> AL = 00 Success
>   = 01 Disk is full
>   = 02 Not enough space in DTA segment

INT 21H, Service 23H — File Size

Input

> DS:DX points to an unopened FCB
> AH = 23H

Output

> AL = 00 Success
>   = FF No file found that matched FCB
> Random record field set to file length in records, rounded up

INT 21H, Service 24H — Set Random Record Field

Input

> DS:DX points to an opened FCB
> AH = 24H

Output

> Random record field set to match current record and current block

INT 21H, Service 25H — Set Interrupt Vector

Input

```
AH   =  25H
AL   =  Interrupt number
DS:DX  =  New address
```

Note: This service can help you intercept an interrupt vector.

INT 21H, Service 26H — Create a New Program Segment (PSP)

INT 21H, Service 27H — Random Block Read

Input

```
DS:DX points to an opened FCB
Set FCB's random record field at DS:DX+33 and DS:DX+35
AH   =  27H
```

Output

```
AL   =  00 Success
     =  01 End of file, no more data
     =  02 Not enough space in DTA segment
     =  03 End of file, partial record padded with 0s
CX   =  Number of records read
Random record fields set to access next record
```

Note: The data buffer used in FCB services is the DTA, or Disk Transfer Area.

INT 21H, Service 28H — Random Block Write

Input

```
DS:DX points to an opened FCB
Set FCB's random record field at DS:DX+33 and DS:DX+35
CX=  Number of records to write
AH   =  28H
```

Output

```
AL   =  00 Success
     =  01 Disk is full
     =  02 Not enough space in DTA segment
Random record fields set to access next record
```

CX = 0 → file set to the size indicated by the random record field. The data buffer used in FCB services is the DTA, or Disk Transfer Area.

INT 21H, Service 29H — Parse Filename

Input

DS:SI	=	Command line to parse
ES:DI	=	Address to put FCB at
AL	=	Bit 0 = 1 → Leading separators are scanned off command line
		Bit 1 = 1 → Drive ID in final FCB will be changed ONLY if a drive was specified
		Bit 2 = 1 → Filename in FCB changed ONLY if command line includes filename
		Bit 3 = 1 → Filename extension in FCB will be changed ONLY if command line contains a filename extension
AH	=	29H

Output

DS:SI	=	1st character after filename
ES:DI	=	Valid FCB

Note: If the command line does not contain a valid filename, ES:[DI+1] will be a blank.

INT 21H, Service 2AH — Get Date

Input

AH	=	2AH

Output

CX	=	Year – 1980
DH	=	Month (1 = January, etc.)
DL	=	Day of the month

INT 21H, Service 2BH — Set Date

Input

CX	=	Year – 1980
DH	=	Month (1 = January, etc.)

DL   =   Day of the month

AH   =   2BH

Output

AL   =   0, success

AL   =   FF, date not valid

INT 21H, Service 2CH — Get Time

Input

AH   =   2CH

Output

CH   =   Hours (0 – 23)

CL   =   Minutes (0 – 59)

DH   =   Seconds (0 – 59)

DL   =   Hundredths of seconds (0 – 99)

INT 21H, Service 2DH — Set Time

Input

AH   =   2DH

CH   =   Hours (0 – 23)

CL   =   Minutes (0 – 59)

DH   =   Seconds (0 – 59)

DL   =   Hundreds of seconds (0 – 99)

Output

AL   =   0, success

AL   =   FF, time is invalid

INT 21H, Service 2EH — Set or Reset Verify Switch

Input

AH   =   2EH

DL   =   0

AL   =   1 → Turn verify on

=   0 → Turn verify off

INT 21H, Service 2FH — Get Current DTA

Input

> AH = 2FH

Output

> ES:BX = Current DTA address

Note: The data buffer used in FCB services is the DTA, or Disk Transfer Area.

INT 21H, Service 30H — Get DOS Version Number

Input

> AH = 30H

Output

> AL = Major version number (3 in DOS 3.10)
> AH = Minor version number (10 in DOS 3.10)
> BX = 0
> CX = 0

Note: If AL returns 0, you are working with a version of DOS before 2.0.

INT 21H, Service 31H — Terminate Process and Keep Resident

Input

> AH = 31H
> AL = Binary exit code
> DX = Size of memory request in paragraphs

Note: Exit code can be read by a parent program with Service 4DH. It can also be tested by ERRORLEVEL commands in batch files.

INT 21H, Service 32H — Internal to DOS

INT 21H, Service 33H — Control-Break Check

Input

> AH = 33H

AL   = 0 → Check state of ^Break checking
     = 1 → Set the state of ^Break checking
             DL   = 0 → Turn it off
             DL   = 1 → Turn it on

Output

DL   = 0 → Off
DL   = 1 → On

INT 21H, Service 34H — Internal to DOS

INT 21H, Service 35H — Get Interrupt Vector

Input

AH   = 35H
AL   = Interrupt number

Output

ES:BX   = Interrupt's vector

INT 21H, Service 36H — Get Free Disk Space

Input

AH   = 36H
DL   = Drive number (0 = Default, 1 = A, ...)

Output

AX   = 0FFFH → Drive number invalid
AX   = Number of sectors/cluster
BX   = Number of available clusters
CX   = Size of a sector (512)
DX   = Number of clusters

Note: Files are stored in clusters — the smallest allocatable unit on a disk.

INT 21H, Service 37H — Internal to DOS

INT 21H, Service 38H — Returns Country-dependent Information

Input

    AH   = 38H
    DS:DX = address of 32-byte block
    AL   = 0

Output

Filled in 32-byte block (see below)

The 32-byte block looks like this:

2	Bytes DATE/TIME format.
1	Byte of currency symbol (ASCII)
1	Byte set to 0
1	Byte thousands separator (ASCII)
1	Byte set to 0
1	Byte decimal separator (ASCII)
1	Byte set to 0
24	Bytes used internally

The DATE/TIME format has these values:

    0 = USA (H:M:S M/D/Y)
    1 = Europe (H:M:S D/M/Y)
    2 = Japan (H:M:S D:M:Y)

Note: In DOS 3+ you can set, as well as read, these values.

INT 21H, Service 39H — Create a Subdirectory

Input

    AH   = 39H
    DS:DX point to ASCIIZ string with directory name

Output

    No Carry → Success
    Carry →   AH has error value:
                 AH = 3 Path not found
                 AH = 5 Access denied

INT 21H, Service 3AH — Delete a Subdirectory

Input

AH   = 3AH
DS:DX point to ASCIIZ string with directory name

Output

No Carry → Success
Carry → AH has error value:
AH = 3 Path not found
AH = 5 Access denied or subdirectory not empty

INT 21H, Service 3BH — Change Current Directory

Input

AH   = 3BH
DS:DX point to ASCIIZ string with directory name

Output

No Carry → Success
Carry → AH has error value:
AH = 3 Path not found

INT 21H, Service 3CH — Create a File

Input

DS:DX points to ASCIIZ filename
CX= Attribute of file
AH   = 3CH

Output

No Carry → AX = File Handle
Carry → AL   = 3 Path not found
= 4 Too many files open
= 5 Directory full or previous read-only file exists

INT 21H, Service 3DH — Open a File

Input

DS:DX points to ASCIIZ filename.

AL = Access Code ⌐

AH = 3DH ↓

Access Codes:AL = 0 File opened for reading

AL = 1 File opened for writing

AL = 2 File opened for reading and writing

Access Codes, DOS 3+ — isssraaa:

i = 1 → File is not to be inherited by child processes

i = 0 → File handle will be inherited

sss= 000 → Compatibility mode

sss= 001 → Deny all

sss= 010 → Deny write

sss= 011 → Deny read

sss= 100 → Deny none

r = Reserved

aaa = 000 → Read access

aaa = 001 → Write access

aaa = 010 → Read/write access

Output

No Carry → AX = File handle

Carry → AL = Error code (check error table)

INT 21H, Service 3EH — Close a File Handle

Input

BX holds a valid file handle

AH = 3EH

Output

Carry → AL = 6 → Invalid handle

INT 21H, Service 3FH — Read from File or Device

Input

    DS:DX = Data buffer address
    CX   = Number of bytes to read
    BX   = File handle
    AH   = 3FH

Output

    No Carry → AX = Number of bytes read
    Carry → AL = 5 Access denied
    AL = 6 Invalid handle

INT 21H, Service 40H — Write to File or Device

Input

    DS:DX = Data buffer address
    CX   = Number of bytes to write
    BX   = File handle
    AH   = 40H

Output

    No Carry → AX = Number of bytes written
    Carry → AL = 5 Access denied
    AL = 6 Invalid handle

Note: Full disk is NOT considered an error. Check the number of bytes you wanted to write (CX) against the number actually written (returned in AX). If they do not match, the disk is probably full.

INT 21H, Service 41H — Delete a File

Input

    DS:DX = ASCIIZ filename
    AH   = 41H

Output

    No Carry → Success
    Carry → AL = 2 File not found
    AL = 5 Access denied

Note: No wildcards allowed in filename.

INT 21H, Service 42H — Move Read/Write Pointer

Input

    BX   = File handle
    CX:DX = Desired offset
    AL   = Method Value ⸺
    AH   = 42H
    Method Values (AL):
        AL = 0 Read/write pointer moved to CX:DX from the start
                  of the file
        AL = 1 Pointer incremented CX:DX bytes
        AL = 2 Pointer moved to end-of-file plus offset (CX:DX)

Output

    No Carry → DX:AX = New location of pointer
    Carry → AL = 1 Illegal function number
    AL = 6 Invalid handle

INT 21H, Service 43H — Change File's Attribute

Input

    DS:DX = ASCIIZ filestring
    AL   = 1 → File attribute changed; CX holds new attribute
    AL   = 0 → File's current attribute returned in CX
    AH   = 43H

Output

    No Carry → Success
    Carry → AL = 2 File not found
            AL = 3 Path not found
            AL = 5 Access denied
    If AL was 0, CX returns the attribute

INT 21H, Service 44H — I/O Control

INT 21H, Service 45H — Duplicate a File Handle

Input

    BX   = File handle to duplicate
    AH   = 45H

Output

No Carry → AX = New, duplicated handle
Carry → AL = 4 Too many files open
　　　　　AL = 6 Invalid handle

INT 21H, Service 46H — Force Duplication of a File Handle

Input

BX　=　File Handle to duplicate
CX　=　Second file handle
AH　=　46H

Output

No Carry → Handles refer to same "stream"
Carry → AL = 6 Invalid handle

INT 21H, Service 47H — Get Current Directory on Specified Drive

Input

AH　=　47H
DS:SI point to 64-byte buffer
DL　=　Drive number

Output

No Carry → Success, ASCIIZ at DS:SI
Carry → AH = 15 Invalid drive specified

Note: Drive letter is NOT included in returned ASCIIZ string.

INT 21H, Service 48H — Allocate Memory

Input

AH　=　48H
BX　=　Number of paragraphs requested

Output

No Carry → AX:0000 memory block address
Carry → AL　= 7 Memory control blocks destroyed
　　　　AL　= 8 Insufficient memory; BX contains maximum
　　　　　　　allowable request

INT 21H, Service 49H — Free Allocated Memory

Input

```
AH   = 49H
ES   = Segment of block being freed
```

Output

```
No Carry → Success
Carry → AL   = 7 Memory control blocks destroyed
             = 9 Incorrect memory block address
```

INT 21H, Service 4AH — SETBLOCK

Input

```
AH   = 4AH
ES   = Segment of block to modify
BX   = Requested size in paragraphs
```

Output

```
No Carry → Success
Carry → AL   = 7 Memory control blocks destroyed
             = 8 Insufficient memory; BX holds maximum
                 possible request
             = 9 Invalid memory block address
```

INT 21H, Service 4BH — Load or Execute a program — EXEC

Input

```
AH    = 4BH
DS:DX = ASCIIZ string with drive, pathname, filename
ES:BX = Parameter block address (see below)
AL    = 0  → Load and execute the program
        3  → Load but create no PSP, don't run (overlay)
```

Parameter Block for AL = 0:

Segment Address of environment to pass (Word)
Address of command to put at PSP+80H (DWord)
Address of default FCB to put at PSP+5CH (DWord)
Address of second default FCB to put at PSP+6CH (DWord)

Parameter Block for AL = 3:

Segment address to load file at (Word)
Relocation factor for image (Word)

Output:

No Carry → Success
Carry:
AL   =   1 Invalid function number
2 File not found on disk
5 Access denied
8 Insufficient memory for requested operation
10 Invalid environment
11 Invalid format

INT 21H, Service 4CH — Exit

Input

AH   =   4CH
AL   =   Binary return code

Note: This service can end a program.

INT 21H, Service 4DH — Get Return Code of Subprocess

Input

AH   =   4DH

Output

AL   =   Binary return code from subprocess
AH   =   0 If subprocess ended normally
1 If subprocess ended with a ^Break
2 If it ended with a critical device error
3 If it ended with Service 31H

INT 21H, Service 4EH — Find First Matching File

Input

> DS:DX → ASCIIZ filestring
> CX   = Attribute to match
> AH   = 4EH

Output

> Carry →AL = 2 No match found
>   AL = 18 No more files
> No Carry → DTA filled as follows:
> > 21   Bytes reserved
> > 1   Byte found attribute
> > 2   Bytes file's time
> > 2   Bytes file's date
> > 2   Bytes low word of size
> > 2   Bytes high word of size
> > 13   Bytes name and extension of found file in ASCIIZ form
> >   (NO pathname)

Note: The data buffer used in FCB services is the DTA, or Disk Transfer Area. See earlier services.

INT 21H, Service 4FH — Find Next Matching File

Input

> Use Service 4EH BEFORE 4FH
> AH   = 4FH

Output

> Carry → AL = 18 No more files
> No Carry → DTA filled as follows:
> > 21   Bytes reserved
> > 1   Byte found attribute
> > 2   Bytes file's time
> > 2   Bytes file's date
> > 2   Bytes low word of size

    2   Bytes high word of size

   13   Bytes name and extension of found file in ASCIIZ form (NO pathname)

Note: The data buffer used in FCB services is the DTA, or Disk Transfer Area. See earlier services.

INT 21H, Services 50H-53H — Internal to DOS

INT 21H, Service 54H — Get Verify State

Input

AH = 54H

Output

AL = 0 → Verify is off.
          1 → Verify is on.

INT 21H, Service 55H — Internal to DOS

INT 21H, Service 56H — Rename File

Input

DS:DX = ASCIIZ filestring to be renamed
ES:DI   = ASCIIZ filestring that holds the new name
AH   = 56H

Output

No Carry → Success
Carry → AL = 3 Path Not Found
AL = 5 Access Denied
AL = 17 Not same device

Note: File CANNOT be renamed to another drive.

INT 21H, Service 57H — Get or Set a File's Date and Time

Input   **Output**

BX= File handle   No Carry:
AL= 0 → Get date and time ——→ CX returns time
                                                    DX returns date

AL= 1 → Set time to CX   ——→ File's date and time set
              Set date to DX

                                    Carry → A= 1 Invalid function
                                                            number
                                                    6 Invalid handle

The time and date of a file are stored like this:

Time=2048×Hours + 32×Minutes +Seconds/2
Date=512×(Year-1980) + 32×Month + Day

INT 21H, Service 58H Internal to DOS

INT 21H, Service 59H — Get Extended Error DOS 3+

Input

AH   = 59H
BX   = 0

Output

AX   = Extended error
BH   = Error class
BL   = Suggested action
CH   = Locus

This error handling service is very lengthy and involves the many DOS 3+ extended errors.

INT 21H, Service 5AH — Create Unique File DOS 3+

Input

AH   = 5AH
DS:DX = Address of an ASCIIZ path (ending with "\")
CX= File's attribute

Output

    AX   = Error if carry is set
    DS:DX = ASCIIZ path and filename

INT 21H, Service 5BH — Create a New File DOS 3+

Input

    AH   = 5BH
    DS:DX = Address of an ASCIIZ path (ending with "\")
    CX   = File's attribute

Output

    AX   = Error if carry is set
          = Handle if carry is not set.

INT 21H, Service 5CH — Lock and Unlock Access to a File DOS 3+

Input

    AH   = 5CH
    AL   = 0 → Lock byte range
            1 → Unlock byte range
    BX   = File handle
    CX   = Byte range start (high word)
    DX   = Byte range start (low word)
    SI   = No. bytes to (un)lock (high word)
    DI   = No. bytes to (un)lock (low word)

Output

    If Carry = 1, AX = Error

INT 21H, Service 5E00H — Get Machine Name DOS 3+

Input

    AX   = 5E00H
    DS:DX = Buffer for computer name

Output

    DS:DX = ASCIIZ computer name
    CH   = 0 → Name not defined

CL   = NETBIOS number
AX   = Error if carry set

INT 21H, Service 5E02 — Set Printer Setup DOS 3+

Input

AX   = 5E02H
BX   = Redirection list index
CX   = Length of setup string
DS:DI = Pointer to printer setup buffer

Output

AX = Error if carry is set

INT 21H, Service 5E03 — Get Printer Setup DOS 3+

Input

AX   = 5E03H
BX   = Redirection list index
ES:DI = Pointer to printer setup buffer

Output

AX   = Error if carry is set
CX   = Length of data returned
ES:DI = Filled with printer setup string

INT 21H, Service 5F03 — Redirect Device DOS 3+

Input

AX   = 5F03H
BL   = Device type
       = 3 → Printer device
       = 4 → File device
CX   = Value to save for caller
DS:SI = Source ASCIIZ device name
ES:DI = Destination ASCIIZ network path with password

Output

AX   = Error if carry is set

INT 21H, Service 5F04H — Cancel Redirection DOS 3+

Input

AX   = 5F04H
DS:SI   = ASCIIZ device name or path

Output

AX   = Error if carry is set

INT 21H, Service 62H — Get Program Segment Prefix DOS 3+

Input

AX   = 62H

Output

BX   = Segment of currently executing program

INT 21H, Service 67H — Set Handle Count DOS 3.30

Input

AX   = 67H
BX   = Number of allowed open handles (up to 255)

Output

AX   = Error if carry is set

INT 21H, Service 68H — Commit File (Write Buffers) DOS 3.30

Input

AX   = 68H

Output

BX   = File handle

Note: 68H is the last of the DOS 3.3 INT 21H services.

INT 22H Terminate Address

INT 23H Control Break Exit Address

INT 24H Critical Error Handler

AH filled this way:

0   Diskette is write-protected
1   Unknown unit
2   The requested drive is not ready
3   Unknown command
4   Cyclic redundancy check error in the data
5   Bad request structure length
6   Seek error
7   Media type unknown
8   Sector not found
9   The printer is out of paper
A   Write fault
B   Read fault
C   General failure

If you just execute an IRET, DOS will take an action based on the contents of AL. If AL = 0, the error will be ignored. If AL = 1, the operation will be retried. If AL = 2, the program will be terminated through INT 23H.

INT 25H — Absolute Disk Read

Input

AL   = Drive number
CX   = Number of sectors to read
DX   = First logical sector
DS:BX = Buffer address

Output

No Carry → Success
Carry → AH   = 80H Disk didn't respond

AH = 40H Seek failed
AH = 20H Controller failure
AH = 10H Bad CRC error check
AH = 08 DMA overrun
AH = 04 Sector not found
AH = 03 Write-protect error
AH = 02 Address mark missing
AH = 00 Error unknown

Note: Flags left on stack after this INT call because information is returned in current flags. After you check the flags that were returned, make sure you do a POPF. Also, this INT destroys the contents of ALL registers.

INT 26H — Absolute Disk Write

Input

AL = Drive number
CX = Number of sectors to write
DX = First logical sector
DS:BX = Buffer address

Output

No Carry → Success
Carry → AH = 80H Disk didn't respond
AH = 40H Seek failed
AH = 20H Controller failure
AH = 10H Bad CRC error check
AH = 08 DMA overrunR AH=04 Sector not found
AH = 03 Write-protect error
AH = 02 Address mark missing
AH = 00 Error unknown

Note: Flags left on stack after this INT call because information is returned in current flags. After you check the flags that were returned, make sure you do a POPF. Also, this INT destroys the contents of ALL registers.

INT 27H — Terminate and Stay Resident

Input

DS:DX = point directly after end of code which is to stay resident

INTs 28H-2EH — Internal to DOS

INT 2FH — Multiplex Interrupt

INT 30H-3FH — DOS Reserved

INT 40H-5FH — Reserved

INT 60H-67H — Reserved for User Software

INTs 68H-7FH — Not Used

INTs 80H-85H — Reserved by BASIC

INTs 86H-F0H — Used by BASIC Interpreter

INTs F1H-FFH — Not Used

Index

A

A command, 394, 396
accepting keyboard input, 415–418
access keywords, 378
ADD instruction, 416–418
Add With Carry instruction, 482
addem ( ) function, 78, 318, 319
adding color to painter. c program 148–152
adding data to PRINTZ.ASM program, 408–412
adding second modules to libraries, 506–510
addition operator, 21
addresses, 80, 81, 114
advance procedures with for loops, 65–69
advanced pointers, 271–302
ah register, 200, 201, 202
al register, 201, 415, 430
allocating memory in Microsoft C, 256
allocating memory in Turbo C, 256–257
Alt key combinations, 307
Alt-v, 328
American National Standard Institute (ANSI), 3
ANSI C, 3, 350
ANSI standard, 4, 123, 184
& character in C functions, 42
& operator, 81, 414
_ANALOG constant, 141
_ANALOGCOLOR constant, 141
_ANALOGMONO constant, 141
AND logical operator, 53, 190
ANDing, 231
animation example, 158–159

animation in C, 152–157
argc parameter, 196, 324, 331
arguments, 12
argv [ ] array, 196
arithmetic operators, 18–24, 27, 189
arrays, 83, 85, 271–278
ASCII arrow characters, 234
ASCII characters, 164, 425, 434
ASCII codes, 28, 42, 43, 45, 81, 126, 232, 415, 416, 417, 418
ASCII files, 172–174
ASCII strings, 174, 429
ASCIIZ format, 42
.ASM files, 403, 404, 406, 414, 436
assembler directives, 403–406
assemblers, actions of, 391
assembling PRINTZ.ASM program, 407–408
assembly language, 389–442
assembly language example, 393–396
assembly language instruction, 390
assembly language procedures, 437–442
assembly language routines, 481–511
assertion statement, 303
assertions, definition of, 303
assignment operators, 18, 19, 20
automatic variables, 244, 245, 246, 260–264
ax register, 200, 201, 203, 392, 393, 428, 430, 483

B

B programming language, 2
backslash codes, 13

backslashes, in C, 110
base type of pointers, 115
BASIC assembly language, 268, 471
BCPL programming language, 2
.BGI extension, 145
bh register, 201
biases, definition of, 455
BIOS interrupts, 513–533
    INT 0, 513
    INT 1, 513
    INT 2, 5134
    INT 3, 514
    INT 4, 414
    INT 5, 514
    INT 6, 514
    INT 7, 514
    INT 8, 514
    INT 9, 514
    INT 0AH, 514
    INT 0BH-0FH, 515
    INT 10H, Service 0, 515
    INT 10H, Service 1, 516
    INT 10H, Service 2, 516
    INT 10H, Service 3, 516
    INT 10H, Service 4, 516
    INT 10H, Service 5, 517
    INT 10H, Service 6, 517
    INT 10H, Service 7, 517
    INT 10H, Service 8, 517
    INT 10H, Service 9, 518
    INT 10H, Service A, 518
    INT 10H, Service B, 518
    INT 10H, Service C, 519
    INT 10H, Service D, 519
    INT 10H, Service E, 519
    INT 10H, Service FH, 519
    INT 10H, Service 10H, 520
    INT 10H, Service 10H, Function 0, 520
    INT 10H, Service 10H, Function 1, 520
    INT 10H, Service 10H, Function 2, 521
    INT 10H, Service 10H, Function 7, 521
    INT 10H, Service 10H, Function 8, 521
    INT 10H, Service 10H, Function 10H, 521
    INT 10H, Service 10H, Function 12H, 522
    INT 10H, Service 10H, Function 13H, 522
    INT 10H, Service 11H, 522
    INT 10H, Service 12H, 522
    INT 11H, 523
    INT 12H, 523
    INT 13H, Service 0, 523
    INT 13H, Service 1, 524
    INT 13H, Service 2, 524
    INT 13H, Service 3, 525
    INT 13H, Service 4, 525
    INT 13H, Service 8, 526
    INT 13H, Services 0AH and 0BH, 526
    INT 13H, Service 0CH
    INT 13H, Service 0DH, 527
    INT 13H, Service 0EH and 0FH, 527
    INT 13H, Service 10H, 527
    INT 13H, Service 11H, 527
    INT 13H, 527
    INT 13H, Service 19H
    INT 14H, AH=0, 528
    INT 14H, AH=1, 528
    INT 14H, AH=2, 529
    INT 14H, AH=3, 529
    INT 15H, 530
    INT 16H, Service 0, 530
    INT 16H, Service 1, 530
    INT 16H, Service 2, 531
    INT 17H, Service 0, 531
    INT 17H, Service 1, 531
    INT 17H Service 2, 531
    INT 18H, 532
    INT 19H, 532
    INT 1AH, Service 0, 532
    INT 1AH, Service 1, 532
    INT 1BH, 532
    INT 1CH, 532
    INT 1DH, 533
    INT 1EH, 533
    INT 1FH, 533
binary code, 390
binary files, 172–174
binary operators, 53
binary streams, 164
bitwise operators, 18, 189–195
bl register, 201, 430
blocks, definition of, 11
Borland C++ program, 6, 7, 350, 505
Borland program, 4
bp register, 203
break statement, 58, 62
break statement in loops, 63–64
breakpoints, 335–337
Breakpoints option, 306
Break/Watch menu, 306, 310
buffer variable, 310, 311
bx register, 200, 201, 210, 219, 392, 393, 425, 426,
    430, 478, 485, 494, 495, 498, 499
bytes, 28, 90, 115, 119, 164, 390, 404, 412

C

C calling convention, 268–270, 457
'c' command, 148
C compiler, 5, 12, 444
C functions, 6, 74–81
C language, 1, 2, 7
C libraries, 6, 7
C's portability, 163
C type conversions, 34–37
C++ I/O class libraries, 351
C++ program, 1
CAP.COM program example, 415–416
capitalizing lowercase letters, 43
carriage return, 67
carry flags, 452, 492
Central Processing Unit (CPU), 200
cerr stream, 350

cflags register, 203
ch register, 201
changing the mouse cursor appearance,
229–234
char data type, 28–30
character strings, 12, 83, 412, 446
CI/O system, 165
cin stream, 350, 351, 355
circular buffers, 302
CL command, 7
cl register, 201, 428
classes, 355
clearing the keyboard buffer, 67
clog stream
close ( ) function, 184, 185
CMP instruction, 418–420, 487
code area, 236–239
code blocks, 49
.CODE directive, 404
code segment register, 401, 474
CodeView debugger, 320, 321
_COLOR constant, 141
Color Graphics Adapter (CGA), 124, 138, 140
_CGA constant, 141
CGA driver, 148
CGA palettes, 144, 147, 148
CGA_PIXEL program example, 499
CGA video buffers, 493
CGA video controller, 494
color mixing, 143
coloring a screen pixel, 125–128
columns in two-dimensional arrays, 88
.COM file shell, 415, 420
.COM files, 200, 403, 404, 406, 407, 408,
409, 413
combining arithmetic and assignment
operators, 21–22
comma operator, 68, 69, 87
comments, 9
Compile File option, 6
concatenation, definition of, 98
Condition option, 341
conditional jumps, 415, 418–420, 421, 492
conditional operators, 100–107
conditions in if statements, 45, 46
connecting assembly language to C, 443–480
constants, 5
continue statement, 62–63
converting four-digit hex numbers to decimal
numbers, 420–437
coordinates in drawing rectangles, 131, 132
copier. c program example, 194–195, 197
coping files, 185–189
cout stream, 350, 351, 354, 355
CP/M operating system, 2
.cpp extension, 355
curly braces in C, 50, 51, 69
cursor, 67
cursor keys, 125, 126, 129, 130
cursor mask, definition of, 229

CV.EXE, 320
cx register, 200, 201, 210, 219, 392, 393, 398, 494,
495, 499

D

data area, 236, 239–248
.DATA directive, 475
data segment register, 401, 402, 475
data sets, 83, 84
data storage, 15
data structures, 83, 107–114
data type modifiers, 31, 32–34
data types, 15, 27, 28–32
database program example, 91–95
databases, 1
Debug menu, 306, 310
DEBUG.COM program, 393, 394, 395, 396, 397,
398, 399
debugged program example, 345–347
debugging actions, 306
debugging C programs, 303–347
debugging hotkeys, 306
debugging techniques, 1
DEC instruction, 22, 426
decimal digits, 429, 430, 431, 432, 433
decrement operator, 22, 23
dedicated debuggers, 320–347
define byte directive, 408, 409–412, 422, 443, 448
#define directive, 155–157
define word directive, 408, 409–412, 443, 448
defining pointers to functions, 295–299
DEHEXER.ASM program, 420–437
delimiter pairs, definition of, 11
detect graph ( ) function, 146
dh register, 201
di register, 203
displaying the mouse cursor, 206–208
DIV instruction, 430, 485
divide algorithm, 484, 486
dividing in code, 489–493
division operator, 21
dl register, 201, 425, 426, 428, 429
do-while loop, 71–74
'$' terminating character, 413
DOS, 168, 173, 191, 199, 407, 421
DOS commands, 200
    COPY, 200
    FORMAT, 200
    TIME, 200
    VER, 200
    XCOPY, 200
DOS interrupts, 533–563
    INT 20H, 533
    INT 21H, 533
    INT 21H, Service 0, 533
    INT 21H, Service 1, 533
    INT 21H, Service 2, 534
    INT 21H, Service 3, 534
    INT 21H, Service 4, 534
    INT 21H, Service 5, 534

INT 21H, Service 6, 534
INT 21H, Service 7, 537
INT 21H, Service 8, 535
INT 21H, Service 9, 535
INT 21H, Service A, 535
INT 21H, Service 0BH, 536
INT 21H, Service 0CH, 536
INT 21H, Service 0DH, 536
INT 21H, Service 0EH, 536
INT 21H, Service 0FH, 536
INT 21H, Service 10H, 537
INT 21H, Service 11H, 537
INT 21H, Service 12H, 537
INT 21H, Service 13H, 538
INT 21H, Service 14H, 538
INT 21H, Service 15H, 538
INT 21H, Service 16H, 539
INT 21H, Service 17H, 539
INT 21H, Service 18H, 539
INT 21H, Service 19H, 539
INT 21H, Service 1AH, 539
INT 21H, Service 1BH, 540
INT 21H, Service 1CH, 540
INT 21H, Service 1DH-20H, 540
INT 21H, Service 21H, 540
INT 21H, Service 22H, 541
INT 21H, Service 23H, 541
INT 21H, Service 24H, 541
INT 21H, Service 25H, 542
INT 21H, Service 26H, 542
INT 21H, Service 27H, 542
INT 21H, Service 28H, 542
INT 21H, Service 29H, 543
INT 21H, Service 2AH, 543
INT 21H, Service 2BH, 543
INT 21H, Service 2CH, 544
INT 21H, Service 2DH, 544
INT 21H, Service 2EH, 544
INT 21H, Service 2FH, 545
INT 21H, Service 30H, 545
INT 21H, Service 31H, 545
INT 21H, Service 32H, 545
INT 21H, Service 33H, 545
INT 21H, Service 34H, 546
INT 21H, Service, 35H, 546
INT 21H, Service 36H, 546
INT 21H, Service 37H, 546
INT 21H, Service 38H, 547
INT 21H, Service 39H, 547
INT 21H, Service 3AH, 548
INT 21H, Service 3BH, 548
INT 21H, Service 3CH, 548
INT 21H, Service 3DH, 549
INT 21H, Service 3EH, 549
INT 21H, Service 3FH, 550
INT 21H, Service 40H, 550
INT 21H, Service 41H, 550
INT 21H, Service 42H, 551
INT 21H, Service 43H, 551

INT 21H, Service 44H, 551
INT 21H, Service 45H, 551
INT 21H, Service 46H, 552
INT 21H, Service 47H, 522
INT 21H, Service 48H, 522
INT 21H, Service 49H, 522
INT 21H, Service 4AH, 553
INT 21H, Service 4BH, 553
INT 21H, Service 4CH, 554
INT 21H, Service 4DH, 554
INT 21H, Service 4EH, 555
INT 21H, Service 4FH, 555
INT 21H, Service 50H-53H
INT 21H, Service 54H, 556
INT 21H, Service 55H, 556
INT 21H, Service 56H, 556
INT 21H, Service 57H, 557
INT 21H, Service 58H, 557
INT 21H, Service 59H, 557
INT 21H, Service 5AH, 557
INT 21H, Service 5BH, 558
INT 21H, Service 5CH, 558
INT 21H, Service 5E00H, 558
INT 21H, Service 5E02, 559
INT 21H, Service 5E03, 559
INT 21H, Service 5F03, 559
INT 21H, Service 5F04H, 560
INT 21H, Service 62H, 560
INT 21H, Service 67H, 560
INT 21H, Service 68H, 560
INT 22H, 561
INT 23H, 561
INT 24H, 561
INT 25H, 561
INT 26H, 562
INT 27H, 562
INT 28H-2EH, 563
INT 2FH, 563
INT 30H-3FH, 563
INT 40H-5FH, 563
INT 60H-67H, 563
INTs 68H-7FH
INTs 80H-85H, 563
INTs 86H-F0H, 563
INTs F1H-ffH, 563
DOS prompt, 424
DOS redirection commands, 351
double data type, 28, 30–32
double quotation marks in C, 30
double quotation marks in strings, 97
doubly linked lists, 301
drawing colors, 143
drawing ellipses, 134–136
drawing lines, 127–131
drawing rectangles, 131–134
DUP directive, 422
dx register, 200, 210, 219, 392, 393, 428, 431, 485,
    495, 496, 497

E

EGAHI mode, 154
8-bit compilers, 2
8-bit registers, 201
80 X 86 registers, 201
ellipse ( ) function, 134, 135
_ellipse ( ) function, 134
end-of-file (EOF) marker, 171–172, 422
Enhanced Graphics Adapter (EGA), 124, 138, 140, 143
_EGA constant, 141
EGA_PIXEL program example, 500–503
encapsulation, definition of, 350
END directive, 406
ENDP directive, 437, 438
_ENHCOLOR constant, 141
Enter key, 5, 6, 7, 67
entry points, 406
equal sign, 18
_ERESCOLOR mode, 154
errno ( ) function, 182, 183
error messages, 182, 184
.EXE file, 237, 326, 407, 475, 504
Exit label, 419
Expression True option, 341
external variables, 246
extra segment register, 401, 402

F

F2 key, 335
F5 key, 126
F7 key, 307, 309, 329
F8 key, 307, 309
F9 key 335
'f' command, 136
false condition in if statements, 47, 51
farfree ( ) function, 257
farmalloc ( ) function, 253, 256, 257
fast sorting techniques, 285–295
fclose ( ) function, 168, 175, 181, 184
fgetc ( ) function, 165, 171
fgets ( ) function, 168, 169
File Allocation Table (FAT), 301
file errors, 182–185
file handle, 192
file handling, 1, 163–198
file opening options, 166
file pointer, 192
file pointer position, 178–182
file_pointer stream, 166, 167, 169
file reading example, 168–170
file records, 174–182
file writing example, 165–168
files, 163–165
filling shapes with color, 136–138
finding a two's complement, 452–453
finding the video mode, 470, 471
float cast, 87

float data type, 27, 96, 119, 454
float point numbers, 87, 174, 454
floating point formats, 454–456
floodfill ( ) function, 136
_floodfill ( ) function, 136
fopen ( ) function, 165, 166, 175, 181, 184, 312
for loop, 59–69, 86, 155
format specification, 16, 31
format strings, 16, 41
FORTRAN language, 81, 268, 471]
fprint ( ) function, 164, 165, 167
fprintf ( ) function, 175
fptr variable, 310, 312
fread ( ) function, 175, 177, 182, 184, 312
free ( ) function, 257
freeing memory, 257
fscanf ( ) function, 165
fseek ( ) function, 179, 180, 181
function overloading, 353, 369–378, 381
function overloading example, 376–377
function pointer, 297, 298
function pointer use example, 299
function prototypes, 75
fwrite ( ) function, 175, 177, 182, 184

G

_GBORDER constant, 132, 134
_get_char ( ) function, 74, 75, 76, 77
getc ( ) function, 165, 326
getch ( ) function, 125, 126, 171
getche ( ) function, 67, 74, 125, 126, 171
getimage ( ) function, 152
_getimage ( ) function, 152, 153, 156
gets ( ) function, 96, 421
_getvideoconfig ( ) function, 140, 141
_GFILLINTERIOR constant, 132, 134
Global option, 341
global variables, 77, 241
global versus local variables, 241–244
Go key, 335
goto statement, 64–65
graph. h header file, 124, 141
graphic output position, 129
graphics, 1, 123
graphics driver file, 124
graphics drivers, 145
graphics images, 152
graphics video buffer, 493
graphics viewports, 158–162
graphics.h header file, 124, 145
grdriver constant, 146
grmode constant, 145, 146
grpath variable, 145, 146

H

halloc ( ) function, 253, 256, 260
head of keyboard buffer, 302
header files, 8, 185

heap area, 236, 248–260
hex digits, 428, 432
hex numbers, 399, 424, 428, 436
hexadecimal values, 31
_HGC constant, 141
hiding the mouse cursor, 208–210
high precision addition, 482
high precision division, 484–493
high precision multiplication, 483–484
high precision subtraction, 482–483
high resolution mode, 139, 493
hotkeys, 307

I

IBM mouse, 200
identifiers, 15
if statement, 39, 45–51
if-else-if ladders, 48–49, 52, 54, 56, 59
imagesize ( ) function, 152
_imagesize ( ) function, 152, 153, 154
in-line assembly language, 443, 444
in-line code, 443, 445, 449
INC instruction, 22
#include instruction, 8
increment operator, 22, 23
indentation in C, 50
indirect addressing, 426, 427
indirection operator, 115, 116
inheritance, definition of, 378
inheritance example, 384–387
inheritance in C++, 378–387
init ( ) function, 361
initgraph ( ) function, 145
initialization, definition of, 60
initialized arrays and structures, 241
initialized data, 236, 238, 239, 240, 241, 263
initializing multidimensional arrays, 90
initializing single-dimensional arrays, 90
initializing the mouse, 200
initializing the variable, 15
initializing two-dimensional arrays, 89
int data type, 30, 96, 141
integer variables, 19
integers, 15, 449–451
int86 ( ) function, 200, 201, 204, 222
int86x ( ) function, 201, 204–206
interactive debugging, 306–320
internal data formats in C, 448–456
I/O functions, 165

J

JA jump instruction, 419, 421, 492
JB jump instruction, 419, 421, 492
JBE jump instruction, 420, 421
JCXZ jump instruction, 421
JE jump instruction, 421
JMP instruction, 412
JNA jump instruction, 420, 421
JNAE jump instruction, 420, 421

JNB jump instruction, 420, 421
JNBE jump instruction, 420, 421
JNC jump instruction, 495
JNE jump instruction, 421
JNZ jump instruction, 421
jump instruction, definition of, 411
jumps, 411, 415, 418–420, 421
JZ jump instruction, 421

K

kbhit ( ) function, 67
keeping data in arrays, 84–87
keyboard buffer, 67
keyboard data, 41
keyboard input in C++, 353–355
keyboard-input functions, 41

L

'l' command, 130 131
labels, 404–405
left shift operator, 351, 354, 355, 428
LIB command, 505
.LIB extension, 505
.LIB files, 511
LIB.EXE program, 504
line feeds, 67
lineto ( ) function, 129, 131
_lineto ( ) function, 158
LINK command, 468, 509, 510, 511
linked lists, 299
linking assembly language functions to C, 470–477
linking C into assembly language, 477–480
linking files, 466–470
linking in external assembly language, 465–470
loading mouse driver software, 200
loading the CGA driver, 146
local variables, 77, 241, 243
logical operators, 18, 51–54, 189
Logitech mouse, 200
long division, 485
long integers, 450–451
long modifiers, 32, 33
loop counter, 60
loop index, 60, 61, 64, 65
LOOP instruction, 436–437
loops, 39, 59
low resolution mode, 124, 139
lowercase sensitivity in C, 5
lseek function, 185

M

machine language, 237, 389–390
machine language instruction, 390
main ( ) function, 4, 6, 10–12, 55, 77, 195, 319, 365, 384, 406
Make EXE File option, 6
Make menu, 6
making programs faster, 276–277

malloc ( ) function, 153, 186, 236, 248, 249, 256, 257, 259
managing blocks of code, 49–51
manipulators, definition of, 353
MAXX constant, 155
MAXY constant, 155
_MCGA constant, 141
_MDPA constant, 141
medium resolution mode, 124, 493, 494
member functions, 361, 362
memory, 15
memory addresses, 390
memory allocation, 153
memory control, 1
memory management, 249–253
memory model definitions, 251
memory models, 249–253
memory segmentation, 399–403
Microsoft C libraries, 123
Microsoft C painter.c program, 149–150
Microsoft C program, 7, 123
Microsoft program, 4
Microsoft debugger, 320
Microsoft mouse, 200
mixed-model programs, 254–256
modular code, 10
modularity of objects, 349
module, definition of, 506
modulus operator, 21
_MONO constant, 141
Monochrome Display Adapter, (MDA), 138, 140
mouse, 199–234
mouse cursor, 206, 207, 208, 209, 210
mouse driver, 205
mouse driver software, 199, 200
mouse_button variable, 218, 221, 222
MOUSE.COM file, 200
mouse_hide cursor function, 208, 209–210
mouse_horizontal_range, 225–227
mouse_information ( ) function, 211–215
mouse_initialize ( ) function, 200, 206, 208, 221
mouse_move_cursor ( ) function, 215–217
mouse_set_cursor ( ) function, 206, 231, 234
mouse_show_cursor ( ) function, 205, 207, 208, 221
MOUSESYS.COM file, 200
mouse_times_pressed ( ) function, 218–221, 222, 223
mouse_times_released ( ) function, 222–224
mouse_vertical_range ( ) function, 227
MOV AX, 5 instruction, 390, 393, 395, 396
MOV format, 391
MOV instruction, 391–392
_moveto ( ) function, 129, 158
moving the mouse cursor, 215–217
_MRES4COLOR constant, 124
MUL instruction, 430, 483
multiplication operator, 21
myvid fields, 141

N
NEG instruction, 453
new line backslash code, 16
new.vars. bat batch file, 6
NOT instruction, 453
Not logical operator, 53, 128, 453
NULL pointer, 167, 170, 186, 300
null strings, 146
NULL value, 167
number variables, 316, 317
numeric indexes, 86
numerical value of keys, 45

O
.OBJ files, 407, 444, 504, 506
object file, 6
objects, definition of, 349
_od switch, 326
offset address, 250
OFFSET directive, 413, 414
open ( ) function, 184, 185, 186, 189, 192
open ( ) function flags, 189
operands, 26
operator overloading, 351
operator precedence, 25–27
OR operator, 189, 190, 231
organizing data, 83–122
organizing pointers, 83–122
origin value, 181
ORing, 189, 499
OS/2 computers and .COM files, 403
O_TRUNC function flag, 189

P
'p' command, 125, 127, 128, 129, 130, 132, 133
padding variable in breakpoints, 341, 342
painter.c program, 126, 128, 138, 148
palettes, 144, 147
parameter list, 44
parantheses in operator precedence, 26, 27
Pascal assembly language, 268, 471
passing long parameters, 460–462
passing parameters, 456–462, 472–474
passing parameters to functions in C, 80–81, 260, 269
passing structures, in C, 109
PC computers, 123, 185
PCjr computer, 140
% c format specifier, 29, 44
% d format specifier, 29
perror ( ) function, 182, 183, 184
PgDn key, 327
PgUp key, 327
pixel graphics in assembly language, 493–503
pixels, 124, 125, 493, 494
pointer operator, 115
pointers, 81, 112, 114–122
polymorphism, definition of, 353
pop ( ) function, 360, 361, 362, 363, 372, 380
POP CX instruction, 431

popping values off stacks, 267, 366, 432

positioning code in the code segment, 405–406

post fix operators, 23, 24

precision specifier, 31

predefined I/O streams, 350–353

prefix operators, 23

preprocessor directives, 8

pressing the mouse button, 218, 219, 220, 221

print ( ) and the C library, 12–14

print ( ) format specifications, 32

printf ( ) function, 5, 6, 7, 8, 9, 29, 41, 74, 76, 96, 102, 103, 164, 165, 350, 413, 478

PrInTf function, 5

print_number_in_hex ( ) function, 380

printing strings, 413–414

private classes, 357

PROC directive, 437, 438

PS/2 computers, 123, 138, 185

public classes, 357

push ( ) function, 360, 361, 363, 372, 380

PUSH DX instruction, 431

pushing values onto stacks, 267, 366, 432

putc ( ) function, 326

putimage ( ) function, 152

_putimage ( ) function, 152, 158

PUT_PIXEL program, 494–503

Q

'q' command, 127

Quick C compiler, 5, 6

Quick C debugger, 307

Quick C linker, 6

Quick sort sorting method, 289

R

R command, 393, 394, 395, 398

'r' command, 132, 133, 134

random versus sequential file access, 182

read ( ) function, 184, 185, 194

reading command line parameters, 195–198

reading file records, 177–178

reading from the keyboard, 39–81

reading mouse information, 210–215

reading the mouse button pressed queue, 218–221

reading the mouse button released queue, 222–224

realloc ( ) function, 257

rectangle ( ) function, 131

_rectangle ( ) function, 131, 134

recursion at work, 264–266

register return values, 462

register storage class, 238–239

register variables, 246

registers, 200, 201, 202

Registers option, 328

relational operators, 18, 46, 47, 51–54, 99, 189

restricting the mouse cursor horizontally, 225–227

restricting the mouse cursor vertically, 227–229

RET instruction, 439, 440

return statements, 78–79

return (0) function, 14

return 0 statement, 62

returning values from functions, 462–465

rewind ( ) function, 179

right shift operator, 351, 354, 355

ring buffers, 302

rows in two-dimensional arrays, 88

Run menu, 6, 7, 355

Run option, 6, 355

S

saving memory space, 277–278

scan codes, 126

scanf ( ) function, 40, 41, 42, 54, 67, 80, 81, 103, 165, 186, 187, 350, 415

scope resolution operator, 361

screen attribute character, 231

screen attributes, 229–234

screen mask character, 231

screen mask, definition of, 229

screen modes, 138–152

screen output in C++, 350–353

segment address, 250

segment override type modifiers, 255

segment registers, 401, 402

segment selectors, 250

_select pallet ( ) function, 144

selecting colors in Microsoft C, 143–145

selecting colors in Turbo C, 147–148

_setbkcolor ( ) function, 144

setcolor ( ) function, 137, 147

_setcolor ( ) function, 129, 136, 138, 143, 144, 145

setgraphmode ( ) function, 124, 147

setting video modes in Microsoft C, 124, 140–143

setting video modes in Turbo C, 124, 145–147

setvideomode ( ) function, 124

setvideomode function, 142, 143

setviewport, 160

_setviewport, 160, 161

shell sorts at work, 287–295

Shift-F5 key, 126

short modifiers, 32, 33

SHL instruction, 428

SHR instruction, 428

si registers, 204

sign bit, 451

signed modifiers, 32, 33

signed numbers at work, 451–452

single quotation marks in C, 30

16-bit registers, 201

sizeof ( ) operator, 169, 291

sorting with pointers example, 294–295

source files, 192, 196

stack area, 236, 260–270

stack overflow, 186

stack pointer, 267, 358

stack segment register, 401, 402

stacks at work, 266–268

stacks at work in C++, 358–369

standardized C language, 3–4

start label, 405, 406, 411, 412
statement terminators, 12
statements in programs, 11
static global variables, 245
static variables, 241, 244, 245, 246
static variables versus automatic variables, 244–248
stderr stream, 350
stdin stream, 171, 350
stdio.h function header, 165
stdlog stream, 350
stdout stream, 164, 350
storing data, 15, 163
storing automatic variables, 26
storing images, 152
storing return addresses, 260
strcat ( ) function, 96, 98
strcmp ( ) function, 96, 99
strcpy ( ) function, 96, 110
streams of data, 163–165
strings, 30
strings in memory, 412–415
strlen ( ) function, 96, 98
struct, 203, 355
SUB instruction, 416–418
subtract with borrow(SBB) instruction, 482, 483
subtraction operator, 21
summer ( ) function, 269
switch statement, 56–59, 330, 331, 334, 339

T

T command, 396
tail of keyboard buffer, 302
target files, 192, 196
TD.EXE, 320, 321, 327
temp [ ] function, 168
text streams, 164
TLIB command, 505
TLINK command, 469
the_operator variable, 56, 57
toupper ( ) function, 43, 74
true conditions in if statements, 51
Turbo Assembler, 350
Turbo Debugger, 307, 320
Turbo C graphics drivers, 145
Turbo C graphics modes, 146
Turbo C libraries, 123
Turbo C painter.c program, 150–152
Turbo C program, 6, 7, 505
Turbo C++ program, 6, 7, 123, 350
Turbo C++ Pro program, 350
turning pixels on, 494–503
two's complement math, 452
two-dimensional arrays, 87–90, 122, 278–283
type casts in C, 35–37

U

unary operators, 53
union data type, 203–205

unitialized data, 236, 238, 239, 240, 241, 263
UNIX file functions, 185–195
UNIX operating system, 2, 173, 184
unresolved externals, definition of, 504
unsigned modifiers, 32, 33
updating library files, 510–511
updating the copier.c program, 258–260
user_guess read-in value, 70, 72
using addition with pointers, 118–122
using assertions, 303–306
using break in loops, 63–64
using C++ classes, 355–358
using comments, 414–415
using data in-line assembly language, 445–448
using data types, 28–32
using files in C, 163–198
using in-line assembly language, 443–448
using memory in C, 235–270
using pointers to structures, 283–284
using subtraction with pointers, 118–122

V

_v option, 326
variables, 15
Variables option, 331, 341
video buffer 8k blocks, 495
video buffers, 493, 495
Video Graphics Adapter (VGA) monitor, 124, 138, 140, 143
video modes in C, 124–125
videoconfig, 140
vidmode ( ) function, 470, 471
View menu, 328, 331
viewports, 160
void data type, 28

W

W command, 398
Watch Values option, 306, 311, 313
while loop, 69–71
while ( ) statement, 194
"whitespace" characters, 68
write ( ) function, 184, 185
writing C functions, 74–81
writing file records, 174–177
writing in-line assembly language, 44
writing procedures, 437–442

X

XGA monitor, 139
XOR operator, 190
XORing, 190, 231

Z

Zi option, 326

C Programming
Disk Offer

A companion disk is available for this book. The companion disk contains:

- All of the programs described in the book
- A Quicksort program, showing how the Quicksort works in C
- A program that lets you customize the mouse graphics cursor
- A C++ example showing how to create and use string classes in C++
- An 80x87 assembly language interface

To order your disk, simply fill out coupon below and mail it to MICROSERVICES, 200 Old Tappan Road, Old Tappan, NJ 07675.

C Programming

I am ordering the companion disk for this book and have enclosed my check for $15.00 payable to Simon & Schuster, Inc.

Please send a   ☐   3.5-inch disk   ISBN: 0-13-118027-4

☐   5.25-inch disk   ISBN: 0-13-663154-1

Name_____

Address_____

City _____ State _____ Zip_____

Phone Number (   ) _____

Please mail this request to MICROSERVICES, 200 Old Tappan Road, Old Tappan, NJ 07675. For more information call (201) 767-5054.